WHEN AMERICA STOPPED BEING GREAT

WHEN AMERICA STOPPED BEING GREAT

A History of the Present

NICK BRYANT

BLOOMSBURY CONTINUUM
LONDON · OXFORD · NEW YORK · NEW DELHI · SYDNEY

BLOOMSBURY CONTINUUM
Bloomsbury Publishing Plc
50 Bedford Square, London, WC1B 3DP, UK
29 Earlsfort Terrace, Dublin 2, Ireland

BLOOMSBURY, BLOOMSBURY CONTINUUM and the Diana logo are trademarks of
Bloomsbury Publishing Plc

First published in 2020 in Australia by Viking, an imprint of Penguin Books
First published in Great Britain 2021

A catalogue record for this book is available from the British Library

Library of Congress Cataloguing-in-Publication data has been applied for

ISBN: HB: 978-1-4729-8548-4; TPB: 978-1-4729-9140-9;
eBook: 978-1-4729-8549-1; ePDF: 978-1-4729-8550-7

2 4 6 8 10 9 7 5 3

Typeset by Deanta Global Publishing Services, Chennai, India
Printed and bound in USA by Berryville Graphics Inc., Berryville, Virginia

Bloomsbury Publishing Plc makes every effort to ensure that the papers used in the
manufacture of our books are natural, recyclable products made from wood grown
in well-managed forests. Our manufacturing processes conform to the
environmental regulations of the country of origin.

To find out more about our authors and books visit www.bloomsbury.com
and sign up for our newsletters

*For Honor Wood Bryant, our American daughter,
the brightest of lights in the darkest of times*

Contents

INTRODUCTION

Face to Face with 'The Donald'

'It's a great honour,' said Donald Trump, proffering a welcoming hand and tipping slightly his feather-light wedge of corn-coloured hair, as we greeted each other outside the golden elevators on the 25th floor of his skyscraper. Expecting this germophobe to recoil at the possibility of physical contact, I was surprised he was prepared to take my hand, let alone grip it so firmly. Expecting to be confronted by a wall of bombast, I found his humility disarming.

In the flesh, Donald Trump seemed a more likeable and sophisticated version of his crass reality-television self: less brash, more intelligent, unexpectedly charming. The conference room he ushered us into also defied his corporate image: not the wood-panelled firing chamber of *The Apprentice* but a modern and airy space with tasteful office furniture and corner-window views down Fifth Avenue all the way to Central Park.

We met in the autumn of 2014, when the pleasure palaces he once operated in Atlantic City, the Trump Plaza and Trump Taj Mahal, were about to close their doors. Amidst a swirl of negative publicity – he hadn't yet coined the phrase 'fake news' to discredit unwelcome coverage – he was determined to distance himself from the failed casinos, which had been emblazoned with his name until he sued the new owners and forced them to haul down the garish 'T-R-U-M-P' signage.

The Trump Taj Mahal, much like the Indian subcontinent during the British Raj, had once been the jewel in his crown, a monument to his vanity. The 'eighth wonder of the world', he even called it, as he paraded Michael Jackson at its grand opening in April 1990. Now, though, this decaying eyesore on the Jersey Shore was a derelict folly, a landmark of a business empire that had become something of a standing joke.

These days Donald Trump was better known as a television personality than as a property tycoon, someone who traded on his name through global licensing deals and his primetime TV show rather than constructing his own skyscrapers or gambling halls. Sitting for an interview with the BBC gave him an opportunity to demonstrate to the outside world that the sun still reflected off his golden signage.

He seemed to regard appearing on the British Broadcasting Corporation as a status symbol, airtime more rarefied than the flatulent fog of *The Howard Stern Show*, one of his more regular haunts. It was as if he looked upon us as an offshoot of the monarchy, which may have explained his near-courtly manner. A celebrity whose candidacy would be defined by contempt for institutions – the presidency, Congress, the Republican Party, *The New York Times*, the media more broadly and the snooty bi-coastal elites living in California and New York – was respectful, for now at least, of a pillar of British life.

Turning on the camera instantly made him more recognisable. The red light activated his showman self, his performative persona. It was as if he had inhaled some intoxicant. Over the course of the interview I witnessed first-hand the traits and tics that would soon be transferred from the business realm to the political.

There was his unabashed boastfulness: 'When I was in Atlantic City it was a great thing. It was a heyday for Atlantic City. It was primetime.'

The hyperbole: 'There was nothing like it. It was the Las Vegas of the East Coast. There was nothing like it.'

The inflated claims about his business acumen and negotiating skills: 'A lot of people are giving me credit for good timing ... I decided years ago to get out. It was a good decision, and very interestingly it coincides with Atlantic City going down.'

The blaming of others for personal failure: 'A lot of it has to do with poor political management and too much competition ... very bad political decisions over many years.'

His disregard for science and war on windmills: 'Wind turbines. They are terrible. They're obsolete. They ruin neighbourhoods. They reduce the value of everybody's houses. They raise everyone's taxes. They're very bad. They kill the birds and hurt the environment.'

His prowess at gleaning free advertising from major news organisations: 'Want to ask a question about Turnberry [his championship golf club on the Firth of Clyde in Scotland] by any chance? It's rated the number-one course. We're going to do something amazing. The hotel is going to be one of the great hotels in the world. We will do a terrific job for the people of Scotland.'

Evident, too, was his wistfulness for the mythic glory days of Atlantic City, a Jersey Shore version of the sentimental nationalism he would peddle in 2016 for those who sought refuge in a misremembered past.

To watch the tape back now is to be reminded of how interchangeable was his sales patter. Though the topic was his casinos, he could just as easily have been hawking Trump steaks, Trump University, Trump wine, the Trump board game, the Tour de Trump cycling race, the Trump candidacy or the Trump presidency.

Most of his boasts and rationalisations did not withstand close scrutiny. His Atlantic City business ventures were such a financial disaster they had turned him into a six-time bankrupt. However, his answers were uttered with such complete conviction I felt sure he could have passed a lie-detector test.

What the camera did not record that day was Trump's roving eye. 'Booootiful' was his libidinous reaction to my producer, as he looked her slowly up and down after the interview was over. It was the kind of rich-man sleaziness that revealed both his shamelessness and his misogyny. The fact that we let it go, and lightly laughed it off, also anticipated some of the recurring journalistic failings of the presidential campaign: a hesitancy on the part of reporters to hold him to account, a tendency to be overawed by his Trumpian aura and a cravenness in handing over airtime to this proven ratings winner, whatever the moral outlay. Even my subconscious choice of attire that day, a white silk tie that would not have looked out of place at a mob wedding in Queens or New Jersey, hinted at how ingratiatingly we entered his orbit.

So often it came to be said that Trump defied the laws of political gravity that this commonplace became a cliché. But were we not complicit as journalists in letting him so effortlessly achieve weightlessness?

For all his faults, I left that day with a sense that he was self-aware enough to be in on the Trump joke: that his public persona was a deliberately cartoonish shtick; that the tycoon who appeared each week on *The Apprentice* was an exaggerated rendering of a more reasonable self; that he was laughing up his own sleeve.

As for the possibility of him making a run for the White House, it never even cropped up in our conversation. The notion he could monopolise media attention, seize control of the Republican Party, upend the US political system and swap Fifth for Pennsylvania Avenue seemed risible.

When the interview was over, and our story went to air, I never again expected to report on Donald J. Trump, or to mention him much in passing. Indeed, I left with the firm impression that his best days and grandest designs were in the past. The idea that my first waking act, day after day, month after month, year after year, would be to check his Twitter feed was farcical. So I was not in the least bit perturbed, despite a long-held paranoia about missing breaking stories, to be on holiday the day he descended that golden escalator to announce his bid for the presidency. It seemed like a brand-boosting stunt. A narcissistic pseudo-candidacy. A novelty act. An entertainment rather than political story: one that might provide the lead for *Access Hollywood* but not the evening news, although admittedly the two were becoming harder to tell apart. The BBC did not even dispatch a camera crew to Trump Tower.

In any case, within 36 hours of his campaign launch, cable news channels were consumed by the horror unfolding in Charleston, South Carolina. There, a 21-year-old had walked into a prayer meeting at the Emanuel African Methodist Episcopal Church, sat for an hour during the Wednesday-night devotions and even expressed opinions about the scriptures, then pulled out a Glock 41 .45 calibre handgun and shot dead nine African-American worshippers.

When it emerged that the shooter, Dylann Roof, was a white supremacist who lauded the Confederate flag and intended his massacre to ignite a race war, Charleston took on an even more malign historical significance. Referred to as 'Mother Emanuel', this was the oldest AME church in Dixie, the country's first independent black denomination and a cradle of black activism stretching from a nascent slave revolt in the early nineteenth century to the struggle for black equality of the '60s. The Reverend Dr Martin Luther King Jr had spoken from its pulpit; so, too, had Booker T. Washington, the great African-American educator. Its black-tiled spire could be seen from the ramparts of Fort Sumter in Charleston Harbor, where in 1861 the first shots of the American Civil War had rung out. So in addition to the ritual calls for tighter gun controls came fresh demands for a racial reckoning and, in particular, the banishment of the Confederate battle flag from the grounds of the State House in Columbia, a row that had rumbled on in South Carolina for decades.

Over the coming weeks the arc of the moral universe seemed more pliable than usual, and for progressives it bent decisively towards justice. Barack Obama, in one of the more electrifying moments of his presidency, surprised mourners at the funeral of the Reverend Clementa Pinckney, the slain pastor of Mother Emanuel, by launching into 'Amazing Grace'. So often hesitant to explore publicly the racial meaning of his political ascent, it was as if he had belatedly decided to assume fully the role of America's first black president.

'For too long, we've been blind to the way past injustices continue to shape the present,' Obama said on a day remembered not for his lyricism but rather for his song. 'Perhaps we see that now.'[1]

That very evening, the president returned to a White House bathed in rainbow colours, a floodlight display celebrating the Supreme Court's ruling earlier in the day, codifying same-sex marriage as a nationwide right. For jubilant members of the LGBT community the ruling was akin to the *Brown* decision of the '50s, which signalled the end of southern school segregation. It promised first-class citizenship and the sharing of a now universal right. Only the day before, the conservative-leaning Supreme Court had delivered another victory for progressives by rejecting a constitutional challenge to the Affordable Care Act, or 'Obamacare' as it came to be known, the signature health reform that promised to make him a genuinely transformational president.

A few weeks later I returned to South Carolina, this time to watch the Confederate colours being lowered at the State House grounds from the ten-metre flagpole. On a stiflingly hot day, amidst tears of joy and relief, a multi-generational crowd of African-Americans bore witness as the battle flag of an army fighting to preserve slavery was furled and packed off to a nearby museum.

Such culminating moments lend themselves to over-extrapolation, especially for foreign correspondents, who tend to work in bold colours rather than pastel shades. So it was tempting to view the coming down of the flag as a final surrender of the American Civil War, the end of a long defeat. At the very least, it seemed like the closing of a chapter in which the white nationalists who revered this fabric of hate ended up once more firmly on the wrong side of history, a lost cause lost again.

What was soon dubbed the 'summer of love' felt in some ways like a belated fulfilment, six years after entering the White House, of Obama's 'Yes We Can' America. A triumph of progressivism; even a reformist 'end of history' moment, in which liberal gains, while far from being universally accepted, were nonetheless irreversible.

Victories had been achieved in two climactic fights, over the hateful iconography of the Confederacy and the rainbow colours of same-sex marriage. Just as emblematic was success in the legal battle over Obamacare, a legislative trophy beyond the grasp of Harry Truman, John F. Kennedy, Lyndon Johnson, Jimmy Carter or Bill Clinton. With 'God, gays and guns' America reeling, the Democrats looked forward to the upcoming presidential race with preening self-confidence. Not only did history seem to be on their side, but so too did the demographics of a fast-changing America. The 2016 electorate would be the most racially and ethnically diverse polity America had ever seen, with nearly a third of voters either Hispanic, African-American, Asian or another racial or ethnic minority.

Thus it seemed preordained that the first female president would follow the first black president into the White House.

Here, though, we erred. In the end, 17 June 2015, the day Dylann Roof massacred those defenceless parishioners, altered history much less than 16 June 2015, the day Donald Trump launched his presidential campaign. What we were witnessing that summer was not some liberal Eden but the beginning of a rage-filled blowback. Many of us – most of us – had badly misread the zeitgeist. The coming down of the Confederate flag no more marked the defeat of racism than the election of Barack Obama. The Affordable Care Act, rather than being immutable, would soon come under renewed attack. Evangelical Christians, for whom the rainbow flag was a red rag, were newly galvanised. Seemingly we were seeing the victory of racial and LGBT identity politics, where marginalised groups achieved singular goals. However, its counterpoint was the resurgence of something that historically had always been more dominant, the politics of white resentment.

In Donald Trump, those who felt marginalised and maligned now had a figurehead. Just as millions of Americans had projected their hopes onto Obama, many now channelled their muttered fears through the billionaire: of immigrants taking their jobs, of Mexicans contaminating their communities with narcotics and gangsterism, of African-Americans advancing too fast, of political correctness smothering their culture, of liberal do-gooders seizing their guns, of transnational corporate capitalism laying waste to their once thriving towns.

'Make America Great Again' and 'Build the Wall'. Two slogans neatly summed up the nationalism, nativism and nostalgia that fuelled his candidacy. The addition of the word 'again' proved to be a masterstroke, for it turned the slogan into a sentimental catch-all. Trump, rather than sketching out a timeline himself, let voters decide for themselves when America had last been great. He was a revivalist who did not specify precisely what he was seeking to revive. This gave his supporters the historic licence to conjure up kingdoms of the mind, places that existed only in the abstract, for the country to revisit. For some, American greatness was found in the post-Cold War peace and prosperity of the '90s. For others it was the early '70s, before automation started killing off so many manufacturing jobs. For many it was those supposed sunny uplands of the '50s, before the civil rights movement had granted African-Americans first-class citizenship and women's liberation had challenged the patriarchy.

Asked in January 2016 to be more specific about when America was great, Trump pinpointed the '80s, the decade he rose to national prominence. 'I think during the Reagan years we were very good,' he said. 'We felt good about our country.'² But such specificity was rare.

Personifying the moment, mirroring the spirit of the times, had long been Donald Trump's particular genius. If decades have personalities, then he came to embody them over and over. In the '80s, not even Ronald Reagan embodied the era of Reaganism quite like Trump. In the 1990s, the decade of tabloid sensationalism, his divorce from Ivana Trump and his affair with Marla Maples, who became his second wife, made him a front-page 'Best Sex I've Ever Had' fixture in *The New York Post* and *New York Daily News*, thereby magnifying his fame. In the noughties, the decade of reality television, social media and the celebrity-worshipping fad of being famous for being famous, *The Apprentice* and Twitter amplified his stardom.

As for his political rise, it came in the post-Great Recession decade of grievance and populist vengeance. In his latest spirit-of-the-age makeover, he became a cipher for Rust Belt rage in America's old industrial heartland, a billionaire recast as a working-class hero. In this age of disruption, he emerged as the ultimate disruptive politician, a one-man particle collider for the political, cultural, economic and technological changes that had reshaped the country with such manic suddenness.

Because the 2016 presidential election was decided by fewer than 78,000 votes in three industrial battleground states – Michigan,

Wisconsin and Pennsylvania – it was easy to see his freak victory as a historical accident. However, it also seemed historically inescapable: as much a culmination as an aberration. As the politically impossible became real on 20 January 2017, and Donald Trump raised his hand to take the presidential oath of office, the words used by the Frenchman Alexis de Tocqueville to describe the revolution in his homeland in 1789 also seemed to match this earth-rattling moment: 'So inevitable, yet so completely unforeseen.' Arguably, the bigger surprise, given the direction America had been travelling for the previous 40 years, was that Barack Obama became America's 44th president, rather than Trump becoming its 45th. Both were figureheads, but of two very different Americas.

If the coverage of the 2016 election had been based on the false assumption that Donald Trump could not possibly win, there was a widespread perception early in 2020 that he might not lose. His political vital signs were strong. He had survived his impeachment trial. His presidential approval rating matched its highest ever level. Polls measuring national satisfaction suggested the most buoyant mood in nearly 15 years. He could boast a strong economy and benefit from the advantages of incumbency, a combination that usually yields a first-term president four more years. The betting markets anointed him the favourite.

Clearly, many Americans yearned for a presidency they could have on in the background: Joe Biden's soft jazz after the round-the-clock heavy metal of the Trump years. But at the beginning of election year it was questionable whether the 77-year-old former vice-president could hold a tune. In Iowa and New Hampshire, the more voters saw of him, the more they witnessed his fragilities. For those of us who watched him on the campaign trail, struggling sometimes to finish sentences and regularly losing his train of thought, his fourth- and fifth-place showings in those early contests came as no surprise.

There was also the question of whether America would countenance as president Biden's main Democratic rival, Bernie Sanders. The notion of a one-time socialist sitting behind the desk in the Oval Office arguably required a greater leap of imagination than the thought of a Trumpian second term. Donald Trump stood a strong chance of renewing his lease on the White House.

Then, of course, everything changed. The coronavirus reached American shores. The United States eventually went into lockdown. The country confronted the gravest public health crisis since the Spanish Flu a hundred years earlier, its most jolting economic shock since the Great Depression and, following the killing of George Floyd, the most widespread racial turbulence since 1968. Covid-19 paralysed much of the country, and completely upended the race for the White House. It granted Joe Biden a cloak of invisibility, a useful concealment for a candidate often so fumbling and frail. Donald Trump, meanwhile, wrapped himself in the mantle of a wartime president, but in a battle that America quickly started to lose.

Faced with this viral onslaught, Trump became more specific about when America was great. He identified a date. He instructed us exactly where to travel back in time. 'Before the plague', he kept telling his campaign rallies, in an ever more self-pitying tone, when the United States had had what he boasted was the strongest economy in the history of the world.

But even his mishandling of Covid-19 did not completely doom Donald Trump. As America's death toll spiralled upwards, soaring past 100,000 and then 200,000 fatalities, the president remained politically viable. And though polls repeatedly suggested Joe Biden enjoyed a commanding lead, nobody was entirely sure whether those surveys could be trusted. In the final weeks of campaigning, when Trump drew huge crowds of adoring and mask-less supporters, he believed another upset was in the offing. Few pundits felt confident enough to flatly contradict him, because America had become so hard to read and the polling was so unreliable.

On election night I was in Wilmington, Delaware, the Biden HQ, and in regular touch with members of his inner circle who had studied the actual voting data and were convinced they had won. Unlike the Clinton team four years earlier, which sensed early on that it had lost, Biden was hitting his targets in key battleground states. Yet as the early results started coming in, there was panic from Democrats watching on television when Trump took Florida and opened up a 500,000-vote lead in Pennsylvania. Many experienced a stomach-churning sensation: the freak-out fear that they were reliving the horror of 2016.

This red mirage of early Trumpian success was quickly followed, of course, by a blue shift, as an unprecedented number of postal ballots were counted. Biden gained Arizona. Trump's lead in Georgia evaporated. Clawing back Wisconsin, Michigan and finally Pennsylvania, Joe Biden started to take a joyride through the Rust Belt on his road to the White House. By mid-morning on Saturday, when four days after Election Day the US networks finally called the race, he could claim victory.

Yet the 2020 election could hardly be described as a repudiation of Donald Trump. Nowhere near. This presidential outlier received more than 74 million votes, an almost 18 per cent increase from four years earlier. Like Joe Biden, he smashed the record set by Barack Obama in 2008 for the most votes received by a presidential candidate. He took 25 states and recorded a higher share of the vote, 46.8 per cent, than when he won the White House. Out of the more than 159 million votes cast, Biden's winning margins in key states were relatively small. In Arizona, it was 10,457 votes; in Georgia, 11,779; and in Wisconsin, 20,608. Had Trump won those three states, which would have required a shift of less than 43,000 votes, he would have remained as president.[3]

Trump's strong showing buried once and for all the notion that his victory in 2016 had been some cosmic fluke. Close to half of voting Americans had studied the fine print of his presidency and clicked on the terms and conditions.

That Saturday night in Delaware, Joe Biden held a drive-in victory party in the car park of a convention centre, which was as much a catharsis as a celebration. To honks of car horns and the muffled cheers of supporters wearing masks, the president-elect called for an end to the 'grim era of demonisation' and said it was 'time to heal'. 'We are not enemies,' he told his flag-waving supporters. 'We are Americans.' Yet even as he spoke, there was still no agreement on who had won the presidential election. The two Americas were at loggerheads.

How did the United States arrive at this point of disunion? Why was this fading superpower unravelling before our eyes? What brought us to this point?

To locate the origins of this divisiveness one could justifiably reach back to the revolutionary era. It was the founding fathers, after all, who, in something of a constitutional afterthought, came up with the Electoral College, a flawed mechanism that enabled Trump to win the presidency in 2016 despite a three million deficit in the popular vote. His insurgent candidacy also benefited enormously from the dysfunction on Capitol Hill, partly the fault of an imperfectly designed system that established the Senate as a bulwark against change and a House whose members had to seek re-election every two years, forcing them to engage in a relentless permanent campaign.

Nor would a journey through the battlefields of the Civil War be a needless detour, given how they continue to shape the contours of American life. Gettysburg, Antietam, Manassas and Fort Sumter remind us that polarisation is not a new phenomenon. Rather, it is America's default setting. The United States has always been a fight between liberal and illiberal forces, and an unending tug-of-war between the expression of individual rights and encroachment of national government. Modern-day presidential elections have often felt like referendums on the '60s, that tumultuous decade of divergence, so it is worth remembering that the '60s themselves were in many ways a referendum on the Civil War and the nettlesome notion that every citizen should be treated equally regardless of their pigmentation. Disunion has long been as much a feature of American life as union.

In search of traceable roots, we could dig into the Know Nothing movement, the nativist party that flourished briefly in the mid-nineteenth century, or the isolationism of the pre-war years, which gave rise to demagogues such as the celebrity aviator Charles

Lindbergh, who popularised the phrase 'America First'. But the prime focus of this book, a personal journey as well as a historical exploration, is the post-war years, when an age of collaboration came to be supplanted by an age of confrontation.

This kind of enterprise runs the risk of becoming a journalistic version of reverse engineering, where the plot mechanics build neatly and automatically towards a known outcome. But even with the benefit of hindsight, some of the moving parts remain fairly well hidden.

For anyone trying to make sense of the present, the question is always how far to reach back. But to explain how Donald Trump made it to the White House in 2017, and came close to renewing his tenancy in the 2020 election, I am going to retrace my own steps. So I'll begin with my first trip to the United States, when the mood was more buoyant. It was the time of Ronald Reagan's 'It's morning again in America', a wholly different place from the dark dystopia of Donald Trump's 'American carnage' inaugural address, the mass mourning of Covid-19 and the storming of the US Capitol.

1

It's Morning Again in America

Flying into Los Angeles, a glide-like descent that takes you from the desert over the mountains to the outer suburbs dotted with kidney-shaped swimming pools and finally to the rim of the Pacific Ocean, always brings on a near-narcotic surge of nostalgia. For this was the flight path I followed over 30 years ago, as I fulfilled a boyhood dream to visit the United States.

America had always fired my imagination, as a place and as an idea, so it was hardly love at first sight. My infatuation had started long before with cop shows, westerns, superhero comic strips and movies – *Batman*, *West Side Story*, *Starsky & Hutch*, *Grease*. Gotham exerted more of a pull than London. Washington was of more interest than Westminster. My 16-year-old self could quote more presidents than prime ministers. Like so many wide-eyed new arrivals, like so many of my British compatriots, I felt an instant sense of belonging, a fealty borne of familiarity.

Eighties America lived up to its billing. From the multi-lane freeways to the cavernous fridges; from drive-in movie theatres to drive-through burger joints; from pizza slices that required origami folds to consume to steaks the size of frisbees. Coming from a country where too many people were reconciled to their fate from too early an age, the animating energy of the American dream was seductive and unshackling. Upward mobility was not a given amongst my schoolmates. Also striking was the absence of resentment: the belief success was something to emulate not envy. The glimpse of a passing Cadillac aroused wholly different feelings than the sight in my homeland of a Rolls-Royce.

From the moment I passed through the arrivals hall at LAX, under the winsome smile of the country's movie-star president, I loved the bigness, the brashness and the boldness of this land of plenty. The smog-piercing skyscrapers of downtown LA seemed double the height of anything I had seen before. Tomorrowland at Disneyland back then really did seem like a portal into the future. Mega-churches came not with flying buttresses but with stadium-style seating, giant illuminated crosses on their roofs and, as at the Crystal Cathedral in Garden Grove, 10,000 panes of reflective glass shaped like a four-pointed Star of Bethlehem and giant doors that opened up for car-borne worshippers.

The family hosting me, who had emigrated from Britain at the end of the '60s, had a spacious house in the nearby suburb of Fountain Valley, a flat, largely featureless conurbation set amidst the urban sprawl of Orange County. Their home had a garage that could accommodate three cars, sofas that turned corners, an open-plan kitchen that looked out over a poolside terrace, and an array of household items I had never before seen: an ice-maker, telephone answer machine and super-sized television with a super-sized number of channels. These included MTV, whose looping stream of music videos vied with the endless hum of air-conditioning units straining to refrigerate the Southern Californian heat.

My father's best man, an engineer in the aeronautics industry who rode to work every day along the freeway on his motorbike – even his commute exemplified the rugged individualism of his adopted country – had clearly prospered. Now I became the beneficiary of his family's Californian dream. On arrival, I toasted my good fortune with a tall glass of luminous yellow soda with the nutritious-sounding name of Mountain Dew and took a dip in the pool. America really did seem to be a land of infinite choice and possibility.

It was 1984. Los Angeles was hosting the Olympics, and I arrived in the country just in time to watch the opening ceremony. In this festival of Americana, a marching band blasted out Broadway show tunes and the rousing martial anthems of John Philip Sousa. An African-American gospel choir, swaying from side to side in billowing fuchsia robes, sang 'When the Saints Go Marching In'. In a gambolling portrayal of manifest destiny, a troupe of ballet dancers dressed as wranglers, ropers and cowgirls pushed westward to the strains of 'Hoedown' from Aaron Copland's *Rodeo*. Eighty-four pianists at 84 grand pianos answered the siren call of the soaring clarinet to thump out Gershwin's 'Rhapsody in Blue'. A pilot even rocketed into the stadium with a jetpack affixed to his back, the cue for a Disney-style mascot called Sam the Eagle to shuffle awkwardly onto the running track dressed in a red, white and blue Yankee Doodle Dandy outfit. For the host nation, the games of the XXIII Olympiad were a modern-day gold rush. In the absence of the Soviet Union, boycotting in retaliation for America's refusal to compete in the Moscow Games four years earlier, US athletes dominated the medals table as never before. McDonald's had a 'When the US wins, you win' scratch-card promotion, planned before Eastern bloc countries announced they were staying away, offering Big Macs, French fries and regular Cokes if Americans won gold, silver or bronze in the event concealed under those grey metallic strips. So for weeks I feasted on free fast food, the calorific accompaniment to chants of 'USA! USA!'

This was the summertime of American resurgence. After the long national nightmare of Vietnam, Watergate and the Iranian hostage crisis, the United States demonstrated its capacity for renewal. 1984, far from being the dystopian hell presaged by George Orwell, was a time of optimism and contentment. Uncle Sam seemed happy again in his own skin – even the plastic feathers of that opening ceremony mascot. 'Born in the USA', Bruce Springsteen's protest song about Rust Belt decline, which topped the charts that summer, was repurposed as a hymn of national self-love.

For millions, truly it was morning again in America, the slogan of Ronald Reagan's 1984 re-election campaign and the title of the most successful campaign ad in political history. Filmed in California, this Rockwellian montage showed a paperboy hurling a newspaper onto a perfectly manicured front lawn, a family drawing up outside their new white clapboard home in a wood-panelled station wagon, and a wedding ceremony officiated by an elderly pastor cupping in his hands an open Bible, who looked like he had stepped from the set of a Frank Capra movie. It ended with a patriotic tableau of Americans peering skyward, as the Stars and Stripes were unfurled, the only time people of colour featured in the minute-long film.

'Today more men and women will go to work than ever before in our country's history,' claimed the caramel commentary. 'Under the leadership of Ronald Reagan, our country is prouder and stronger and better.' The sentimentalism, it was said, reduced members of Reagan's Secret Service detail to tears.[1]

Prouder, stronger and better. After emerging from its deepest recession since the Great Depression, the country had witnessed a stunning economic turnaround. Reagan had also staged a dramatic political comeback, for even after an attempt on his life 70 days into his presidency, which boosted his popularity following a troubled start, there were stretches when he looked like becoming a one-term president.

'The stench of failure hangs over Ronald Reagan's White House,' declared *The New York Times* in the aftermath of the Republicans' dismal showing in the 1982 congressional midterms, when his approval rating slumped to 35 per cent.[2]

Seemingly the Democrats also had a potential candidate with the star power, personal narrative and name recognition to beat him: the former astronaut Senator John Glenn of Ohio.

By the start of 1984, however, as he announced his bid for re-election, Reagan could boast, 'America is back and standing tall.' No longer was there double-digit unemployment. Inflation had been tamed. Taxes were lower. Business confidence was high. The 'Reagan recession' was a thing of the past. The Olympics generated a red, white and blue wave that swept across the country. Chants of 'USA! USA!' became the sound-bed for Reagan's rallies, along with the country singer Lee Greenwood's anthem 'God Bless the USA' and Springsteen's 'Born in the USA', which Republicans shamelessly appropriated.

On Election Day, this patriotic surge completely overwhelmed his Democratic opponent, Walter Mondale. Reagan won 58.8 per cent of the popular vote and 49 out of 50 states. Even though the Democrats had, for the first time, included a woman on a major party ticket, the New York congresswoman Geraldine Ferraro, Reagan managed to win 58 per cent of the female vote – an early indication women would not necessarily favour a fellow female.[3]

Even in one-time Democratic strongholds, Reagan was triumphant. Back in 1960, Macomb County, just north of Detroit, handed John F. Kennedy his biggest victory in any suburban county. In 1984, its heavily unionised electorate went two to one to Reagan and thus became the spiritual home of the 'Reagan Democrat'.[4] Had it not been for 3,761 votes in Minnesota, Mondale's home state, Reagan would have become the first presidential candidate to complete an Electoral College state sweep.[5] This ideological election traumatised Democrats, inflicting psychological scars that have never fully healed, not least because Reagan's anti-government populism severed the umbilical link between the party and the working class.

The United States could hardly be described as politically harmonious. With the Democrats keeping their three-decade stranglehold on the House of Representatives, there was the usual divided government. But the president's campaign poster from four years earlier had proven prophetic: 'America: Reagan Country'.

The re-elected president brought his cheerfulness to his second inaugural, which was held inside the Capitol Rotunda because of the arctic temperatures outside.

'My fellow citizens, our nation is poised for greatness,' he declared. 'Let history say of us, "These were golden years when the American Revolution was reborn, when freedom gained new life, when America reached for her best."'

The country was in the ascendant again. Not so paranoid as it was in the 1950s, not so restive as it was in the 1960s and nowhere near as demoralised as it had been in the 1970s.

Underpinning the Olympic celebrations was a commonality of spirit and purpose. From Gershwin's 'Rhapsody in Blue' to a polyglot team of US athletes bedecked with medals. From that pilot who buzzed the LA Memorial Coliseum in his space-age jetpack to those McDonald's customers who left with free Big Macs. There was reason for rejoicing. The present was golden. The future was something to welcome, not fear. America felt like America again. The United States seemingly had a president around whom the states could unite. When Reagan claimed 'today is better than yesterday, and tomorrow will be better than today,' most Americans believed him.

It was only years later, when the souvenir Olympic editions of the *Los Angeles Times* I shipped back to Britain had started to fray and yellow, that I realised Ronald Reagan was in actual fact one of the founding fathers of America's modern-day polarisation.

———

Had it been a screen test, he probably would have flunked it. Absent was the usual poise that was a hallmark of his appearances on the *General Electric Theater*, his weekly Sunday-night CBS television show in the '50s. Lacking was his usual jaunty rhythm. Galloping through sentences and failing to pause between them, he seemed uncharacteristically nervous. Agitated even.

The setting, a Los Angeles television studio dressed to resemble a political convention hall, right down to the red, white and blue bunting draped from the speaker's podium, added to his awkwardness. The audience, in which some women, as well as men, wore cowboy hats, was strangely passive, as if it was made up of extras yet to receive stage direction. Camera cutaways showed one man in a chequered shirt, looking distracted and bored. Others were expressionless. Not even Ronald Reagan's first attacks on big government, high taxation and intellectual elites lifted them. The actor had been speaking for almost ten minutes before receiving his first smattering of applause, which came after a sideswipe at President Lyndon Johnson. Thereafter, the partisan audience became more responsive to Reagan's attacks on Washington. 'When the government tells you you're depressed, lie down and be depressed' got a ripple of laughter. 'A government bureau is the nearest thing we'll ever see to eternal life on earth' got those cowboy hats bobbing up and down. Now that Reagan had hit his stride, the audience behaved more like fans outside a movie premiere, cheering what essentially became his presidential manifesto. A political star was born.

Airing just a week before the 1964 presidential election, this infomercial paid for by the Barry Goldwater campaign came too late to rescue the Arizonian senator from electoral annihilation. In the retelling of Goldwater's defeat, however, it was nonetheless rendered glorious. It came to be known simply as 'The Speech'. Over the 26 minutes it took to deliver, Reagan demonstrated how it was possible in the television age to become an overnight sensation, and create a political brand with a single, well-received performance. 'The Speech' thus became the crucible moment in his conservative canonisation. Afterwards, a group of rich, right-wing Californians urged him to run for the governorship, a summons that altered the course of modern-day conservatism and set the Grand Old Party on the path it travels to this day. As the waspish columnist George Will famously observed, Goldwater lost 44 states but won the future. In 1980, Ronald Reagan became the belated victor.

The Lazarus-like tale of how right-wing Republicans turned the most humiliating defeat in the party's history into a takeover of the conservative movement doubles as the foundation story for the polarised state of modern-day US politics. Everything changed, of course, with the passage of the 1964 Civil Rights Act, the landmark legislation that dismantled southern segregation and reshaped America's political landscape. Lyndon Johnson reportedly predicted, as he added his signature to the legislation, that the Democrats had kissed goodbye to the south for a generation.

It ended up being a permanent divorce rather than a trial separation. The Solid Democratic South, the old slave states of the Confederacy that hated the party of Abraham Lincoln, became reliably Republican in presidential elections, an astonishing historical inversion.

Even though a higher proportion of Republican senators voted for the Civil Rights Act than Democratic senators, Goldwater and

Reagan had both been firmly opposed. So from the ruins of the 1964 landslide came the southern strategy, which exploited white unease about black advance to turn Democratic voters Republican, the basis of the GOP's domination of presidential politics for the next two decades. The Republican Party became the home of white voters anxious about the pace of racial reform. It won five of the next six presidential elections largely as a result.

As part of this dramatic realignment, dyed-in-the-wool segregationists, such as Senator Strom Thurmond of South Carolina, who in 1957 had launched a 24-hour solo filibuster in an attempt to block a civil rights act, defected from the Democrats to the Republicans, a switch that forever altered the character of both parties. Before then, the schisms in post-war politics were primarily within the parties, rather than between them: white supremacists versus non-south progressives in the Democratic Party, internationalists against isolationists in the Republican. Now there was a stark divide between Democrats and Republicans.

At the start of the decade the political theorist Daniel Bell published *The End of Ideology*, a set of essays arguing that, in the absence of a philosophical battle between left and right, elections would focus on managerialism, a candidate's expertise rather than ideas. Now it became more ideologically charged.[6] Following the passage of the Civil Rights Act and its companion reform the 1965 Voting Rights Act, the parties became more uniform and antagonistic towards each other, even though there remained considerable overlap between liberal Republicans and conservative Democrats.

Just as the 1964 Civil Rights 'Act transformed the political geography of America, so the 1965 Immigration and Nationality Act had the unintended consequence of radically altering the country's demographics. Signed by Lyndon Johnson with the Statue of Liberty as his epic backdrop, the act ended national origin quotas that favoured white immigrants from northern Europe, and for the first time accepted all nationalities on a more equal basis.

At the start of the 1960s, 87 per cent of immigrants came from Europe. Fifty years later, 90 per cent came from other corners of the globe. The browning of America would take decades, but LBJ had set the country on course to have a non-white majority population by the middle of the 21st century. Ultimately, these three landmark acts had an overlapping effect: to make white Americans fear their dominant position in society was under threat from people of colour.

The repercussions of the Vietnam War, yet another splintering event, also reverberated for decades afterwards. The sight each night on the evening news of so many young American conscripts being killed had an especially radicalising effect on the left. Conversely, the sight each night on the evening news of so many young American protesters burning the US flag had a reactionary effect on the right. Blue-collar Americans especially became more suspicious not just of anti-war protesters but also of feminist activists, black agitators and liberal-minded journalists who gave them sympathetic coverage.

By the end of the '60s, then, the battle-lines in presidential elections came to be more unambiguously drawn. Ahead of the 1960 contest, the liberal historian Arthur M. Schlesinger Jr felt it necessary to dash off a quick campaign book, *Kennedy or Nixon? Does It Make Any Difference?*, outlining points of divergence between the two candidates, which to many voters were not immediately obvious.

In 1964, true to Goldwater's promise to offer 'a choice not an echo', the differences were blatant, as they have been in most elections since. Goldwater, a hawk faced former army pilot who buzzed his own convention at the Cow Palace in San Francisco in a rented light plane, signalled the change with one electrifying line from his acceptance speech: 'Extremism in the defense of liberty is no vice. And let me remind you also that moderation in the pursuit of justice is no virtue.'

What made the rise of the New Right all the more noteworthy was the likelihood in the early '60s that the GOP would become the party of Rockefeller, rather than the party of Reagan. When the Republican National Committee conducted a post-mortem of its defeat in 1960, it blamed Nixon for being too stridently conservative. It looked, then, as if the moderate Governor of New York, Nelson Rockefeller, another billionaire who wanted to swap his residence on Fifth Avenue for the White House, would become the party's standard-bearer. Liberal Republicans seemed poised to beat Goldwater Republicans. Yet the scandal surrounding Rockefeller's messy divorce from his wife, Mary, and remarriage to his one-time secretary, 'Happy', altered that trajectory.

The cumulative effect of Johnson signing the Civil Rights Act and, less momentously, Rockefeller filing his divorce papers in 1962 was to shift the Republican Party's centre of gravity. Over the coming years, it moved from Wall Street to the Sunbelt, the region stretching from Florida through the other Old Confederate states to Southern California; from East Coast Episcopalians and Presbyterians to 'Bible Belt' evangelicals and Pentecostals; from golf clubs, chambers of commerce and Connecticut commuter trains to gun ranges, NASCAR racetracks and eventually mega-churches.

For Reagan to emerge as the frontman for Goldwaterism and the genial face of Sunbelt radicalism required considerable political shapeshifting. As a young man, he had idolised Franklin Delano Roosevelt, describing himself as a 'haemophiliac liberal'. Also he was a union leader, the president of the Screen Actors Guild. In 1952, though, he voted Republican for the first time, having failed to persuade General Dwight D. Eisenhower to run as a Democrat, and did so again in the 1956 presidential election, when the former Supreme Allied Commander trounced the liberal darling Adlai Stevenson for a second time.

As the '50s progressed, and Reagan's role as a spokesman for the American conglomerate General Electric deepened, his conservatism became more pronounced. On flights between speaking appearances, he consumed GE's in-house pamphlets trumpeting American free enterprise. He also railed against what he saw as the moral superiority and intellectual condescension of liberal elitists. Though in 1960 he remained a registered Democrat, he voted for Richard Nixon over his fellow Irish-American Jack Kennedy. 'Under the tousled boyish haircut is still old Karl Marx,' Reagan wrote to Nixon.[7] Finally, aged 51, he registered as a Republican.

After the 1964 election, Reagan blamed Goldwater's defeat on moderate Republican traitors rather than the radical right. Other conservatives felt the same. 'Far from admitting that Goldwater-style conservatism spells disaster at the polls,' wrote the influential columnists Rowland Evans and Robert Novak, who had started to take a close interest in Reagan, 'the conservatives now contend all they need is a candidate to package the doctrine in a more appetizing fashion.'

That candidate, conservatives thought, was Reagan. As Evans and Novak pointed out, he brought together 'Barry Goldwater's doctrine with John F. Kennedy's technique.'[8]

When Reagan announced his bid for the California governorship in 1966 with a 30-minute infomercial in which he mounted his usual broadsides against the growth of 'big brother, paternalistic government', the Democratic incumbent, 'Pat' Brown, could scarcely believe his luck. Thinking he was guaranteed a third term in Sacramento, he mocked Reagan as a B-list actor who was on set making movies such as *Bedtime for Bonzo* while he was in the Governor's Mansion tackling the state's problems (a forerunner of the jibe aimed by Hillary Clinton at Donald Trump that he was appearing on *Celebrity Apprentice* while she was in the basement Situation Room complex on the night of the Osama bin Laden raid).[9]

Reagan, however, benefited from the lawlessness unleashed during the Watts riot in 1965, when 34 people lost their lives and 4,000 members of the National Guard had to be deployed on the streets of Los Angeles, and from anti-war unrest on California's campuses. 'They chant like Tarzan, look like Jane and smell like Cheetah,' was a go-to line for Reagan when confronted by 'hippie' protesters.

Because he had been cast as the good guy in so many films, the Democrats found it hard to portray him as a right-wing extremist. Reagan won by almost a million votes, a portent of victories to come. After the 1984 landslide, Pat Brown opined, 'We Democrats in California made the same mistake [in 1966] the whole Democratic party made a dozen years later: we mightily underrated him as a politician, as a leader.'[10] The same would be said of Donald Trump.

Two years after entering the Governor's Mansion in Sacramento, Reagan made a half-hearted bid for the Republican presidential nomination. In the aftermath of Robert Kennedy's assassination in Los Angeles in 1968 during his campaign for the Democratic presidential nomination, however, even amiable right-wingers were regarded as too divisive.

Political friends therefore urged him to be patient. 'Young man, you'll be president some day,' Strom Thurmond prophesied during a campaign swing through Dixie. 'But not this year.'[11] Not yet ready for Reagan, the party opted for the relative moderate, Richard Nixon, who ran for the presidency making shrill calls to restore law and order on the campuses and in the inner cities, but who governed as a centrist.

By the time Reagan launched his second bid for the White House in 1975, an audacious attempt to oust the incumbent president Gerald Ford, politics had changed in his favour. Nixon's reliance during the 1968 campaign on consultants, pollsters and *Mad Men*-style marketeers accelerated its professionalisation. Politics became more of an exercise in marketing and branding, with Nixon packaging himself as a cipher for what he called the 'Silent Majority'.

As part of this image makeover, the GOP set about shedding its staid image as the party of Wall Street and projecting more Main Street appeal. Messaging became sharper and more disciplined. Hard-nosed political operatives came to the fore, such as the young Roger Ailes, the future head of Fox News, who believed the political future belonged to candidates who could perform on television and who relished cultural conflict.

In that poisoned vein, Ailes packed Nixon's town hall meetings with anti-war activists, knowing they would barrage his candidate with hostile questions. Not only did it make for riveting television, it framed the election as a choice between law and order and counter-cultural chaos. This was verdant terrain for Reagan, and a winning formula for conservative politics and right-wing broadcasting for decades to come.[12]

Nixon chose Spiro Agnew as his running mate, a pugilistic populist who referred to anti-war protesters as 'pigs', boasted he did not need to visit black ghettoes because 'if you have seen one city slum, you've seen them all' and later on maligned the media as 'the nattering nabobs of negativity' – a fancy forerunner of 'the fake news media'. As the 1968 campaign got more ugly, the Governor of Maryland seemed in a race to the bottom with the former Governor of Alabama George Wallace, an avowed white supremacist running as a third-party candidate, to see who could cause most offence. Both were practitioners of what the historian Dan Carter labelled 'the politics of rage'.

The rise in the early 1970s of the modern-day primary system, with its series of state contests starting in Iowa and New Hampshire, meant presentational skills and showmanship became more of a prerequisite. No longer were nominations negotiated in smoke-filled rooms – Hubert Humphrey, the Democratic nominee in 1968, had not contested a single primary. Instead, they were decided increasingly on television.

The Watergate scandal and Nixon's resignation was another boon for Reagan, for it made his anti-Washington rhetoric all the more resonant. Outsiders, such as the little-known Governor of Georgia Jimmy Carter, suddenly became viable. The newly invigorated primary process, where voters in Iowa and New Hampshire became almost as influential as party bosses, gave them the opportunity to mount insurgent bids for the presidency.

All the time the conservative movement was becoming more godly, doctrinaire and less tolerant of opposing values and ideas, an anti-pluralistic impulse that made it more narrowly partisan. Nixon's courtship of America's most prominent preacher, Billy Graham, brought about a closer collaboration between the GOP and the Southern Baptist Convention, the country's largest Protestant denomination.

The backlash against bra-burning feminists and the campaign for the Equal Rights Amendment brought to the fore unbending activists such as Phyllis Schlafly, who was as proud to be called a 'housewife' as 'the first lady of the conservative movement'.

After the *Roe v. Wade* Supreme Court ruling in 1973, which gave women the right to choose whether they wanted to terminate their pregnancies without excessive government restriction, abortion became a wedge issue, making the GOP the natural home for pro-lifers. Battle-lines were sketched out that have shaped US politics ever since.

Even though Jimmy Carter was a bona-fide born-again Christian and the most openly spiritual president of the twentieth century, his party increasingly rejected social and religious dogmatism: those slick-talking TV evangelicals such as Oral Roberts, Jimmy Swaggart, Pat Robertson and Jim and Tammy Faye Bakker, who railed against pro-choicers, communists, homosexuals and the permissiveness of post-'60s America. Conservative evangelicals, who had been politically dormant in the post-war years, saw how church leaders had lent such moral and institutional support to the civil rights movement and sought to mobilise in favour of right-wing causes. Even though Reagan rarely went to church, he enthusiastically aligned himself with the Religious Right.

Reagan formally announced his candidacy in November 1975 with a bold defence of Goldwaterism. 'The only thing wrong in 1964 was that the voters of this country were still in something of a New Deal syndrome,' he argued, referring to the Great Depression reforms of President Franklin Delano Roosevelt. 'They still believed that federal help was free and that federal programs did solve problems. Now the change has come, and the people no longer have to be convinced that the federal government is too big, too costly and hasn't really solved any problems.'[13]

While the Washington press corps continued to view him as a lightweight – 'The Candidate from Disneyland: Ronald Duck for President,' sneered *Harper's* – the Ford White House took him more seriously, especially after Reagan won the Texas primary. 'We are in real danger of being out-organized by a small number of highly motivated right-wing nuts,' warned an internal memo.[14] Sure enough, Reagan ended up running Ford close, receiving the backing of 1,070 delegates compared to the president's 1,187. However, he could not quite overcome an incumbent president with the backing of the party establishment.

Had it not been for a miscommunication between Ford and Reagan staffers, the former governor might have ended up on the Republican ticket, which could have wrecked his chance of ever becoming president. As it was, the Republican Senator Bob Dole became the vice-presidential nominee after Nelson Rockefeller, Ford's deputy, agreed to step down in recognition of the growing strength of the Republican right. Rockefeller Republicanism had lost its talisman. Ford's subsequent defeat to Jimmy Carter dealt an even more terminal blow to middle-of-the-road Republicanism.

Between the elections of 1976 and 1980, the modern-day conservative movement came into being and took on the form we recognise today. In 1979, the Reverend Jerry Falwell Sr founded the Moral Majority, the organisational home of the Religious Right. The National Rifle Association, following a 1977 coup that ousted its moderate leadership dubbed the 'Revolt at Cincinnati', became more hard-line and partisan. Whereas in the '60s it had supported common-sense gun controls, such as bans on purchasing firearms via mail order and carrying loaded weapons in public, following the assassinations of John F. Kennedy, Robert Kennedy and Martin Luther King, now it fiercely resisted any encroachment on the right to bear arms. In 1980, Reagan became the first presidential candidate to be endorsed by the NRA. Like abortion, gun control became an angry new fault line in American politics.

Right-wing think tanks, such as the Heritage Foundation and American Enterprise Institute, became more ideologically influential, even as the GOP became more overtly anti-intellectual. The most significant was the Federalist Society, founded in 1982, which promoted checks on government power, the protection of individual liberty and an originalist interpretation of the Constitution, which maintained the only way to understand the meaning of this eighteenth-century text was to discern the framers' original intent.

In the rightward shift of the US judiciary, the Federalist Society became the driving force. Almost all of Reagan's judicial appointees were members, foremost amongst them Antonin Scalia, his second appointee to the Supreme Court. This new reading of the Constitution, which rejected liberal ideas about acting in the spirit of the founding fathers, the basis of judicial activism during the civil rights era, became as central to New Right thinking as supply-side economics.

A relaxation of campaign finance laws in the late 1970s, which allowed for the infusion of 'soft money' to fund parties rather than specific candidates, also fuelled the rise of political action committees, which made politics more combative. The National Conservative Political Action Committee, founded in the mid-'70s by a dandyish dirty trickster, Roger Stone, who later had a tattoo of Richard Nixon inked between his shoulder blades, was one of the more aggressive. In 1980, it played a major role in unseating four of the six liberal Democratic senators it targeted, including the Democrats' former presidential nominee George McGovern and the highly respected Indiana senator Birch Bayh, who was beaten by a 33-year-old baby boomer called Dan Quayle. For the first time since the 1950s, the Republicans won back control of the Senate. *Time* magazine's Joe Klein later claimed it marked the start of the modern-day political war.[15]

That year, Reagan became the standard-bearer for this motley crew of conservatives and the spokesman for a movement he had personally done so much to create. In the primaries, he easily overcame the establishment favourite, George H. W. Bush, and was crowned the nominee at the GOP convention in Detroit. Afterwards, he launched his general election campaign in Philadelphia, Mississippi, close to where three civil rights workers, Michael Schwerner, James Chaney and Andrew Goodman, had been murdered by white supremacists in 1964, with a dog-whistle call for 'states rights'. It was rhetorical shorthand, conservative trigger words of widely understood meaning, for allowing the south to take care of race relations without interference from Washington.

This kick-off event at the Neshoba County Fair, days after Reagan had received and rejected the endorsement of the Ku Klux Klan, was a sign both of how the party's centre of gravity had shifted southward and of how aggrieved white voters had become its target demographic.

Gerald Ford was pessimistic about Reagan's chances. 'A very conservative Republican can't win a national election,' he reckoned.[16] Yet in a country reeling from high unemployment and soaring inflation, led by a president who rarely flashed his toothy smile any more, Reagan won the election by asking a brilliantly simplistic question, which he posed in the sole presidential debate: 'Are you better off than you were four years ago?'

Voters in 44 states said no, and handed Reagan 489 of the 538 Electoral College votes, a record number for a non-incumbent presidential candidate. Thus started a political era that would soon come to bear his name.

The galvanising speech. The parlaying of celebrity. The admonishment of the Washington establishment. The takeover of the party. The enunciation of a few gut beliefs. The skill at tapping into white anxieties. The use of race to mobilise the base. The unapologetic patriotism. The improbably close relationship with the Religious Right. The disbelief and mocking tone of Washington reporters. Though Ronald Reagan took 16 years to achieve what Donald Trump managed in a little over 16 months, America's first movie-star president laid the path for America's first reality-TV-star president. In 1980, Reagan even rolled out the slogan that Trump refined and repurposed decades later: 'Let's Make America Great Again.'

Ronald Reagan not only restored faith in America: admirers claim he also made the presidency great again. Unlike Jack Kennedy, whose time in office was tragically cut short, he was not cowed by Congress or hobbled by a schism within his party. Unlike Lyndon Johnson, he was not overwhelmed by war or haunted by the phantom presence of his predecessor. Unlike Richard Nixon, he was not a crook. Unlike Gerald Ford, he was not an accidental – and accident-prone – stand-in. Unlike Jimmy Carter, he was not a pious killjoy. When Reagan left office in January 1989, wistfully peering down as his helicopter banked over 'our little bungalow', as he described the White House to his adoring wife, Nancy, he became the first president since Dwight

D. Eisenhower to complete two terms.[17] After four failed or truncated presidencies finally came a success.

Whereas his predecessor had gone from room to room in the White House switching off lights to save energy, Reagan and his image-makers wheeled in the movie-set kliegs. Alert to the theatrical requirements of the office, he applied the presentational skills he learned as a film star to the presidency. His success lay in amalgamating these two jobs. When the journalist David Brinkley asked in a valedictory interview whether he had learned anything from his career as an actor that had helped him as president, Reagan delivered a telling response: 'There have been times in this office when I've wondered how you could do the job if you hadn't been an actor.' He was the great communicator long before arriving in Washington.[18]

In his first inaugural, various Reaganite traits came together: his cheerleader optimism; his confidence behind a podium; his ability to encapsulate a governing philosophy in bumper-sticker slogans; his relish for the grandest of stages, even if he didn't insist, as Washington lore has it, that the inauguration ceremony be moved for the first time from the east side of the US Capitol to the west, so he could peer out towards California.[19]

From this magnificent pulpit, the new president outlined the Reaganite holy trinity of limited government, lower taxation and a strong military. 'Government is not the solution to our problem, government is the problem,' he famously stated, setting the tone for the next eight years and framing the political debate for the next three decades. From the moment he took the oath of office, he looked and sounded ideally suited to perform what his finest biographer, Lou Cannon, called 'the role of a lifetime'.

By embracing some of the monarchical trappings of the presidency, the former actor dressed the White House as a more epic set. Presidents Ford and Carter, as part of the post-Watergate clean-up, had sought to curb the excesses of Nixon's imperial presidency, with small but symbolic acts such as dropping the playing of 'Hail to the Chief' when they entered the room. Not only did Reagan restore the presidential anthem, but he also summoned back the US Army Herald Trumpets, a ceremonial brass ensemble which sometimes dressed in breeches banished during the Carter and Ford years. The look, however, was more Tinseltown pizazz than eighteenth-century pomp.

Carter, showing the traits of a good neighbour rather than a strong leader, had suburbanised the White House by wearing Mr Rogers-style cardigans in the Oval Office and turning off all those lights. Reagan restored it to being a stately home and the focal point of national attention. Never did he step foot in the Oval Office without first donning a jacket and tie. Visitors to the White House left with gifts of cufflinks embossed with the presidential seal, trinkets that were part of the new paraphernalia of power.[20] His intention always was to refurbish this battered institution.

In the process, Reagan reinvented the modern presidency. He provided the model for the presidential commemorative speech – the oration he delivered on the 40th anniversary of D-Day atop the cliff overlooking Omaha and Utah beaches. 'These are the boys of Pointe du Hoc,' he said, paying tribute to the old men before him who had clambered up the cliffs under a hail of enemy fire. 'These are the men who took the cliffs. These are the champions who helped free a continent. And these are the heroes who helped end a war.' Also, he perfected the 'nation-in-mourning' Oval Office address, his speech after the Challenger disaster in 1986 providing the stencil his successors would follow.

'We will never forget them,' he said of the seven space-shuttle astronauts killed 73 seconds after lift-off, 'nor the last time we saw them, this morning, as they prepared for their journey and waved goodbye and "slipped the surly bonds of earth" to "touch the face of God".'

He invented the contemporary State of the Union address, with its 'heroes in the balcony' and appropriation of stirring personal narratives that belonged to others. 'We don't have to turn to our history books for heroes,' he said in his 1982 State of the Union, as he introduced the first of these human props – a freed POW from Vietnam and a fearless federal worker, Lenny Skutnik, who dived into the freezing waters of the Potomac to rescue a flight attendant after an Air Florida Boeing 737 crashed shortly after take-off from what later became Ronald Reagan National Airport.

Working like location scouts, his White House advance team regularly came up with telegenic settings for set-piece speeches – none more so than the Brandenburg Gate in West Berlin in 1987. Reagan's immortal line, 'Mr Gorbachev, tear down this wall!', would not have conveyed such moral force had it not been delivered in front of the concrete monolith that symbolised Soviet oppression. Thereafter, every presidency aspired to these made-for-television moments.

In contrast to his predecessor, Reagan understood the inspirational power of speech. Serving as Jimmy Carter's speechwriter was not unlike being Franklin Delano Roosevelt's tap-dancing teacher, joked James Fallows, the journalist who occupied that role. In the Reagan team, Peggy Noonan, his most poetic wordsmith, and Michael Deaver, who helped choreograph many of the memorable set-pieces, were more central to Reagan's success than all but a few members of his Cabinet. This was a presidency of images as much as ideas.

Even when Reagan had poor material to work with, he instinctively knew how to squeeze the best out of every lifeless word. A case in point came during that opening ceremony in Los Angeles, when he was restricted to delivering 16 perfunctory words: 'I declare open the Games of Los Angeles celebrating the 23rd Olympiad of the modern era'. Reagan felt the obvious applause line, 'I declare open', was buried at the beginning, so he switched it to the end. Reporters in the White House press pool, who had been handed copies of the script he was supposed to read out, ridiculed him for fluffing his lines.

'The press having a copy of the lines as written are gleefully tagging me with senility & inability to learn my lines', Reagan penned in his diary that night.[21] Ever the showman, however, Reagan knew precisely what he was doing. When they came from his lips, even banalities sounded polished.

His pep talk to the US Olympic team hours before the opening ceremony was also classic Reagan. Invoking George Gipp, the Notre Dame football legend he played in the movies, he implored the athletes, 'Go for it! For yourselves, for your families, for your country. And, you can forgive me if I'm a little presumptuous, do it for the Gipper.'[22]

It demonstrated not only the patriotic optimism that voters found so attractive but also his habit of purloining lines from films. 'Go ahead – make my day,' he warned, Clint Eastwood-style, when Congress threatened to raise taxes. 'The evil empire,' his label for the Soviet Union, sounded like it had been plucked from the opening scroll on the *Star Wars* movies that referred to 'the evil Galactic Empire.'[23]

During a sound-test for a speech to the nation in 1985 on the release of 39 Americans held in Beirut, picked up and later broadcast by the major networks, Reagan joked, 'Boy, I saw *Rambo* last night. I know what to do the next time this happens.'[24]

Reagan looked to the movies for policy inspiration as well. The Matthew Broderick film *War Games* was the spur for the 'Star Wars' defence initiative. And Reagan was so obsessed with the imminence of an alien invasion that he proposed to Gorbachev at the Geneva summit in 1985 that the United States and the Soviet Union join forces to repel any extra-terrestrial threat, an idea inspired by the 1951 science-fiction movie *The Day the Earth Stood Still*.[25] Colin Powell, Reagan's National Security Advisor, would roll his eyes when his boss talked about 'the little green men'.

In the jumble of Reagan's mind, the extra-terrestrial mingled with the astrological as well. The most startling revelation of his White House Chief of Staff Don Regan's memoir, *For the Record*, was that a San Francisco astrologer was sometimes responsible for the president's diary and schedule changes – part of what the journalist Hendrik Hertzberg memorably described as 'government of, by, and for the stars'.[26]

When we talk of how much Donald Trump is influenced by what he watches on television, it is worth recalling how much Reagan was influenced by the 363 films he saw in the White House movie theatre and screenings at Camp David, the president's country retreat.

Just as Reagan understood the sway of a well-performed speech, so he also grasped the power of a well-timed joke. As with some of his most memorable lines, many of his best zingers originated in Hollywood.[27]

'All in all, I'd rather be in Philadelphia,' he quipped in the recovery room after surgery on his gunshot wounds following the attempt on his life in 1981, paraphrasing a W. C. Fields punchline. 'Honey, I forgot to duck,' his one-liner to Nancy as he was wheeled into the operating theatre at the George Washington University Hospital, and 'Please tell me you're Republicans,' his joke to the team of surgeons, sounded like wisecracks from Bob Hope.

Fittingly, his 1984 re-election was sealed with a gag, when he neutralised the age issue raised by his doddery performance in the first televised debate with a zinger he remembered from a stage show in Las Vegas. 'I will not make age an issue of this campaign. I am not going to exploit, for political purposes, my opponent's youth and inexperience.'

Mondale, his 56-year-old opponent, joined the audience in laughter, knowing his chance of becoming president had just evaporated.

Reagan was by no means the first occupant of the White House to smudge the lines between politics and entertainment, but he was unquestionably the most adept at bringing these two worlds together. Whereas Jack Kennedy embraced high culture to lend his administration more élan – hosting Pablo Casals for a cello recital and also a state dinner in honour of 49 Nobel laureates – Reagan deliberately was more middlebrow.

He launched his presidency with an All-Star Inaugural Gala featuring Jimmy Stewart, Ethel Merman and Bob Hope, which prompted the MC, Johnny Carson, to deadpan, 'This is the first administration to have a premiere.'[28]

Ever alert to stars with box-office appeal, the Reagans awarded Michael Jackson, the 'King of Pop', with a presidential commendation after the singer allowed the White House to use 'Beat It' in a drink-driving campaign – Jackson turned up in shades, a shimmering blue uniform, with a gold sash and epaulettes, looking like the potentate of a small tropical island. They also made sure John Travolta, the star of *Saturday Night Fever* and *Grease*, was on hand to dance with Princess Diana during a royal visit in 1985 – with a determined nudge from Nancy.

Maybe the zenith came in the first year of his second term, when Ron and Nancy featured on the front cover of *Vanity Fair*, the newly revived glossy which has done more than any other publication to glamorise politics and ordain the marriage between celebrity and power. Photographed on their way to a state dinner, dressed in black tie and evening wear, the portrait showed them in a heel-kicking pose that evoked Fred Astaire and Ginger Rogers.

The Reagans understood 'the pitfalls of wooden productions', wrote the conservative intellectual William F. Buckley Jr in an essay that accompanied the photo spread, and had created 'their own version of Camelot'. Norman Mailer, grasping the president's mass-market appeal, put it better. Reagan 'saw that the President of the United States was the leading soap opera figure in the great American drama, and he had better possess star value'.[29]

Thus Reagan established the intricately choreographed presidency of the modern era: with evocative scripting, polished production values, a filmic eye for dramatic photo opportunities and a variety-show-like mix of spectacle, entertainment and gags.

The problem was that Reagan created a flawed blueprint, and showed that a president could achieve historical greatness without even mastering some of the basics of the job. When Americans saw him on television, he performed the role with aplomb. Behind the scenes, however, in many of the back-office aspects of the presidency, he fell pitifully short.

He was intellectually incurious, often comically ill informed and overly reliant on the cue cards he read from in meetings, without which he was often reduced to incoherence or silence. Gerald Ford, in his 1979 memoir, *A Time to Heal*, described him as 'one of the few political leaders I have ever met whose public speeches revealed more than his private conversations'. Ford also identified Reagan's 'penchant for offering simplistic solutions to hideously complex problems'.[30]

When Reagan met Carter during the transition, he declined the offer of a writing pad to take notes. 'He displayed utterly no interest,' recalled one of Carter's aides.[31] Often the president neglected to do his homework. When James Baker, his first chief of staff, chided him for failing to go through his briefing book on the eve of an important economic summit, Reagan gave the exquisite response, 'Well, Jim, *The Sound of Music* was on last night.'[32] Even short position papers went unread: hence his nickname 'The Great Delegator'.

On fundamental matters of foreign affairs and national security, he was often clueless. He did not understand, just as Donald Trump failed to do 30 years later, the concept of the Pentagon's nuclear triad, which simply meant warheads could be delivered by submarines and strategic bombers, as well as land-based intercontinental ballistic missiles. He mixed up Afghanistan and Pakistan. During the 1980 campaign, when asked by NBC's Tom Brokaw about the then French president Giscard d'Estaing, Reagan evidently had no idea who he was.[33] During the Iran-Contra scandal, when senior administration officials facilitated the sale of weapons to Iran, circumventing an arms embargo, and then used the proceeds to illegally fund the right-wing rebel group the Contras in Nicaragua, his defence was that he didn't know what was going on. This sounded eminently believable, though it was more a case of plausible ineptitude than plausible deniability. Reagan was also something of a part-time president. He arrived at the office late, left early and spent large amounts of time at his ranch in the mountains above Santa Barbara in California – Rancho del Cielo, the 'heavenly ranch', the First Couple called it. 'It's true, hard work never killed anybody,' he used to joke, 'but, I figure, why take the chance?'

Reagan so often confused reality with fiction that he pursued a post-truth presidency. His truth twisting began with his inaugural address, when he invoked the memory of Martin Treptow, a soldier on the Western Front during World War I who was killed under heavy artillery fire as he ferried messages between two US battalions.

Peering out across the Potomac towards Arlington National Cemetery, 'with its row on row of simple white markers bearing crosses or Stars of David', Reagan described how 'under one such marker' lay Treptow. Upon his dead body was found a diary, and in it a handwritten pledge: 'America must win this war. Therefore, I will work, I will save, I will sacrifice, I will endure, I will fight cheerfully and do my utmost, as if the issue of the whole struggle depended on me alone.'

Here was a mission statement for these troubled times, but when Reagan's speechwriters spent a day at Arlington National Cemetery trying to locate Treptow's grave, they could not find it. Treptow, as reporters quickly uncovered, had been interred more than a thousand miles away, in Bloomer, Wisconsin.[34] The words 'under one such marker' were deliberately ambiguous. Nonetheless, they felt like the work of a screenwriter stretching a real-life story to breaking point, an unwelcome import from Hollywood.[35]

Throughout his presidency, Reagan traded in these kinds of falsehood. In a meeting with the Israeli Prime Minister Yitzhak Shamir, he claimed to have filmed the liberation of the concentration camps, even though he never stepped foot outside the United States for the duration of World War II.

At a presidential Medal of Honor event, he told the story of a B-17 bomber that went down over Europe after coming under enemy fire, whose commander ordered the evacuation of the plane but stayed gripping the hand of a young soldier as it nose-dived towards the ground. Reagan quoted the commander's reassuring last words, 'Never mind, son, we'll ride it down together.' Yet this was a scene not from the pages of history but from the World War II movie *A Wing and a Prayer*.

When pressed by reporters, the then White House spokesman Larry Speakes, who later admitted to making up quotes from the president, offered a superlative definition of post-truth politics: 'If you tell the same story five times, it's true.'[36] Harmless sentimentality was how administration officials, such as Pat Buchanan, the White House communications director, tried to explain away these mistruths. 'For Ronald Reagan, the world of legend and myth is a real world. He visits it regularly, and he's a happy man there.'[37]

These falsehoods, however, could also be malevolent. Take Reagan's demonisation during the 1980 campaign of a 'Chicago welfare queen', who had supposedly fraudulently accumulated $150,000 in payments with her 80 aliases, 30 different addresses and 12 social security cards. In actuality, the woman in question had just two aliases. Her haul of deceitful claims amounted to $8,000.[38] Reagan paid little political price for this blurring of fact and fiction. If anything, it helped him camouflage the contradictions of his presidency. Thus he proselytised about tax cuts while at the same time increasing the tax burden. He portrayed himself as a deficit hawk while overseeing the ballooning of the federal budget. This divorcee who rarely attended church was beloved of the Religious Right. Reagan's acting skills, his proficiency in taking on different guises, surely helped make him a Janus-like president.

Indeed, one of the paradoxes of Reagan's split-screen life is how a B-movie actor came across as such an authentic president. It also helped during the crises of his presidency, not least the Iran-Contra affair during the second term. 'He walks away from more political car crashes than anyone,' noted John Sears, who managed his 1976 presidential campaign.[39]

So a leader who elevated the stature of the presidency also ended up dumbing it down, producing an inadequate prototype in the process: one which cast the president primarily as a frontman and cheerleader, but not a full participant in his own administration. The Reagan-inspired emphasis on star power devalued expertise. Name recognition became key. Likeability trounced know-how. Presidential debates increasingly came down to who could deliver Reagan-style one-liners – the jokes or putdowns that would be rerun endlessly on the news in the days afterwards. Elections increasingly felt like auditions for the role of leading man. Presidents came to be judged on presentation: the ability to deliver State of the Union addresses or to articulate and emote the thoughts of the nation in times of grief and sorrow. Into this charisma trap fell Mike Dukakis, Bob Dole, Al Gore, John Kerry and Mitt Romney, all of them losing candidates eminently qualified to perform the practical tasks of the presidency.

Nor is it a coincidence that the only one-term president for thirty-plus years, George H. W. Bush, was a poor communicator who mutilated the English language, even though he was one of the better chief executives. Reagan changed the qualities and qualifications that the American people looked for in their president, and not for the better. A chief beneficiary was Donald Trump, who would also come to play the role of his lifetime.

———

That ice-maker, telephone answer machine and jumbo television. Shopping trips to mega-malls in Orange County, such as South Coast Plaza, which had become America's new Main Street. Breakfasts at the International House of Pancakes. The all-you-can-eat salad bar at Sizzler, with its bewildering array of dressings. Family suppers at Benihana, where a knife-wielding chef would serve up teppanyaki at polished wood tables.

Rampant across America was the same consumerism, the same great affluence, I witnessed during that first summer in Southern California. Reaganism promoted an individualistic sense of happiness and contentment built on conspicuous consumption, instant gratification and the celebration of wealth. The very term Reaganism spoke of the selfish individualism of the age, and was starkly different in tone from the communal coinage of the Roosevelt, Truman, Kennedy or Johnson years – the New Deal, the Fair Deal, the New Frontier, the Great Society.

If the 1970s were, as the novelist Tom Wolfe suggested, the 'Me Decade', the 1980s might be called the 'Mine Decade', given the accumulation of possessions and wealth. Madonna's anthem 'Material Girl', which came out in 1984, the year of Reagan's re-election, captured the national mood. Relationships were not primarily romantic, it suggested, but transactional, where the boy with the dollars was always 'Mister Right'.

The end of the worst recession since the Great Depression brought on a buying binge. In the last six years of the Reagan presidency, as Lou

41

Cannon noted, Americans purchased 105 million colour televisions, 62 million microwave ovens, 57 million washers and dryers, 46 million refrigerators and freezers, 31 million cordless phones and 30 million telephone answering machines.[40] Between 1982 and 1986, imports of luxury cars doubled.[41] In this 'I-consume-therefore-I-am' culture, ostentation was no longer frowned upon.

Even the LA Olympics became a showcase for capitalism, from the commodification of the Sam the Eagle mascot to the corporate ubiquity of US giants such as Coca-Cola and McDonald's. The head of the organising committee, Peter Ueberroth, was determined the games should turn a profit and to showcase that America could put on a better Games than the communists in Moscow or the socialistic French Canadians in Montreal, who had almost driven their city into bankruptcy.

Spurred by the money motive, there was a boom in demand for MBAs and law degrees. Talking openly about salaries – ideally six-figure salaries – became more socially acceptable. Millionaires proliferated. At the beginning of the '80s, 4,414 tax returns filed with the IRS listed adjusted gross earnings of more than a million dollars. By 1987, there were 34,944 such returns.[42] The millionaires even had their own television show, *Lifestyles of the Rich and Famous*, which debuted in 1984. Its over-the-top presenter, Robin Leach, became the godfather of reality shows such as *Keeping up with the Kardashians*.

'Yuppies' made their entrance, a surprisingly large proportion of them hippies from the '60s who transferred their social libertarianism into the commercial and political worlds, turning liberals into Reaganites. The 'Masters of the Universe' so brilliantly satirised by Tom Wolfe in *The Bonfire of the Vanities* and Oliver Stone in the movie *Wall Street*, both of which came out in 1987, also made their debut. 'Greed, for lack of a better word, is good,' proclaimed the corporate raider Gordon Gekko, played by Michael Douglas, in the film's era-defining monologue: 'Greed is right, greed works. Greed clarifies, cuts through.'

The dialogue was based on a commencement speech delivered at the University of California, Berkeley, one of the country's most liberal campuses, by the stock trader Ivan Boesky, in which he told the graduating class, 'Greed is all right, by the way. I want you to know that. I think greed is healthy. You can be greedy and still feel good about yourself.'

Boesky was sentenced to three years in prison for insider trading a week after *Wall Street* premiered in movie theatres. Yet Oliver Stone was alarmed to discover that many of those who saw the film were inspired afterwards to pursue careers in banking and finance. Thus, a parody intended to skewer the excesses of Reaganism inadvertently ended up glorifying them.[43] 'Greed is good' became the unofficial dictum of the decade. Few remember the liberal counterblast, 'Greed is not enough.'

It was not just Madonna and Sherman McCoy, the antihero from *The Bonfire of the Vanities*. Popular culture more broadly came to reflect this materialist moment. I came from a country where soap operas, such as *Coronation Street* and *EastEnders*, focused on the working class and the grittiness of everyday life. By contrast, the primetime soap-opera hit of the 1980s in America was *Dallas*, which focused on a wealthy Texas oil family.

Dynasty, with its catfights and caviar, even more perfectly captured the zeitgeist. The story of the Carringtons of Colorado debuted the month Reagan was sworn in as president and aired its finale months after he left office. Its spin-off, *The Colbys*, starred Charlton Heston, a Democrat and civil rights activist in the 1960s who had become a prominent supporter of Reagan and a leading gun advocate by the 1980s.

Falcon Crest, a primetime soap opera about the feuding factions of the Gioberti and Channing families, starred the president's first wife, Jane Wyman. Its creator, Earl Hamner, was better known for producing *The Waltons*, a drama of simpler pleasures and more homely parables set in rural Virginia during the Great Depression. The last 'Goodnight John-Boy' came in June 1981, just as the Reagan era was cranking into gear.

The sitcom of the decade, *The Cosby Show*, featured the Huxtables, an upwardly mobile African-American family who lived in a brownstone in Brooklyn Heights. Though it challenged stereotypes and gave the black middle class more visibility in the media, it also created a falsely self-congratulatory sense of racial progress and shied away from confronting white viewers with the inconvenient realities of life for African-Americans who had not been able to climb the economic ladder.

Just as Bill Cosby emerged as America's dad, Michael J. Fox, playing the character Alex P. Keaton in *Family Ties*, became Reaganism's son. Keaton – the offspring of hippie parents who'd served in the Peace Corps and graduated from Berkeley – read the *Wall Street Journal*, kept a framed photograph of Richard Nixon on his nightstand and was a passionate advocate of supply-side economics. Set in the heartland city of Columbus, Ohio, this culture-clash show, which aired from 1982 to 1989, was Reagan's favourite sitcom.

Michael J. Fox parlayed his success in *Family Ties* into a starring role in Steven Spielberg's *Back to the Future*, a film in which Reagan's improbable political ascent became a running gag. When Marty McFly travelled back to the 1950s, the Hill Valley movie theatre was showing *Cattle Queen of Montana*, the names of its stars, Ronald Reagan and Barbara Stanwyck, up in lights on the marquee. When McFly informed 'Doc' Brown that the actor had made it to the White House, the crazy-haired scientist scoffed, 'Yeah, and Jerry Lewis is vice-president.' However, when Doc discovered Marty's JVC camcorder, the penny dropped. 'No wonder your president has to be an actor,' he said. 'He's gotta look good on television.'

Reagan loved *Back to the Future*, partly because it reminded him of Frank Capra's films, and told aides after a viewing at Camp David it was the kind of movie the big studios should make more of.[44] The title of the film, with its mix of nostalgia and modernity, described his presidential mission. He even gave it a nod in his 1986 State of the Union address, and purloined a script line from a scene where Doc Brown gripped the steering wheel of the stainless steel DeLorean and accelerated into the next century: 'As they said in the film *Back to the Future*, "Where we're going, we don't need roads."' It showed the extent to which Washington and Hollywood were now on a feedback loop.

Box-office blockbusters mirrored Reaganite tropes. *Top Gun* reflected the militaristic patriotism of the era, and led to a 500 per cent increase in the number of young men who applied to become navy aviators. The *Rocky* movies, which started out as a gritty blue-collar drama, became ever more bombastic and nationalistic, and used Cold War tensions to reinvigorate the franchise. *Rocky IV* opened with a shot of two giant boxing gloves, one emblazoned with Old Glory, the other with the hammer and sickle of the Soviet flag. The movie, promoted with a poster showing Rocky draped in the flag and wearing stars-and-stripes shorts, was the highest-grossing film in the series.

Broadcasting changed as well, with the demise of the Fairness Doctrine, a rule which had come into effect in 1949 and been amended in the late 1950s, mandating broadcasters to air 'honest, equitable and balanced programming' to offer 'varying opinions on the paramount issues facing the American people'.

When the Federal Communications Commission voted to abolish it in 1987, some within the Reagan administration feared it would lead to a liberal onslaught. The polar opposite was true. Almost a year to the day later, Rush Limbaugh launched his nationally syndicated show, ushering in the boom in right-wing talkback radio. By 1992, there were 900 talk radio stations, almost a four-fold increase from 1987.[45] Attempts by Democrats in Congress to bring back the Fairness Doctrine were repeatedly met with the threat of vetoes by Reagan and George H. W. Bush.

The '80s witnessed the privatisation of American life. Home computers and games consoles kept people inside – in 1982, *Time* temporarily ditched its 'Man of the Year' award in favour of a 'Machine of the Year', the computer. So, too, did the proliferation of cable news channels, which had the additional effect of fragmenting audiences and eroding the power of the three main TV networks that had done so much to shape public consciousness.

VCRs meant people could watch movies from their sofas. They could also work out. The transformation of Jane Fonda from the Vietnam War protester 'Hanoi Jane' to millionaire fitness guru, selling workout videos, spoke of the reordering of national priorities.

The rise of the TV evangelists meant worshippers did not even have to leave home to go to church or make a credit card donation. Religion became more individualistic, with the emphasis on personal salvation rather than social justice. From his opulent Crystal Cathedral, Robert Schuller preached the gospel of prosperity and self-esteem, a Reaganite theology. Challenging Jesus's injunction that it was easier for a camel to pass through the eye of a needle than for a rich man to enter the kingdom of heaven, Schuller himself built a money-spinning ecclesiastical empire. Christianity had become more closely linked to consumerism.

The profit motive became not only the driving force for US companies but their singular obsession, as the economist Milton Friedman's 'agency theory' about maximising shareholder returns and minimising civic responsibility became boardroom gospel. 'There is one and only one social responsibility of business,' he had written in a seminal column for *The New York Times* in 1970, 'to use its resources and engage in activities designed to increase its profits.' By the 1980s, Friedman's apostles ran some of America's leading corporations.

Jack Welch, who took over at General Electric in the same year Reagan entered the White House, became the most prominent advocate of maximising shareholder value. Later, Welch boasted callously about killing off American jobs. 'Ideally, you'd have every plant you own on a barge to move with currencies and changes in the economy,' he said in 1998. GE also became masters of tax avoidance. In 2010, it made $5.1 billion in profits but managed to exploit loopholes so that it paid zero in federal tax.[46]

Corporate responsibility was cast aside. US companies had lost their public purpose. Swashbuckling corporate titans topped the bestseller lists. The most popular hardback non-fiction book in 1984 and 1985 was the memoir of the auto-industry king Lee Iacocca, *Iacocca: An Autobiography*. As Chrysler battled with Japanese carmakers, Iacocca became the frontman for his company, and tried to appeal to the patriotism of American consumers with the slogan 'Let's make American mean something again.'

Iacocca's chief rival as America's celebrity CEO was Donald Trump, whose 1987 book *The Art of the Deal* topped the *New York Times* bestseller list for 13 weeks and sold more than a million copies in hardback alone. Trump was not only a creature of the '80s, who dined at the 21 Club and partied at Studio 54, but also a creation of them. In real life, no one better personified the ego-driven, hyper-individualism of the Reagan era or the rapacious appetite for acquisitions.

Trump's decade began with the reopening of The Commodore Hotel on East 42nd Street between the Chrysler Building and Grand Central Station, which built his reputation as a dealmaker extraordinaire. In an architectural form of power dressing, Trump encased the building in mirror glass, much to the consternation of conservationists. Nonetheless, it became a landmark demonstration of his business acumen. Trump, who was not yet 30, became the first commercial developer in New York to receive a tax abatement from the city government in a project his property tycoon father Fred likened to 'fighting for a seat on the *Titanic*'.[47] The Trump myth was born.

A string of headline-grabbing acquisitions followed. Of the New Jersey Generals in 1983, a franchise of the short-lived United States Football League. Of Trump Plaza, the flashy hotel and casino on the boardwalk in Atlantic City that came to host the world heavyweight boxing match between Mike Tyson and Michael Spinks, a bout Trump described as 'one of the great events of the '80s', even though it lasted just 91 seconds.[48] Of the classy Plaza Hotel overlooking Central Park, which was run by his first wife, Ivana, for 'one dollar plus all the dresses she can buy'. Of the Trump Shuttle in 1989, which operated hourly flights between New York, Washington and Boston, in jetliners with gold-plated taps in the bathrooms and his name inscribed in red letters on the fuselage.

If Trump was the living embodiment of the winner-takes-all ethos of the decade, Trump Tower, which opened in 1983, became its totem. The million-dollar fountain in the atrium, fashioned from peach rose and pink Breccia Pernice marble tiles, spoke of the showiness. The doormen dressed as palace guards, wearing scarlet tunics and white pith helmets in the summer and black bearskin hats in the winter, spoke of the vogue for status symbols. The jackhammering of the Art Deco sculptures that had ornamented the building on Fifth Avenue, bulldozed to make way for the skyscraper, spoke of the civic vandalism and disdain.

A tenant list handed to reporters that included Sophia Loren, Johnny Carson and Steven Spielberg spoke of the glorification of celebrity. The black-tied pianist playing in the lobby on a pink piano was a nod towards Liberace and the showmanship of the era, whether in Vegas or Washington. The shipping of $75,000 worth of palm trees from Florida for the foyer, which were then chain-sawed because Trump did not like the look, spoke of the wastefulness. The tower's concrete frame, constructed using materials supplied by mob-run firms, spoke of the shady business practices. The eponymous skyscraper, with the tycoon's name rendered in bronze capital letters above the door, spoke of the narcissism and fantastical self-belief.

No other building more accurately depicted the '80s than this bastion of decadence, which is perhaps why, on my first trip to New York in the late '80s, I visited Trump Tower before I went up the Empire State. To this day, its atrium feels like a kitschy time capsule.

A fixture already in New York, Trump became a nationwide celebrity in the '80s. His first appearance on *60 Minutes* came in 1985, in which he complained to the anchor Mike Wallace about his treatment in the press: 'I believe they make me out to be something more sinister than I really am.'

Fortune magazine put him on its cover in 1986, describing him as a 'high-roller'.[49] Trump also made his debut in January 1989 on the front cover of *Time*. 'Flaunting it is his game, and Trump is the name,' read the headline, alongside a portrait of Trump brandishing an ace of spades and wearing his trademark red silk tie. Inside, *Time* called him a 'Flashy Symbol of an Acquisitive Age', and published various Trumpian pearls of wisdom: 'I love to have enemies. I fight my enemies. I love beating my enemies to the ground.'[50]

So central was Trump to the cultural zeitgeist that a character was based on him in the sequel to *Back to the Future*: the casino owner, Biff Tannen, who made a political run as a Republican with the slogan 'America's greatest living folk hero'.[51]

His renovation in the mid-'80s of the Wollman Skating Rink in Central Park, which was portrayed as the triumph of free enterprise over government inefficiency, fuelled his fame. When City Hall was in charge, the six-year project was a $12 million cost blowout. After Trump intervened, skaters took to the ice within four months for under $1 million. *The New York Times* sang his praises, calling the completed ice rink 'one of the boldest feats of civic bravado tried in New York in recent years'. How the tycoon must have loved the headline: 'New York Hopes to Learn from Ice Rink Trump Fixed'.[52]

What was striking about the early press coverage of Trump was the starry-eyed fascination and laudatory tone. In 'The Empire and Ego of Donald Trump' in 1983, *The New York Times* described him as 'a brash Adonis from the outer boroughs bent on placing his imprint on the golden rock' of Manhattan, whose name 'has in the last few years become an internationally recognized symbol of New York City as mecca for the world's super-rich'.[53]

In a profile published the following year under the headline 'The Expanding Empire of Donald Trump', *The New York Times* pronounced: 'Donald J. Trump is the man of the hour.' 'Spending a day with Donald Trump is like driving a Ferrari without the windshield,' noted the reporter William Geist, who spoke of Trump's genius for negotiation and skill at selling super-rich apartments in Trump Tower during a difficult phase for Manhattan real estate.

'You sell them a fantasy,' said Trump, who was described by one of his admirers as 'the Michael Jackson of real estate'. Four years later, following his acquisition of The Plaza, a follow-up profile in the *Times* further embroidered the master dealmaker narrative: 'What Trump wants, Trump gets'.[54]

What made this favourable press all the more remarkable was that Trump did not employ a public relations firm. He generated all of this publicity himself, though sometimes under the guise of 'John Barron', a pseudonym he often used when briefing reporters over the telephone in a barely disguised voice.[55] The media willingly, and often gullibly, helped create and fuel the Trumpian myth. In a reworking of Oscar Wilde's famous dictum about not being talked about, Trump wrote in *The Art of the Deal*: 'Good publicity is preferable to bad, but from a bottom-line perspective, bad publicity is sometimes better than no publicity at all. Controversy, in short, sells.'[56]

Some of the early coverage seemed to will the property tycoon to fix his gaze on the country's most prized political real estate.

'Would you like to be president of the United States?' asked the celebrity reporter Rona Barrett in 1980, evidently the first time he was asked on screen whether he harboured presidential ambitions.

'I really don't believe I would, Rona,' he replied, coyly. 'Why wouldn't you dedicate yourself to public service?' she asked, having suggested he could 'make America perfect'. 'Because I think it's a very mean life.'

In that first *New York Times* profile, the writer admitted how far-fetched was the notion of a Trump presidency, but entertained the possibility nonetheless. 'The idea that he would ever be allowed to go into a room alone and negotiate for the United States, seems the naïve musing of an optimistic, deluded young man who has never lost at anything he has tried,' he wrote. 'But he believes that through years of making his views known and through supporting candidates who share his views, it could someday happen.'[57]

The BBC's legendary chronicler of American life, Alistair Cooke, also predicted great things of 'the young, bouncy blond tycoon whose aspirations to take over hotels, casinos, airlines, resorts, cities – why not the country? – appear to be boundless'.[58]

As the '80s progressed, and Trump's celebrity ballooned, he became more overtly political. In September 1987, he forked out almost $100,000 for a full-page ad in *The New York Times*, *Washington Post* and *Boston Globe* to publish an open letter to the American people headlined: 'There's Nothing Wrong with America's Foreign Defence Policy That a Little Backbone Can't Cure.'

Outlining themes he would return to almost 30 years later, he explained 'why America should stop paying to defend countries that can afford to defend themselves' and how 'Japan and other nations have been taking advantage of the United States' for decades.

'Why are these nations not paying the United States for the human lives and billions of dollars we are losing to protect their interests?' he asked. 'The world is laughing at America's politicians as we protect ships we don't own, carrying oil we don't need, destined for allies who won't help.'

The letter had apparently been the idea of Roger Stone, that Forrest Gump of the right who served now as his unofficial political advisor. In conclusion, Trump noted, 'Let's not let our great country be laughed at any more.' At the end, he added his signature written with a thick black pen in handwriting that looked like a seismograph during a medium-sized quake.[59]

The attention the letter received showed once more Trump's gift for self-publicity and his ease at securing column inches, usually without paying a dime. The editorial board of *The New York Times* even published a 'Dear Donald Trump' riposte. The thrust of his argument about burden-sharing was valid, it acknowledged, but claimed it was the price of US global leadership.

'The terms of friendship may often be maddening,' it noted, 'but Americans surely like having those friends.'[60]

The following month his hometown broadsheet published a news report under the headline 'Trump Hints of Dreams Beyond Building', which spoke of a possible presidential run. 'I love what I do,' he opined. 'I've built the best private company in the world at a very early age.' That said, 'I believe that if I did run for president, I'd win.'[61]

Amidst this swirl of presidential speculation, Trump descended on New Hampshire in October 1987, aboard his French-made helicopter, for his first political campaign speech. Dressed in a dark blue suit and a red silk tie, he addressed the Rotary Club of Portsmouth at the invitation of a local businessman who had formed a 'Draft Trump' committee.

'We are being ripped off and decimated by foreign nationals who are supposedly our allies,' he said, repeating what was now becoming a familiar refrain. 'The Japanese, when they negotiate with us, they have long faces. But when the negotiations are over, it is my belief – I've never seen this – they laugh like hell.' Substitute China for Japan, and he was basically previewing the script for his 2016 run.[62]

Given that *The Art of the Deal* was about to hit bookstores, Trump's flirtation with presidential politics was clearly a naked marketing ploy. Yet this brief, aborted foray demonstrated the strength of his convictions on trade and freeloading allies, and also indicated he was unafraid to take on the political establishment.

Somewhat surprisingly for a tycoon who came to be regarded as the embodiment of Reaganism, *The Art of the Deal* took a swipe at the president, who was now more vulnerable following the Iran-Contra affair. Reagan has been 'so smooth, so effective a performer', the book noted, but 'only now, seven years later, are people beginning to question whether there's anything beneath that smile'.

Above all, the presidential speculation demonstrated how easy it would be to mount a more serious bid. In this media-saturated age, Trump was a ratings gift. Invited onto *The Oprah Winfrey Show* the following year, he vented once more about America being taken for a ride by its trading partners and allies.

'We're really making other people live like kings,' he complained, 'and we're not.'

Then he fielded from Oprah what now felt like the obligatory question about the presidency.

'Probably not,' he answered, when asked if he would ever run. 'But I do get tired of seeing the country ripped off.'

As for his prospects? With trademark immodesty, he claimed he 'would have a hell of a chance of winning'.

An appearance on another daytime talk show, *Donahue*, drew praise from an unexpected quarter. 'I did not see the program,' wrote Richard Nixon, 'but Mrs Nixon told me that you were *great* on the *Donahue* show. As you can imagine, she is an expert on politics, and she predicts that whenever you decide to run for office you will be a winner!'[63]

Certainly, Trump had started to take himself seriously as a political entity. In 1988, as the Reagan years drew to a close, he suggested to Lee Atwater, George H. W. Bush's campaign chief, that he should join the Republican ticket as the vice-presidential nominee. Bush considered the idea 'strange and unbelievable'.[64]

However, no longer did the prospect of a Trump run seem so ludicrous. By the late '80s, Reagan had normalised the idea that a show-business personality could become president, and the billionaire clearly believed he had the self-promotional prowess that had become so elemental to the presidential skill set.

'I play to people's fantasies,' he wrote in *The Art of the Deal*. 'People may not always think big themselves, but they can still get very excited by those who do. That's why a little hyperbole never hurts. People want to believe something is the biggest and the greatest and the most spectacular. I call it truthful hyperbole. It's an innocent form of exaggeration.'[65]

Inside the rotunda of the US Capitol, the site of Reagan's weather-hit second inaugural, tens of thousands queued to file past his flag-draped casket, which rested on a catafalque constructed in 1865 to display Abraham Lincoln's coffin. On the morning of his funeral, the New York Stock Exchange ceased trading, giving some of Wall Street's Masters of the Universe the day off. At his boyhood home in Dixon, Illinois, mourners left packets of jelly beans, his beloved candy, at the foot of a life-sized statue.

The public and political reaction to Ronald Reagan's death in June 2004 demonstrated how widely accepted was his claim to presidential greatness. Tributes honoured a leader who, in the clichéd retelling, had looked the Soviet Union in the eye and refused to blink; a president who had rescued America from economic ruin; an optimist who had rallied the country after years of malaise.

Much like the response to the passing nine years later of his ideological soulmate, Margaret Thatcher, criticisms were softened, old antagonisms set aside. Longstanding opponents acknowledged America needed the shock therapy of the Reagan revolution. No longer was Reagan a joke. Nor was Reaganism a term of derision. In the red-and-blue America of the new millennium, his legacy transcended politics.

From leading Democrats, eulogies came gushing in. Bill Clinton said his predecessor 'personified the indomitable optimism of the American people'. Ted Kennedy observed 'his infectious optimism gave us all the feeling that it really was "morning in America"'. Senator John Kerry, the party's presidential nominee that year, added his voice to the Democratic chorus of praise. Failing to pay homage would have offended Reagan Democrats the party was still trying to wrench back. 'He was our oldest president,' said Kerry, 'but he made America young again.'[66]

Ten years earlier, following the announcement from his Bel-Air retirement home he was suffering from Alzheimer's disease, the country had conducted a dress rehearsal for Reagan's death. Even in his infirm state, the Gipper executed the most graceful of exits, penning a handwritten letter to the American people that was pitch-perfect Reagan. 'I now begin the journey that will lead me into the sunset of my life,' he wrote in a scrawl that revealed the ravages of his disease. 'I know that for America there will always be a bright dawn ahead.'

Thereafter, it seemed cruel to question his legacy, or reassess his record, not least since the great communicator had lost the capacity to answer back. His incapacitation offered inoculation against disparagement. His presidency came to be encased in amber.

Long before his retreat from public life, Reagan hero-worship had reached the level of deification within the conservative movement. Only Abraham Lincoln had been a more consequential Republican president, decreed The Heritage Foundation. The Ronald Reagan Legacy Project, set up in the late '90s by the conservative ideologue Grover Norquist, succeeded in renaming National Airport, and continued to press for a park, statue or road to be named after him in every one of America's 3,140 counties. The Reaganite anthem, 'God Bless the USA', came to be played at every GOP convention. It was as if he was not just great but supernatural. A quadrennial ritual of the Republican primary season became the battle to claim his mantle. Ahead of the 2000 election, George W. Bush described himself as a Reagan Republican, even though it meant besmirching his father. Ahead of the 2010 midterm congressional elections, the RNC proposed that prospective candidates had to sign up to a 'Reagan Resolution', agreeing to at least eight out of ten conservative principles, in order to receive help from the party.[67] During the 2016 campaign, the second Republican debate was held at his presidential library, during which his name was mentioned, worshipfully, no fewer than 45 times. 'So how Reaganesque exactly are these Republicans?' intoned the moderator, CNN's Jake Tapper, as if it was the all-important litmus test.[68] To this day, Republican primary voters will tolerate many transgressions, but not the cardinal sin of desecrating Reagan's memory – perhaps it should be called the 12th commandment, an addendum to Reagan's 11th commandment, decreeing that Republicans should not speak ill of any fellow Republican.

Donald Trump liked to claim he had almost been anointed by Reagan in the Blue Room of the White House in 1987, and popularised a meme featuring what the then president was supposed to have told aides after shaking the tycoon's hand, 'For the life of me, and I'll never know how to explain it, I felt like the one shaking hands with the president.' However, there is no record of Reagan ever having uttered these words, and this is almost certainly a made-up quote.

In all personality cults, followers can be blind to the flaws of their idols. This has been especially true of the misty romanticism enshrouding Reagan. Modern-day Republicans continue to regard him as a leader of unbending beliefs, overlooking the pragmatism central to his political success. They recall, for instance, that he reduced taxes in his first and last year as president, but forget that he raised them in the other six.

His landmark 1982 Tax Equity and Fiscal Responsibility Act, which slashed rates on the wealthiest Americans from 70 per cent to 50 per cent, was followed in 1982 and 1984 by what was cumulatively the largest tax hike in peacetime history.[69] Nor do Reagan's disciples place his tax cuts in a proper historical or economic context. When he entered the White House, the highest rate of personal income tax was 70 per cent. When he left that 'little bungalow', it was 28 per cent.[70] Slashing such punitive tax rates in the early '80s was justifiable. Continuing to cut them when they were already low compared to other western countries has proven fiscally reckless. Republicans have come to see tax cuts as the remedy for every economic ill, regardless of the impact on the country's finances. As well as accumulating more debt, they have always disproportionately favoured the rich, exacerbating the problem of income inequality.

Reagan is often remembered as a fiscal conservative, but he ran up more debt than any of his predecessors. It tripled during his time in office. For all his anti-government rhetoric, the number of federal employees actually grew during his eight years in office. Again, this was partly due to the Pentagon build-up, but he reneged on his promise to shut down the Departments of Education and Energy, and actually ended up adding another Cabinet-level agency, the Department of Veterans Affairs.

Reagan repeatedly committed Reaganite apostasy. Never did he vigorously seek a constitutional ban on abortion, offering only tepid support to the religious right's efforts to push through the 'Human Life Amendment'. Anti-abortion rallies he addressed by phone over a public address system rather than in person. By appointing Sandra Day O'Connor as the country's first female Supreme Court Justice, a jurist who believed in a woman's right to choose, he safeguarded *Roe v. Wade* for a quarter of a century.

On immigration, Reagan was a moderate. Believing their arrival offered proof that America was a city on a hill, he welcomed the 'millions of immigrants from every corner of the earth'. In 1986, he signed the Immigration Reform and Control Act granting amnesty to more than a million illegal immigrants. A follow-up executive order legalised the status of children whose parents had been granted amnesty. This to Reagan made moral and political sense. 'Hispanics are conservatives,' he was fond of saying. 'They just don't know it.'

In foreign affairs, it was not chiefly his militarism that brought the Soviet Union to heel, but rather his willingness to negotiate arms reductions agreements with Mikhail Gorbachev. After decrying the détente advocated by Nixon and Ford, he ended up embracing it. His ambition to rid the world of atomic weapons, every single warhead, placed him in the same camp as the peaceniks of the nuclear-freeze movement.

Though remembered as a strongman, Reagan's response to the 1983 bombing of the marine barracks in Lebanon, an attack in which 241 US service personnel were murdered, was to quietly pull out US forces, rather than mount retaliatory strikes. 'Phased redeployment', Reagan called it, the sort of defeatist euphemism Republicans would have pounced upon had it come from the lips of Jimmy Carter.

As bodies were still being pulled from the wreckage, he then ordered the invasion of Grenada, a military adventure in a tiny chain of islands in the Caribbean that seemed like a deliberate attempt to deflect from the carnage in the Middle East. Thus the great communicator became the great distractor. The only time Reagan took military action in retaliation for a terror attack came when, in response to the 1986 bombing of a discotheque in West Berlin that killed two Americans, he ordered air strikes against Libya.[71] Another inconvenient truth for contemporary Republicans was Reagan's bipartisanship, a word Grover Norquist, the driving force behind the Reagan Project, has likened to date rape. Reagan regularly clashed with his fellow Irish-American, the Democratic House Speaker, Tip O'Neill, who castigated the president as a 'cheerleader for selfishness'. Often at the end of the day, however, they shared a tumbler of Irish whiskey and started to cut deals.

'Tip, you and I are political enemies only until six o'clock,' Reagan would joke. 'It's four o'clock now. Can we pretend it's six o'clock?'[72]

Reagan's bipartisanship was born of necessity. For the entirety of his presidency, he confronted a Democrat-controlled House. Yet both Reagan and O'Neill understood the founding fathers had hard-wired compromise into their design for government, and that Washington was unworkable without give-and-take.[73]

Reagan was also respectful of his opponents. In his acceptance speech at the Republican convention in 1980, he quoted Franklin Delano Roosevelt, and reminded supporters he had once been a

'New Deal Democrat'.[74] His respect for New Deal reforms extended to creating a bipartisan commission to save Social Security, FDR's greatest achievement. 'Reagan Democrats' supported him not only because of his cultural conservatism, but also because he preserved so much of the New Deal.

Often forgotten as well is the criticism Reagan faced from conservative contemporaries, especially before his personal popularity gave him a protective shield. Were he on the political scene today, he would probably be dubbed a RINO, a Republican in name only – or, more appositely, a Reaganite in name only. Reagan would find it hard to sign up to the Reagan Resolution.

Even his popularity has been inflated. His average Gallup job-approval rating over his eight years in office was 52.8 per cent. That put him behind Kennedy (70.1 per cent), Eisenhower (65 per cent), George H. W. Bush (60.9 per cent), Lyndon Johnson (55.1 per cent) and Bill Clinton (55.1 per cent). At the height of the Iran-Contra scandal, polls suggested a third of Americans thought he should resign.[75] Yet Republicans have created a fabulist figurine, a paragon faithful to the truth-twisting of his presidency but not the man himself. Arthur M. Schlesinger called Reagan 'the president as master illusionist'. To this day, Republicans remain spellbound.[76]

Reagan altered the Democratic Party almost as much as he transformed the Republicans. Bill Clinton launched his 1992 campaign with a stinging rebuke of Reaganism: 'The 1980s ushered in a gilded age of greed and selfishness, of irresponsibility and excess, and of neglect.' However, the centrist Democratic Leadership Council, of which the Governor of Arkansas became a leading light, came into existence to meet the philosophical and electoral challenge posed by a Republican president who in 1980 and 1984 won almost a third of white Democrats.[77] Clintonism became a progressive response to Reaganism, which recognised how much he had altered the terms of political debate and changed American minds about the relationship between citizens and the government.

Much of the DLC's thinking was predicated on Reagan's critique of the post-'60s Democrats: that the party had left him, not that he had left the party. As a result, Clinton's political philosophy was shaped by the belief that the only way to contend with Reaganism was to ape it. His Third Way was a synthesis of New Deal government intervention and the regulatory retrenchment of the Reagan years, a balancing of the rights agenda of the '60s with the values agenda of the '70s.

When Clinton spoke, as a candidate, of ending welfare as we know it, he was essentially endorsing Reagan's contention in 1988 that 'the federal government declared war on poverty, and poverty won'. Following the Republican Revolution led by the conservative firebrand Newt Gingrich in 1994, Clinton ended up almost ventriloquising Reagan. 'The era of big government is over,' he declared in his 1995 State of the Union address, in what sounded more like a capitulation rather than accommodation.

When the former president visited Washington shortly afterwards for his 84th birthday celebrations, he joked to a crowd of cheering Republicans, 'Watching the State of the Union address the other night, I'm reminded of the old adage that imitation is the sincerest form of flattery. Only in this case, it's not flattery, but grand larceny.'[78] Just as Eisenhower had normalised Rooseveltism, so Clinton regularised Reaganism.

More surprising was how enthusiastically Barack Obama participated in the veneration of the most conservative president of the post-war years. Campaigning for the presidency in 2008, the then senator made no secret of his admiration. 'I think Ronald Reagan changed the trajectory of America in a way that Richard Nixon did not and in a way Bill Clinton did not,' he told the *Reno Gazette-Journal* in March 2008 during an interview which gained traction in the national press. 'He put us on a fundamentally different path because the country was ready for it.'[79] Later, in 2010, when he convened a White House symposium of presidential historians to glean lessons from his predecessors, he was intrigued most by what Reagan could teach him. That Christmas, aides let it be known the president's vacation reading in Hawaii was Lou Cannon's *President Reagan: The Role of a Lifetime*, the superlative biography.

Afterwards, he happily put his name to a personal tribute published in *Time*. 'Reagan recognized the American people's hunger for accountability and change,' the 44th president wrote admiringly of the 40th. In a 2011 cover story, *Time* even went as far as to describe Reagan as Obama's 'role model'.[80] After all, he yearned to be a transformational president who renewed America's faith in itself and revived a moribund economy.

By praising their Republican predecessor so unreservedly, both Obama and Clinton contributed to the ideological shift rightwards, the process through which Roosevelt's America became Reagan's America. But were they right to concede so much to a president with so many negative entries in the historical ledger?

His trickle-down economics brought about a massive redistribution of wealth upwards. As Obama could have learned from Lou Cannon, 'By 1989, the richest two-fifths of families had the highest share of national income (67.8 per cent) and the poorest two-fifths the lowest share (15.4 per cent) in the 40 years since the Census Bureau had been compiling such statistics.' One out of five children lived in poverty, a disproportionate number of them African-American.[81] In the mid-1970s, bosses earned 35 times as much as their workers. By the end of the '80s, as Milton Friedman's ideas took hold and the phrase 'greed is good' gained wider coinage, they were raking in 120 times as much.[82]

The tax giveaway of 1981 not only further inflated the deficit balloon but also helped create the 1980s real-estate bubble. In an ever more decadent society, pleasure and consumption edged out innovation and industry, the drivers of America's post-war growth. The market was king.

Reagan ignored the AIDS epidemic, opposed a national holiday for the Reverend Dr Martin Luther King Jr and was a flat earther on climate change who once claimed trees emitted more pollution than cars. Admirers recall his appearance in front of the Brandenburg Gate, but not his highly controversial visit in 1985 to the Bitburg cemetery in West Germany where members of the Nazi SS were buried. They forget how long it took him to disavow the extreme right John Birch

Society when he was running for the governorship of California, just as they overlook his decision to launch his 1980 campaign in Mississippi with that rallying cry for states' rights. In 2019, a tape emerged of a phone conversation with President Nixon in which Reagan described African delegates at the United Nations as 'monkeys' who were 'still uncomfortable wearing shoes', but it was quickly dismissed as an aberration rather than a moment that revealed his true self.[83]

Democrats who have reached the White House have all made major ideological concessions to Reagan. His scapegoating of government is a case in point. For much of the past 30 years Democrats have so often let one of his favourite one-liners go unchallenged, the old chestnut about the most frightening words in the English language being 'I'm from the government and I'm here to help'.

In the absence of a counter-narrative, the perception of government changed. Prior to the Reagan era, government was seen as a force for good: the saviour of capitalism and rescuer of the poor after the Great Depression, the defender of democracy during World War II, the architect of nation-building infrastructure in the '50s, the helping hand when Americans fell sick or lost their jobs.

Afterwards, it has been harder to make a positive case for the government. Rare are the occasions when Bill Clinton or Barack Obama mounted a forceful defence, even though the Reagan years abound with egregious examples of lax regulation, whether it was the defanging of the Environmental Protection Agency, the Justice Department's Civil Rights Division or the Food and Drug Administration. Financial deregulation contributed to the Savings and Loans crisis in the late '80s and early '90s, a forerunner of the 2008 crash when more than a thousand 'thrift' associations failed, partly because they were allowed to sell more exotic products such as high-risk securities and junk bonds. Under Reagan, regulatory reform invariably meant regulatory relaxation.

For the past 30 years, strident critics of government have outgunned its timid defenders. Small wonder Hillary Clinton was confronted during the 2016 campaign by protesters brandishing placards reading: 'Get your government hands off my Medicare.'

Some of those most dependent on government had been encouraged to hate the government, which had corroded the social compact between Washington and the people that had been a feature of American life since the New Deal. As the political scientists Lloyd Free and Hadley Cantril have correctly pointed out, Americans have become 'operational liberals' who benefit from government support but 'ideological conservatives' who resent government intervention.

For Bill Clinton, the end of the era of big government translated into the light-touch regulatory framework of the '90s, a deregulation binge that contributed to the 2008 financial meltdown. For Barack Obama, it meant a Wall Street-friendly stimulus package that left untouched the Masters of the Universe whose recklessness brought capitalism to the point of collapse.

Somewhat perversely, many of the most biting criticisms of Reagan came not from his Democratic successors but from his vice-president. No one has ever bettered the phrase 'voodoo economics' that Bush came up with during the 1980 fight for the Republican nomination to describe the self-contradictions of Reaganomics, which claimed it was possible simultaneously to slash taxes and balance the books. George H. W. Bush's kinder, gentler America was meant as a course correction for the materialism and selfishness of the Reagan years.

So, just as Democrats underestimated Reagan at the time, they have overestimated him in retrospect. Likewise, Republicans have put him on such a lofty pedestal they have succumbed to historical altitude sickness in assessing his record. In the national memory, Reaganism has come to be equated emotionally with that glorious Olympian summertime, and politically by his 'Morning in America' landslide victory afterwards. For both Republicans and Democrats, 1984 has ended up having an imprisoning effect. Contemporary US politics would benefit from a more sober-minded appraisal of the Reagan years, stripped of the soft-heartedness and devoid of the rose-tinted remembrances: a realistic evaluation of his presidency, rather than a Hollywood-style romance where there can never be anything other than a happy ending.

2

Goodbye to the Greatest Generation

The city of Angels was now ablaze, for the acquittal of three of the four Los Angeles Police Department officers videotaped in the spring of 1991 clubbing the black motorist Rodney King 56 times in 81 seconds provoked a howl of rage. Fires of fury engulfed sections of the sprawling metropolis that had crackled with so much energy and pride during the Olympian summer of 1984. Not far from the LA Memorial Coliseum stadium, which had reverberated with those looping chants of 'USA! USA!', came screams of anger. The fireworks gave way to plumes of acrid smoke and piles of grey ash.

Now a student in Boston, I watched the evening news those April nights with unblinking horror, as footage was broadcast of stores being looted, entire blocks being torched and a white truck driver, Reginald Denny, being dragged from the cabin of his truck and viciously beaten by a group of rioters, one of whom repeatedly pummelled his face with a brick. So proud were his attackers that they performed victory dances for the news helicopters hovering above, as if celebrating a last-minute touchdown. It was hard to watch, but impossible to take your eyes off. Sixty-three people were killed, 2,383 were injured.

Walking on the night of the riots through Central Square in Cambridge, an African-American enclave sandwiched between the campuses of Harvard and the Massachusetts Institute of Technology (MIT), a British friend who had arrived on a coveted academic scholarship angrily declared he wanted to turn his back on America that very instant and leave without completing his studies. The mood of locals drifting through the streets, however, was of numb resignation. So commonplace was injustice, even following the civil rights reforms of the '60s, that few expected fair treatment from the criminal justice system. What was shocking, then, was the absence of shock. For the first time, the thought entered my mind that American exceptionalism, the idea that the United States was inherently special and unique, could also be a negative construct. The phrase 'Only in America' could be a term of derision. Even at this time of multiplying divisions, however, I remained confident about America's future.

During a visit to my family friends in Orange County a few months later, we ended up having a heated discussion on the terrace overlooking the pool about the acquittal of the LAPD officers. Like many white Angelinos, my father's best man sympathised with the cops. So I got hold of a copy of a speech delivered in Congress by Senator Bill Bradley – the lanky former basketball star who had played alongside the greats of the NBA before going into politics – slipped it into a manila envelope and posted it to their address in Fountain Valley.

'Fifty-six times in 81 seconds,' thundered Bradley. 'Fifty-six times in 81 seconds.' Then he repeated the word 'pow' 56 times, striking his mahogany Senate desk with a pencil every time he uttered it.

'Pow, pow, pow, pow, pow, pow, pow, pow, pow, pow, pow, pow, pow, pow, pow, pow, pow, pow, pow, pow, pow, pow, pow, pow, pow, pow, pow, pow, pow, pow, pow, pow, pow, pow, pow, pow, pow, pow, pow, pow, pow, pow, pow, pow, pow, pow, pow, pow, pow, pow, pow, pow, pow, pow, pow, pow.'

These kinds of dinner-table post-mortems took place across the country, as Los Angeles became the latest proxy combat zone of the culture wars. The city where in 1984 athletes such as Carl Lewis, Edwin Moses, Valerie Brisco-Hooks and a young Michael Jordan had lifted the spirits of a beleaguered nation now became a symbol of America's racial divisiveness and pervasive sense of gloom.

It was 1992. National self-doubt again weighed heavy. Japan looked set to outpace the United States economically and technologically.

Germany was resurgent. America had won the Cold War only to see other countries prosper. With the country mired in recession, the standard-of-living gains of the Reagan years, if not quite a chimera, seemed superficial. Even Donald Trump was now in financial trouble. The Trump Taj Mahal in Atlantic City, his trashy eighth wonder of the world, now resembled a Potemkin village. After its flashy opening in 1990, Trump was forced the next year to file for Chapter 11 bankruptcy protection. With creditors at his golden doors, the New Yorker had to sell off his airline and yacht, *The Trump Princess*. The Trump Castle Hotel and Casino in Atlantic City filed for bankruptcy the following year, as did the Trump Plaza, which had opened in 1984.

By some measures, America had more to celebrate in the early '90s than the mid-'80s. The Berlin Wall was demolished by the very people it once enclosed. The Iron Curtain, following the 1989 revolutions in East Germany, Poland, Hungary, Bulgaria, Czechoslovakia and Romania, had been ripped down. Earlier that year, the Red Army completed its humiliating retreat from Afghanistan. By the summer of 1991, the Warsaw Pact, the communist counterpoint to NATO, had been dissolved. By the New Year, the Soviet Union no longer existed, after morphing peacefully into the Russian Federation and 14 separate republics.

'You can have a very quiet Christmas evening,' Mikhail Gorbachev informed President Bush during a telephone call to Camp David on 25 December 1991, after handing over authority of the nuclear arsenal to the new Russian president, Boris Yeltsin.' The Russian bear had been declawed. After a 40-year fight, the United States could claim an ideological victory in the Cold War. The American system was dominant. George H. W. Bush was in a position to craft his 'New World Order', a phrase both he and Gorbachev used to describe a harmonious new era based on great power collaboration not conflict.

A lightning conquest in the first Gulf War in 1991 underscored America's new pre-eminence. In Operation Desert Storm, some 543,000 US military personnel took just 100 hours to liberate occupied Kuwait.[2] Threatened with 'the mother of all battles', the US-led forces not only annihilated the Iraqi army, which suffered some 20,000 deaths, but also slayed the phantoms of Vietnam. For all the concerns beforehand about wading into a Mesopotamian quagmire, America lost 148 troops. 'By God, we've kicked the Vietnam syndrome once and for all,' the president told state legislators at the White House in a rare public show of self-congratulation.[3]

The Gulf War was also a diplomatic triumph, in which the United States stood at the head of a multilateral coalition drawing together 28 countries. The United Nations Security Council authorised the military operation. Bush also had the strategic insight to bring military action to a timely end. Alert to the dangers of regime change, he halted the blitzkrieg advance down the 'Road of Death' to Baghdad and made no attempt to topple Saddam Hussein.

By no means was Operation Desert Storm flawless. Bush should have compelled the Iraqi dictator to sit at the table in Safwan when 'Stormin' Norman' Schwarzkopf accepted his country's surrender, a public shaming that would have dramatically undercut his power. When Shiites and Kurds rose up against the Iraqi dictator, Bush left them at the mercy of the dictator's army. However, not since the end of World War II had America been so sure-footed in projecting its military and diplomatic power.

'When you left, it was still fashionable to question America's decency, America's courage, America's resolve,' Bush told returning troops at Sumter, South Carolina, in March 1991. 'No-one in the whole world doubts us any more.'[4]

The university campus I was on at MIT exuded confidence and spoke also of America's ambition to conquer the remaining new frontiers. On arrival I was given something called an 'email address', and told it was possible to communicate with professors via a device called the Intranet, which connected all the computers. To my impressionable eyes, Americans seemed to be in a hurry to win the future.

At the very moment America had most to cheer, however, it no longer had a cheerleader as president. Throughout his career, Bush had obeyed the directive of his patrician mother against boastfulness, a commendable trait in the white-flannelled tennis clubs of Maine, maybe, but not one rewarded in modern-day politics.

When the Berlin Wall was demolished in 1989, Bush was reproached by the White House press corps for failing to rejoice in America's victory; for missing the historical moment; for not rushing to Berlin. 'You don't seem elated,' said a mystified reporter. 'I'm just not an emotional kind of guy,' the president protested in his buttoned-down way. Bush also knew triumphalism in Washington would strengthen hardliners in Moscow looking for an opportunity to oust Mikhail Gorbachev. A trip to Berlin may have won a few news cycles, but made it harder to bring the Cold War to a peaceable conclusion.

By refusing to attend a victory celebration in New York, Bush showed the same self-effacement in the aftermath of the Gulf War. Troops deserved the ticker-tape adulation, he told advisors, not their commander-in-chief. Nor did the highest presidential approval ratings Gallup had ever recorded, a stratospheric 89 per cent – a poll in *USA Today* put his popularity even higher at 91 per cent – go to his head.[5]

When he left for Camp David after the war was over, hundreds of White House aides gathered on the South Lawn waving signs that read 'The Great Liberator' and '91 per cent'. Bush, though, was careful to avoid a 'Mission Accomplished' moment. 'I haven't yet felt this wonderfully euphoric feeling that many of the American people felt. I'm beginning to,' he told a gathering at the White House. But he admitted to needing 'more time to sort out in my mind how I can say to the American people: "It's over. The last 't' is crossed, the last 'i' is dotted."'[6] He was a better statesman than showman.

Far from sharing in the euphoria, Bush ended up suffering from a post-war funk, a Churchill-style 'black dog', that led him to consider quitting politics altogether. 'I want to get out of this,' he wrote in his diary in February 1991. 'I want to walk into a drugstore in Kennebunkport; build a house in Houston; or teach at the library at A&M [Texas A&M University], with less pressure.'[7]

A year out from the start of the primary season, his mood remained bleak: 'I've lost heart for a lot of the gut political fighting, as a result of trying to lead this country and bring it together in the Gulf. It's strange but true.'[8] In his moment of maximum triumph and popularity, he temporarily lost his way. Thereafter, it was extraordinary how quickly things unravelled for Bush. Here was a president with the foreign policy acumen and diplomatic skills to forge that 'New World Order'. But it was the new political order he found more perplexing. The reunification of Berlin had a schismatic effect on Washington. The loss of America's post-war organising principle brought to mind the prophetic words of Georgy Arbatov, a Soviet expert on the United States, speaking before the break-up of his homeland: 'We are going to do a terrible thing to you. We are going to deprive you of an enemy.'[9]

The son of a patrician senator and scion of a blue-blood banking family who reinvented himself as a Texan oil man and Lone Star politician, George H. W. Bush could easily have been the poster boy for the geographic reorientation of the Republican Party. There was always the sense, though, that he was faking it: that he enjoyed darting around the waters off Walker's Point on the Maine shoreline in his cigar boat more than hurling horseshoes; that he felt more comfortable in preppy loafers than cowboy boots; that he was a Yankee, rather than a true son of the south. For nearly a quarter of a century, he kept a mailing address at the Houstonian Hotel that allowed him to vote in Texas, but his ancestral and spiritual home was the Bush compound in Kennebunkport. 'This is home,' he admitted in 1988. 'This is where I am really me.'[10] Dana Carvey, the comedian who pilloried the president each week on *Saturday Night Live*, described Bush as Mr Rogers, the children's TV presenter, trying to be John Wayne. Never, though, was he *True Grit*.

Rather than its southward tilt, what Bush truly embodied was the mounting tensions within the Republican Party between the establishment and insurgent right. Throughout his 30-year career, as this private struggle played out in the public arena, we saw two contradictory Bushes: on the one hand, the well-mannered Ivy Leaguer advocating a kindler, gentler politics; on the other, a ruthless opportunist who fought like a scrappy redneck. In Washington, he tended to behave like an aristocrat – once, during the 1984 primary season, he told Senator Gary Hart, the Democratic frontrunner, that if he needed rest ahead of the Maine caucuses he was more than welcome to use the nearby Bush residence. To get to Washington, however, Bush often fought ugly, even as he tried to maintain a veneer of civility.

Battling for a Senate seat in Texas during his first political campaign in 1964, he opposed the Civil Rights Act, derided Martin Luther King as a 'militant' and remained staunchly loyal to Barry Goldwater.[11] But in a state populated by ranch hands and oil workers, he also wore preppy striped ties on the campaign trail, and appeared at rallies alongside the Bush Bluebonnet Belles, the musical cousins of the Yale Whiffenpoofs, an a cappella ensemble that performed at his father's political events.[12] His campaign manager considered him the worst candidate he'd ever worked for.

After his defeat, Bush regretted aligning himself so closely with Goldwater and bemoaned the malign influence of the far-right John Birch Society.[13] 'This mean humourless philosophy which says everybody should agree on absolutely everything is not good for the Republican Party or for our State,' he wrote, foreshadowing battles that lay ahead. 'When the word moderation becomes a dirty word we have some soul searching to do.'[14]

As the conservative movement veered further right, Bush often sounded more like an outlier than the radicals. During the 1980 Republican primaries, his taunting description of Reaganomics as voodoo economics raised the hackles of supply-siders, who believed in reducing taxation and lessening government regulation. Even after serving for eight years as Reagan's loyal deputy, he was seen as a Rockefeller Republican masquerading as a Reagan Republican, which is essentially what he was – a lamb in wolf's clothing.

Aware of his right-wing image problem, Bush tried to make amends by professing his love of pork rinds and beef jerky, testifying to becoming a born-again Christian and even inviting Jim and Tammy Faye Bakker for supper at the Naval Observatory, his vice presidential residence. Yet right-wingers knew these mating rituals were performed through gritted patrician teeth. His true feelings surfaced after being harangued at a campaign event in Tennessee by a supporter of the TV evangelist Pat Robertson who refused to shake his hand, an affront for a gentleman of such refined manners.

'They're scary,' Bush wrote in his diary, 'they're religious fanatics and they're spooky. They will destroy this party if they're permitted to take over.'[15] So repulsive did he find the New Right that in 1987 he turned down an invitation to address the Conservative Political Action Conference. 'Fuck 'em, I ain't going,' he reportedly told aides. 'You can't satisfy these people.'[16]

As he launched his campaign for the Republican nomination in 1988, his early mis-steps recalled that first, striped-tie campaign in Texas. Explaining away his poor performance in an early Iowa straw poll, he noted his supporters had to drop off their daughters at debutant balls.[17] At a truck stop in New Hampshire, he requested 'a splash' of coffee.[18]

Bush benefited, however, from the absence of an obvious Reaganite heir. His main rival, Bob Dole, who won the 1988 Iowa caucus, was pilloried by New Right conservatives as 'the tax collector for the welfare state', having helped enact the tax hike that kept Social Security solvent. So despite being humiliated in Iowa, where Pat Robertson pushed him into third place, Bush rebounded in New Hampshire by portraying Dole as a tax raiser. On Super Tuesday he won 16 of the 17 states contested, and wrapped up the nomination. Thus, this pillar of the establishment became the standard-bearer of an anti-establishment party. For the next 30 years, the Republican right yearned for its Excalibur moment, when the true heir to Ronald Reagan would pull from the stone the sword. Instead, the primary process kept on selecting establishment candidates rather than true believers.

When the Republican Party gathered for its 1988 convention in New Orleans, Bush delivered a speech best remembered for the six-word pledge that ended up ensnaring his presidency. 'Read my lips, no new taxes,' he snarled, trying to sound more like John Wayne than Mr Rogers. In passages composed with the help of Reagan's most eloquent West Wing wordsmith, Peggy Noonan, he also outlined his vision of a kinder, gentler America illuminated by a thousand points of light.

For all the high-mindedness of his convention speech, however, Bush ended up taking the gutter route to the White House. Roger Ailes became one of his chief image-makers. Lee Atwater, a pit-bull terrier of a political consultant and a down-and-dirty proponent of the southern strategy, served as his campaign manager. The South Carolinian, who on his deathbed apologised to opponents for his venality, produced a 312-page memorandum, 'The Hazards of Duke', that outlined the weaknesses of his opponent, the Massachusetts Governor Mike Dukakis. Then Bush set about assassinating his character.

He questioned the patriotism of this Greek-American first-generation immigrant, and sought to capitalise from a notorious ad featuring Willie Horton, an African-American convicted murderer who twice raped a white woman while furloughed from prison under a Massachusetts programme in place while Dukakis was governor.

'If I can make Willie Horton a household name, we'll win the election,' said Atwater, licking his South Carolinian lips at the prospect of depicting Dukakis as a liberal elitist who was soft on crime 'The only question is whether to portray Willie Horton with a knife,' Ailes told *Time* magazine.[19] Even well-mannered moderates such as Bush were prepared now to prosecute the politics of personal destruction.

What the 1988 campaign also revealed was the extent to which elections were coming to be fought on cultural terrain. Candidates deliberately sought to divide the country. Emotive wedge issues had more sway than dry policy questions. All politics was personal. On education, it was whether children should recite the Pledge of Allegiance. On health, it was reproductive rights. Bush even toured a flag factory to wrap himself in the Stars and Stripes. 'Every single thing I did,' Ailes later explained, 'from debates to rhetoric to speeches to media was to define the two [candidates] and push them farther apart.'[20]

Witnessing my first campaign, I was shocked not just by the unscrupulousness but also by the effectiveness of negative campaigning. When I interviewed Dukakis afterwards on the Boston campus where he taught classes in public policy, he seemed still to be suffering from a political form of PTSD. Winning 40 states, including California, and more than 53.4 per cent of the vote, the Republicans scored not just their third victory in a row but their third lopsided win. The GOP had now won five of the last six presidential elections, fuelling talk of a permanent electoral lock on the White House. It said much about the pitiful state of Democratic presidential politics that Dukakis's 45.6 per cent share of the vote was the party's second-best performance in 20 years. The District of Columbia was the Democrat's only impregnable stronghold. Not a single state was deep blue.[21]

In his inaugural address, Bush tried to rekindle those thousand points of light, and lamented the rancorous state of politics. 'There has grown a certain divisiveness,' he said. 'We have seen the hard looks and heard the statements in which not each other's ideas are challenged, but each other's motives.'[22] Yet Bush's nationalistic, scorched-earth campaign accelerated that trend. A genial patrician had foreshadowed what post-Cold War politics would look like. And it was ugly.

The early post-war years could hardly be described as an idyllic age of American consensus, a non-partisan Shangri-La. However, the Cold War imposed a discipline on Washington politics that produced a level of comity unrecognisable today and also a steady stream of sound public policy. The country experienced outbreaks of paranoia, such as the McCarthyite witch-hunt aimed at rooting out alleged communists in the US government and Hollywood, fuelled by the ideological intensity of East–West tensions. On Capitol Hill, a reactionary – and bipartisan – coalition of dyed-in-the-wool Republicans and segregationist southern Democrats continued to block long-overdue reforms, most flagrantly civil rights.

Nonetheless, much of the 1950s and early 1960s witnessed a surprising degree of constructive cooperation, as partisanship was subordinated to the collective aim of containing communism. The cloakrooms of Capitol Hill were crowded with veterans, such as the former patrol-boat skipper Jack Kennedy and navy reservist Richard Nixon, who had experienced combat in Europe and the Pacific. Now, the Soviet Union was the enemy. At a time when domestic politics was inseparable from foreign affairs, Democrats and Republicans were rivals not mortal foes. Legislators went to Washington to legislate.

Defeating the Soviets, and demonstrating the superiority of the US system, provided the spur for most of the bipartisan achievements of the age. The national freeway system, that bitumen landmark of the Eisenhower years, was the result of the National Interstate and Defense Highways Act, a measure designed, as its title suggested, to make it easier to move troops around the country.

In a Sputnik induced panic, following the Soviet Union's successful launch in 1957 of the world's first satellite, Congress didn't pass a straightforward education act to improve science teaching, but rather the 1958 National Defense Education Act, again with bipartisan backing. The mission to the moon was an attempt to make sure an American astronaut planted the Stars and Stripes before a Soviet cosmonaut unfurled the hammer and sickle. Even the civil rights reforms of the '60s had a Cold War dimension, since 'whites only' signs and the protests they sparked gifted the communists a propaganda coup at a time when Washington and Moscow were competing to extend their spheres of influence on the newly decolonised continent of Africa.

Throughout this period, the country's leaders were refreshingly pragmatic. Dwight D. Eisenhower was such a non-ideological figure – 'his smile was his philosophy', it was once said – that in 1952 both Republicans and Democrats tried to draft him as their presidential candidate.[23]

In winning the Republican nomination, the former general beat Senator Robert Taft of Ohio, or 'Mr Conservative' as he was known, an era-defining defeat in which the GOP opted for moderation and internationalism over hard-line conservatism and isolationism. Eisenhower, sounding like an early advocate of Third Way politics, promised to take America 'down the middle of the road between the unfettered power of concentrated wealth ... and the unbridled power of statism or partisan interests'. During his eight years in office, he made no concerted attempt to dismantle FDR's New Deal.[24]

Eisenhower's successor, John F. Kennedy, far from being the crusading liberal idealist of lore, was also a cautious pragmatist. His election in 1960 heralded generational change, but hardly a major ideological shift. Unexpectedly, Lyndon Johnson enacted more liberal legislation than Kennedy, but remained a moderate at heart who tried to steer a course between northern progressives and his fellow southerners.

Even Richard Nixon, for all his law-and-order shrillness during the 1968 campaign, governed much like his former boss, President Eisenhower. Federal spending and federal regulation grew faster under Nixon than under Johnson. For a politician who pioneered the southern strategy, his civil rights record was unexpectedly enlightened. So, too, was his environmentalism. Nixon authored the 1970 Clean Air Act, the most ambitious green legislation yet passed, and created the Environmental Protection Agency. From president to post-war president, consensualism provided a continuous thread.

Congressional leaders were also surprisingly cooperative. During the Eisenhower years, the then Senate Majority Leader Lyndon Johnson and his Texan mentor House Speaker Sam Rayburn came in for criticism, not because they stymied the president's legislative agenda but because they lent too much support. The 1964 Civil Rights Act, as we have seen, would not have been enacted had it not been for the support of moderate Republicans led by the then Senate Minority Leader Everett Dirksen.

Even Nixon's resignation from office, the biggest political commotion of the post-war years, produced a surprising degree of bipartisanship. Though there was a cabal of Nixon loyalists, including Ronald Reagan, who stayed with him almost to the end, members of his own party were instrumental in his downfall. It was a Republican, Fred Thompson, the minority counsel on the Senate Watergate Committee and a future Hollywood actor and GOP presidential candidate, whose line of questioning revealed publicly for the first time that Nixon kept a secret taping system in the Oval Office (another Republican staffer had uncovered its existence). The conservative *National Review*, under the editorship of William F. Buckley, demanded that Nixon hand over the 'smoking gun' tapes.

Howard Baker, a Republican senator from Tennessee, posed the legendary Watergate question, 'What did the president know, and when did he know it?' Baker expected the question to help exonerate Nixon, but after discovering the president knew an awful lot more than he had previously let on, he backed impeachment. When the House Judiciary Committee voted on five articles of impeachment, three passed with Republican support. Finally, it was Republican elders, such as the Senate Minority Leader Hugh Scott and Barry Goldwater, who drove down Pennsylvania Avenue to implore Nixon to resign.

Watergate prompted a series of reforms intended to fumigate Washington. Campaign finance laws curbed the corrupting influence of money and made it harder to pull off Nixonian dirty tricks. Constraints were imposed on executive power, limiting the president's authority to start new wars and impound funds appropriated by Congress. There was a push to raise ethical standards and provide greater government transparency.

Politics in Washington, however, became more combative. The influx of 'Watergate Babies' in the 1974 midterm elections, the vast majority of whom were 30-somethings who came of political age during the culture wars of the 1960s and had been participants in the civil rights and anti-war movement, had a radicalising effect on the House.

The lingua franca of politics also changed. The Class of '74 talked of rights and values, rather than the pocketbook dollars and cents of the New Deal era. For progressives, it was the right to have an abortion or the right to drink clean water. For conservatives, it was the rights of an unborn foetus and right to bear arms.

All these issues aroused powerful passions, which meant feelings started to trump objective facts and politics became more emotive. Debates also came to be framed in a more binary way, often as moral and even mortal clashes. As the historian John Lawrence has observed, 'Elevating policy goals to the status of rights would prove to be a crucial step in the evolution of ideological partisanship in the United States.'[25]

Because of their moral absolutism, the new generation of lawmakers was often allergic to compromise. From the mid-'70s onwards, the voting gap between congressional Democrats and congressional Republicans became more pronounced. Progressives became more secular and conservatives became more devout. Cultural relativism clashed with religious dogma.

On both sides of the aisle, congressional oversight increasingly came to be used as a political cudgel, paving the way for the televised hearings that have become such a permanent – and polarising – feature of Washington. The enactment in 1978 of the independent counsel statute, another post-Watergate reform, placed in the hands of lawmakers powerful new weapons that could be used for partisan purposes.

First, the new law was used to investigate whether Jimmy Carter's chief of staff, Hamilton Jordan, and campaign manager, Timothy Kraft, had used cocaine. Then, in what felt like a reprisal attack, the Democrats deployed independent counsels to hound members of Ronald Reagan's inner circle, namely his attorney general, Edwin Meese, and chief image-maker, Michael Deaver.

Public life became criminalised. Congressional oversight hearings became show trials. A classic of the genre was the Iran-Contra hearings, which featured an exotic array of cast members, including Lieutenant Colonel Oliver North, resplendent in his full dress Marine Corps uniform; his beautiful assistant Fawn Hall, who helped him shred incriminating documents; and Admiral John Poindexter, Reagan's National Security Advisor, who was convicted of lying to Congress and obstructing its committees.

Televising Congress, where the klieg lights were intended to have the same cleansing effect as sunshine, further raised the partisan temperature. Soon after the Cable-Satellite Public Affairs Network went to air in 1979, with a speech from a thrusting Tennessean congressman named Al Gore, a young freshman grasped its potential for promoting himself and his aggressive brand of Republicanism. Taking advantage of rules that prohibited C-SPAN cameras from showing wide shots of an empty chamber, Newton Leroy McPherson Gingrich started delivering incendiary late-night speeches with little or no live audience, but a growing one in American living rooms (by 1984, almost 20 million homes received C-SPAN). In the process, Gingrich and his allies created a new style of late-night political television, a prototype, in conservative content at least, for Fox News.

Gingrich's grandstanding had long irked the House Speaker, Tip O'Neill, whose breaking point came in the spring of 1984, when the Georgian accused him of pursuing 'a McCarthyism of the Left'. O'Neill responded with finger-wagging rage. 'It is the lowest thing that I've ever seen in my 32 years in Congress,' he thundered.

By mounting a derogatory personal attack on Gingrich, however, O'Neill breached House rules, and thus became the first Speaker since 1798 to be rebuked for violating its honour code. When this David-and-Goliath clash aired on the evening news, Gingrich instantly became a right-wing folk hero. 'I am now a famous person,' he told *The Washington Post*.

His guerrilla tactics worked to asymmetrical perfection. 'The number-one fact about the news media is they love fights,' Gingrich afterwards told a group of conservative activists. 'You have to give them confrontations. When you give them confrontations, you get attention. When you get attention, you educate.'[26]

For O'Neill, all politics was local. For Gingrich, all politics was confrontational. Bipartisanship, he believed, buttressed the status quo by reducing the incentive to change course, which was a problem for a party that had not held the Speakership since the 1950s.

Democrats were hardly shrinking wallflowers. This they showed in the battle in 1987 to block the nomination of Ronald Reagan's Supreme Court nominee Robert Bork, who as Nixon's solicitor general had fired the Watergate special prosecutor Archibald Cox after the notorious 'Saturday Night Massacre', when the attorney general and deputy attorney resigned rather than do so.

A constitutional originalist who opposed the 1964 Civil Rights Act, *Roe v. Wade*, and a string of Supreme Court rulings on gender equality, Bork was the first nominee to find himself in the midst of the kind of confirmation knife-fight commonplace today (paradoxically, the year before, the Senate had confirmed the arch-conservative Antonin Scalia by 98 votes to 0).

In an epoch-making fight between liberals and conservatives, Ted Kennedy marked out the battle-lines. 'Robert Bork's America is a land in which women would be forced into back-alley abortions,' he roared on the Senate floor, 'blacks would sit at segregated lunch counters, rogue police could break down citizens' doors in midnight raids, schoolchildren could not be taught about evolution. Writers and artists would be censored at the whim of government.'

The hearings could hardly have been more polarising, with the opposing sides even resorting to paid advertising as if it were an election campaign. The die was cast.

For the next climactic nomination fight, when in 1991 President Bush nominated the black jurist Clarence Thomas to replace the civil rights icon Thurgood Marshall, I was living in America. Like the rest of the country, I was spellbound by the televised hearings, in which Thomas claimed to be the victim of 'a high-tech lynching' and the law professor Anita Hill accused him of sexual harassment.

Viewers sniggered at the porn films he allegedly discussed with her, starring Long Dong Silver, an actor with an eponymously large penis. There was a collective sense of cringe at the revelation that he reportedly asked Hill, 'Who put the pubic hair on my Coke?'

What I failed to realise at the time was that we were watching a trailer for an internecine future, a movie we would watch many times over, when the struggle for control of the Supreme Court would produce some of the nastiest and most divergent clashes.

A former congressman, Bush preferred the old ways of Capitol Hill. The backslapping camaraderie. The weekend mini-league games and supper parties. The wives' clubs that brought together political spouses from both sides. The co-sponsored legislation. On becoming president, though, he was confronted by the new spitefulness when the Senate rejected his choice of defense secretary, the former Texas Senator John Tower. In more collegiate times, Tower's transgressions, which included drunkenness, womanising and links to defence contractors, would probably have been forgiven or ignored. Capitol Hill, after all, was home to more than its share of drunken letches. For only the third time in the twentieth century, however, the Senate blocked a president's Cabinet pick.

Though unforeseen at the time, Tower's withdrawal ended up having consequences that would impact American life for decades to come. Congressman Dick Cheney, who had been serving as the Republican minority whip, filled the vacancy at the Pentagon, which speeded his rise. This in turn created an opening in the GOP House leadership. By just two votes, Newt Gingrich beat Ed Madigan, a moderate from Illinois favoured by the party establishment. The headline in *The Washington Post* served as a forewarning: 'Gingrich Elected House GOP Whip: Increased Partisan Polarization Seen'.[27] His aim, after all, was to turn the Republican Party into a fully fledged opposition party.

Immediately, Gingrich ramped up his campaign to bring down O'Neill's successor as House Speaker, Jim Wright, who was alleged to have breached ethics rules over income received from his autobiography. Wright, a veteran of World War II, became the first Speaker to resign because of scandal. In a fiery resignation speech, he bemoaned the 'harsh personal attacks' and 'mindless cannibalism' of partisan warfare: 'It is grievously hurtful to our society when vilification becomes an accepted form of political debate, when negative campaigning becomes a full-time occupation, when members of each party become self-appointed vigilantes carrying out personal vendettas against members of the other party. In God's name, that's not what this institution is supposed to be all about.'[28]

Gingrich saw things differently. 'This war has to be fought with a scale and a duration and a savagery that is only true of civil wars,' he told the Heritage Foundation during a speech in 1988. The new politics in a nutshell.

In his next fight, over the 1990 budget, Gingrich took on the president himself. Bush, in a grand bargain with the Democratic leadership, had jettisoned his 'no new taxes' pledge in return for deficit-reducing cuts in government spending. Naturally, Gingrich believed Bush had committed conservative apostasy. 'I think you may destroy your presidency,' he told Bush at a White House meeting on the day congressional leaders inked the final deal.[29] Then he stormed out of the West Wing.

When CNN broadcast Bush's budget deal announcement, it did so on a split screen. One side showed Bush in the Rose Garden flanked by Democratic congressional leaders. The other showed Gingrich exiting the White House and heading back to Congress, where he was greeted by cheering supporters. The schism within the conservative movement was being broadcast in real time. When the budget deal came to a vote in the House, 71 Republicans remained loyal to the president. A hundred and five sided with Gingrich.[30] The Republican Party was split in two: the pragmatists pitted against the purists.

The bipartisan budget, which slashed the deficit by $500 billion over the next five years, put the country's finances on a sounder footing and helped usher in the economic boom of the '90s. In terms of policy, it provided Bush with one of the most long-lasting achievements of his presidency. Politically, however, it was disastrous. As president, he could claim still to be the titular leader of the Republican Party, but Gingrich was in true command of the conservative movement. At the GOP convention two years later, Bush was forced to make a pitiful apology. 'Well, it was a mistake to go along with the Democratic tax increase. And I admit it.' The baby-boomers had usurped the greatest generation. The age of moderation was coming to an end.

When I arrived in Boston in the late summer of 1991, Bush continued to enjoy the kind of dizzying approval levels that made him a shoo-in for a second term. Governor Mario Cuomo of New York, the president's most threatening Democratic opponent, was doing his 'Hamlet on the Hudson' act, as he dithered over whether to mount a challenge. Al Gore, after his dress rehearsal four years earlier, considered Bush invincible. So, too, did Lloyd Bentsen, Dukakis's vice-presidential running mate and the sole Democratic star of the dismal 1988 campaign, who had already beaten Bush once before in the 1970 Texan Senate race.

By Labor Day, the traditional end of the American summer, the only candidate in the race was a charisma-less no-hoper, the former Senator Paul Tsongas – another Greek-American from Massachusetts, no less – who introduced himself to the American people with a campaign ad showing him doing laps in a swimming pool in skin-tight Speedos. Not until October did the Governor of Arkansas, Bill Clinton, enter the race, vowing in his down-home drawl to fight for 'the forgotten middle class' and to 'make America great again'. Clinton, evidently, did not think he could win. As he revealed to Washington insiders, this was primarily a warm-up for 1996.[31]

For reporters eager to cover a contest not a crowning, Clinton was the most eye-catching Democrat. An all-you-can-eat buffet of a candidate, he was Georgetown University, Yale and Oxford-educated with a folksy, popular touch; the partner of a talented and equally ambitious wife, saddled with a 'Slick Willie' reputation for womanising; a telegenic governor who had turned backward Arkansas into a laboratory of centrist reform; a preening overachiever with a junk-food habit.

Back at the 1988 Democratic convention, Clinton had suffered a near-death experience after delivering an interminably long primetime speech where the words 'in conclusion' were met with mordant applause. Displaying the survival instinct and pop-culture smarts that saved him four years later, afterwards he went on *The Tonight Show with Johnny Carson* to poke fun at himself, an act of contrived self-deprecation that probably rescued his career.

What also made Clinton so intriguing was his leading role in the Democratic Leadership Council, the group founded in 1985, the year after the Reagan landslide, to win back Reagan Democrats. Indeed, an irony of Bill Clinton is that a politician who became such a polarising figure rose to prominence as the prime architect of centrist Third Way politics. Clinton became the chairman of the DLC in 1990, the year of its inaugural conference, and was a driving force behind the New Orleans Declaration that spoke of 'expanding opportunity, not government' and noted 'the promise of America is equal opportunity, not equal outcome'.[32] Jesse Jackson ridiculed the DLC as the 'Southern White Boys' Caucus'. Yet the only Democrats to win a presidential election in the previous 28 years had been two southern boys, Lyndon Johnson and Jimmy Carter. Small wonder the Arkansan was seen as the Democratic Party's great white hope.

During this early phase of the race, I myself got to see the governor up close – felt his firm handshake, was affixed by his empathetic gaze, was flattered to momentarily become the focus of what struck me even then as his transactional attentiveness. Our first encounter came outside the doors of the JFK Presidential Library in Boston, a pilgrimage of sorts for a candidate who, like most ambitious Democrats, yearned to be seen as the next Jack Kennedy. Clinton, though, believed he had a special claim on this moniker, having shaken hands with the young president during a Boys Nation visit to the Rose Garden in 1963 when he was 16 years old. If anything, the black-and-white photograph capturing this moment for posterity showed Clinton looking more like the senior partner.

Buttonholing the candidate, I suggested he sit for an interview with his old university newspaper in Britain, *Cherwell*, and asked if we could schedule some time. Clinton liked the idea – or at least gave the people-pleasing impression of liking the idea – and handed me the number of his media handlers in Little Rock.

The next time I ran into him was at another stopping point on Boston's Camelot trail, the John F. Kennedy School of Government at Harvard. This time he suggested I contact his chief of staff, Betsey Wright, whose fictionalised character, Libby Holden, was played in the movie *Primary Colors* by Kathy Bates. For the second time, however, I failed to make any headway.

The third time I saw him was in the back corridor of a downtown hotel, one of those kitchen escape routes favoured by candidates seeking a quick getaway. Again I introduced myself as the bothersome student reporter keen to nail down an interview, but this time Clinton looked alarmed, as if he was being ambushed. Even the hitherto magic word 'Oxford' seemed to terrify him. The headlines a few days later made more sense of his startled reaction. Clinton's controversial draft letter written during his year as a Rhodes Scholar in Britain, in which he stated no government should have the power to compel a citizen to fight in a war they opposed, had been leaked to the press, and now read, to his critics at least, like a suicide note.

Already by then, Clinton's candidacy was imperilled. Days earlier, *Star*, the supermarket tabloid, had published an exposé featuring Gennifer Flowers, a cabaret singer from Arkansas who claimed to have had a 12-year affair with the governor. Four years earlier, Gary Hart, the then Democratic frontrunner, had been forced to withdraw when the *Miami Herald* reported on his trysts with the model Donna Rice aboard the pleasure boat *Monkey Business*.

Clinton, though, was determined to withstand what were then called 'bimbo eruptions', an ugly misogynistic term coined, ironically, by Betsey Wright. Activating a pre-planned strategy of containment, Bill and Hillary Clinton agreed to sit for an on-the-couch interview for *60 Minutes* that acknowledged marital difficulties without delivering a full-blown confessional. This we all watched, dipping chips into bowls of guacamole and sipping on flavourless American beer, in a special Super Bowl Sunday edition of the programme, which attracted some 50 million viewers.

Gary Hart, in his valedictory speech announcing his exit from the race, warned that politics had become 'another form of athletic competition or sporting match'. On *60 Minutes*, it was being used as a pre-match curtain raiser ahead of the biggest sporting event on the calendar. Under persistent questioning from the presenter Steve Kroft, the Clintons demonstrated the new skill set required of ambitious politicians: the ability to withstand scandal and determination to fight back.

Though the governor survived the onslaught, the couple suffered lasting collateral damage. In Bill Clinton, conservatives saw a skirt-chasing draft-dodger. In his wife, Hillary Rodham Clinton, they saw a self-righteous feminist who sneered at women who had not pursued careers of their own. 'You know, I'm not sitting here, some little woman standing by my man like Tammy Wynette,' she said on *60 Minutes*, a condescending line that haunted her for decades afterwards.

In her primetime debut, she had been forced to introduce herself to the American people in the most appalling of circumstances, the curse of the wronged political wife. Gone was the chance to create a more favourable first impression solely on her own terms. Bill Clinton, who came second in the New Hampshire primary three weeks later, became the Comeback Kid. His wife was cast as Lady Macbeth. My sense is that Hillary Clinton lost the 2016 election almost a quarter of a century before she ran.

Gone by the start of election year was President Bush's air of unassailability, something he himself had predicted would evaporate. 'The common wisdom today is that I'll win in a runaway,' he wrote in his diary in March 1991, 'but I don't believe that. I think it's going to be the economy [which] will make that determination.'[33] As unemployment rose, his personal approval rating came back down to earth.[34] By Christmas, it had dipped below the all-important 50 per cent mark. The New Year brought worsening economic news, and an unhappy trip to Japan, during which he vomited over the Japanese

Prime Minister Kiichi Miyazawa at a state banquet. The pictures of him slumped back in his chair, his body askew, his chin resting on his dinner shirt, his wife holding a napkin up to his gaping mouth, seemed to depict a president heading for enforced retirement.

Reporters who previously trumpeted his invincibility, now treated the president like roadkill. 'Bush encounters the supermarket, amazed,' was the front-page story in *The New York Times* in early February, a snarky piece on how the president had apparently been bamboozled by the barcode scanner he was shown at a mock-up of a checkout at a grocers' convention.

It fed the narrative, as the *Times* put it, that Bush 'is having trouble presenting himself to the electorate as a man in touch with middle class life'.[35] This widely referenced story, which is still cited to illustrate Bush's aristocratic detachment, was wrong. Bush had actually been shown a state-of-the-art checkout, with features, such as the capability to read mangled barcodes, then considered ground-breaking.

On other occasions, Bush essayed his own negative headlines. 'Message I care,' the 67-year-old told a town hall meeting in Exeter, New Hampshire, mistakenly reading aloud from his cue cards. 'Don't cry for me Argentina,' he said cryptically at an event in Dover.

As Bush struggled even to string a coherent sentence together, we watched Pat Buchanan, a former speechwriter for Richard Nixon and communications director for Ronald Reagan, give word-perfect expression to the malcontents on the insurgent right – his 'Pitchfork Brigade', as it came to be known. Though Buchanan had never held elective office, television had made him a conservative celebrity. CNN's *Crossfire*, which he co-hosted, and *The McLaughlin Group*, on which he appeared as a panellist, provided antagonistic arenas to hone his pugilistic style. Naturally confrontational – he was a street brawler as a child – he depicted himself as an isolationist up against a globalist, the renegade outsider against the establishment blue blood.

Buchanan attacked the trade deal Bush had negotiated with Mexico, railed against Japan for its predatory trade policies, linked rising levels of crime to rising levels of immigration, castigated

European allies for sponging off the Pentagon and threatened to withdraw the United States from multilateral organisations such as the World Bank and International Monetary Fund. 'He would put Americans' wealth and power at the service of some vague new world order,' Buchanan grumbled in his announcement speech. 'We will put America first.'[36]

Demonising illegal immigrants was central to his political brand. 'Take a look at what's happened to the people of California,' he said in an interview on *This Week with David Brinkley*. 'One in five felons in a federal prison is an illegal alien. The immigrants are coming in such numbers that they're swamping the schools, and you have to raise taxes.'[37] Buchanan also staged a photo-op at the southern border, to make the case for fortifying the frontier with a concrete-buttressed fence and ditches. 'I am calling attention to a national disgrace,' he said, after a tour from the Border Patrol guards, 'an illegal invasion that involves a million aliens a year.'[38] 'Pitchfork Pat' came up with a mocking nickname for his opponent: 'King George'. 'Make America First Again' was his campaign slogan.

At times, his nativism spilled over into blatant racism. 'I think God made all people good,' he told Brinkley, 'but if we had to take a million immigrants in, say Zulus, next year, or Englishmen, and put them in Virginia, what group would be easier to assimilate and would cause less problems for the people of Virginia?'[39]

For right-wingers who could not quite bring themselves to support David Duke, the former Grand Wizard of the KKK who had entered the race for the Republican nomination, the anti-Semitic Buchanan was the more palatable option.

Bush limped over the finish line in the New Hampshire primary, but Buchanan's 36.5 per cent share of the vote was nonetheless startling. 'I think King George is getting the message,' he declared on the night of this glorious defeat. 'When we take America back, we are going to make America great again, because there is nothing wrong with putting America first.'[40] So similar was the language, so echoing the message, that it seemed almost 20 years later he was being plagiarised by Donald Trump.

The 1992 New Hampshire primary rewrote the rulebook. Clinton demonstrated it was possible to weather multiple personal scandals if a candidate was shameless enough to brazen them out and come up with a counter-narrative. For Clinton it was his 'Comeback Kid' storyline, all too easily embraced by a pliant press, which helped him wrap up the nomination over the coming months as the contest moved south. His survival helped desensitise the electorate to philandering politicians and thus normalised bad behaviour.

For the GOP, Pat Buchanan demonstrated the populist lure of nativism, nationalism and protectionism. In so doing, he shattered the Republican consensus on mass immigration and internationalism. In the aftermath of the Cold War and in the absence of Ronald Reagan, he showed, too, that the future of the conservative movement was very much up for grabs.

For now, the Republican establishment was strong enough to withstand this insurgent assault. New Hampshire was Buchanan's high point, and Bush swept the remaining primaries. Nonetheless, the president had to appease Buchanan and his 'Pitchfork Brigade' of two million voters by granting him a speaking slot at the Republican convention in Houston. This he used to devastating effect.

With the imprimatur of primetime, Buchanan framed the election as a 'cultural war' in which American values were under attack from the 'homosexual rights movement', the 'radical feminism' of Hillary Clinton and 'the most pro-lesbian and pro-gay ticket in history'. The Democratic agenda, he claimed, meant 'abortion on demand, a litmus test for the Supreme Court, homosexual rights, discrimination against religious schools [and] women in combat units'. To clamorous cheers from the Houston delegates, Buchanan declared, 'There is a religious war going on in this country. It is a cultural war, as critical to the kind of nation we shall be as the Cold War itself, for this is a war for the soul of America.' The Texas journalist Molly Ivins sneered that 'the culture war speech', as it came to be known, was 'better in the original German'. The president's son, George W., shocked by its extremism, called it 'disastrous'.[41] That night, however, Buchanan achieved a personal victory, by bringing the intolerant, values-based language voiced by so many grassroots conservatives into the Republican mainstream.

If Buchanan provided a script for Donald Trump, Ross Perot, another presidential aspirant, offered a field guide for billionaire populism. The pint-sized, jug-eared Texan, a former IBM salesman who amassed his fortune by founding a data company at the start of the computer age, had the same gift for self-publicity – he had once sent Christmas baskets to POWs held in Vietnam and then flown to Hanoi to personally demand they be delivered. He did not feel bound by normal rules – he organised a commando team to rescue two of his employees being held in Iran, a paramilitary escapade dramatised in the popular 1986 television mini-series *On Wings of Eagles*. His unexpected popularity also demonstrated how it was possible to upend politics in a single moment, just as Reagan had done in 'The Speech'.

For the Texan, it came two nights after the New Hampshire primary during an appearance on CNN's *Larry King Live* show, when he invited viewers to place his name on the presidential ballot in all 50 states. Even before the programme ended, the signatures came gushing in.

Like Buchanan, Perot railed against cheap Japanese imports and destructive global trade deals. But it was his outsider attacks on Washington, his positioning as an anti-politician, his insistence on putting American interests first and his business acumen that fuelled his rise. 'The people are concerned that our government is still organised to fight the Cold War,' he told a country worried about US decline. 'They want it reorganised to rebuild America as the highest priority.'[42] Again, the language sounded emphatically 'America First'.

By the time the primary season drew to a close, Perot led the national polls, pushing Clinton into third place. Never before in the history of Gallup polling had a third-party candidate led the presidential race.[43] All the polls suggested he was drawing equally from the Democrats and Republicans and mobilising independent voters who felt the traditional parties had made them politically homeless.[44]

The Perot honeymoon, so adoring in the spring, did not survive the summer. His policy of firing corporate employees who cheated on their spouses seemed puritanical. Employing a staff member to measure the skirt length of his employees seemed not just autocratic but theocratic. Facing the kind of scrutiny he was completely unused to, he suspended his eccentric campaign in mid-July, and blamed his withdrawal on Republican dirty tricksters he accused of trying to sabotage his daughter's wedding.

As Perot faltered, Clinton surged. The turning point came in the early summer with his carefully orchestrated attack on the African-American hip-hop activist Sister Souljah, who in the aftermath of the Los Angeles riots had railed, 'If black people kill black people every day, why not have a week and kill white people?'

Sister Souljah became a proxy for Clinton's true targets, traditional left-wing black leaders such as Jesse Jackson and the identity politics they personified. The attack offered proof of his centrism, and showed he was unafraid of offending the very groups white working-class voters complained had hijacked the Democratic Party. (Clinton had hitherto played the race card during the New Hampshire primary when he returned to Arkansas to oversee the execution of Ricky Ray Rector, a lobotomised black felon who told his lawyer the night before he was 'gonna vote Clinton' and then asked for the pecan pie from his last meal to be set aside to eat after his execution.)

The selection as his running mate of Al Gore, a fellow southern moderate, underscored his New Democrat credentials. On the eve of their convention in New York, Clinton even received what sounded like a tacit endorsement from Perot. 'The Democratic Party has revitalised itself,' remarked the Texan. 'They've done a brilliant job, in my opinion, in coming back.'[45]

On the black-and-white television in my student billet in Boston, I tuned in every night to see the Democrats stage their most successful convention since Kennedy stood in the Los Angeles Memorial Coliseum, the sun setting over the Pacific Ocean, to unveil his 'New Frontier' reform programme. Clinton's 'The Man from Hope' convention biopic, which evoked the mood of a Norman Rockwell painting as it told the story of his humble origins in Hope, Arkansas, was a soft-focus triumph. It set the scene for his sunny speech – 'I believe in a place called Hope' that brought Madison Square Garden to its feet. The first poll afterwards showed him with a lead of 27 points.

Scornful still of Bill Clinton, Bush thought he was too much of a 'Slick Willie' to win. 'The American people are never going to elect a person of Bill Clinton's character,' he wrote in his diary. But the charisma gap with the youthful candidate continued to plague him. Whereas Clinton happily donned his shades and lifted a saxophone to his lips to play 'Heartbreak Hotel' on *The Arsenio Hall Show* – the pop-culture moment of the campaign – the White House said Bush considered the show too lowbrow to appear on.

Arsenio Hall, in a statement that spoke of the generational gulf between the two main candidates, hit back. 'Excuse me, George Herbert, irregular-heart-beating, read-my-lying-lipping, slipping-in-the-polls, do-nothing, deficit-raising ... sushi-puking Bush! I don't remember inviting your ass on my show. My ratings are higher than yours.'[46] In an ever more celebritised politics, pop-culture figures now helped make the political weather.

The televised debates laid bare Bush's failure to master the presentational requisites of the presidency. His emotional aloofness, at a time when Oprah Winfrey had become the queen of daytime talk, was a further handicap. In the second debate, held for the first time in a town-hall format, an audience member asked the candidates how the national debt affected them personally. Clinton, who understood the intimacy of the medium, was masterful, purposefully edging closer to the questioner with the stagecraft of Elvis and the empathy of Dr Phil. 'Tell me again how it's affected you,' he purred. By contrast, a tongue-tied Bush confessed to being confused by the question. When the cameras caught him peering uncomfortably at his wristwatch, this awkward gesture suggested his time had passed.

By this late stage, in an October surprise of sorts, Perot had re-entered the race, following another appearance on *Larry King Live* in which he displayed again his unusual messianic energy. And voters disaffected with the two main parties remained enthralled.

On Election Day, he attracted almost 20 million votes, or 18.9 per cent of the vote. Not since Theodore Roosevelt in 1912 had a third-party candidate done so well, a performance made all the more remarkable by his absence from the campaign for two months during the summer and his decision to stump in only 16 states.[47] Clearly there was an appetite for a billionaire businessman in the Oval Office, whatever their eccentricities and excesses. Perot's strong showing prompted a warning from his one-time spokesman Jim Squires. 'The next time round the man on the white horse comes, he may not be so benign. He could be a real racial hater or a divider of people.'[48]

By winning only 37 per cent, President Bush suffered the ignominy of receiving the lowest share of the popular vote of any incumbent in more than 100 years. To add to his humiliation, some on the Republican right celebrated his defeat. 'Oh, man, yeah, it was fabulous,' reflected the future House Majority Leader, Tom 'The Hammer' DeLay, a hard-line acolyte of Newt Gingrich. Had Bush won, he reckoned, it would have meant 'another four years of misery' for House GOP conservatives.[49] Moderate conservatism would have received a boost. Radical Republicans would have been side-lined. The New Right had to lose in order to win.

Bill Clinton's 43 per cent share of the vote was lower than Mike Dukakis's, but finally he had managed to pick the Republicans' electoral lock on the White House. Demonstrating once more that southern Democrats were the party's most feasible presidential candidates, Clinton won four states of the Old Confederacy, and polled highly below the Mason–Dixon line.

In doing so, he broke apart the Nixon and Reagan coalitions and redrew the electoral map. California went Democrat for the first time since the Johnson landslide in 1964, and has remained so ever since. Michigan, Connecticut, Maine, Vermont and Delaware, which had been reliably Republican since the mid-'60s, now became reliably Democratic. The party of McGovern, Mondale and Dukakis returned as a serious force in presidential politics. Before Clinton, the Republicans won five out of six presidential elections. After his victory, the Democrats won the national popular vote in six out of the next seven.

1992 is rightly viewed as a watershed election, because it ended the Republicans' domination of the White House. Also there were portents of the rise a quarter of a century later of Donald Trump, whether it was Buchanan's ethno-nationalism, Perot's billionaire populism, Clinton's imperviousness to scandal or the collapse of Bush-style moderation.

To stand outside Washington's National Cathedral in November 2018 for the funeral of George H. W. Bush was to watch a tableau of modern history file past. All the living former presidents were there: Jimmy Carter, George Bush Jr, Barack Obama and Bill Clinton, who by now had become a close friend of his one-time adversary. Also in that front-row pew, albeit cold-shouldered by the others, was the latest commander-in-chief to carry the nuclear codes in his suit pocket, who was invited to attend, but pointedly not asked to speak.

The former Soviet leader Mikhail Gorbachev was too ill to make the journey, but Lech Wałesa, the hero of Gdansk and leader of the Solidarity movement in the 1980s, had flown in from Poland to salute a president globally regarded as the leader of the free world. The German Chancellor, Angela Merkel, a protégée of Helmut Kohl who had grown up in East Germany, also crossed the Atlantic to pay tribute to Bush's skilful handling of the peaceful reunification of her homeland, a feat the late president regarded as his greatest accomplishment.

From London had come the former British Prime Minister John Major, another moderate conservative short of charisma, who had struggled to escape the oversized shadow of a domineering predecessor. Diplomatic luminaries of the Cold War years made their slow way down the nave: elder statesmen such as Henry Kissinger, who was pushed in a wheelchair, Bush's National Security Advisor Brent Scowcroft, who was hunched over a walking frame, and the former Secretary of State James Baker, by far the most sprightly and commanding of the three. Dick Cheney and Colin Powell walked briskly past the tiered bank of television cameras outside, heroes of the first Gulf War whose reputations had been sullied by the second.

In this rare act of political ecumenism, Bush was farewelled with affection, humour and near universal respect. George W. described his father, tearfully, as a 'great and noble man', the 'brightest of a thousand points of light'. Jon Meacham, whose sympathetic 2015 biography of Bush had done so much to rehabilitate his reputation, saluted 'America's last great soldier statesman'. He also told of how he had rehearsed his eulogy in front of its recipient, a reading met with the patrician self-effacement that had sometimes hobbled his presidency: 'That's a lot about me, Jon.'[50]

Many Americans that day mourned not just the passing of a former president but also the vanishing of a lost politics. To them, Bush was a war hero who personified the patriotic bipartisanship of the post-war years; a moderate who genuinely wanted to make America a kinder and gentler country, even if he was prone to political viciousness; and a pragmatist who disdained the ideological purists in the Republican Party who fetishised tax cuts and demonised government.

Like Harry S. Truman, another great foreign-policy president underappreciated at the time, Bush offered a prime example of how presidential reputations evolve over the passing decades: how legacies are reassessed and how traits characterised contemporaneously as weaknesses can be judged by future generations as virtues.

Posterity was certainly more generous than the headline writers of the time – *Newsweek* spoke of his 'wimp factor', even though he had flown 58 missions over the Pacific and been shot down by the Japanese over Chichi-Jima. Nor was he now so easily dismissed as a White House placeholder sandwiched awkwardly between the more consequential Reagan and Clinton presidencies. In his less showy way, he could also lay claim to being an era-defining politician: those fleeting years of unrivalled US global dominance, when its military seemed invincible, its multilateralism was widely applauded, its finances were more robust and its politics was more level-headed.

Because he was a one-term president, a transitional rather than transformational leader, his achievements, especially in the domestic sphere, had often been overlooked. Bush himself saw parallels with Babe Ruth, the baseball legend famed for his batting but who for 50 years held the record for pitching the most consecutive scoreless innings in a World Series.[51] Much like the music of Wagner, to bastardise Mark Twain, his presidency was better than it sounded.

Posthumously, his policy contributions came to be reassessed. Among the dozen or so major bills he signed into law were crucial amendments to the Clean Air Act raising emissions standards, the 1991 Civil Rights Act and his great legislative achievement, the Americans with Disabilities Act. Most consequential perhaps was the 1990 budget deal, which laid such a firm fiscal foundation for the economic growth of the '90s. The Bush years were a reminder of what could be achieved through a boring presidency that unfolded mostly in the background.

Politically, too, his success has been underestimated. No one since has won 40 states, or a 53 per cent share of the vote (although Barack Obama came close in 2008). Bill Clinton, the beneficiary of the peace and prosperity that Bush helped deliver, never cracked 50 per cent. He was the last president to be regarded universally as legitimate, which owed much to the fact he was the final greatest-generation commander-in-chief, and also the final president of the pre-internet age. This was very much an offline presidency.

Bush had the misfortune to occupy the White House in the age of television, a looking-glass that magnified the gulf in star power with Reagan. Nor did his accomplishments necessarily make for good TV. Coalition building, whether at home or abroad, took place away from the cameras. The evening news shows rarely rewarded detail, nuance or modesty. Instead, they hungered for the kind of dramatic imagery Bush was so reluctant to confect. Prioritising foreign over public relations, he shied away from a Brandenburg Gate moment in order to make sure the Iron Curtain moment passed off peacefully.

Nor was he well suited for the shock-jock age, even though he made clumsy attempts to court the cultural warriors of the conservative airwaves. Carrying the bag of Rush Limbaugh when he invited the radio host to spend the night in the Lincoln Bedroom – a stay negotiated by Roger Ailes – was never going to pacify right-wing blowhards.[52] Instead, it made him look needy and weak. From start to finish, Bush was the New England blueblood ill at ease in an ever more populist and southern party.

On the international front, he was the last president to enter office with a rounded grasp of foreign affairs, expertise that brought into sharper focus his eldest son's abject ignorance. His multilateralism buttressed the diplomatic architecture, such as NATO and the United Nations, which America had constructed after the war, and which became the foundation of its pre-eminence. Understandably, it pained him not to get more recognition at home for his success abroad.

'My opponents say I spend too much time on foreign policy, as if it didn't matter that schoolchildren once hid under their desks in drills to prepare for nuclear war,' he said in his 1992 convention speech. 'I saw the chance to rid our children's dreams of the nuclear nightmare, and I did.'[53] Alas for Bush, domestic politics had become uncoupled from foreign affairs.

Even though Bush was ideally qualified to bring the Cold War to a peaceful end, he was inept at articulating a post-Cold War mission at home. He admitted as much when he spoke so derisively of 'the vision thing'. Voters expecting to enjoy the spoils of victory were sorely disappointed when the economy went into recession. He was a man of his time, and his time was the epochal struggle between the United States and the Soviet Union. After receiving that Christmas Day phone call from Gorbachev, it was almost as if he no longer had a *raison d'être*. His New World Order turned out to be an empty slogan.

Much was made in the aftermath of his death of the gracious letter Bush wrote in his own hand to Bill Clinton that he placed on the Resolute desk in the Oval Office on inauguration day in January 1993. 'Your success now is our country's success.'

Magnanimous though that gesture doubtless was, Bush did not think Clinton possessed the rectitude to be president. Those feelings came to the fore on his final morning as commander-in-chief when an admiring soldier flashed him a thumbs-up. 'I must say I thought to myself, "How in God's name did this country elect a draft dodger?"' he asked in his diary. 'I didn't feel it with bitterness. I just felt it was almost generational. What am I missing?'[54] He was missing that the torch had just been wrenched from the hands of the greatest generation. The age of decency had come to an end. Baby-boomers were now in the chair. Those who had never donned military fatigues. Those who viewed Washington as a theatre of war.

3

Bill and Newt

Not since the transfer of power from Dwight D. Eisenhower to JFK had Washington witnessed such a profound generational shift, as a 68-year-old grandfather made way for a successor more than 20 years his junior. Bill Clinton's inaugural celebrations, rather than alluding subtly to this changeover, sledgehammered the point home. Shortly after arriving in the capital, Clinton made a pilgrimage to Jack Kennedy's graveside in Arlington National Cemetery, a visit not included ahead of time on his official schedule and witnessed by only a select group of reporters – the sort of stealth arrangements sure to attract more media attention.

This séance like visit suggested a shared lineage: that the Clintons were somehow an offshoot of the Camelot clan. Blurry black-and-white footage of the 'torch has been passed to a new generation' passage from the Kennedy inaugural bellowed from big screens erected either side of the Lincoln Memorial, which again implied an ancestral affinity. 'Clinton stared in wonderment and mouthed the words,' wrote the journalist John Harris, the finest chronicler of the Clinton years.[1]

Just as Kennedy had got Frank Sinatra to sing at his pre inaugural gala, so Clinton turned to the pop-culture idol of the day, Michael Jackson, who moonwalked at the Lincoln Memorial. Maya Angelou, who recited 'On the Pulse of Morning', became only the second poet to perform at an inaugural ceremony, emulating Robert Frost, who in 1961 delivered from memory 'The Gift Outright'.

Clinton's New Covenant speech, replete with Kennedy-esque imitations, was a reworking of JFK's New Frontier: 'This ceremony is held in the depth of winter. But, by the words we speak and the faces we show the world, we force the spring. Now we must do the work the season demands.' Its nimblest line relied on the kind of rhetorical inversion favoured by Kennedy's phrasemaker, Ted Sorensen. 'There is nothing wrong with America that cannot be cured by what is right with America.' Lest anyone be in any doubt this was an epochal event, a carillon of gongs rang out from coast to coast to herald this new Clintonian age.

Because my then girlfriend had worked at campaign headquarters in Little Rock just down the corridor from the famed 'War Room', I was a guest that night at the Arkansas inaugural ball, and watched through a bobbing mass of blow-dried hair as Bill Clinton once again raised his saxophone to his lips to riff with B. B. King. This not only recalled his star turn on *The Arsenio Hall Show* but also signalled that after the somnolence of the Bush interlude a president who understood the show-business requirements of the job was back in the Oval Office – even if the Clinton years would end up feeling more like tawdry daytime television.

For a president who had reached the White House with the smallest share of the vote since Woodrow Wilson in 1912, the celebrations – which also included a stop at Monticello, the Virginian residence of America's third president, on the tenuous pretext that his mother had given him the middle name Jefferson – were ludicrously over the top. A narcissistic delusion.

The inaugural festivities also glossed over another parallel with Kennedy: the unconvincing nature of their respective victories. In 1960, when Kennedy edged out Nixon by just 112,827 votes, or 0.17 per cent of the electorate, the popular vote was a virtual dead heat. Clinton's victory was more comfortable – he received five million more votes than Bush – but his 43 per cent of the vote was hardly resounding.

As with Kennedy in 1961, Clinton's mandate immediately came into question. Now, though, the GOP went further by raising doubts about his very legitimacy, something Nixon had shied away from doing in 1960, despite allegations that Chicago's then mayor, Richard J. Daley, had spirited up enough phantom votes to put Illinois in the Democrat column (Kennedy, it is often forgotten, would have won without the Prairie State). The day after the 1992 election, the Senate Minority Leader Bob Dole pledged to be 'a watchdog for the 57 per cent' of the electorate who had not supported Clinton. Republicans labelled him 'a minority president'. Instead of a political honeymoon, he received a partisan hazing. So began the modern-day habit of losing political parties refusing to admit they had lost.

Another JFK storyline the Clintons would have preferred not to repeat was the lamentable start to his presidency. The mists of Camelot have obscured the early mis-steps that exposed the 43-year-old's callowness: from the calamity of the Bay of Pigs, when a CIA-backed invasion force was easily repelled by Fidel Castro's ragtag army, to his first disastrous summit with Nikita Khrushchev in Vienna, which encouraged the Soviet premier to believe he could construct the Berlin Wall months later without any serious push-back from Washington.

Clinton's early slip-ups were less momentous, partly because with the Cold War consigned to history the world was a less perilous place. Nevertheless, he ran into immediate trouble over his choice of attorney general, gays in the military and his attempts to pass a budget. Each controversy exhibited the ugliness of post-Cold War Washington. Each fight brought to mind the old adage about academia, where the politics are said to be so vicious because the stakes are so small. From start to finish, a pettiness pervaded the Clinton years.

Newt Gingrich, who was then still the House whip, immediately signalled an escalation of political hostilities in the confirmation battle over Clinton's pick as attorney general, Zoë Baird, who looked set to become the first woman to head up the Justice Department. Originally, when *The New York Times* reported that she and her husband had employed illegal immigrants as household help, senior Republicans such as Senator Orrin Hatch, the ranking member of the Judiciary Committee, described it as 'no big deal'.[2]

Gingrich, however, that master of contrived controversy, eyed her as quarry. *How could the Senate confirm an attorney general who had knowingly broken the law?* he asked, showing his skill for sketching out battle-lines. *Was this not a case of the Washington elite protecting its own?* The Gingrich effect was instantaneous. Republican senators hitherto prepared to green-light Baird's nomination now vowed to block it, forcing her to withdraw her name from consideration. It was an example of trickle-down polarisation: of how Gingrich took a controversy that few really cared about and turned it into a moment of political truth.

In a second culture wars flare-up, which opened him up to the criticism that he had hoodwinked the electorate by pretending to be a centrist, Clinton clashed with the Pentagon over his promise to allow homosexuals to serve openly in the military. 'There never was a sign on the wall in Little Rock that said, "It's the gays in the military, stupid,"' complained an unnamed Democratic consultant, bemoaning the kind of cultural liberalism and identity politics that was so off-putting to Reagan Democrats.[3] The 'Don't Ask, Don't Tell' policy which emerged was a classic Clintonian fudge.

If the criticism in those fledging weeks was of a leftward lurch, Clinton's apprehension during the first budget battle of his presidency was of moving too far to the right.

'You mean to tell me that the success of my program and re-election hinges on the Federal Reserve and a bunch of fucking bond traders,' he famously fumed, after his economic team produced a budget designed to reassure Wall Street and appease the Fed Chairman, Alan Greenspan.[4] 'I hope you're all aware we're all Eisenhower Republicans,' he also complained. 'We're Eisenhower Republicans here, and we are fighting the Reagan Republicans.'

The budget battle was a watershed moment: a Democratic president took his cues on economic policy from Wall Street rather than the union movement, an approach repeated by Barack Obama and Hillary Clinton. Clinton's first Treasury Secretary, Robert Rubin, a Goldman Sachs alumnus, joked that if the president had been a Republican, 'they'd be building a monument to him on the National Mall'.[5]

Despite Clinton's fiscal probity, Republicans nonetheless bemoaned the inclusion of tax hikes. For the first time they deployed a filibuster to obstruct an incoming president's economic programme. Not a single GOP lawmaker in either chamber supported the White House budget plan.[6] Nor could Clinton corral his own party. In the House, where the Democrats had what should have been an ironclad majority of 257 seats to 177, the budget plan passed by a solitary vote.

This Republican wall of opposition suggested that the delegitimisation of modern-day presidents had a corollary: the legitimisation of the politics of no. Even though the GOP held just 43 seats in the Senate, the minority party attempted to exert as much control as the majority party. Filibusters, sparingly used in the past, now became routine, a 'weapon of mass obstruction', in the words of Thomas Mann and Norm Ornstein, two highly respected Washington commentators who, justifiably, blamed the Republicans more than the Democrats for this partisan polarisation.

Blocking major legislation, rather than working to amend it, became the new modus operandi. 'You need 60 votes to get anything done around here,' crowed Bob Dole, of the supermajority needed to override a filibuster. The GOP blocked measures, such as new restrictions on lobbying, that previously it had supported, and even withdrew backing for the global trade pact, the General Agreement on Tariffs and Trade – an abnormal posture for the party of business and free trade.

Gridlocking Capitol Hill was the best way to sabotage the Clinton presidency. 'Stop it, slow it, kill it, or just talk it to death,' was how Clinton described the blocking strategy,[7] not that the Republicans cared. 'It's not obstructionism,' claimed Gingrich. 'It's interpreting the will of the American people.'[8] Mitch McConnell, an up-and-coming senator from Kentucky, who over the years turned obstructionism into a political art form, claimed the blocking tactics gave 'gridlock a good name'.[9] Since then, political scientists have used the term asymmetrical polarisation, because the Republicans were the prime instigators of the present-day destructiveness. Likewise, we talk of top-down polarisation, of how political divisiveness has been orchestrated rather than organic. Hyper-partisans, such as Gingrich, deliberately sought to divide the American electorate in the hope of winning over the bigger half.

Clinton's frustrations spilled out into the open at a political fundraiser in Boston in 1994. The Republicans were 'dedicated just to being against everything we are for, and dedicated to the politics of personal destruction', he griped, self-pityingly. Then, getting more visibly angry as he spoke, he complained the GOP had become 'an opposition party that just stands up and says, "No! No! No! No! No! No! No! No! No!"'[10]

This incontrovertibly was true. Yet the Clinton team added to the toxicity by importing its 'War Room' campaign philosophy from Little Rock, and by treating every day as a battle to win the news cycle. Opponents were looked upon as adversaries.

'What are you doing inviting these people in my home?' complained Hillary Clinton when the presidential aide Rahm Emanuel organised a White House event involving moderate conservatives, such as James Baker, to drum up bipartisan support for the North American Free Trade Agreement (NAFTA). 'These people are our enemies. They are trying to destroy us.'

Even friends deemed disloyal or uncooperative were cast as foes. 'We'll roll right over him if we have to,' an unnamed White House aide told *Time* magazine when the Democratic Senator Daniel Patrick Moynihan, the chair of the influential Senate Finance Committee, complained about not being consulted by the new president.[11]

A string of scandals and pseudo-scandals intensified this bunker mentality in the West Wing. 'Travelgate' centred on the firing of seven employees in the White House Travel Office and their replacement by friends of the president and First Lady. 'Troopergate' involved claims from several Arkansas State Troopers, published by the right-wing magazine *The American Spectator*, that they had arranged sexual liaisons involving dozens of women. The most potentially damaging centred on a real-estate investment on the banks of the White River in the Ozark Mountains by the Clintons in the late 1970s.

'Whitewater' crossed a Rubicon, since it was not just suspected sins in office that were now under investigation but alleged transgressions from the pre-presidential past. It led to the appointment in 1994 of a special counsel, Robert B. Fiske, who was later replaced by Ken Starr, a bespectacled former federal judge, who began by investigating the land deal and ended heading up a sexual inquisition.

The suicide in July 1993 of Vince Foster, one of the Clintons' closest aides and a former partner of Hillary Clinton in the law firm they worked for in Little Rock, showed how even a personal tragedy could blow up into a political firestorm. 'Here ruining people is considered sport,' wrote Foster in a resignation letter, found in his briefcase torn into 27 pieces, that read like a suicide note. The discovery of the letter brought calls for a dialling back of the heated rhetoric. If anything, however, it became more incendiary.

'Vince Foster was murdered in an apartment owned by Hillary Clinton,' Rush Limbaugh told his 20 million listeners. Later on he fumed, 'the only difference between Watergate and Whitewater is that Whitewater has a dead body'.[12]

The Arkansas Project, a shady outfit funded by the ultra-conservative billionaire Richard Mellon Scaife to dig up dirt on the Clintons, claimed the president had organised a hit. The Republican Congressman Dan Burton fired a bullet into a watermelon to prove, through crude ballistics, that Foster's wounds could not have been self-inflicted.[13] Five separate official investigations found that the former Little Rock attorney had shot himself in the head, but even Gingrich announced he could not accept the verdict of suicide.[14]

The conduct of the Clintons in the aftermath of their friend's death fuelled the right-wing conspiracy theories. The White House, after finding those torn scraps of paper in Foster's briefcase, took more than 24 hours to report them to the police. Having first agreed to let the Justice Department search Foster's office, the Clintons reneged. While investigators were kept at bay, several files relating to the First Couple's private business were removed. The Clintons' desire for privacy was understandable, given the sensitive nature of these personal documents, but it heightened the sense that they had something to hide and did not feel bound by the law – criticisms that would hound them years later.

In hungrily reporting each plot twist, the press began to rival the Republican Party in its contempt for the Clintons. This was part of a broader industry shift. Post-Watergate, newsrooms came to be populated by reporters who arrived in Washington dreaming of becoming the next Woodward or Bernstein; hoping for clandestine meetings in underground car parks with their own 'Deep Throat's; yearning to be played by a Hoffman or Redford in the sequel, *All the President's Women*.

In many respects, the lack of deference from this new generation of muckrakers marked an improvement on the chumminess of the '50s and '60s, when the relationship between politicians and the Fourth Estate could be horribly incestuous (so close was the friendship between Jack Kennedy and Ben Bradlee, the hero of Watergate, that they watched a porn flick together in downtown Washington while awaiting the results of the 1960 West Virginia primary).

Often, though, the determination to topple presidents elevated what should have been C-grade imbroglios into full-blown scandals. As reporters looked for smoking guns, even the faintest whiff of cordite turned newsrooms into states of near apoplexy. Debased through overuse, the '-gate' suffix became a dreary journalistic cliché. Just as Richard Hofstadter had spoken during the mid-'60s of the paranoid style in American politics spawned by conspiracy theorising, so it was possible now to identify a paranoid style in American journalism. The predicate for so much reporting during the Clinton years was the suspicion that the President and First Lady had committed felonious or potentially impeachable acts: the presumption of guilt. Some White House correspondents almost saw themselves also as crime beat reporters, an after-effect of the Nixon years that added again to the criminalisation of presidential politics.

The tone of the press coverage was different too. With phrase-twirling reporters such as Maureen Dowd and Thomas Friedman of *The New York Times* assigned to the White House, the writing became sassier, snarkier and more comedic. Press pile-ons became more common, such as when Bill Clinton reportedly held up air traffic at LAX airport so the celebrity hairdresser Cristophe could board Air Force One to give him a $200 trim – a story given front-page prominence by *The New York Times, Washington Post, Boston Globe* and *Los Angeles Times*. The *Post* dubbed it 'the most famous haircut since Samson's'. Tom Friedman called it 'the most expensive haircut in history'. *Time*, inevitably, dubbed it 'Haircutgate'. The story, however, was fake news. Rather than two of LAX's runways being shut down, and dozens of flights delayed, the Federal Aviation Administration later revealed just one plane took off two minutes late.[15]

True to the adage that a lie can travel half-way around the world while the truth is getting its boots on, the story was parroted by late-night comedians and right-wing shock jocks, and instantly became part of Clinton lore. Here we were witnessing the convergence of news and comedy, a cycle of cynicism that daily made the president the butt of the joke.

This 'comedy-first culture', as the author Ken Jennings later called it, made late-night talk shows even more central to the political conversation.[16] So much so that by 2016 a higher percentage of Americans got their information about the presidential campaign from late-night TV comedy than from national newspapers.[17]

Alas for the Clintons, there was no shortage of comic material The First Lady was supposed to have thrown a lamp at her husband – or was it an urn, a briefing book or even the Bible? (Each of these objects appeared in various print stories about the alleged incident.) When the president appeared with a scratch on his face – a shaving wound, said the White House press office – rumours abounded that Hillary had physically attacked him after returning from an out-of-town trip to discover Barbra Streisand had stayed overnight in the Executive Mansion. In a post-Cold War America that could enjoy the luxury of being unserious, we were witnessing the trivialisation of national life.

The informality of the Clinton White House further undercut his standing; likewise his awkwardness with some of the ceremonial rituals of the office. His rookie attempts at military salutes, even after coaching from Ronald Reagan, who originated the practice, were so feeble they prompted what was dubbed 'the great salute flap'.[18] Pre-dawn jogs along the National Mall, his flabby pink legs jiggling in the unforgiving glare of the television lights, did little to enhance his presidential aura. Even his baby-boomer dress code raised eyebrows. Observing him in 'threadbare jeans, a check wool shirt, unzipped windbreaker, bulging Reeboks', Alistair Cooke wryly commented, 'Along with the passing of George Bush, we shall see, I fear, the passing of the blue blazer.'[19]

His casualness bred even more contempt, and never more so than when he breezily fielded a question from a 17-year-old female high-school student during an MTV-sponsored forum in the spring of 1994. 'Boxers or briefs?' he was asked. 'Usually briefs,' the 42nd president of the United States unabashedly replied.

This undressing peeled away the mystique of the office, and showed how the traits that gave him a populist touch on the campaign trail could seem indecorous for a president. It was both a strength and weakness, which went some way to explaining why he was so polarising. As James Carville, his 'Ragin' Cajun' political consultant, pointed out, 'He is not remote in the way presidents have been, so you are more free to love him or hate him the way you would anyone.'[20] In trying to humanise the presidency, he ended up undermining the prestige of the office.

The disorderliness of the Clinton White House added to the sense of dishevelment. There was an essay crisis feel to the West Wing, typified by the incoming president staying up until 4.30 a.m. on the morning of his inaugural to make witching-hour alterations to his address. All-night policy discussions, strewn with half-eaten slices of pizza, often ended indecisively, which brought to mind Robert Frost's definition of a liberal as someone so open-minded they wouldn't take their own side in an argument. A session on Bosnia lasted for eight hours without reaching a conclusion. Multiple meetings were held to decide upon trivialities, such as whether the former vice-president Walter Mondale should be appointed as the US ambassador to Poland. Lost in these endless vacillations was a sense of the big picture.

Just as he struggled to make headway pushing his domestic agenda, so Clinton's early foreign policy made a travesty of America's claim to global pre-eminence. Lacking a clear sense of how to project US power in the post-Cold War world, there was no Clinton doctrine. In the absence of an animating vision, the young president merely told advisors foreign policy should be an extension of domestic policy. This 'It's the economy, stupid' principle meant promoting trade deals, such as NAFTA, which came into effect on 1 January 1994, and advancing globalisation, the process of international economic interconnectedness that moved into top gear after the defeat of communism.

Ever since World War II, successive presidents had dealt with the first-tier problem of containing the Soviet Union, and for the most part were instinctively interventionist and hawkish. Clinton's foreign-policy team struggled with second- and third-tier trouble spots, and were squeamish about projecting US power. In Haiti, an angry mob prevented a US warship from docking in Port-au-Prince, which led to a humiliating turnaround. In Bosnia, the Clinton administration continued the Bush administration's policy of non-intervention, despite the ethnic cleansing conducted by the Bosnian Serbs and Croatians. To his eternal dishonour, Clinton did nothing to curb the genocidal fury of the Hutus against the Tutsi minority in 1994, where up to a million Rwandans were slaughtered at the rate of six men, women and children every minute.

The Battle of Mogadishu in October 1993, when Somali tribesmen shot down two US Black Hawk helicopters, killing 19 and wounding 73, was formative. So traumatised was Clinton by the television footage of American casualties being dragged through Mogadishu's streets that he withdrew US forces and became reluctant to insert the military anywhere else. The Gulf War had supposedly vanquished the Vietnam syndrome, but for years afterwards the Mogadishu syndrome had an immobilising effect on Clinton. Less than four years after the fall of the Berlin Wall, America no longer looked so dominant, while its young president looked ineffectual. As Jacques Chirac, the new French president, mocked, 'The position of the leader of the free world is vacant.'[21]

It became clear in the early months of the Clinton presidency that America was vulnerable on the home front too. In February 1993, terrorists detonated a truck bomb in the car park under the North Tower of the World Trade Center, killing six people and injuring more than a thousand. Masterminded by Ramzi Yousef, a jihadist trained at an Al Qaeda camp in Afghanistan and a nephew of Khalid Sheikh Mohammed, the architect of the September 11 attacks, the intention was to topple the North Tower and send it crashing into its twin to the south. Then they planned to blow up the Holland and Lincoln tunnels, along with other New York landmarks. An international Islamist terror network had declared war on the United States, but Clinton was slow to grasp the magnitude of the threat.

Politically, the low point of Clinton's first two years in office came in the battle over healthcare, that post-war liberal lodestar. True to his promise of getting 'two for the price of one', Bill Clinton announced three days into his presidency that the First Lady would head up a health task force to 'hammer out a consensus' on this intractable issue.

Rather than seek compromise, however, she disregarded the advice of Democratic lawmakers, who recommended a gradualist approach instead of a single mammoth reform. Hillarycare ran to 1,342 pages and 240,000 words. Even health-policy experts struggled to make sense of it. Its convoluted design rested on universal coverage, and was unworkable without it, which made Hillary Clinton resistant to compromise.[22] Republicans were implacably opposed, partly out of ideological zealousness but also because they feared it might be a political boon for the Democrats, in much the same way as social security had been for FDR.

Throughout the Hillarycare debate, the psychodrama of the Clinton marriage was almost as significant a factor as the power dynamics of Washington. Clinton's threat during his 1994 State of the Union address to veto any healthcare bill that did not provide 100 per cent coverage came just months after the Troopergate scandal, and White House aides, such as David Gergen, suspected his maximal position was part of a marital quid pro quo. 'Watching him at the time,' said

Gergen, 'was very much like watching a golden retriever that has pooped on the rug and just curls up and keeps his head down.'[23]

After Daniel Patrick Moynihan suggested 95 per cent coverage was the most that could be achieved – 'something like this passes with 75 votes or not at all', he wisely warned – Bill Clinton signalled during a speech in Boston that he was open to compromise. His wife, though, instantly shot him down. 'What the fuck are you doing up there?' she shouted at the president over the phone. The following day Clinton walked back his remarks. With the White House again not willing to compromise, Hillarycare stood no hope of passage. Five weeks before the 1994 congressional midterms, it was pronounced dead. Ignominiously, it did not even reach a vote in either chamber.

The Hillarycare debacle made a hate figure out of Hillary Clinton. During hearings on Capitol Hill, she clashed with Dick Armey, then the third-ranking Republican in the House. 'I have been told about your charm and wit,' Armey said icily, 'and let me say the reports on your charm are overstated, and the reports on your wit are understated.'[24]

The personal animus towards her was evident, too, when she appeared at an event in Seattle. Demonstrators held aloft placards reading 'Impeach Hillary' and 'Heil Hillary', forerunners of the 'Lock Her Up!' banners of the 2016 campaign. So worried was her Secret Service detail that agents persuaded her to wear a bulletproof vest.[25] Hillarycare reinforced the storyline from the 1992 campaign that she was too powerful, too manipulative, too secretive and, to many men *and* women, too much of a threat to the male status quo.

Time derided her as 'ever the best girl in class'. *People* magazine labelled her 'the perpetual A student'. The underlying message of these sexist tropes was that it was entirely acceptable to abhor this she-devil of a First Lady. All this suggested America was not ready for a strong feminist First Lady, let alone a strong feminist president.

Healthcare was not only a demoralising defeat for the Clintons but also a ringing *ex post facto* victory for Ronald Reagan. In post-Reagan America it was harder to enact big government reform, and even to make the case that government could be a force for good. In 1964, 62 per cent of Americans had trusted Washington to do the right thing most of the time. By 1994, that figure was 19 per cent.[26]

Surveying the setbacks of his first two years, it became intellectually fashionable to describe Bill Clinton as America's first post-modern president, and to reflect on how the end of the Cold War, the quickening globalisation of the world economy and the fragmentation of the US media made it harder for any occupant of the White House to shape events at home and abroad. All this was true, but Clinton's faltering start to his presidency magnified his problems, whether it was the miscalculations over Hillarycare, the indiscipline of his White House or his feebleness abroad. In that first year there was also the botched response to the Waco siege, when 76 members of the Branch Davidian cult died – including more than 20 children – after the FBI brought to an end the 51-day stand-off. A *Time* cover in June 1993 neatly captured the powerlessness of a leader widely touted as the most gifted politician of his generation: 'The incredible shrinking president'.[27]

Since the word 'tsunami' was not then in common usage, the scribes of the Beltway, those framers of the conventional wisdom, settled on the term 'earthquake' to describe the Republican Revolution in the 1994 congressional midterm elections. The volcanic terminology was apt. By picking up 54 seats the Republicans ended 40 uninterrupted years of Democratic dominance in the House of Representatives and also won the Senate.

It was the first time since 1954 that both chambers had changed hands simultaneously, and the first time since the start of Eisenhower's presidency that the GOP had monopolised power on Capitol Hill. The Republicans even picked up the governorship of New York, where George Pataki defeated the liberal hero Mario Cuomo.

Trampling all over Tip O'Neill's dictum that all politics is local, Newt Gingrich successfully nationalised the congressional elections. His 'Contract with America', a legislative agenda proposing the shrinkage of government, term limits for lawmakers and welfare reform, served both as an indictment of the Clinton presidency and a declaration of war on Washington. The Republicans' sweeping victory proved there was no political downside for the obstructionism of the past two years, an ugly lesson the GOP drew on time and again thereafter.

Inevitably, given the seismic scale of the landslide, the political ground shifted. By identifying more strongly with Republican candidates, conservative voters became politically less promiscuous. In the 1990 midterms, almost a quarter of voters who described themselves as Republicans voted for Democratic House candidates. In 1994, it was less than 10 per cent. (By 2010, as the American political historian E. J. Dionne has noted, 3 per cent of liberal Democrats and 2 per cent of conservative Republicans voted for candidates from opposing parties.[28])

Regional divides were delineated more sharply, with the states of the Old Confederacy embracing the party of Lincoln like never before. After 1992, Republican House members from below the Mason Dixon line outnumbered Democratic House members for the first time since Reconstruction, the period after the Civil War. Evangelical Christians voted more strongly for the GOP – almost 80 per cent of white, born-again Protestants – as did lower-income whites, showing how the politics of beliefs and values increasingly trumped the politics of the wallet. The Republican Revolution therefore became another important milestone in the ideological sorting of America.

Newt Gingrich's elevation to the Speakership crowned a generational shift in the Republican Party (born two years before the end of the war, the Georgian was technically not a baby-boomer, but was regarded as one nonetheless). On the eve of the midterms, he had replaced Bob Michel, a veteran of the Battle of the Bulge who had served 14 years as minority leader. Though Michel considered himself a staunch conservative, he frequently played golf with Tip O'Neill, took part in card schools with Democrats and moved legislation in a bipartisan way.

'My style of leadership, my sense of values, my whole thinking process is giving way to a new generation, and I accept that,' said Michel, as he handed over the torch to Gingrich prior to the election, in the knowledge that the GOP caucus would yank it away from him afterwards.[29] Gingrich described politics as 'war without blood'.[30] Michel, the recipient of two Bronze Stars and a Purple Heart after being wounded by machine-gun fire, had experienced the real thing first-hand. Whereas Michel had prioritised the defeat of Soviet communism, Gingrich was dedicated to the defeat of American liberalism. Washington became the new Berlin.

Instantly, Gingrich changed the character of the Republican caucus. At his victory party in November, a local Atlanta talk-show host, Sean Hannity, told the crowd that Tylenol had been delivered to the White House because Bill Clinton was about to 'feel the pain'.[31] When the new Congress convened in January, Rush Limbaugh addressed the freshman class. This was the 'Limbaugh Congress', proclaimed the Republican Congressman Vin Weber, the new House Speaker's wingman. The 'Dittoheads', as Limbaugh's unquestioning listeners were known, had sent so many of their ideological fellow travellers to Washington.[32]

The man of the moment, though, was 'King Newt', who believed he was the saviour not just of the Grand Old Party but of American civilisation itself. As he rounded out his first 100 days as Speaker, he even decided to deliver a quasi-presidential address, which CBS and CNN granted him 30 minutes of airtime to deliver.

At the other end of Pennsylvania Avenue, the real president struggled to justify his existence. There was even conjecture about him being dumped from the Democratic ticket in 1996. 'Can Bill Clinton – should Bill Clinton – be the party's presidential nominee in 1996?' asked *The New York Times*'s legendary political commentator, Johnny Apple.[33]

At a primetime news conference on 15 April, carried by just one US network, a reporter even asked Clinton how to ensure his voice would still be heard. "The president is still relevant," he implored. "The Constitution gives me relevance." Now a BBC trainee, with hopes one day of covering the White House, I happened to be in Washington that night, and watched agog. It was the first time I had been back in the US capital since Clinton's inaugural celebrations, and it was extraordinary to see how quickly his power had drained away.

Had it not been for what happened the next morning, his presidency might never have recovered from this pitiful show of insignificance. That day was the first time I had ever set foot in the BBC Washington's bureau, my journalistic home for so much of my career. It was alive with activity, with hurried conversations and staccato telephone calls. From my seat in reception, I thought, thrillingly, I was observing the normal tumble of a busy Beltway news day. The press conference the night before had been startling, after all. Then the receptionist said something that confused me. Reports were coming through of a bomb attack in Oklahoma, a sleepy state where nothing much happened. What we were truly witnessing was one of the most tragic and transformative 48 hours in modern-day US politics.

Clinton's revival began in the rubble of the Alfred P. Murrah Federal Building in Oklahoma City, where a truck bomb was detonated, killing 168 people, including 19 children in day-care, and injuring more than 600 others. As soon as it emerged that the bomber was Timothy McVeigh, an anti-government extremist seeking revenge for the FBI's storming of the Branch Davidian compound in Waco, Gingrich's own revolutionary rhetoric came to be cast in a more sinister light. A president who had pleaded for relevance now became the country's most reassuring and reasonable voice.

'People should examine the consequences of what they say, and the kind of emotions they're trying to inflame,' said Clinton during an appearance on 60 Minutes, in which he avoided naming Newt Gingrich but left no one in any doubt about whom he was talking. Americans should resist 'the purveyors of hatred and division' and the 'promoters of paranoia'. Clinton mounted a further attack during a commencement address at Michigan State University, again without mentioning the House Speaker directly. 'There is nothing patriotic about hating your country, he told graduates, 'or pretending that you can love your country but despise your government.'

Clinton's consoler-in-chief pitch to the moderate middle received a further boost from the National Rifle Association, when it emerged that Wayne LaPierre, its leading propagandist, had issued a statement ahead of the attack labelling officers from the Bureau of Alcohol, Tobacco and Firearms 'jackbooted government thugs' who wore 'Nazi bucket helmets and black storm trooper uniforms'. When the NRA refused to withdraw those remarks, George H. W. Bush, a gun owner and avid hunter, resigned his membership in protest.[34]

As Clinton reflected afterwards, 'The American people sort of began to move back to the vital centre after Oklahoma City.' It 'broke the spell in the country as people began searching for common ground again.'[35] Up until Oklahoma, Clinton looked like he would be a one-term president. Afterwards, he looked like a shoo-in for a second term.

Even before the bombing, Clinton had turned in secret to his old friend Dick Morris, a Republican political consultant who helped salvage his career in the early '80s after voters in Arkansas had made him, aged 34, the country's youngest former governor. Morris, as has oft been told, advised the president that triangulation was the key to winning a second term. This involved positioning himself between the congressional Democrats and Republicans and then staking out a policy above and between the two – the apex of a triangle.

At Morris's urging, Clinton put the triangulation strategy into effect during the 1995 budget battle, which came to be the defining fight of his first term. First he co-opted the Republican idea of balancing the budget. Then he cast himself as the saviour of Medicare and Medicaid, two of the more popular government programmes that Gingrich wanted to cut. This appeal to the Great American middle worked perfectly.

When Clinton vetoed the Republican spending bills, Gingrich retaliated by shutting down the government, first in November and then for 21 days over the holiday season. In the blame game that followed, Gingrich made the mistake of admitting to reporters that he was motivated in part by his fury at being told to exit Air Force One from the rear door rather than the front, after flying home from the funeral of Yitzhak Rabin in Jerusalem. 'Cry Baby!' was the famous headline in the *New York Daily News*, which infantilised the House Speaker, enhanced Clinton's presidential aura and helped turn the public against the Republican revolutionaries who had stormed Congress.

Clinton now became a more imposing leader. 'He had stopped acting like a governor, and he had become the president,' reckoned Donna Shalala, his Secretary of Health and Human Services.[36] In foreign affairs, he became more interventionist. Appalled by the Srebrenica massacre in July 1995, where Ratko Mladić's Bosnian Serb army butchered more than 8,000 Bosniak men and boys, Clinton was finally shamed into action. 'Our position is unsustainable,' he told aides. 'It's killing the position of the US in the world. This is larger than Bosnia.'[37] NATO's bombing campaign forced the Serbs to the negotiating table in Dayton, Ohio, where in December 1995 an American diplomat, Richard Holbrooke, hammered out a peace deal on American soil.

In his 1996 State of the Union speech a month later, Clinton capped his presidential comeback with his seven-word treatise of triangulation, 'The era of big government is over.' Then in the summer, over the vehement objections of liberal Democrats, he burnished his centrist credentials by finally signing welfare reform into law (he had vetoed two earlier versions). In one of the biggest shifts in social policy since the New Deal era, Clinton had made good his 1991 campaign promise to 'end welfare as we know it'. To do so, he adopted what might be called toxic bipartisanship that prioritised political over national gain. Clinton and Gingrich hated each other. The president was trying to outmanoeuvre his opponents, by neutralising an issue upon which Democrats had long been vulnerable.

During his first two years in office, Clinton had suffered from a political identity crisis. 'Was he the fiscally restrained free-trade centrist?' asked William Galston, one of his White House policy advisors. 'Or was he a New Deal, Great Society Democrat trying to push national healthcare? Or was he a George McGovern 1972 Democrat trying to insert gays into the military?'[38]

Clinton had described himself, disparagingly, as an Eisenhower Republican. Now, though, he could finally present himself as a bona fide New Democrat, the Bill Clinton he had always promised to be. From the moment he sounded the death knell of big government until Election Day, he was never behind in the polls.

A year into the Republican Revolution, the GOP now looked like losing the 1996 presidential election. In this astonishing political turnaround, the conservative movement struggled even to coalesce around a half-decent candidate. With Gingrich ruling himself out of contention, there was no obvious Newtonian candidate.

The Texas Senator Phil Gramm, a dour former economics professor who spoke like Elmer Fudd, was philosophically aligned but completely devoid of charisma. The billionaire publisher Steve Forbes attracted attention because of his proposal for a flat tax, but, like Gramm, seemed too nerdy to be president. Colin Powell, following his retirement as chairman of the Joint Chiefs of Staff, became the darling of the press, but was too moderate for conservative tastes. Pat Buchanan this time won a surprise victory in New Hampshire, but faded thereafter. Almost by default, Bob Dole, an elder who commanded the respect if not adoration of his party, dominated the rest of the primary calendar.

Both a generational throwback and ideological misfit, the septuagenarian senator knew in his heart he was hardly the man for these radical Republican times. He admitted as much during a campaign stop at – of all places – Barry Goldwater's ranch in the McDowell Mountains of Arizona.

'Barry and I – we've sort of become the liberals,' he joked to reporters. Goldwater, now in his late eighties, laughingly concurred. 'We're the new liberals of the Republican Party. Can you imagine that?'[39]

Dole bravely proved the point during his acceptance speech at the GOP convention in San Diego, when he took on the nativists in the party who had backed Buchanan. 'If there is anyone who has mistakenly attached themselves to our party in the belief that we are not open to citizens of every race and religion,' he intoned, 'then let me remind you: tonight this hall belongs to the party of Lincoln. And the exits, which are clearly marked, are for you to walk out of as I stand this ground without compromise.'[40]

His error that night was to draw attention to his age. 'Let me be a bridge to an America that only the unknowing call myth,' said the veteran, who still suffered from limited mobility in his right arm and numbness in his left after being wounded by German machine-gun fire in the Allied advance through Italy. 'Let me be a bridge to a time of tranquillity, faith and confidence in action.' For the baby-boomer duo of Clinton and Gore, the line came gift-wrapped. As an alternative to Dole's bridge to the past, they offered a bridge to the 21st century.

Victory for Bill Clinton meant he became the first Democrat since Franklin Delano Roosevelt to win re-election. For all his prodigious political skills, however, he failed to pass the psychologically important 50 per cent threshold in the popular vote, partly because Ross Perot took 8 per cent. Turnout, at just 49 per cent, was also the lowest in a presidential election since 1924. While the Republicans maintained their majorities in the House and Senate, Clinton nonetheless claimed with some justification that his re-election offered proof the 'vital American centre' wanted a more consensual form of politics than the extreme partisanship of the previous four years.

Defeat for Dole was also a rejection of Gingrichism. With suburban white professionals and women deserting the new hard-edged Republican Party, GOP moderates warned that the party might not return to the White House unless it curbed the influence of Christian evangelicals and the radical right. Conservative hardliners, however, drew a very different lesson. For the third election in a row, they complained, the Republican Party had made the mistake of fielding an establishment candidate out of step with the grassroots.

In a quarter of a century covering US politics, only twice have I ever got round to framing newspaper front pages. The first was when Bill Clinton was impeached in December 1998. The second was when he was acquitted the following February at the conclusion of his Senate trial.

Washington in the late 1990s was my first foreign posting. The Monica Lewinsky scandal, as it was unjustly labelled, was my first big American story. The picture framing was partly a vanity project to mark this personal milestone. Yet this also felt like a once-in-a-lifetime story. Clinton was the first US president to be impeached since 1868, when Andrew Johnson also avoided being removed from office by the Senate after his indictment by the House.

Evidently, more seasoned Washington colleagues also wanted mementoes of what we should have called the Bill Clinton scandal. As I came to discover over the following months, the same framed black-and-white newsprint, with the same *Washington Post* headlines 'Clinton Impeached' and 'Clinton Acquitted', adorned their study and toilet walls.

Once-in-a-lifetime stories seemed to come along every few years thereafter: the disputed 2000 election, the attacks of September 11, the election of Barack Obama and the rise of Donald Trump. Nonetheless, the impeachment trial of Bill Clinton remains seminal. The further poisoning of the Washington well. The criminalisation of the modern-day presidency. Post-truth politics, and the rise of political lying. The advent of polarised news. The tabloidisation of national life. The corrosive impact of the internet. All were evident in that Clinton melodrama, which saw *The New York Times* ploughing the same furrows as the *National Inquirer* and reporters filing genre-busting news stories in which quotes from constitutional-law experts interpreting what the founding fathers meant by high crimes and misdemeanours were interspersed with the most salacious snippets of the sex scandal – the snap of Monica Lewinsky's thong, the soiled blue dress, the gift from the president to his intern of Walt Whitman's *Leaves of Grass*, the same anthology of poetry he had once given to a young Hillary Rodham. An epic constitutional showdown was interlaced with a tabloid scandal, showing once more how frivolous national life had become since the demise of the Soviet Union. Would Congress have impeached Bill Clinton, ostensibly for having an affair with an intern, had America still been waging the Cold War?

Also it provided a fitting coda to the sensationalist '90s, dubbed by *Vanity Fair* the tabloid decade, that had brought Pamela Anderson and Tommy Lee's sex tapes, Tonya Harding, Anna Nicole Smith, the murder trial of the Menendez brothers, Elizabeth Taylor's marriage to her seventh husband, Larry Fortensky, the arrest of Hugh Grant on Hollywood's Sunset Boulevard for having sex in his car with the prostitute Divine Brown, the William Kennedy Smith trial, when the nephew of JFK was acquitted of rape, the killing of JonBenét Ramsey, the first accusations against Michael Jackson, the Mike Tyson rape conviction, the death of Princess Diana, the South Beach murder of Gianni Versace, John Wayne Bobbitt and his penis-severing wife, Lorena, and the O. J. Simpson trial; not to mention the divorce of Donald and Ivana Trump and his affair with Marla Maples.

Just as the O. J. Simpson trial brought about the symbiosis of crime and entertainment, so politics and sensationalism became similarly synergetic in the W. J. Clinton trial. Watching the first, much-replayed pictures to emerge showing Monica Lewinsky and Bill Clinton together — the famed 'beret moment' when she hugged him on a South Lawn rope line the day after he won re-election – had the same transfixing effect as seeing O. J being driven down the freeway in Los Angeles. The White House became the white Bronco, although the car chase lasted an entire year. When the author Toni Morrison labelled Bill Clinton America's 'first black president', it had nothing to do with his empathy for African-Americans, which was always inflated. Rather, it was because he was treated like a black perp.[41] The Bill Clinton scandal brought much of the same voyeurism and luridness to the nation's capital, where scandal has always been the highest – and often the basest – form of recreation. Washington, then, was at fever pitch. In the explosive first days of the scandal, ABC's legendary White House correspondent Sam Donaldson predicted Clinton might be forced to resign 'perhaps this week'. Even George

Stephanopoulos, his one-time press secretary, suggested the scandal could provide grounds for impeachment. Clinton's enemies, abetted by the independent counsel Ken Starr, seized upon the president's affair with the 22-year-old intern as their 'gotcha' moment.

For cultural warriors, it was another opportunity to litigate the '60s, one that pitted the modern-day puritans of the right against the permissive peaceniks of the left. Newt Gingrich, seemingly forgetting Watergate and adopting the sensationalist language of the times, called it 'the most systematic, deliberate, obstruction-of-justice cover-up and effort to avoid the truth we have ever seen in American history'. Viewing it as the chance to terminate the Clinton presidency, he added to his partisan arsenal the constitutional mechanism of impeachment, the indictment of a sitting president by the House of Representatives.[42]

Just as impeachment roused Republicans, it rallied Democrats: not so much out of fondness for Clinton as out of contempt for his conservative accusers. 'What kept us close to the president was the Republicans,' remarked Chuck Schumer, then a leading light on the House Judiciary Committee, where the impeachment proceedings originated. 'Their extreme nastiness pushed Democrats into Bill Clinton's arms, even those who didn't like him very much.'[43]

Democratic critics of the president such as the House Minority Leader, Dick Gephardt, a bitter opponent of his welfare reform, circled the wagons.[44] Prominent feminists, such as Gloria Steinem, also defended him, partly because they did not want to hand his pro-life accusers a victory. Partisanship helped save the Clinton presidency. As a result, impeachment solidified the battle-lines on both sides of the aisle, hardening the trench warfare dynamic that has become a permanent feature of Washington life.

As they fought to save their joint political project, the President and First Lady turned this into a partisan confrontation. They did so by altering the question at the heart of the national debate from 'Who do you believe?' to 'Whose side are you on?' That was the strategy behind Hillary Clinton's famed interview on the morning of her husband's State of the Union address with Matt Lauer of *The Today Show*, in which she claimed 'the great story here for anybody willing to find it and write about it and explain it is this vast right-wing conspiracy that has been conspiring against my husband since the day he announced for president'.

The White House went to DEFCON 2. 'We just have to win,' Clinton told Dick Morris, who had conducted secret polling to test whether the president should lie or tell the truth, the quintessence of Clintonian cynicism.

It was during the impeachment crisis that post-truth politics, the appeal to feelings rather than the marshalling of facts, gained a firmer foothold. Clinton also relied on shameless lying. From his tense-parsing 'there is no improper relationship' answer to Jim Lehrer on the *PBS Newshour* in the opening days of the scandal to his finger-jabbing falsehood, 'I did not have sexual relations with that woman, Miss Lewinsky,' Clinton's early dishonesty worked to his advantage. They bought him time to shore up Democratic support. As the president confided to a close friend, 'The lie saved me.'[45] Not until the summer of 1998, when *ABC News* broke the story that Monica Lewinsky had preserved the blue dress stained with his semen, did the president grudgingly admit to the affair. His untruthfulness now exposed, Clinton requested airtime from the networks for a televised confessional.

'Indeed I did have a relationship with Miss Lewinsky that was not appropriate,' he admitted. But then he mounted an unsparing attack on his accusers for pursuing a 'politically inspired' investigation led by Ken Starr. "This has gone on too long, cost too much, and hurt too many innocent people.'

In the early stages of the scandal, polls showed a majority of Americans were not that concerned about Clinton's alleged infidelities. Of his primetime petulance, they were less forgiving. Afterwards, his personal approval rating plummeted by 20 points. More than 30 House Democrats voted to launch a formal impeachment inquiry. Senator Kent Conrad, a North Dakota Democrat, warned one of

Clinton's aides, 'You are about three days from having the senior Democrats come down and ask for the president's resignation.'[46]

However, party unity held, largely because Democrats were so reluctant to hand victory to Newt Gingrich. No senior Democrat publicly called for his resignation. Even Senator Joe Lieberman, the Orthodox Jew who became Clinton's most voluble and moralistic Democratic critic, said impeachment would be 'unjust and unwise'. So strong was party allegiance that minutes after the House of Representatives passed two articles of impeachment, Bill Clinton held a pep rally on the South Lawn of the White House with Democratic lawmakers, Vice-President Al Gore and his wronged wife, Hillary, ranked behind him – this ungainly tableau featured on the front page of *The Washington Post* hanging on my wall.

Public opinion also split along party lines. At the time of Clinton's impeachment in the House of Representatives in December 1998, 84 per cent of Democrats opposed it. Two-thirds of registered Republicans supported it.[47] After his acquittal in 1999, his approval rating amongst Democrats hit 92 per cent, proof that the 'Whose side are you on?' strategy had worked. When he left office, he enjoyed the highest approval rating of any departing president.

The only politicians to lose their jobs during the impeachment crisis were Republicans. Newt Gingrich, who had turned the 1998 midterms into a national referendum on the president's behaviour, was the first casualty, because the GOP unexpectedly suffered a net loss of five seats. Afterwards he resigned, bemoaning the savagery of a Republican Caucus that he had made so bloodthirsty – he called them 'cannibals'. He also admitted to an extramarital affair with a young Congressional aide, his future wife, Callista.

The fall of Bob Livingston, Gingrich's replacement, was also personally humiliating, for he was impaled on his own penis. On the very morning of Clinton's impeachment, the Louisianan resigned after Larry Flynt's *Hustler* magazine exposed his own extramarital affair. 'I must set the example that I hope President Clinton will follow,' he said in a dramatic speech on the House floor. A grotesque irony was that the Speakership then passed to Dennis Hastert, a former teacher considered back then to be irreproachable, who was later exposed as a child molester.

My framed front pages, now slightly yellowed with age, captured much of this drama, but hardly the media zeitgeist. For the Clinton scandal completely altered the metabolism of news, speeding the shift from print to digital and fuelling the growth of cable news channels and talk radio. Public reality, which traditionally had been curated by the major TV networks and prominent newspapers, that tended to be more impartial and consensual, was now being moulded by new start-ups.

With the internet beginning to bypass the longstanding gatekeepers of information, it was the fledgling Drudge Report, an obscure website in the wilds of cyberspace, which broke the story. 'Newsweek Kills Story On White House Intern: Blockbuster Report: 23 Year Old, Sex Relationship With President' read its industry-changing headline posted at 11.27 p.m. on Saturday, 17 January 1998, after its iconoclastic founder, Matt Drudge, caught wind that the news magazine had suppressed explosive details of Monica Lewinsky's affair with the president.

Racing to catch up, Newsweek published a digital piece by its investigative reporter Michael Isikoff, the author of the scoop, on its America Online site, rather than wait for its next magazine issue to hit the newsstands. White House reporters, such as Peter Baker, who was then with The Washington Post, posted their first online stories, even though many of their newsroom colleagues did not at the time have permission to access the internet.

When the Starr Report was published on 11 September 1998, it became America's first internet moment. Downloads of its explicit details accounted that day for a quarter of internet traffic. In what became the first 'clickbait' sensation, CNN got 300,000 hits a minute, a number in those days that was not just unprecedented but unimaginable.

Easier to obtain than printed copies, the digital version of the 453-page report doubled as online porn. Oral sex was mentioned 85 times. Maybe the Clinton saga was the gateway drug to our modern-day information addiction, and perhaps the first recorded case of the screen-time epidemic. It was just that the delivery systems back then were not particularly efficient – dial-up internet and bulky laptops – and the most powerful stimulants, Twitter and Facebook, had not yet flooded the market.

Just as the early online news sites experienced a surge in traffic, so cable news channels enjoyed a ratings bonanza.

Before the Clinton scandal, Fox News, which launched two years earlier, was something of a niche broadcaster available in just 10 million homes. By 2000, in large part because of its blanket coverage of the impeachment process, that figure had mushroomed to 56 million homes. Stoking anger and outrage became its business model – or its 'radicalisation model', as the historian Nicole Hemmer described it.[48] Firebrand anchors such as Bill O'Reilly, Glenn Beck, Laura Ingram and Sean Hannity became the tribunes of this armchair conservative insurgency. By 2002, Fox News had overtaken CNN as the highest-rated cable news network. MSNBC, which also launched in 1996 with an interview with Bill Clinton (something the president pointedly refused to give to Fox News, because it was owned by Rupert Murdoch and run by Roger Ailes), would eventually emerge as its liberal counterpoint.[49] Cable's polarisation industrial complex had been born.

To sustain their 24/7 coverage of the scandal, continuous news channels softened the lines between reportage and comment. Partisan pundits trading in shrill sound-bites helped fill airtime, and quickly realised that the more outspoken their comments, the more they would be invited back. Green rooms came to be packed with what the journalist Joe Klein labelled para-journalists, 'people whose main function was not to report but to perform – whose bilious on-air patter required immediate, simplistic answers to complicated questions'.[50] The argument culture of modern-day cable news, with its peanut gallery of pundits eager to talk but less willing to listen, came of age. One commentator who could also be relied upon for a pithy quote and an entertaining few minutes was Donald Trump, who called Clinton's televised statement 'a disaster' and suggested he should have taken the Fifth Amendment, the constitutional protection against self-incrimination.[51]

Because there was now such a feedback loop between the right-wing media and right-wing politics, Fox News and talk radio heightened the bloodthirstiness of Republicans. So even though polls suggested the push for impeachment was damaging the GOP, and the results of the 1998 midterm elections proved it without question, the pressure from the right was irresistible. Despite various exit ramps being available to Republican leaders, they kept on pressing down a road so rarely travelled, even though they knew it was unlikely to end in Clinton's ousting.

The political ramifications of impeachment would stretch long into the future. Though Clinton suffered the ignominy of becoming only the second president to be impeached, the biggest long-term Democratic casualty was his wife. When the email imbroglio broke early in the 2016 campaign, focused on her use of a private server as Secretary of State, voters already suffering from Clinton fatigue understandably questioned whether they wanted to live through another scandal-prone presidency. The lies from that era hardened the impression that the couple was evasive, untrustworthy and entitled.

Hillary Clinton's attacks on Donald Trump's misogyny, and her ability to capitalise on the notorious *Access Hollywood* tape in which he bragged about sexually molesting women, were undercut by her husband's affairs. Not unreasonably, she was accused of enabling Bill Clinton's behaviour and of showing little sympathy towards the women involved. Clinton defender James Carville gave the game away when he sneered, 'You drag $100 bills through trailer parks, there's no telling what you'll find.'

One of Donald Trump's first lines of defence after the 'grab 'em by the pussy' *Access Hollywood* tape first surfaced was to claim he had heard Bill Clinton saying worse things about women on the golf course, an accusation which, even if not true, had the ring of plausibility. The billionaire even paraded some of Clinton's accusers, including Paula Jones and Juanita Broaddrick, ahead of the first presidential debate, a stunt that many commentators considered monstrously exploitative but which for others raised legitimate questions about her husband's history of sexually abusive behaviour. Hillary Clinton complained in her 2017 campaign memoir *What Happened*, 'He was just using them.' But those women, all of them credible, had accused her husband of far worse – in Juanita Broaddrick's instance, a brutal rape in 1978.

To survive the *Access Hollywood* scandal, the billionaire adopted the 1998 playbook. Like Clinton, he pleaded for partisan allegiance and framed the question as 'Whose side are you on?' Just as Clinton held that South Lawn pep rally hours after his impeachment, so Trump waded into a crowd of placard-waving supporters who had gathered at the foot of Trump Tower in the darkest hour of his campaign. The candidate's counter-attack won him time, mobilised his base and preserved his political viability. Trump also benefited from the seedier side of Bill Clinton's legacy: the redefinition of what constituted disqualifying behaviour for presidential candidates. 'Slick Willie' had dramatically lowered the bar.

The double paradox of the Clinton impeachment, then, was that it made it harder for his wife to shatter the glass ceiling and easier for Donald Trump to become president. Hillary Clinton became a repeat victim of her husband's infidelities.

In those twilight years of the second millennium, the USA looked to be enjoying the same dominance it achieved at the Los Angeles Olympics. The fall of the Berlin Wall, the disintegration of the Soviet Union and that whirlwind victory in the Gulf War emphasised its status as the hegemon in a unipolar world. France's Foreign Minister, Hubert Védrine, described the United States, not altogether affectionately, as a 'hyperpower'. James Baker, the former Secretary of State, referred to a global hub-and-spoke system, with America as the central hub through which every country would now have to go.[52] In this Pax Americana, Madeleine Albright, the first female to head the State Department, described the US, justifiably, as 'the indispensable nation'.

With a reformist leader, Boris Yeltsin, installed in the Kremlin, Russia was expected to spurn authoritarianism and embrace meaningful democracy. Even after the Tiananmen Square massacre in 1989, there were hopes China might follow suit, as Deng Xiaoping's economic reforms moved the country inexorably towards a more market-based economy – which partly explained the Clinton administration's support for its entry into the World Trade Organization.

The thesis of Francis Fukuyama's 1989 essay *The End of History*, which proclaimed 'the universalization of Western liberal democracy as the final form of human government', seemed prescient rather than precipitate. Democracy was on the march. At the beginning of the '90s, 65 countries were truly free, according to Freedom House, a group promoting democratic change. By the end of the decade that number had jumped to 85.

For all the forecasts Japan would overtake the United States to become the world's richest nation, the US economy became the global star performer. In 1997, the economy grew by a staggering 8.2 per cent. By the end of the decade, the Dow Jones Industrial Average had soared by 309 per cent. The country enjoyed full employment while productivity levels exceeded those of the post-war boom.[53] Out of America came almost a quarter of global economic output.

With the Cold War over, the US Treasury enjoyed a peace dividend. By 2001, military spending accounted for just 3 per cent of GDP, the lowest level since the 1940s. Still, America spent more on defence than the rest of the world combined. 1999 saw the first balanced federal budget since 1969, the year of the moon landing. America's winning streak as the world's largest economy, which stretched back to the 1880s, looked set never to end. So buoyant was the mood that some economists peddled a business-cycle version of Fukuyama's end of history thesis, a utopian end to recessions.[54]

Bill Clinton's much-vaunted bridge to the twenty-first century looked impressively sturdy, even if the true engineers were emergent tech giants such as Microsoft, Apple, Google and Amazon.[55] Whereas it once looked like Sony, Toyota, Mitsubishi and Honda might dominate the corporate world, Silicon Valley became its new high-tech workshop. On 31 December 1999, the NASDAQ Composite closed at 4069. On the same date ten years earlier, it had ended trading at 455.[56] In the BBC Washington bureau at the time, all of us correspondents became amateur day traders. The profits from a batch of Silicon Valley shares purchased at breakfast would often pay for a decent lunch and dinner. Bill Gates, the 44-year-old founder of Microsoft and nerdy avatar of the New Economy, ended the century as the world's richest man.

Thirty years after planting the Stars and Stripes on the Sea of Tranquillity, America dominated cyberspace too. The internet passed through 13 servers, nine of which were in the US. ICANN (Internet Corporation for Assigned Names and Numbers), an organisation founded in 1998 with the backing of the US government to maintain the core infrastructure of the worldwide web, was headquartered in Los Angeles. Americans rushed to explore and conquer this new frontier. At the beginning of the '90s, just 2 per cent of the population were online. By 2002, most Americans had access.

America seemed to be making a painless transition from the industrial to the information age, and from a manufacturing-based to a service-based economy. The emergence of this New Economy, focused on information technology, the internet, globalisation and high-tech companies, fuelled talk of this new paradigm of indefinite growth.

As the new millennium approached, the country looked confidently to the future and proudly on the past. A welter of books celebrated the American Century, a contestable term when first coined by the magazine magnate Henry Luce in 1941 that now was undisputed.

Amidst this wave of patriotic nostalgia, a site was finally allotted in 1995 for the World War II Memorial at the opposite end of the Reflecting Pool from the Lincoln Memorial. Three years later, the *NBC News* anchor Tom Brokaw published his runaway bestseller *The Greatest Generation*, a tribute to the Americans who stormed the beaches of Normandy and hauled up the flag at Iwo Jima. The Spielberg epic *Saving Private Ryan*, another homage to the thousands of veterans who confronted the wall of bullets at Omaha and Utah beaches, followed shortly afterwards. Senator John McCain's 1999 autobiography, *Faith of My Fathers*, recounting his family's wartime service and his selfless heroism in Vietnam, was a central reason why he emerged the following year as such an arresting presidential candidate. Vietnam vets, often ostracised following their return from South-East Asia, were repurposed as all-American heroes.

As part of this national stocktaking, the contribution of presidents neglected or maligned by history came to be re-evaluated. The author David McCullough published *Truman*, a revisionist tome that transformed the reputation of the prime architect of the post-war liberal order that underpinned US authority.

Following his death in 1994, the country also made peace with Richard Nixon. All five living US presidents attended the commemorations in California, the first presidential funeral since LBJ's in 1973. Speaking on behalf of the nation, Bill Clinton readily conferred forgiveness: 'May the day of judging Richard Nixon on anything less than his entire life and career come to a close.' Bob Dole, who broke down in tears, claimed 'the second half of the twentieth century will be known as the age of Nixon'. Through all these mawkish eulogies, the word Watergate was never uttered, another sign of America's self-contentment.[57]

On the world stage, Clinton continued to assert himself more assuredly. In Northern Ireland, he was pivotal in bringing to an end The Troubles. Had it not been for his personal lobbying, and his wise decision to appoint as his Northern Ireland envoy the former Senate Majority Leader George Mitchell, the 1998 Good Friday Agreement would not have been finalised. My favourite moment during the Clinton years came that historic night in Belfast, when BBC colleagues whose entire careers had been spent covering The Troubles lined up to get Mitchell to sign photocopies of the newly minted agreement.

The president also pushed successfully for the enlargement of NATO, with the Soviet Union's former clients Poland, the Czech Republic and Hungary joining its 12 founding members. Having absorbed some of the lessons from Bosnia, he acted more decisively in Kosovo, even though he was still squeamish about inserting US troops and preferred to fight war from the air.[58]

In South Asia, he calmed tensions in the nuclear showdown between India and Pakistan, which again displayed the skills as a peacemaker he learned in his alcoholic boyhood home. In his final months, with an eye on a Nobel Peace Prize, he tried to pull off his own Camp David. However, although Clinton pressured the Israel Prime Minister, Ehud Barak, into offering Yasser Arafat what was arguably the best deal the Palestinians could reasonably hope for, the PLO leader balked. From the West Bank to West Belfast, the United States had indeed become the indispensable nation. No other country came close to boasting its diplomatic leverage, unique convening power or military might.

At the dawning of the new millennium, America continued on with its victory lap. So self-congratulatory was the mood that organisers of the midnight gala on the National Mall in Washington dispensed with the term 'The American Century' and opted instead to call it 'America's Millennium' – a bold claim for a country that had made a negligible impact for 776 of the previous 1,000 years.

That night I was on the steps of the Lincoln Memorial for a concert that brought together a rag-bag roster of performers – Kenny Rogers, Bono, Aretha Franklin, Luther Vandross, Diane Keaton, John Glenn, Jack Nicholson, Muhammad Ali, Will Smith and even the Welsh crooner Tom Jones. Top billing, though, went to Bill Clinton, the notoriously late-running president who, out of respect for the Gregorian calendar, managed for once to turn up on time.

'Never before has our nation enjoyed, at once, so much prosperity, social progress, and national self-confidence with so little internal crisis or external threat,' he boasted in a short speech, which on a night of drunken revelry served also as sober analysis. America's primacy went unchallenged, and as fireworks skipped from the Lincoln Memorial down the Reflecting Pool to illuminate the Washington monument, it was entirely fitting that this mighty obelisk resembled a bright shining number 1.

Thereafter, the hangover was quick in coming. From the outset of the new century, America experienced a dramatic and unexpected turnaround. Even though doomsday predictions of a Y2K bug failed to materialise, it felt nonetheless as if the United States had been infected with a virus causing its operating code to malfunction. A harbinger came on 31 December, before the touch-paper had been lit on those fireworks in Washington, with the unexpected announcement from the Kremlin that Yeltsin had nominated Vladimir Putin as his successor. Here perhaps was the Y2K bug in human form: a former KGB spymaster and ultra-nationalist authoritarian, whose arrival on the world stage single-handedly turned the end of history thesis into a pumpkin, even before the clock had struck midnight.

At home, the run-up to the new millennium brought a timely reminder of America's vulnerability to Islamist transnational terror. Al Qaeda had plotted to usher in the New Year by bombing LAX International in Los Angeles, an attack thwarted at the Canadian border when a vigilant US Customs and Border Protection officer stopped a vehicle packed with explosives. In October, however, there was no stopping the jihadists who successfully carried out an attack on the USS *Cole* during a routine refuelling stop in Yemen. Seventeen US sailors were killed when two suicide bombers rammed a small boat packed with high explosives into its hull.

On the home front, the New Economy was revealed to have the same frailties as the old. In March, the heads of the New York Stock Exchange and NASDAQ took the unusual step of issuing a joint statement urging brokerage firms to review how much credit they were extending to investors.

A few weeks later, the dotcom bubble, inflated by overvalued Initial Public Offerings (IPOs) and the stampede to invest in the digital trailblazers of the New Economy, burst like a party balloon in the hands of an over-eager toddler. In a single week in April, the NASDAQ fell by 25 per cent, bringing to an end a 17-year bull market run. Even the digital economy, it became evident, had ultimately to adhere to old-fashioned rules of profit and loss.

A string of corporate scandals over the coming years involving New Economy giants such as Enron, the Houston-based commodities and energy corporation, and WorldCom, the Mississippi-based telecommunications behemoth, exacerbated the effects of the crash. America was paying the price for what Alan Greenspan described in December 1996 as the 'irrational exuberance' of an overvalued stock market. All that intoxicating talk of business cycles being relegated to history now sounded like an inebriated boast. In March 2001, the US economy went into recession for the first time in a decade.

The turn of the century brought unmistakable signs of a nascent backlash against globalisation, as American workers grew more concerned about threats from abroad to their livelihoods. At the Battle of Seattle in November 1999, some 50,000 demonstrators shut down a meeting of the World Trade Organization, a siege blamed on anarchists and extreme environmentalists but which also involved organised labour – a combination of union muscle and green activism dubbed 'Teamsters and turtles'.[59] The following year, blue-collar protesters again took part in the A16 demonstrations in Washington DC, targeting the spring meetings of the International Monetary Fund and World Bank. In Seattle and Washington, we were seeing the first stirrings of a blue-collar revolt.

For workers in the Rust Belt, that bridge to the twenty-first century more resembled a new highway that bypassed their decaying towns. Disruptive technologies, dramatically altering the ways in which businesses, industries and consumers operated and behaved, turned out to be a jobs killer in the old industrial heartland. Between 1990 and 2007, machines replaced up to 670,000 US manufacturing jobs. A 'digital divide' had also opened up, a phrase first coined in 1996 to describe the discrepancy between the haves and have-nots of the information age, which was aggravated by the lack of affordable access to the internet in poor and rural areas.

The labour market had changed, and not necessarily for the better. Over the previous 25 years, employment growth had been focused on the upper and lower strata of the economy, in highly paid professional occupations and low-wage service jobs. Missing were the manufacturing jobs that had traditionally helped workers without college degrees to enter into the ranks of the middle class. Increasingly there were good jobs and bad jobs, with fewer opportunities between the two. 'Job polarisation', as economists started calling it, became more pronounced in the 1990s, a process attributed to deindustrialisation, deregulation and deunionisation. From the end of World War II to the late '90s, union membership fell from a third of the American workforce to just 13.9 per cent.[60] Attitudes towards unions also evolved. In the public mind they went from being organisations that protected workers to organisations that burdened US corporations with unnecessary costs, paving the way for more lay-offs, plant closures and foreign outsourcing.

By the end of the '90s, disparities in wealth were becoming more glaring – what the economist Paul Krugman dubbed the 'Great Divergence'. In 1970, the CEOs of America's top 100 companies had earned 39 times the pay of the average worker. By 1999, they were paid 1,000 times more than ordinary workers. In the 1990s alone, remuneration for senior executives rose by 442 per cent. From the early '70s to the late '90s, the only income group not to experience a decline in real wages was the top 10 per cent. 'We are now living in a new Gilded Age,' observed Krugman in 2002. 'The America of Wall Street and Bonfire of the Vanities was positively egalitarian compared with the country we live in today'.[61]

As the new century dawned, there were warnings America's social fabric was not just fraying but ripping apart; that the country was becoming more atomised as well as more polarised. In his seminal 2000 study, Bowling Alone: America's Declining Social Capital, Robert D. Putnam drew attention to how lower participation rates in organisations such as unions, parent–teacher associations, the Boy Scouts and women's clubs had reduced person-to-person contacts and civil interaction. Institutions of American association were in decline. Also of concern for Putnam was what he called the 'individualising' effect of television and the internet. The proliferation of cable channels, fragmentation of the media and explosion of websites brought to an end the simpler, more communal era when Americans gathered around their television sets to watch, say, the final edition of *M*A*S*H*, *The Waltons* or the 'Who Shot JR?' episode of *Dallas*, and then talked about it the next day around the water cooler. An increasingly rare exception was the farewell episode in 1998 of *Seinfeld*, a show famously about nothing that became a cultural touchstone for the carefree aimlessness and national stasis of the '90s when history had supposedly run its course.

During this period, it was noticeable how I spent more time covering bizarre 'Only in America' stories. The rise, for instance, of creationism, the literal belief in the origin story set out in the Book of Genesis, as opposed to Charles Darwin's heretical theory of evolution. Then there was the war on Harry Potter. One autumn afternoon, I recall heading to a bookstore in suburban Washington, where a conga-line of children dressed in the red and gold colours of Gryffindor were waiting to meet J. K. Rowling. This was newsworthy not only because of the phenomenal success of the Harry Potter books, but because Rowling, a church-goer herself, had been accused of promoting witchcraft. Both biblical literalism and the demonisation of Harry Potter spoke of a decline of reason and a rejection of science, trends that were accelerating, and not just in the Bible Belt. No longer were these fringe views. In some conservative states, they had become mainstream thinking.

With the clarity offered by hindsight, it has become increasingly clear that, for all the peace and prosperity, the '90s were in fact pregnant with America's post-millennium decline. The celebratory mood in which the country greeted the new millennium looked more and more like decadence before the decay. The transition from the old economy to the new was anything but pain-free. Reforms presented as being in step with the march of modernisation proved to be terrible slip-ups. Talk of a new economic paradigm sounded like the pitch for seed money from an overambitious Silicon Valley start-up.

Clearly, the Clinton years were a period of excessive and reckless financial deregulation. By far the most egregious mistake was the repeal of the Depression-era Glass–Steagall Act, which tore down the firewall between commercial and investment banking. Financial institutions such as Citigroup and even the insurer AIG became buyers and sellers of the most risk-laden products, derivatives and credit default swaps. Commercial banks, which had long been pillars of financial rectitude, became infected with the risk culture of investment banks. To compound this error, the Clinton administration signed into law the Commodity Futures Modernization Act in December 2000, which exempted credit default swaps from regulation – contracts that Warren Buffett, the billionaire and fabled 'Oracle of Omaha', described as 'financial weapons of mass destruction'.[62]

During this regulatory free-for-all, accountancy standards upheld by the Financial Accounting Standards Board were loosened, partly to enable big practices, such as Arthur Andersen, to rake in consultancy fees from the very companies they audited, a blatant conflict of interest. Even well-intentioned policies, such as initiatives by the Department of Housing and Urban Development to boost home ownership amongst the poor, had ruinous consequences. In credit-deprived areas, loans were granted to borrowers with a high risk of defaulting, a heedless lending policy that fuelled the subprime crisis, when a sharp fall in property prices after the burst of the housing bubble led to four million foreclosures Whether to those struggling to get a foot on the housing ladder or to Wall Street's Masters of the Universe, the Clinton administration acted like a barman lining up shots to the drunk before closing time and then handing him the keys of his car to drive home.

When it came to regulating the New Economy, Clinton opted for the same laissez-faire approach. It should be 'kept to a bare minimum', in the words of Assistant Attorney General Joel Klein, the head of the Antitrust Division at the Justice Department.[63] The rules for the twenty-first century would be lax.

Technology firms were not given an entirely free rein. In the late 1990s, the Clinton Justice Department mounted a landmark prosecution against Microsoft for illegally maintaining its monopoly in personal computers. But the New Economy would create dozens of new Microsofts, giant big-tech monopolies such as Amazon (founded in 1994), Google (1998) and eventually Facebook (2004).

Partly because there were so many early high-tech casualties, the erroneous belief took hold that market forces would serve as a regulator. Another mistake was to think online companies would be additive rather than alternative, that they would duplicate rather than destroy. The Clinton administration did not foresee the devastating impact of e-commerce: of how Amazon, for instance, would kill off bricks-and-mortar bookshops, and then, as its online inventory expanded, cripple entire shopping malls – and end up paying zero corporation tax. Nor did they predict how company names would become verbs. Reluctant to act as sheriff, Washington allowed Silicon Valley to become a regulatory Wild West. The 'move fast and break things' ethos trumpeted by the Facebook founder Mark Zuckerberg spoke of its cowboy culture. 'Fake it until you make it' became another mantra of the New Economy. The tech start-ups were not so much the workshop of the world as its chaos factory.

The same utopianism that surrounded the creation of the New Economy fuelled idealistic claims about the democratic potential of the internet. Digital citizenship and e-politics would bolster public participation and make lawmakers more attentive and responsive. New civic spaces would open up, the online equivalent of public squares and town-hall meetings. Crowdsourcing would make political candidates less dependent on super-rich donors, reducing the corrupting influence of big money. It could even heal the partisan rift.

'Partisanship, religion, geography, race, gender and other traditional political divisions are giving way to a new standard – wiredness – as an organizing principle for political and social attitudes,' wrote Karen Breslau of *Wired* magazine in the spring of 2000 in a wildly optimistic essay entitled 'One Nation, Interconnected'.[64]

Even in the infant years of the internet, there were portents of how it would degenerate into a forum for division, cynicism, hate, crazed conspiracy theories and the dissemination of misinformation. Of how algorithms promoted anger, and connected people sharing the same prejudices and fears and turned them into keyboard warriors. Of how the decision to exempt Facebook and Google from the 1996 Communications Decency Act, which gave them legal protection from publishing false and defamatory content, would allow the conflict culture to metastasise. The paranoid style in American politics had now found its natural home.

Just consider the rise of Alex Jones, a shock jock who had accused the US government of faking the moon landing and planning the Oklahoma City bombing, and who in 1999 founded infowars.com. This widely read site turned him into one of the web's most demented purveyors of conspiracy theories, the untitled head of what the author Kurt Andersen called 'a confederacy of paranoids'. By 2016, Jones's YouTube channel had 2.4 million subscribers, while his Infowars Facebook page had drawn more than 650 million views.[65] Jones would later claim 9/11 was an inside job and the 2012 Sandy Hook Elementary School shooting, where a gunman murdered 20 first-graders, was a 'false flag' attack perpetrated by the Obama administration as a predicate for stricter gun controls. Yet that did not stop Donald Trump, a fraternal conspiracy theorist, from appearing on his show when running for presidency. Jones even claimed that President-elect Trump called him after the election to thank him for his help – the fanciful boast of a deranged liar, maybe, but tellingly not one that was denied by the Trump camp.[66]

What seemed in 2000 like major Clinton legacy items – NAFTA, welfare and criminal justice reform – arguably ended up doing more harm than good. It was when the administration was functioning at its optimal level, with the president triangulating with Pythagorean glee, that some of the more lasting damage was done. NAFTA was widely perceived as a jobs killer. Even as economists trumpeted the benefits of the pact in lower consumer prices, higher productivity and a tripling of trade between the United States and its closest neighbours, NAFTA was easy to scapegoat for the decline in US manufacturing jobs. Just as Ross Perot had predicted, it came with the 'giant sucking sound' of jobs leaving America. While employment in the Mexico auto industry rose by over 400,000 jobs since 1994, the US auto industry shed a third of its jobs, some 350,000 positions.[67]

Initially welfare reform was deemed a transformative success, slashing welfare rolls and boosting employment. It became central to the peace-and-prosperity narrative. Over time, however, the shrinkage of the safety net meant more Americans fell into poverty. The number of families living on less than $2 per person per day more than doubled between 1996 and 2011.[68] By 2012, more than three million American children spent at least three months each year existing on next to no money.[69]

The impact of the 1994 crime bill, along with the president's support for 'three strike' habitual offender laws, is more clear-cut. It led to the imprisonment of millions of low-level drug offenders and, with the clank of a jailhouse door, presaged the age of mass incarceration. Clinton oversaw the biggest increase in the federal and state prison population in American history. By the end of his presidency, the United States had the highest rate of incarceration in the world. Racially, the policy was flagrantly discriminatory. Crack was virtually identical, chemically, to powder cocaine, and yet its users, who were predominantly black, were treated as 100 times more criminal than the affluent whites who preferred to snort narcotics after cutting up lines with a credit card.

The Telecommunications Act of 1996, which Clinton signed electronically in a ceremony streamed live on the internet from the Library of Congress, paved the way for the biggest overhaul of telecommunications since the New Deal era, and helped speed the rise of the internet. But media ownership came to be consolidated in the hands of fewer corporations, as foreshown by the merger in February 2000 of America Online, the pioneering internet provider, and Time Warner, the dream marriage between the old media and the new. By 2016, 90 per cent of the major media companies were owned by six corporations – Time Warner, Disney, Viacom, CBS, Comcast and Rupert Murdoch's News Corporation – as opposed to 50 companies in the early 1980s.

Liberated from ownership constraints, giant radio conglomerates came into existence, the most influential of which was Clear Channel (which later became iHeartMedia). From coast to coast, it nationalised shrill shock jocks who ended up having such a denationalising effect. In the decade after its enactment, right-wing talk radio exploded. The Telecommunications Act helped make syndicated stars of Sean Hannity, Glenn Beck and the Trump favourite Mark Levin. Beck had an audience of six million listeners a day, bigger than the readership of all the major newspaper mastheads in America.[70]

The origins of the opioid crisis are found in the early 1990s, when doctors over-prescribed powerful painkillers like OxyContin, promoted by misleading ad campaigns from pharmaceutical companies such as Purdue Pharma. Opioids that should have been more strictly regulated by the Food and Drug Administration were handed out like Halloween candy: to kids who had picked up knocks on the American football field; to middle-aged people with mild back ailments; to Rush Limbaugh, who booked himself into rehab after revealing to his Dittoheads that he had become addicted to OxyContin and hydrocodone, prescription drugs dubbed 'hillbilly heroin'. Between 1991 and 2011, painkiller prescriptions tripled and addicts commonly made the deadly switch to harder opioids such as heroin, which were often cheaper and more readily available. Since 1996, the crisis has contributed to the deaths of more than 400,000 Americans from drug overdoses. In 2016 alone, 47,000 people died from overdosing on opioids.

Twenty years on, much of Clinton's foreign policy looks hubristic and ill advised. His aggressive pursuit of NATO expansion, a spoil of Cold War victory, backfired terribly, for it fuelled the feelings of national victimhood exploited by Vladimir Putin. After the Cold War, NATO was pretty much obsolete and foreign-policy thinkers such as George Kennan, the author of the post-war strategy of containment, warned that the enlargement was a 'strategic blunder of potentially epic proportions'.[71]

The Clinton administration's response to the threat from Al Qaeda was inadequate, even negligent. US targets were hit repeatedly throughout the '90s: in November 1995, a car bomb exploded outside an office building in Riyadh, Saudi Arabia, killing five Americans and two others; in June 1996, a truck bomb exploded outside the Khobar Towers apartment complex, again in Saudi Arabia, murdering 19 US servicemen and wounding hundreds; in 1998, the embassy bombings in Kenya and Tanzania killed 224 people, including 12 US citizens. The president retaliated to the embassy attacks by ordering US forces to bomb a pharmaceuticals plant in Khartoum, Sudan, where Osama bin Laden's Al Qaeda network was suspected of manufacturing chemical weapons, and six of the terror leader's bases and training camps in Afghanistan.

Yet although the military action came with a grandiose title – Operation Infinite Reach – it was feeble and counterproductive. As even the State Department admitted, its main effect was to bring the Taliban and Al Qaeda into closer alignment. Up until the strikes, the Taliban had been wary of sheltering Arab jihadists on its soil. Afterwards, it more willingly offered them safe haven. Coming just weeks after Clinton had admitted his affair with Monica Lewinsky, the most perilous phase of his presidency, the cruise missiles were inevitably seen as weapons of mass distraction. Parallels were instantly drawn with the plotline of the 1997 movie *Wag the Dog*, in which a Hollywood producer fabricated a war to deflect attention from a presidential sex scandal.

Throughout his presidency, Clinton failed to comprehend the murderous magnitude of the threat, despite the first attack on the World Trade Center and warnings that jihadists could strike again on American soil. The loudest warning came from three leading national security thinkers, Ashton Carter (a future defence secretary under Obama), John Deutch (a former CIA chief) and Philip Zelikow (who ended up working as the executive director of the 9/11 Commission). In 1998, in the aftermath of the embassy attacks, they published an ominous essay in *Foreign Affairs* outlining their fears of 'catastrophic terrorism' targeting major US cities. Citing the 1993 attack on the World Trade Center, they raised the spectre of a Pearl Harbor-like event that 'would divide our past and future into a before and after'.[72]

The following year, the former senators Gary Hart and Warren Rudman presented a report to Congress that also proved prescient. 'Americans will likely die on American soil,' they warned, 'possibly in large numbers.'

The Clinton administration's response to the most existential planetary threat, global warming, was mixed. Though he signed up in 1997 to the Kyoto Protocol limiting emissions, Clinton made little effort to push for its Senate ratification (in another example of Clintonian diplomatic double-speak, he signed the Rome Statute setting up the International Criminal Court, but did not send it to the Senate to be ratified). Though he cast himself as a modern-day Theodore Roosevelt, protecting more than four million acres of public land in the form of national parks and wilderness, he was criticised for not doing enough to pressure Detroit into manufacturing more fuel-efficient cars. Ralph Nader, the consumer crusader turned environmentalist, exploited these weaknesses in the 2000 election. He polled almost 100,000 votes in Florida, enough to cost Al Gore the presidency.

A trashiness pervaded the '90s, evident not just in the string of supermarket tabloid scandals but also in the rise of tabloid talk shows. Seeking to emulate the success of *The Oprah Winfrey Show*, the networks launched more raunchy rivals *The Maury Povich Show*, *The Jenny Jones Show* and *Ricki Lake*. The former mayor of Cincinnati, a politician who wanted to become a celebrity, presented the most extreme iteration of the format, *The Jerry Springer Show*. In what *TV Guide* called the worst television programme of all time, he became the carnival barker of a modern-day freak show, which featured, among others, 'the man who married his horse', a woman who claimed to have slept with 251 men in ten hours and a self-styled 'breeder for the Klan'.[73] It was aggressive, vulgar, foul-mouthed, unashamedly populist, proudly anti-elitist and a ratings winner. Small wonder Springer complained years later that Donald Trump 'stole my show and took it to the White House'. The members of the studio audience who chanted 'Jerry, Jerry, Jerry' and booed the unfaithful wife or the cheating girlfriend were not dissimilar to the supporters who thronged Donald Trump's rallies and yelled 'Lock her up!'

Television tastes were evolving. In 2000, for the first time, a reality TV show, *Survivor*, became the most watched programme of the year, as presaged by the 1998 Peter Weir classic *The Truman Show*. The show's catchphrase, 'The tribe has spoken,' inadvertently summed up the clannish politics of the moment. Its producer, Mark Burnett, a former British paratrooper and Falklands War veteran, would go on four years later to produce another ratings winner, a business show with a survival-of-the-fittest theme called *The Apprentice*. At the Emmys in 2016 just weeks before the presidential election, the host, Jimmy Kimmel, took aim at the British showrunner. 'Thanks to Mark Burnett, we don't have to watch reality shows any more, because we're living in one.'

So much of what was unattractive about '90s America was on display in the O. J. Simpson trial. The circus-like proceedings. The celebrity culture which made stars out of the attorneys (Johnnie Cochran, Marcia Clark, Robert Shapiro); the judge (Lance Ito, who played to the cameras); a cop alleged to be racist (Mark Fuhrman); bit players (like Kato Kaelin, who parlayed his witness-stand limelight into various appearances on reality TV shows); and even a Kardashian (O. J.'s close friend Robert Kardashian, the father of Kourtney, Kim, Khloé and Rob, sat alongside the defence team throughout the trial, and first appeared before the media on the day of the Bronco car chase, when he read a letter penned by O. J., which sounded like a confession). The extent to which the criminal justice system, like politics, had become performance art reliant on bumper-sticker jargon: 'If the glove doesn't fit, you must acquit'.

There was the post-truthism of a manifestly unjust verdict, a victory of feelings over facts. Though the evidence presented in that LA County courtroom overwhelmingly pointed to Simpson's guilt, some jury members admitted afterwards the evidence presented in court was secondary to their desire to retaliate against the Los Angeles Police Department for the Rodney King beating. Their deliverance of a 'not guilty' verdict was as much a protest as a judgement. As the panellists left the courtroom, one of the African-American jurors, a former Black Panther, even raised his clenched fist in a black power salute.

America's racial divisiveness was again on global view. While a majority of whites were convinced of his guilt, polls showed six out of ten African-Americans thought 'The Juice' was innocent. When the trial ended with his acquittal, jubilant African-Americans celebrated as if O. J. had scored one of his magical, weaving touchdowns.

By contrast, white viewers were stunned and speechless. 'Shit' was Bill Clinton's response, after watching the verdict in the office of his African-American personal secretary, Betty Currie.[74] Here, the US president spoke for the rest of the world. How could America have got it so wrong? Had the country gone berserk? The questions asked incredulously by international onlookers as the 'not guilty' verdict was read to a stunned courtroom found an echo on Election Night in 2016.

In the late '90s there was a warning that politics was not immune from the same hoopla as the O. J. trial. It came from an unlikely quarter, the normally sober-minded state of Minnesota, and in an improbable form, Jesse 'The Body' Ventura, a star of WrestleMania best known for his glittering skin-tight pants and luxuriant pink feather boas. The free-wheeling Ventura, who had first raised the possibility of running for public office on his radio talk show, railed against political correctness and the political establishment – one of his opponents was the Democrat Hubert H. Humphrey III, the son of the former vice-president. Campaigning with the slogan 'Retaliate in '98', his body-slam candidacy took on a populist momentum all of its own. A curio quickly became a phenomenon. His shock victory demonstrated how quickly the political order could be upended by an outsider with name recognition railing against 'politics as usual', who understood how to manipulate the modern media. Not insignificantly, Ventura's grassroots campaign was one of the first to harness the power of the internet.

Having run in Minnesota as a Reform Party candidate, Ventura was talked of as the party's prospective presidential nominee in

2000 – Hulk Hogan, his friend from the pro-wrestling days, suggested they don leotards for one final bout before he took up residence in the White House. Ventura, however, had pledged to serve out his first term as governor, and therefore pushed another celebrity candidate as a kind of placeholder. The luminary he had in mind was his fellow grapple fan and friend from the WrestleMania circuit, Donald Trump.

The '90s had been an unhappy interlude for the struggling New York tycoon. They began on the ski fields of Aspen, Colorado, when his first wife, Ivana, an Olympic skier, ran into her husband and his mistress, Marla Maples. This fractured love triangle produced the first tabloid scandal of the decade, when the break-up of his marriage coincided with the decline and fall of his casino empire.

At the beginning of 1990, Trump owed more than $4 billion to 70 banks. Even an illegal loan from his father, Fred, who bought $3.5 million worth of chips at the Trump Castle in Atlantic City and then walked out of the door without using them, could not save him from insolvency.

The sight in 1991 of a beggar proffering a tin cup outside Tiffany on Fifth Avenue brought home the abject state of his finances. 'I looked at Marla and said, "You know, right now that man is worth $900 million more than I am."'[75] In another retelling of that moment, Trump claimed he said, 'That bum isn't worth a dime, but at least he's at zero.'[76]

After restructuring his mammoth debts, Trump's financial fortunes changed in the mid-'90s.[77] By the summer of 1996, in an article headlined 'An Ex-Loser Is Back in the Money', Fortune celebrated his 'Houdini-like escape'.[78] In his 1997 bestseller The Art of the Comeback, Trump told the story of his financial recovery, and discussed his political prospects. 'The problem is, I think I'm too honest, and perhaps too controversial, to be a politician,' he wrote. 'I always say it like it is, and I'm not sure a politician can do that.' When Jesse Ventura talked up his candidacy, however, Trump started seriously exploring a run.

In a straw poll of delegates at the Reform Party convention in 1999, Trump came a close second to the movement's founder, Ross

Perot. Revelling in his newfound political popularity, he appeared on *Larry King Live* in October and announced, Perot-like, the formation of a presidential exploratory committee headed by his friend Roger Stone. Afterwards, Trump embarked upon a media blitz that once more demonstrated his gift for self-publicity. Oprah Winfrey would be his ideal running mate, he teased. His then girlfriend, Melania Knauss, would become his wife, so she could serve as First Lady.

In another sign of things to come, *Saturday Night Live* lampooned him with a sketch based on an imaginary strategy meeting between Trump, Perot and Pat Buchanan, whose rival campaign for the Reform Party nomination had run into trouble because of his horrific claim that America need not have confronted Hitler.[79] 'The Reform Party needs a new crazy leader,' said a Ross Perot impersonator, looking expectantly at Trump and Buchanan. 'What we need is a real nutbag.'

The *Wall Street Journal* took Trump more seriously, and allotted prime real estate on its op-ed page for a characteristically self-aggrandising column, 'America Needs a President Like Me'. 'Let's cut to the chase,' it began breathlessly. 'Yes, I am considering a run for president. The reason has nothing to do with vanity, as some have suggested.'

In what read like a preview of his Twitter feed, Trump promised to negotiate better trade deals and threatened to bomb Pyongyang. Denouncing the 'striped pants set' running US foreign policy, he vowed to reverse any move to normalise relations with Fidel Castro's Cuba.

In parts, he sounded clairvoyant: 'I believe non politicians represent the wave of the future.' For now, though, he presented himself as a centrist. 'The Republicans are captives of their right wing. The Democrats are captives of their left wing. I don't hear anyone speaking for the working men and women in the center.'

Jesse Ventura was his model: 'the embodiment of the political qualities America needs'. Trump pledged to run solely for a single term, so he could return to the job in New York he loved doing.

'I would center my presidency around three principles,' he concluded, 'one term, two-fisted policies, and no excuses.'

In outlining his presidential manifesto, Trump sounded at times like a New York Democrat. On abortion, he was 'totally for choice'. On healthcare, he was borderline socialistic. 'We must have universal healthcare' based on the Canada model, he wrote in his campaign book, *The America We Deserve*. 'We need, as a nation, to re-examine the single-payer plan, as many individual states are doing.'

On other issues, such as gun control, he claimed to be 'very conservative'. His Cabinet dream team included Oprah, the General Electric CEO Jack Welch, the Teamsters boss Jim Hoffa (the son of James), Jeb Bush and Steven Spielberg.[80]

An irony of his run, given his nativism 15 years later, was that Trump framed his battle with Buchanan as a choice between tolerance and intolerance. To draw more attention to his opponent's anti-Semitism, he toured the Simon Wiesenthal Center's Museum of Tolerance in Los Angeles. 'We must recognise bigotry and prejudice and defeat it wherever it appears,' he said, high-mindedly.[81] Only 'the really staunch right wacko vote' would back a racist like Pat Buchanan, he told Tim Russert on *Meet the Press*.[82] As the political commentator Steve Kornacki cleverly put it, Trump was fighting Trumpism.

Only in his demonisation of the Central Park Five, a group of African-Americans wrongly convicted of the rape and assault of a white female jogger attacked in 1989, were there shades of the racism that lay in store. In response to the attack, he had placed ads in four New York newspapers calling for the state to adopt the death penalty. 'BRING BACK THE DEATH PENALTY AND BRING BACK OUR POLICE,' he wrote in all caps. In *The America We Deserve*, he boasted about demanding the death penalty for the five blacks. Nor did he make any effort to conceal his misogyny. 'The only difference between me and the other candidates,' he said at one point, 'is that I'm more honest and my women are more beautiful.'[83]

Early in election year, Trump decided to end his bid after Buchanan received the endorsement of the former KKK leader David Duke and a self-styled black nationalist Marxist called Lenora Fulani. No longer was he interested in being the figurehead of a party, as he put it, that now included a Klansman, a neo-Nazi and a communist. Nor did he want to be associated with the crackpots he had encountered at a Reform Party event in California, where, he grumbled, 'the room was crowded with Elvis lookalikes, resplendent in various campaign buttons and anxious to give me a platform explaining the Swiss-Zionist conspiracy to control America'.[84]

The Reform Party's then head, Pat Choate, was not unhappy to see the back of him. 'Donald Trump came in, promoted his hotel, promoted his book, he promoted himself at our expense,' he complained. 'All this was was a serious hustle on the media, and I think the media should send him a massive bill on it.'[85] So ended Donald Trump's first semi-serious bid for the presidency.

In 2000, the career trajectory of his future presidential rival was very much on the up. That November, Hillary Clinton won the New York Senate seat left vacant by Daniel Patrick Moynihan, a victory she celebrated in the presidential suite of the Hyatt on 42nd Street, the hotel that had established Trump's deal-making reputation. If the '80s had been the making of the New York billionaire, the Clintons had dominated the '90s. Reflecting on that roaring decade, Hillary Clinton had asked, 'Which part of peace and prosperity didn't you like?'[86] By 2016, voters had compiled a laundry list of complaints.

4

The Three Convulsions

Almost as much a futurist as a politician, Al Gore appeared uniquely well qualified to serve as president at the outset of the new millennium. His prescience on global warming, the most urgent issue facing the planet, was imprinted on every page of his 1992 bestseller, *Earth in the Balance: Ecology and the Human Spirit*. From the 1970s, first as a congressman and then as a senator, he had promoted high-speed telecommunications. All the key legislation paving the way for the 'information superhighway', a phrase he made part of the political lexicon, originated from his office. Though he could not claim to have invented the internet – in fairness to Gore, who was prone to truth-twisting, he never did – no lawmaker anywhere in the world had done more to bring it into existence.

Throughout the 2000 campaign, however, the vice-president made the patronising mistake of thinking voters were incapable of differentiating between the good, the bad and the squalid of the Clinton years. Rather than presenting himself as the continuity candidate best placed to bestow even more peace and prosperity upon the American people, he distanced himself from the Clinton record. Ditching his one-time running mate also meant jettisoning Clintonism, the centrism Gore had advocated throughout his political life.

Instead, he cast himself as a *faux* populist, proclaiming, as the commentator Michael Kinsley brilliantly paraphrased it, 'You've never had it so good and I'm as mad as hell about it.' This 'us versus them' class-warfare message seemed better suited to the start of the twentieth century than the beginning of the twenty-first – although, as recent history has proven, perhaps here, as well, he was ahead of his time.

This 'I'm-no-Bill-Clinton' shtick even extended to subjecting his poor wife, Tipper, to a screen kiss at the Democratic convention in Los Angeles that made Clark Gable's 'You need kissing badly' embrace of Vivien Leigh seem almost loveless. In the press box that night, as the Jumbotron screens in the Staples Center turned unexpectedly into a giant kiss cam, our universal reaction was 'Yuk!'

Gore was a hapless campaigner. After Bill Clinton's touchy-feely presidency, this technology-obsessed technocratic came across as an automaton, a Buzz Lightyear of a politician programmed by consultants to deliver vapid soundbites devoid of emotion or spontaneity. Even the kiss seemed pre-set, although its length and lustiness suggested a software malfunction.

Gore suffered, too, from snarky journalists handicapping the race in favour of George W. Bush, who was inarguably the less qualified candidate of the two. Not only were liberal-leaning reporters determined to demonstrate their impartiality by holding Gore to a higher standard – a problem Hillary Clinton encountered in 2016 – they were prone to 'better story bias'. The Texan possessed more entertainment value than the Tennessean. A Bush restoration, with all its historical echoes and Oedipal overtones, offered a more seductive storyline than a third Clinton term with a dull understudy as lead. The coverage of the 2000 campaign revealed a recurring journalistic dereliction: how reporters commonly produce narratives that comport with the kind of race they ideally want to cover, with a bias in favour of the candidate who delivers the best story arc.

What was also striking about the coverage of Gore was how often he came to be judged on his presentational shortcomings. Those sighs and audible harrumphs during the first presidential debate while his opponent was speaking. His make-up in the second debate, so heavily applied that he resembled the Lord High Executioner from an amateur production of *The Mikado*. His tendency to sweat through his shirts during campaign speeches, creating small archipelagos of perspiration around his ribcage. Harry Truman, Dwight D. Eisenhower, Lyndon Johnson and Richard Nixon could hardly be described as natural campaigners, but nonetheless had other skills and qualities to offer. In the age of the performative presidency, where image management was all, no longer were those attributes so highly valued.

The early stages of the Republican race had offered a stirring narrative, for after the toxicity of impeachment, the candidacy of John McCain felt like a cleansing stream. Thundering around New Hampshire aboard his campaign battle bus the 'Straight Talk Express', a gaggle of reporters hanging on his every unfiltered word, he railed against the corrupting influence of big money and called for an overhaul of the campaign finance rules.

Character became his main selling point, and traits political consultants had to fabricate for lesser candidates, McCain had in spades. The former navy pilot also tapped into the newfound respect for old warriors. His personal story, of selflessly turning down the chance of early release in the Hanoi Hilton, which consigned him to nearly five more years as a POW, provided the core of his stump speech. Even veteran reporters went weak at the knees in his presence, which explained why McCain called the travelling press corps his base. New Hampshire voters, who packed his town-hall meetings, adored him too.

Other than being the establishment favourite, George W. Bush, McCain's main rival, seemed everything his father wasn't. Charismatic. Focused on domestic policy – the early hot take on the Texan governor was that he was a policy wonk with a granular grasp of education policy. A born-again Christian, with a bona fide come-to-Jesus moment – the morning after his 40th birthday, when he woke up vowing never to let liquor pass his lips. A true son of the south who revelled in its good ol' boy politics. To win the Lone Star governorship, Bush had even vanquished his father's tormentor Ann Richards, who had mocked Poppy at the 1988 Democratic convention for being born with a silver foot in his mouth, a zinger for the ages.

'The biggest difference between me and my father,' said George W., in what became a stock line, 'is that he went to Greenwich Country Day and I went to San Jacinto Junior High.'[1]

Just as his embrace of the south made him more attuned to the modern-day Republican Party, so, too, did his religiosity. Bush spoke in the tongue of the mega-churches, and happily testified to his faith. Asked during a Republican debate to name his favourite philosopher, he answered, 'Christ, because he changed my heart.'

Bush Sr, thinking his son had committed an egregious gaffe, called the next day to console him. 'Don't worry, son. I don't think the Jesus answer will hurt you very much.'[2] Yet the conversation revealed GHW's blind spots rather than his son's: his failure to appreciate the extent to which the GOP had become a faith-based movement.

George W. Bush's compassionate conservatism was intended to soften the cold-heartedness of Gingrichism, just as his father's kinder, gentler politics was meant to take the rough edges off Reaganism. Moving towards the centre was also an act of political necessity for a party that had gained a paltry 37 per cent of the presidential vote in 1992 and just 40 per cent four years later. This pitch to the political middle also looked like a vote winner. When Clinton first heard the alliterative phrase 'compassionate conservatism', he thought the Democrats were in trouble.[3]

Bush showcased his new-look GOP at the convention in Philadelphia, which was stage-managed to draw attention to the racial inclusivity of the party. Primetime speaking slots were allotted to his future Secretary of State Colin Powell, and also to his future National Security Advisor Condoleezza Rice. So many black preachers delivered invocations, and so many African-Americans performed musical numbers on stage, that a BBC colleague thought it necessary to remind viewers they were indeed watching the Republican convention and there was no need to adjust their sets. Bush was attempting to create a multiracial coalition of the faithful, to make the GOP a bigger, more welcoming tent.

Just as George H. W.'s kinder, gentler politics speech did not stop him from savaging Michael Dukakis, so George W. reached for the machete after McCain trounced him in the New Hampshire primary. As the race moved to South Carolina, the home state of Lee Atwater, it seemed his entire campaign was paying homage to the Republican Party's master of the dark electoral arts.

Bush fringe groups and surrogates bombarded South Carolinians with robo calls and false messaging that smeared McCain's character. The war hero had not fought hard enough for fellow POWs left behind in Vietnam. His wife, Cindy McCain, had an addiction problem. The senator had fathered an African-American love child.

Then there were his policy sins. McCain had opposed tax cuts. The National Right to Life Committee accused him of being soft on abortion. Bush, meanwhile, brazenly pursued an updated version of the southern strategy. First, he re-launched his troubled campaign at Bob Jones University, an evangelical campus in Greenville where interracial dating was still banned. Then, championing states' rights, he endorsed the flying of the Confederate flag above the South Carolina Statehouse, which back then was a hugely contentious issue (McCain did so too, though he afterwards apologised for his cravenness).

Not until 2016 did I cover a viler campaign, for in South Carolina we witnessed so much of what had become fetid about American politics. The relentless negativity, the personal destructiveness, the pandering to prejudice, the culture wars dog-whistling, the infusion of unregulated money and the trampling of truth.

More depressing still, all those tactics worked. Bush won in a landslide, and went on to wrap up the nomination. 'In retrospect, McCain's 2000 campaign may have represented the last off-ramp for the GOP on the road towards the confrontational and tribal conservatism that has transformed the party over the past two decades,' wrote the political commentator Ron Brownstein afterwards.[4]

Gore versus Bush should have been a battle of the centrists, but just as McCain had pushed Bush to the right, so Clinton's affair with Monica Lewinsky had the effect of pushing the vice-president to the left. A supposed compassionate conservative and a one-time New

Democrat ended up producing one of the most polarising election results in recent history.

The country awoke after Election Night to the sight of yellow police tape stretched across the entrances of polling stations in Florida, as if some terrible crime had been committed. So began a 36-day legal and political fight that went all the way to the US Supreme Court. Nationally, Gore won 500,000 more votes than Bush – he actually polled more votes than any other Democrat in history, while only Reagan in 1984 had got more – but Bush had seemingly won the Electoral College.

After the melodrama of the Clinton impeachment came the slapstick farce of the Florida recount, another civics lesson from hell. Electoral officials peered at ballot papers with giant magnifying glasses, as if studying species of endangered butterflies. Foreigners looked on askance, as if viewing America through a hall of fairground mirrors. At one point, as the road to the White House careered through various appellate courts, a diplomat from Robert Mugabe's Zimbabwe suggested sending international observers to oversee the recount.

Maybe it should have come as little surprise that the election ended in a statistical deadlock, with the candidates separated in Florida by just 527 out of six million votes cast, because America had become so evenly split between Democrats and Republicans. From the early '50s until Reagan's first victory in 1980, there had been 15 per cent more registered Democrats than Republicans. In the years after the Reagan landslide that advantage shrank to just 3 per cent.[5]

The United States had become a 50/50 country, which also went a long way towards explaining the trench-warfare dynamic in Washington. The political middle had become something of a no-man's land of emptying electoral terrain.

In the Reagan years, independent voters who did not identify with a party made up a quarter of the electorate. By 2000, it had shrunk to just 6 per cent. Commentators had started talking about the incredible missing middle.

When a magnifying glass was held up to the American model of electing a president, it showed a voting system in a chronic state of democratic disrepair. The butterfly ballot which had flapped its wings in Palm Beach County and caused so much chaos revealed one of its stranger idiosyncrasies: the lack of uniformity in voting, not just between states, but also between the districts within them.

Elderly voters found this particular ballot, designed by a Democratic election supervisor, especially confusing, prompting hundreds of Jewish seniors to vote for Pat Buchanan by mistake. As for those infamous pregnant and hanging chads, they highlighted the inability of antiquated voting machinery to record voting intentions accurately. Republican-leaning districts had more up-to-date technology that produced fewer ballot-reading errors. Malfunctioning machines were most commonly found in the poorer counties of Florida, with a higher proportion of minority voters. Those Democratic vote banks were short-changed.

The closer journalists looked, the more abnormalities we found. In the run-up to the election, Florida officials sent out to the state's 67 counties a list with 50,000 names of ex-felons barred from voting. More than 12,000 of those names were wrong, and almost half of them belonged to African-Americans.[6] Among those blocked from voting was Willie Steen, a veteran from the Gulf War who had gone to vote with his ten year-old, only to be humiliatingly turned away.

When the US Commission on Civil Rights crunched the numbers, it calculated Al Gore had been deprived of 4,752 black votes, nine times more than his opponent's margin of victory.[7] Given the presence in the Governor's Mansion in Tallahassee of George W. Bush's brother Jeb, this felt more like a conspiracy than a cock-up. His Republican Secretary of State, Katherine Harris, a Cruella de Vil lookalike who certified the election results in Florida and became an unlikely star of the recount, seemed like his accomplice.

Rather than letting democracy take its course with a state-wide manual recount, Florida turned into an electoral version of the O. J. Simpson trial. From across the country came armies of attorneys, parachuting in like screaming legal eagles; among them were future conservative luminaries such as John Roberts (whom George W. Bush eventually made Chief Justice of the Supreme Court), Brett Kavanaugh (another future Supreme Court jurist), and a 29-year-old Texan who had clerked for Chief Justice William Rehnquist called Ted Cruz, who put the team together. For every dollar the Democrats spent on legal fees in Florida, the Republicans spent four.[8]

At times, the Florida recount became an extra-judicial fight. In what became known as the Brooks Brothers riot, a flash mob of paid conservative activists stormed an administrative office to stop the recount in Miami-Dade County, a Democratic bastion. The leader of this chino-clad militia was that self-styled 'GOP hitman', Roger Stone.

Perhaps the most audacious electoral heist was carried out by five elderly jurists dressed in black flowing robes, who halted the manual state-wide recount ordered by the Florida Supreme Court that Republicans feared would hand Al Gore the presidency. Instead, the Supreme Court justices decreed that the disputed election should be settled in the highest court in the land. *Gore v. Bush* resulted in a 5–4 ruling, split along ideological lines, in favour of the Texan.

In an especially mendacious twist, given how many African-American voters had been blocked from voting in Florida, the five justices grounded their decision on the equal-protection clause of the 14th Amendment, ratified after the Civil War to safeguard the rights of former slaves. Perhaps embarrassed by their illogic and inconsistency, they did not put their names to their work, and recommended it should be 'limited to the circumstances' of the 2000 election and therefore not be used as a precedent.

The dissenters in the minority essentially accused their conservative colleagues of an electoral smash and grab. 'Although we may never know with complete certainty the identity of the winner of this year's Presidential election,' wrote John Paul Stevens, a liberal jurist nominated by Gerald Ford, 'the identity of the loser is perfectly clear.

It is the Nation's confidence in the judge as an impartial guardian of the rule of law.'

Ruth Bader Ginsburg, who as time went on looked to her liberal admirers like Clinton's greatest legacy item, drew attention to the rank hypocrisy of Antonin Scalia and his originalist colleagues. In overruling the Florida Supreme Court, they had wilfully interfered in a state's interpretation of state law, an approach diametrically opposed to their judicial philosophy. Like her three colleagues, Ginsburg ended by almost spitting out the words 'I respectfully dissent'.

2000 became a before-and-after moment for US democracy. From the passage of the 1965 Voting Rights Act until the end of the twentieth century, there was common agreement that everyone should be allowed to vote and that deliberately preventing them from doing so was unscrupulous and immoral (prior to 1965, Jim Crow laws, such as literacy tests, had been used across the south to prevent blacks from voting).

After 2000, however, suppressing turnout became as central to electoral strategy as maximising turnout, especially for the Republicans. Half of the states have passed legislation making it more difficult to vote. Between 2011 and 2015, 468 voting restrictions were introduced. Under the guise of combating voter fraud, Republican state legislatures especially have passed a panoply of laws restricting early voting opportunities, closing polling stations, penalising voters who skipped just one election and tightening ID regulations. (In Texas, for instance, a gun licence is considered an acceptable form of identification, while student ID cards are not.)

Big turnouts bringing out minority and young voters favour the Democrats, which is why the Republicans have devoted such legislative energy to barring minorities from voting. In this concerted attempt to suppress turnout, Republican governors and state legislatures have found an active ally in the Supreme Court, which repeatedly rubber-stamped anti-democratic practices.

This culminated in 2013, in the *Shelby County v. Holder* decision, when the Supreme Court weakened dramatically the provisions of the 1965 Voting Rights Act by invalidating a practice known as 'preclearance' that prevented local jurisdictions from making changes to voting without federal approval, which had proved effective in protecting minority enfranchisement in counties with a history of discrimination. In a 5–4 decision, the Supreme Court reasoned preclearance was no longer needed because it had been so successful, a train of thought that Ruth Bader Ginsburg likened to discarding an umbrella because you were no longer getting wet. America had become a democracy where qualified voters were actively barred from voting.

Just as the 2000 recount magnified the mechanical inefficiencies in the voting system, so it also exposed the architectural flaws in the electoral system. The founding fathers, for all their cleverness and erudition, made a terrible hash of deciding how to elect their head of state. To safeguard the office of the presidency from mob rule, the much-feared 'passions of the people', they decided designated electors rather than voters should pick the president, an Electoral College chosen by the states under criteria decided by the states.

By the 1820s, most states enacted laws establishing a winner-takes-all principle based on a state-wide popular vote (although, to this day, Nebraska and Maine remain holdouts). It became possible, then, for a successful candidate to amass a majority in the Electoral College without winning the nationwide vote, as happened in 1824 (John Quincy Adams), 1876 (Rutherford B. Hayes), 1888 (Benjamin Harrison), 2000 (George W. Bush) and, later, 2016 (Donald Trump). In closely fought states, a candidate could also win all the electors with the slimmest of pluralities. In Florida, Bush pocketed all 25 electoral votes, despite winning the state by less than 0.1 per cent of the vote.

Much as the US Senate betrayed a small-state bias, with each state getting two senators regardless of population size – the New York borough of Queens has a bigger population than 16 states – so, too, did the make-up of the Electoral College. Just 4 per cent of the country's population controlled 8 per cent of the Electoral College votes.

Another defect that revealed itself over time was the dearth of competitive states – only a dozen or so by the turn of the century, which did not include some of the most populous states in the land, including California, Texas and New York.

Defenders of the status quo argue that deciding the presidency through a nationwide popular vote would create an urban bias, and unfairly marginalise rural voters. Yet abolishing the Electoral College would bring about a parity of influence for voters everywhere. Besides, presidential candidates who campaign in rural states invariably focus their attention on urban centres, rather than waste precious time campaigning in the sparsely populated countryside. Already there is an urban bias.

Changing the system inevitably means challenging the near-sacred belief the founding fathers were blessed with something akin to papal infallibility, and that the US Constitution they produced was near-perfect. This cherished view, fortified by the conservative creed of constitutional originalism and a conviction that the pages of the Constitution are like biblical tablets, has long acted as a bulwark against change. So, too, has the now outdated notion that America is a young and thrusting republic, when in actual fact it is the oldest democracy in the world, and showing signs of age.

Vitally, the framers themselves looked upon their new republic as an experiment in democracy subject to refinement and improvement, which explains why there was a Bill of Rights immediately afterwards and 17 additional constitutional amendments that followed – including the abolition of slavery, the direct election of senators by popular vote and female suffrage. The problem is that the framers made the Constitution notoriously hard to alter – a two-thirds vote in both houses of Congress and ratification by three-quarters of the states.

The Florida debacle, and the Supreme Court's nakedly partisan intervention, meant the new century began with a democratic and constitutional convulsion that divided the country even more deeply than the impeachment crisis.

The 2000 election also produced a new nomenclature to describe this rupture, for it was the first time all the US networks agreed on a colour scheme for their electoral maps. In the on-screen graphics, Republican states would be shaded red, Democrats blue. 'The result was a brand new shorthand,' wrote Steve Kornacki, 'that would define American political culture in the new century.'⁹

With the country deadlocked, David Letterman joked, 'George W. Bush will be the president for the red states and Al Gore will be the president for the blue states.'¹⁰ With uncanny timing, *The West Wing* TV series, which debuted in 1999, presented disgruntled Democrats with an alternative occupant of the White House. 'Jed Bartlett is my president' T-shirts, featuring the 'made-for-Mount-Rushmore' features of the actor Martin Sheen, became *de rigueur* in the liberal enclaves of Washington. Right-wing critics soon labelled the show 'The Left Wing'.

Though the real new president-elect promised to be 'a uniter not a divider', the Bush team came up with a political plan for his first term in office that prioritised energising the base over persuading swing voters – what the political commentator Ron Brownstein called 'the 51 per cent solution'.¹¹ It was a separatist strategy for a separating country: red and blue America.

For a time it seemed modern America's most awful day might be the catastrophe that returned a sense of civility to national politics, halted the slide into tribalism and unified the country. Under the now silent skies in the days after September 11, stores sold out of the Stars and Stripes, tens of thousands queued for hours to donate blood and people of all ages, faiths, skin colours and political persuasions shed tears together at candlelit vigils.

On Capitol Hill, as bodies were still being dragged from the Pentagon, more than 150 Republican and Democrat lawmakers congregated on the steps of the East Front, where they broke out unexpectedly into a rendition of 'America the Beautiful'. Within days, Congress had passed a bipartisan bill to provide $40 billion for anti-terrorism measures and victim aid, a defiant statement of cross-party intent.

George W. Bush, after struggling in those initial chaotic days to summon words that reflected the magnitude of the attacks, finally asserted himself as a national leader. With bullhorn in hand, amidst the tangled wreckage of Ground Zero, he spontaneously came up with some stirring language. 'I can hear you,' he responded, when a fireman complained his words were being drowned out by the clank of heavy machinery. 'The rest of the world hears you. And the people – and the people who knocked down these buildings will hear from us soon!'

Six days after the attacks, in a well-timed act of ecumenism, he also visited the Islamic Center in Washington DC, where he affirmed 'the face of terror is not the true faith of Islam' and attested to how Muslims 'love America just as much as I do'.

His most commanding performance came before a joint session of Congress on 20 September, when he sought to reassure his shell-shocked compatriots and to outline a new national mission. 'We will direct every resource at our command – every means of diplomacy, every tool of intelligence, every instrument of law enforcement, every financial influence, and every necessary weapon of war – to the destruction and to the defeat of the global terror network.'

After his speech, as the chamber stood in unison to applaud, he exchanged bear hugs with the most senior Democrats in the chamber, Tom Daschle and Dick Gephardt. Patriotic bipartisanship had returned to Capitol Hill, and with it an understanding the national interest was again paramount.

As the attacks unfolded on the east coast, I was out west, asleep in Seattle of all places. I awoke to a changed world, and a career severed in two, the before and after of my working life. With the airspace closed, it took me three days to return to Washington, and by the time I reached the still smouldering Pentagon, the reporters from the US networks I found myself stood alongside had affixed flag pins to the lapels.

Much like Los Angeles on my first trip to America, it was hard not to be swept up in the patriotic wave, and for a time many reporters sounded more like participants in the war on terror than its chroniclers. Normal service eventually came to be resumed, but the suspension of journalistic scepticism across large swathes of the media continued largely unabated until after the fall of Saddam Hussein's statue in Firdos Square.

In the weeks following the attacks, there was an ugly thirst for revenge. Despite Bush's best efforts, American Muslims became the target of a spate of Islamophobic reprisal attacks – within the first ten days, some 600 anti-Muslim incidents were recorded. A Pakistani grocer was murdered in Texas. A gunman in Arizona, hunting down Muslims to slaughter, murdered an Indian-born Sikh. In this climate of fearful recrimination, the culture wars flared up as well, as a number of leading evangelicals claimed that a vengeful God was punishing America for its permissiveness.

'I really believe that the pagans, and the abortionists, and the feminists, and the gays and lesbians who are actively trying to make that an alternative lifestyle, the ACLU [American Civil Liberties Union] ... all of them who have tried to secularise America,' declared the Moral Majority preacher Jerry Falwell Sr. 'I point the finger in their face and say, "You helped this happen."' For the most part, however, 'United we stand' truly meant that, as tragedy nourished togetherness.

Polls offered proof of this political coming together. In the final Gallup survey before the hijackers boarded those four planes, Bush had an approval rating of 51 per cent, which reflected America's 50/50 split. Afterwards, as Americans rallied around their commander-in-chief, it surged to 86 per cent. If not entirely forgiven, the acrimony of the Florida recount and Supreme Court was temporarily forgotten. Two weeks after 9/11, almost nine out of ten Democrats and independents approved of his presidency.[12] As the leader of a country united once again by a common enemy, Bush finally gained legitimacy.

Unified government, however, did not necessarily mean good governance, and whereas the legislation of the Cold War years made the country stronger, the response to 9/11 sometimes had a self-destructive effect. In the legislative rush to respond to the attacks, Congress passed the USA Patriot Act by the end of October, hurried legislation agreed to without sufficient oversight – many lawmakers did not even have time to read its contents – granting the federal government sweeping and draconian powers.

Sneak-and-peek powers enabled FBI agents to search homes or businesses secretly without informing the owners. It became easier for the federal government to scoop up data, such as web-surfing histories and medical records. When investigating a single person, the FBI could seize a hospital's entire database.[13] For now, however, security trumped liberty, scratching at a sacred American ideal.

By the end of November, Bush took further advantage of the blank chequebook he had been handed by issuing a military order decreeing that terror suspects would not be put through the US criminal justice system. Instead, they would be tried and sentenced by military commissions. The breadth of the order, which swept aside US courts and longstanding legal protections including habeas corpus, raised obvious constitutional red flags. All that was needed to hold a non-citizen indefinitely was the 'reason to believe' that they were involved in terrorism.

Even Bush's hard-line Attorney General, John Ashcroft, was shocked by the lack of due process. 'You've got to be kidding me,' he responded, after reading the draft plan for military commissions, which sidelined the Justice Department and came under the purview of the Pentagon.[14] Senior Democrats expressed concerns about the lack of consultation and weakening of constitutional protections, but knew, too, the public was on the president's side, which muffled their opposition.[15]

Next came the establishment in January of the detention camp at Guantánamo Bay: 'the legal equivalent of outer space', as one government official put it. This Cuban outpost was chosen precisely because terror suspects would not be able to apply for protections under US criminal law. 'Gitmo' came to be viewed as an American gulag, but when it first opened there was little outcry from Democrats.[16]

When I visited Guantánamo, an unexpectedly picturesque outpost hemmed in by Cuban minefields and watchtowers, we were told the detainees were given 'Happy Meals' from the McDonald's on the base if they delivered actionable intelligence, but they were also subjected to torture.

There was near unanimous support for the opening phase of the war on terror, the hunt for Osama bin Laden, which led to the ousting of the Taliban after it refused to hand over the Al Qaeda leader. Operation Enduring Freedom had broad international backing and cross-party agreement. Only when the war on terror moved from the necessary war in Afghanistan to the unnecessary war in Iraq did national unity seriously begin to fray. It was then that the Bush administration started to politicise its response to 9/11, turning this national tragedy into a partisan wedge issue.

The strategy was set in January 2002, ahead of that year's midterm congressional elections, when Bush's political Svengali, Karl Rove, told the Republican National Committee that candidates 'can go to the country on this issue [Iraq]' because voters 'trust the Republican Party to do a better job of protecting and strengthening America's military might and thereby protecting America'.[17]

So whereas George H. W. Bush had waited until after the midterms to seek war authorisation from Congress for the first Gulf War, his son demanded a rubber stamp in October 2002, on the eve of the election, in a brazen attempt to corner sceptical Democrats. The authorisation vote passed, and the midterms became a khaki election. For only the fourth time since the Civil War, the president's party improved its showing in the House.

Pushing for war in Iraq came at the cost of national unity. Whereas three-quarters of Americans backed military action in Afghanistan, only half supported the invasion of Iraq. A year after 9/11, the president's approval rating among Democrats plummeted to 50 per cent – 42 per cent lower than among Republicans, which showed how the partisan breach had reopened. By January 2004, less than a quarter of Democrats thought Bush had been right to strike Iraq.[18] Impending war had turned America red and blue again.

In the lead-up to the war, which began with the shock-and-awe bombardment of Baghdad in March 2003, the welter of false and misleading justifications showed how much America was moving away from being a fact-based polity. Rejecting claims repeatedly made by the Bush White House, the bipartisan 9/11 Commission concluded afterwards that Iraq had no cooperative or corroborative relationship with Osama bin Laden with regard to the September 11 attacks. Nor were stockpiles of any weapons of mass destruction ever found, demolishing the main justification for military action. Small wonder 'Bush lied, people died' became the chant of his critics.

Never was the White House embarrassed by its truth-twisting. Instead, it became part of the Bush administration's war-on-terror swank. 'We're an empire now, and when we act, we create our own reality,' a Bush administration aide, widely thought to be Karl Rove, told Ron Suskind of *The New York Times*. 'And while you're studying that reality ... we'll act again, creating other new realities ... We're history's actors ... and you, all of you, will be left to just study what we do.'

The Bush administration was trying to define public reality. Aided by a pliable press, it did so with effortless ease. On the front page of *The New York Times* came alarming stories written by Judith Miller giving prominence to the administration's falsehoods and bolstering the case for war, which most of us, myself included, ended up regurgitating.

After coming up with a dubious *casus belli* for invading Iraq, Bush delivered a false declaration of victory. He did so, of course, from the flight deck of the USS *Abraham Lincoln*, after landing hours before, *Top Gun*-like, in green flight fatigues, having briefly taken the controls mid-flight of a Viking warplane. Sailing back to California from the Persian Gulf having completed the longest naval deployment since the Vietnam War, it was the ship's crew that hung the notorious 'Mission Accomplished' sign.

Yet White House image-makers, happy with staging that looked like the handiwork of Hollywood producer Jerry Bruckheimer (*Pearl Harbor, Black Hawk Down, Top Gun*), kept it as the backdrop. 'Major combat operations in Iraq have ended,' declared the president. Here again, the White House created its own reality, to claim success on the war on terror and also to win an election. The flight deck of the USS *Abraham Lincoln* became the launch-pad for Bush's 2004 re-election campaign.

Had the mission truly been accomplished, history could have been very different. At that time, 104 US troops had lost their lives, a small fraction of the final death toll of 4,424. As it was, Bush turned the American liberators of Iraq into the American occupiers of Iraq, a strategic error of immense scale, an overextension of US power for which the country continues to pay an enormous price.

Military chiefs, such as General Tommy Franks, expected the US military involvement in Iraq to be limited to 90 days. Neither the Pentagon nor the State Department had been instructed to plan for an open-ended US presence in the country. What followed was calamitous, just as old-timers from the first Gulf War, such as Brent Scowcroft, James Baker and General Norman Schwarzkopf had predicted. Once again, America suffered from the shift in leadership at the end of the Cold War away from its greatest generation.

During this period of maximum peril, when the country needed another FDR, America was instead led by a foreign policy neophyte, whose world view was simplistic and uninformed, and whose initial bond with his first National Security Advisor, Condoleezza Rice, was forged through their shared love of American football and the realisation during a get-to-know-you session at Kennebunkport that they both spoke in sporting idioms, such as 'slam dunk'.

Almost 20 years on, after the mistakes of Iraq have been litigated endlessly, the incompetence, the strategic short-sightedness, the blind faith and imperial hubris still beggar belief.

There were the errors of language: the Manichean 'good versus evil' frame purloined from the conservative intellectual Samuel Huntington that implied a clash of civilisations between the

Judaeo-Christian and Islamic worlds. There was the all-embracing term 'war on terror', which instantly made every pound-shop jihadist feel part of a worldwide Holy War and also implied that the conflict would be ceaseless and open-ended. There was the bellicose invective of Bush's 'Axis of Evil' 2002 State of the Union address targeting Iraq, Iran and North Korea, which suggested his unilateralism had no bounds and which accelerated attempts in Pyongyang and Tehran to develop nuclear weapons.

There were the mortifying lapses in knowledge – as he waded into Mesopotamia, Bush did not even understand the difference between Sunni and Shia Muslims, the sectarian line that now divided the Arab world. There was the arrogance of the neo-conservatives pushing for the overthrow of Saddam Hussein, who believed the second Gulf War would be a 'cakewalk'. There was the criminal lack of post-war planning and foresight. After being briefed for the first time by Jay Garner, the former general put in charge of the reconstruction effort, all Bush inquired about was whether he came from Florida. Then, after asking no more questions, the president wished him well with a backslapping 'Kick ass, Jay!'

There was the flawed notion that the Iraq War would curb terrorism, when actually it became a 'cause celebre for jihadists', in the words of a US intelligence report, that was 'shaping a new generation of terrorist leaders and operatives'.[19] There was the misplaced messianic belief it was possible to create western-style democracies in countries such as Afghanistan and Iraq without an electoral tradition. Covering the first presidential election in Afghanistan brought this home. Stirring though it was to see lines of burqa-clad women queuing up outside the polling stations to use their suffrage for the first time, many of them had been browbeaten into voting for certain candidates by their husbands, who themselves had been browbeaten by local warlords or imams. Afghanistan, like Iraq, was a mess, with the Taliban resurgent. In 2008, the final year of Bush's presidency, its black-turbaned holy warriors operated still in 33 out of the country's 34 provinces, and managed to detonate some 7,200 improvised explosive devices (IEDs). That year, 153 US military lost their lives, the most since the Afghan war began. In 2009, fatalities more than doubled to 310.

The situation in Iraq was far worse. The war and its aftermath claimed the lives of 110,600 Iraqis, though many estimates put that number even higher. More than two million Iraqis were forced to flee the country. In addition to the more than 4,000 Americans who lost their lives, 31,952 were wounded in action.

The human cost to the homeland of all those broken bodies and tortured minds is still being tallied. In Afghanistan I saw for myself the fear on the faces of young soldiers who went out on foot patrols knowing they could be ambushed any instant by Taliban snipers; whose convoys of Humvees ventured down tracks regularly booby-trapped with IEDs; who went to surf-and-turf night in the mess hall dressed in their combat helmets and body armour, knowing their steak and lobster dinners could be interrupted by incoming shellfire from insurgents who had learned the dinner tables would be especially crowded those particular evenings.

The US military tried to provide for their troops the comforts of American life, from Seattle-style coffee shops to pizza parlours and burger joints. But this was a bloody war zone. Homecomings could be just as traumatising. Up to a fifth of Iraq War veterans suffered from PTSD. Military suicides started increasing in 2006, and rose to a new record in 2009, when 310 servicemen and women took their own lives, the same number lost in combat that year in Afghanistan. All too frequently we reported on returning servicemen who had either killed themselves or murdered loved ones.

As well as the blood, there was the treasure. The cost of the Iraq War to American taxpayers has been estimated to be between $1.5 trillion and $3 trillion. Books balanced when George W. Bush entered the White House now were drenched in red ink. By 2005, America was borrowing $2 billion a day from abroad.[20] The final budget of the Bush presidency showed a deficit of $1.4 trillion, with the military now accounting for 20 per cent of government spending, or more than 5 per cent of GDP.[21] With America in need of a credit line, China, its geopolitical rival, would come to hold $1 trillion of US debt.

The opportunity cost was incalculable. Dollars allotted to nation-building in Afghanistan and Iraq – the Pentagon banished that term, but constructed roads, schools and communications systems nonetheless – could have been spent on nation-building at home. The social-security system might have been refinanced. America's decrepit electricity grid, revealed to be so fragile during the northeast blackout of 2003, which many of us in New York that day feared was the start of a second wave of terror strikes, was in chronic need of repair. Bridges were collapsing – a report in 2019 found that 47,000 were structurally deficient, including the Brooklyn Bridge – and roads crumbling. In the '50s, the entire US interstate highway system had cost the equivalent of $540 billion to build, a third of what was spent in Iraq.[22] It was not just the debt burden of the Iraq War that ended up having such dire economic consequences. The soaring price of oil, which went from $20 a barrel to $140, ignited a financial chain reaction. With the United States forced to pay so much more for oil, the Federal Reserve had to cut interest rates to guard against an 'oil shock' recession. Awash with so much cheap money, the housing bubble became even more dangerously inflated. Soaring petrol prices were a body blow to the US auto industry. Consumers stopped buying sports utility vehicles, the gas-guzzling SUVs that clogged suburbia but kept Detroit solvent.

The diplomatic cost is well chronicled. 9/11 had presented the opportunity to revive US global leadership, as America became the recipient of a torrent of 'nous sommes tous Américains' goodwill. In prosecuting the war on terror, however, the Bush administration opted for extreme unilateralism. The Bush doctrine came to be based on a crude loyalty test: if countries were not with the United States, slavishly and unquestionably, they were, by definition, against it. Close allies such as France, whose then president, Jacques Chirac, had been the first international leader to visit Ground Zero, were pilloried when they refused to support the Iraq War. Even Air Force One served 'Freedom Fries' rather than French fries, aping *The Simpsons*-inspired 'cheese-eating surrender monkeys' jingoism of the New York tabloids.

While close allies were shunned, Vladimir Putin, a leader deemed to be in the 'with us' camp, was granted *carte blanche* to conduct his own brutal war on terror in Chechnya. The White House also averted its gaze as Putin – whose soul had been peered into by the president and given a clean bill of moral health – started reversing Russia's democratic reforms and consolidating his authoritarian power.

A president who entered office promising a strong but humble foreign policy flouted the international norms and institutions created and enforced by America after the war. Bush bypassed the United Nations Security Council when it refused to pass a resolution authorising the war in Iraq. He violated the Geneva Conventions by subjecting 'enemy combatants' to various forms of torture, including waterboarding. Top-secret CIA black sites, used to interrogate enemy combatants, dotted the world. America was acting, in the words of the historian Michael Burleigh, 'like a rogue state under the flag of high principles'.[23]

None of this troubled Bush or Dick Cheney, who now acted more like a co-president. 'The only legitimacy we really need comes on the back of an M1A1 tank,' the vice-president affirmed during an internal White House debate over Iraq.[24] Raw power, however, was not the same as authoritative power. Other than the most unquestioning allies, Tony Blair, who was dubbed 'Bush's poodle', and John Howard, who described Australia as the US 'deputy' of the Asia-Pacific (Bush later promoted it to 'sheriff'), few countries were saying '*nous sommes tous Américains*' any more.

To America's international reputation the collateral damage was immense, whether it was incurred by the grotesquery of Abu Ghraib, where prisoners were tortured, raped, sodomised and humiliated, and which the Vatican described as 'a more serious blow to the United States than September 11th', or the Haditha massacre, when a group of US marines shot dead 24 unarmed Iraqi civilians in November 2005, a modern-day Mai Lai, the horrific mass murder during the Vietnam War.[25] For millions of international onlookers, and especially those in the Muslim world, the watchtowers and orange jumpsuits of

Guantánamo Bay became as much a symbol of post-9/11 America as the Statue of Liberty.

What was most surprising perhaps was how little 9/11 directly changed the everyday lives of Americans themselves. After the decadence of the '80s, the irrational exuberance of the '90s, the frivolity of impeachment and the smugness of the millennial celebrations, it seemed inevitable that the shock of 9/11 would end what the conservative columnist Charles Krauthammer called its 'holiday from history'.[26]

But for all Bush's rhetorical efforts to imbue the country with a sense of national purpose similar in scope and ambition to the Cold War, there ended up being a gaping discrepancy between the seriousness of the moment and the demands made of the American people by the president. New security measures brought some mild inconveniences – Americans had to queue for longer when they took a flight, making some travellers more afraid of airports than of flying. The Patriot Act curtailed certain civil liberties, not that it generated much concern or outrage.

In the main, however, Americans were not asked to make many sacrifices. There was no repeat of Kennedy's famed Cold War admonition: 'Ask not what your country can do for you – ask what you can do for your country.' Rather, Bush successfully pushed for another multi-billion tax cut, the second of his two-year presidency, even as the bills from Iraq and Afghanistan started to mount.

When Bush's first Treasury Secretary, Paul O'Neill, raised concerns about enacting a $350 billion tax cut in the midst of a costly war, he was fired. 'You know, Paul, Reagan proved deficits don't matter,' O'Neill was told by Dick Cheney in late 2002,[27] a comment that spoke of the obsession with tax cuts and durability of the cult of Reagan.

Over the next ten years, the tax cuts of 2001 and 2003 took $3.2 trillion out of the economy, which is partly why Barack Obama took office facing an annual $1 trillion deficit. As a result, between 2001 and 2010 the national debt saw its biggest decade rise in US history. Moreover, these tax cuts aggravated the problem of income inequality. Up to 45 per cent of the 2001 tax cuts went to the top 1 per cent.[28]

Even as Bush expanded and extended his war on terror, conscription was never seriously considered – although the Harlem congressman Charles Rangel introduced a call-up bill to make the political point that black boys from poor neighbourhoods would be doing much of the fighting. Though far too many Purple Heart families were created by the post-9/11 wars, less than half of 1 per cent of Americans experienced active duty in the decade after the attacks.[29] Army recruitment actually fell by late 2005 to its lowest levels in 25 years, because new recruits understandably were deterred by the bloodshed in Iraq.

The Pentagon was forced to offer cash inducements and the fast-tracking of citizenship for immigrants prepared to sign up. There was an increase, too, in the number of moral waivers granted to convicted felons, which often meant it was easier to fight in Iraq than to vote to select the next commander-in-chief.

Such was the myopic focus on counter-terrorism that other pressing problems were neglected or made worse. This was true of the national debt crisis, climate change (which, in any case, the Bush administration showed little interest in combating) and the response to the workplace revolution wrought by information technology. Other problems, such as the mass-shooting epidemic, Bush actively made worse, in this instance by allowing the ban on assault weapons to lapse in 2004. The 1994 law brought in by the Clinton administration, which had contributed to a drop in gun fatalities, banned the military-style AR-15 semi-automatic rifle, a weapon the NRA promoted as 'America's rifle' that was used with such murderous effect at Aurora, Sandy Hook, Las Vegas and Parkland, among other mass shootings.

After a brief remission, which did not even last until the first anniversary of September 11, it was extraordinary how quickly normalcy returned to American life. And normalcy meant polarisation. The experience of the Texan bluegrass band the Dixie

Chicks served as a post-9/11 parable. In January 2003, the group had performed the national anthem at the Super Bowl. Then in March, during an appearance in London, the band's lead singer, Natalie Maines, dared to criticise George W. Bush over Iraq. 'We do not condone this war,' she said, to cheers from her British audience. 'And we're ashamed that the president of the United States is from Texas.' Within weeks, the Dixie Chicks faced a boycott, with their songs removed from the playlists of country and western radio stations. In blue America, they became folk heroes. In red America, they were persona non grata. The Bush administration's 'for us or against us' doctrine now permeated almost every aspect of national life.

After five manic years covering the presidencies of George W. Bush and Bill Clinton, in late 2003 I left America, but not the 9/11 beat. I headed to South Asia to cover the war on terror from the sharp end, that tip of the spear in Afghanistan and Pakistan. Just before I headed to the departure lounge, however, there was one final American curio to report on: the gubernatorial race in California, which ended with another movie star occupying the Governor's Mansion.

The rise of Arnold Schwarzenegger did not offer a frame-by-frame preview of Donald Trump's ascent to the presidency. For a start, 'The Governator' was a moderate Republican: a champion of climate change who was sympathetic towards Mexican immigrants. Yet he, too, benefited from the fusion of politics and celebrity, and from a voter revolt against the establishment.

In this instance, it was the Democratic Governor Gray Davis, a bland, identikit career politician who suffered the rare humiliation of being recalled, a provision under Californian state law that allowed voters to unseat unpopular governors midway through their term, following a petition of angry citizens. The movie star made himself the face of the recall, after he announced his intention to run on *The Tonight Show with Jay Leno*. Just as Trump claimed only a businessman could mend Washington, so Schwarzenegger sold the idea it would take an action hero to save Sacramento.[30]

173

With Iraq in such a mess, and Osama bin Laden still at large, I flew out of a country facing still the gravest of national challenges. Once again, however, politics seemed frivolous and unserious.

I watched *America Decides 2004* from Islamabad, having travelled there in the expectation that Osama bin Laden would make a last-minute intervention in the election. This the Al Qaeda leader duly did four days before polling day by releasing a 15-minute video, delivered to the nearby Al Jazeera bureau in the Pakistani capital, which mocked George W. Bush for continuing to read *The Pet Goat* to schoolchildren, even after the Twin Towers were aflame. Rather than damage the president, it produced a late surge in his favour that may well have lifted him to victory.

By turning his 500,000-vote deficit from the 2000 election into a two million-vote plurality, Bush became the first presidential candidate since his father to poll more than 50 per cent. His winning margin, though, was slim: the narrowest, at just 2.4 per cent, of any incumbent in history. Had 60,000 votes shifted in Ohio, the Massachusetts Senator John Kerry, whose initials were also JFK, would have become president. When voter irregularities were uncovered in Ohio, the GOP was accused of stealing the election. For a second time, Bush's legitimacy was brought into question.[31] Again, the Democrats found it hard to accept they had truly lost.

Monitoring all this from South Asia was easier than expected, partly because the recreation halls of US bases in Afghanistan piped in Fox News and other cable channels from home, but also because so much of the 2004 campaign played out online. The unexpected rise of the early Democratic frontrunner Howard Dean, a little-known doctor from Vermont who successfully harnessed mounting anti-war sentiment among Democrats, was an internet phenomenon. It showed that in the hands of an insurgent like Dean, who raised money online and also built a nationwide virtual network, the web was something of a magic carpet.

What the internet maketh, however, the internet could just as easily taketh away. The 'Dean scream', that primeval howl disgorged after he trailed a disappointing third in the Iowa Caucus, became the world's first political meme, a viral sensation on the new video-sharing website YouTube. For Dean, death came by a million views.

During the general election campaign later in the year, the Democratic nominee John Kerry also fell victim to the malignancy of the web, when a group calling itself Swift Boat Veterans for Truth slandered his service in the Vietnam War by claiming, speciously, that he had made exaggerated claims about his bravery. His 'swiftboating' introduced a new neologism into the political lexicon, shorthand for a smear campaign based on mistruths. It also illustrated how efficiently the internet could propagate defamatory disinformation.

On television spots for their original attack ad, Kerry's accusers spent just $500,000, chump change in the midst of what became the first billion-dollar presidential campaign. Then, free of charge, they watched their ad light up the web. Soon the Swift Boat Veterans website was receiving more traffic than the John Kerry home page, crashing its servers.

Republicans were especially quick to grasp the potential of this new medium in marrying data acquisition and traditional canvassing techniques. This allowed for customised messaging targeting individuals – the hacking, in effect, of voters based on invading their privacy and both mirroring and altering their behaviour. Though only in its infancy, the internet was already upending politics at breakneck speed and in ways we didn't fully comprehend.

During the campaign, Bush pursued his 51 per cent strategy, after heeding advice from his pollster Matthew Dowd, who had been struck by the vanishing middle in presidential elections. 'It's about *motivation* rather than *persuasion*', Dowd told Karl Rove. 'We maximise the number of Republicans on Election Day and we win.'[32]

Bush therefore moved to the right, and mobilised the conservative base by speaking out strongly against gay marriage in his 2004 State of the Union address. Afterwards, he endorsed a constitutional amendment banning same-sex marriage. True to his 51 per cent strategy, Rove fought an aggressive ground war, building an organisation of 1.4 million volunteers to boost conservative turnout. The Democrats, by contrast, could only muster 233,000 helpers.[33] Bush won by 52 per cent of the vote.

Close though the nationwide result was, the election saw more than a thousand local landslides. Either Bush or Kerry carried a majority of the nation's 3,153 counties by a margin of at least 20 per cent. 'Never before in modern times,' noted *The Washington Times*, 'has so competitive a national election been the sum of so many uncompetitive parts.'[34] Since 1976, the number of these so-called landslide counties had doubled, proof that like-minded Americans were not just attending the same churches and clubs, but making their homes in like-minded communities.[35]

The Democrats were clustering in the cities and suburbs. Republicans were congregating in rural areas and the 'exurbs', neighbourhoods beyond the suburbs in the countryside. The 'Big Sort' was how the political scientist Jim Bishop described this herd-like migration. 'What had happened over three decades wasn't a simple increase in political partisanship,' he wrote, 'but a more fundamental kind of self-perpetuating, self-reinforcing social division.'[36]

Political allegiance could now be predicted not just by whether a voter shopped at Walmart or Wholefoods, listened to National Public Radio or Rush Limbaugh, drank Chardonnay or Coors Light or drove a pick-up truck or a Prius, but also by their postcode. And though the country looked more homogeneous, with its soulless strip malls and ubiquitous Starbucks, Home Depots and Toyota dealerships, the Big Sort was creating two parallel Americas.

As the century progressed, these tribal groups became more ideologically unswerving, with liberals and conservatives embracing liberal and conservative views across a range of issues. Also they became ever more suspicious of each other and antagonistic. 'The Left believes right-wing tribalism – bigotry, racism – is tearing the country apart,' noted the Yale academic Amy Chua. 'The Right believes that left-wing tribalism – identity politics, political correctness – is tearing the country apart.'[37] America was experiencing a political segregation.

The process of gerrymandering, where electoral boundaries were manipulated to favour one party, became an accelerant of polarisation because it increased the number of uncompetitive seats in the House of Representatives. Assured of victory in the general election, incumbents adopted more doggedly partisan positions to guard against a primary challenge from more extreme members of their own party. Moderates who reached across the aisle to forge bipartisan compromise became especially vulnerable, which depleted the already dwindling ranks of pragmatists on Capitol Hill. Gerrymandering was not the primary cause of polarisation, but its effect was to reinforce political tribalism, especially when overlaid with the self-gerrymandering effect of the Big Sort.

Still there were blue states with Republican governors, such as California, New York and Massachusetts, and red states, such as Oklahoma and Montana, run by Democrats, but the 2004 election underscored the trend-lines of recent campaigns: blue states were becoming bluer; red states were becoming redder. The south was becoming more Republican, with Lincoln's Grand Old Party picking up five Senate seats in the states of the Old Confederacy, and leaving Mary Landrieu of Louisiana as the Democrats' sole Deep South senator. The new Congress also reflected this divisiveness. According to *Congressional Quarterly*, 2005 was the most partisan year on Capitol Hill since it had started taking a measure.[38]

For all the talk in 2004 of the rise of a digital democracy, one of the year's most portentous political developments came on television and did not involve a politician. For a season finale of his hit show *Survivor: Marquesas*, the TV producer Mark Burnett hired the Wollman Skating Rink in Central Park, which Donald Trump had renovated in the '80s. Seeing the tycoon in action, Burnett had the idea of making him the frontman in a new format.

The challenge – and, remarkably, it did require persuasion – was getting Trump to sign up. Reality television was 'for the bottom-feeders of society', the tycoon had sneered. His agent – who, fittingly enough, was fired not long afterwards – warned him against doing it. After meeting in Trump Tower, though, the two men shook hands on a deal. Originally, Trump's screen-time would be limited to a brief cameo at the end of each episode. Then, in future seasons, other celebrity entrepreneurs, such as Richard Branson and Martha Stewart, would supersede him. When executives at NBC watched the rushes from Trump's first boardroom scene, however, they realised he, rather than the contestants, should be the star.[39]

Back in Washington, season two of the Bush administration featured a re-emboldened president claiming an emphatic mandate. Along with the White House, the Republicans controlled the Senate, the House and a majority of governorships. The talk again was of that great white whale of American politics, the permanent Republican majority.

'The people made it clear what they wanted,' Bush declared in his first post-election press conference. 'I earned capital in the campaign, political campaign, and I intend to spend it.'

Remodelling social security through partial privatisation became his top domestic priority. This proved to be the first mistake of his error-strewn second term. The harder Bush tried to sell his reform proposals, the more public and congressional support dwindled. By the summer, Bush's plan was flat-lining. After Hurricane Katrina came ashore in August, and caused the flooding that marooned his presidency, it never stood any hope of resuscitation.

That summer the nation's attention, if not initially the president's, was on New Orleans, where the same fatal incompetence that beset the post-war effort in Iraq pervaded the federal disaster response along the battered Gulf Coast. With military helicopters buzzing overhead and columns of Humvees barrelling through the putrid floodwater, the Big Easy became a Baghdad on the Bayou. America's commander-in-chief, however, was AWOL.

When the storm made landfall, Bush was at his Texan ranch on the 27th day of his summer vacation. Then, he flew to sunny San Diego for a few days rather than the Gulf shore. Still in holiday mode, he did not even turn on his television to see the same jolting footage that had horrified the country: of residents stranded on rooftops pleading for help and of the hellish scenes inside the Louisiana Superdome, which was now a lawless thunderdome.

Not until aides compiled a video splicing together these distressing images did Bush begin to get a sense of the horror unfolding on his watch. En route to Washington, Air Force One flew over the devastated area, a change in flight path intended to evidence concern. Instead, the photographs of him taken on board peering through a plane window at the devastation down below underscored his physical and emotional detachment.

Bush's belated visit to the flood zone turned into an even bigger PR disaster when he praised the hapless Federal Emergency Management Agency director Michael Brown with the immortal words, 'Brownie, you're doing a heck of a job.' Thus, he added disaster relief to the lengthening list of functions the US government used to perform competently but now made a hash of. The Republican critique about the ineffectiveness of government had been authenticated by a Republican administration.

The Bush White House tried to shift the blame onto the Democratic mayor of New Orleans and the Democratic governor of Louisiana, which meant partisan point-scoring impeded the relief effort. Calls to the West Wing from Governor Kathleen Blanco went unanswered, she later complained, so she could be scapegoated. Partly in retaliation, Blanco resisted Bush's attempts to federalise the National Guard. 'I've got thousands of people here in the trenches,' Blanco told Bush in an angry phone call, 'while you play politics.'[40] A total of 1,836 people ended up losing their lives.

Hurricane Katrina revealed how the disaster in Iraq had knock-on effects at home. In an early teleconference with FEMA officials, Bush displayed his customary lack of curiosity by failing to ask any questions. Then, he hurried off to prepare for a speech to the nation on Iraq, his overriding priority.[41] The problem, as Michael Brown testified afterwards to Congress, was that Katrina was a natural disaster rather than a terror strike. This made it harder to mobilise a federal government fixated by 9/11.

Whether it was Katrina, Iraq or his failure to elevate a Bush loyalist, Harriet Miers, to the Supreme Court, the president looked powerless. All the political capital accrued through his re-election was now rendered worthless. Less than a year into his second term, he had lost control of his presidency. At the midterm congressional elections the following year, Bush attempted once more to portray his opponents as soft on the war on terror by labelling them the party of 'cut and run' in Iraq. In what was the bloodiest year of the conflict so far, this played into the Democrats' hands by turning the election into a referendum on his wartime leadership. The GOP lost both the House and Senate, and Nancy Pelosi became the first female Speaker in the country's history. The permanent Republican majority had swum off again into the deep.

When the new Congress convened, Bush eyed immigration reform as an area of possible cross-party consensus. Therefore he pushed the biggest overhaul of immigration in 20 years, bolstering border security while at the same time offering the chance of legal status to the 12 million undocumented immigrants. Yet the politics and economics of immigration had changed. Automation meant the business lobby, the most pro-immigrant constituency within the conservative movement, no longer needed so much cheap labour. After the end of the Cold War, taking in refugees from ideological combat zones such as Vietnam and Cuba was no longer such a moral imperative.

The attacks of September 11 heightened suspicions of immigrants, while the influx of unauthorised Hispanics over the southern border aroused nativist concerns and emboldened Republican restrictionists. Right-wing talk-show hosts, who did so much to shape the debate, immediately called Bush's immigration plan, and the path it offered to citizenship, a 'shamnesty'. 'We will not surrender America!' became the talk-show rallying cry.

Washington politics, and the dearth of bipartisan goodwill, played a part in killing off Bush's proposals. Democrats, including the freshman Senator Barack Obama, paid lip service to reform but loaded the White House bill with amendments they knew would destroy it. With only 12 of the 49 Republican senators supporting the president, it was defeated. Bush could have done more to pressure Republican lawmakers into backing reform, but shied away from confronting the right wing of his party. Conservative moderation had suffered another crushing defeat. Hopes the GOP could become a more racially plural party were dashed. Bush and Karl Rove's multiracial coalition of the godly would never come to fruition.

With the failure of compassionate conservatism and the discrediting of neo-conservatism, the muscular and militaristic strain of thought that propelled America into Iraq, the Republican Party faced an intellectual crisis, not that it saw it as such. The thought vacuum came to be filled by what might be called the loudmouth right: talk-shown hosts such as Rush Limbaugh; anchors on Fox News, like Glenn Beck, Bill O'Reilly and Sean Hannity; polemicists such as Ann Coulter, the author of *How to Talk to a Liberal (If You Must)* and *Adios America: The Left's Plan to Turn our Country into a Third World Hellhole*; and online agitators such as Andrew Breitbart, the founder in 2007 of Breitbart News, and Steve Bannon, his alt-right colleague. Ideas were now less important than talking points and articles of faith. Winning whatever was the cultural battle of the hour was paramount. The more extreme the commentary, the more money it made, which prompted the conservative intellectual David Brooks to opine: 'Conservatism went downmarket in search of revenue.'[42] All of these thought leaders, the new profit-driven prophets of the right, led the conservative movement further down the nativist and populist path.

For millions of Americans, the collapse of Lehman Brothers on 15 September 2008 had a more immediate and lasting impact than the destruction of the Twin Towers on 11 September 2001. In some ways, the psychological wreckage was more devastating. Ten million people lost their homes. Unemployment hit double figures, and did not fall below 8 per cent until 2012. Three years after the crash, US house prices were still a third below their peak, and a quarter of homeowners languished in negative equity.[43] Many Americans felt like castaways in a global economy they found increasingly hard to fathom, let alone navigate and prosper from. Just as 9/11 undermined faith in the country's national security, so the financial collapse shattered confidence in its economic security. Twin emotions of fear and desperation were there waiting to be exploited.

This was an especially biting recession, the worst since the Great Depression. Those thrown out of work found it harder to re-enter the labour market. From World War II until 1991, it had ordinarily taken eight months for employment levels to return to their old peak after the trough of a recession. After 1991, it took 38 months, according to Raghuram Rajan, an economics professor at the University of Chicago. Following the Great Recession, it was expected to take five years or more.[44]

In an increasingly automated economy, the downturn provided an excuse for firms to replace workers with robots. Businesses restructured their operations to make them less reliant on human beings. Many Americans found themselves on the wrong side of globalisation, exposed to competition from low-wage unskilled workers abroad and also, for the first time, from low-wage high-skilled workers.

Before the recession, the construction industry absorbed a lot of unskilled labour. The housing crash wiped out those jobs. In an economy configured around highly skilled workers and those with very few skills at all, the MIT economist David Autor identified what he called the missing middle. Inexorably, employment polarisation fuelled income segregation. Between 1999 and 2007, income for the top 1 per cent grew by 275 per cent. For the bottom fifth it was a measly 18 per cent.[45]

America's post-9/11 climate of fear also acted as a brake on recovery. Because of visa restrictions brought in to combat terrorism, it became harder for international students to remain in America after completing their studies, depriving Silicon Valley of some of the finest foreign brains. In a century when America could only hope to maintain its dominance through innovation, creativity and brainpower, visa clampdowns blocked high-end talent. Anxieties about allowing another Mohamed Atta, a ringleader of the 9/11 attacks, into the country made it more difficult, as the commentator Fareed Zakaria observed, for the next Steve Jobs, the son of a Syrian refugee, to make a new life in America.

When the economy did start to recover, the growth was unevenly spread geographically. After the Great Recession, half of new business creation occurred in just 20 counties. Three-quarters of the venture capital went to just three states – California, Massachusetts and New York – all of them reliably Democratic. Just 31 of the country's 3,000-plus counties came to account for a third of GDP. 'It's now clear that geographic inequality is creating another 1 per cent problem,' wrote the journalist Alan Greenblatt, an inequality that could be mapped and which matched the growing political red/blue split.[46]

The missing middle. Job polarisation. A rural-metropolitan divide. The language of economics now mirrored the language of politics. This was no coincidence, for the two were symbiotic. Since the mid-'70s, the widening partisan divide tracked closely with the expanding income divide. Healthy democracies have always relied on a prosperous middle class. Democratic decay was partly a consequence of this economic hollowing out. America's broken politics was tied to America's broken economy.

The Bush administration, like the Federal Reserve, had been slow to see the financial crash coming. When the Treasury Secretary, Henry 'Hank' Paulson, belatedly realised Wall Street was on the verge of a full-blown financial meltdown, he started bailing out the most vulnerable institutions. First, in the spring of 2008, the federal government rescued the investment bank Bear Stearns, which was taken over by JPMorgan Chase. Then in September, Fannie Mae and Freddie Mac, the country's biggest mortgage lenders, were saved from bankruptcy through the largest federal intervention in business since the Great Depression.

When Lehman Brothers faced bankruptcy, however, Paulson refused to intervene, a decision some on Wall Street put down to the firm's longstanding rivalry with his former employer, Goldman Sachs (although the Treasury Secretary claimed that, unlike Bear Stearns, a buyer could not be found). The Bush administration surmised that the 158-year-old investment bank was not too big to let fail, and that the financial fallout could be contained. This was Paulson's fateful blunder. The fall of Lehman Brothers triggered panic around the world.

In handling the financial crisis, President Bush was torn. A drum major for free enterprise and a self-professed Reaganite, he was ideologically averse to government intervention. His instinct, therefore, was to let financial institutions fail. If the federal government continually rode to the rescue, moreover, moral hazard would cease to exist. His overriding fear, however, was of the total collapse of the US financial system: not so much a domino effect on Wall Street as a catastrophic house of cards. Besides, with an eye on history, he preferred to be seen as a modern-day Franklin Delano Roosevelt rather than Herbert Hoover, the Republican president at the onset of the Great Depression. 'I've abandoned free market principles to save the free market system,' pleaded the president in his defence, not that the argument cut much ice with the Republican right.

For hard-line conservatives, the bailouts were a betrayal. When Paulson proposed the Troubled Asset Relief Program, or TARP as it became known, not even Dick Cheney could sell it to a sceptical Republican Caucus. In a House vote, 113 Republicans voted against – compared with 65 in favour – which condemned it to defeat. Two days later, with the country on the verge of a financial abyss, 24 Republicans agreed to set aside their reservations to back the president. Still, it needed the support of the House Speaker, Nancy Pelosi, and her fellow Democrats for it to pass.

Even when US capitalism faced its doomsday scenario, Republican diehards, who venerated the supply-side economics of Milton Friedman, could not bring themselves to embrace a Keynesian, big government solution. Small wonder the official history of the Tea Party movement locates its origin story on 3 October

2008, when Bush signed TARP into law. The president deserves credit for facing down these recalcitrants. 'Ideology was replaced by pragmatism,' noted his biographer, Jean Edward Smith, who concluded, justifiably, that 2008 marked his high point as president, even though his approval ratings plummeted to an all-time low, a miserable 26 per cent. Had a more doctrinaire Republican occupied the White House, one who refused to bring the might of the federal government to bear, the US economy could have disappeared down a mammoth sinkhole.

To the victims of the Great Recession, the Bush bailouts were manifestly unjust. As economists such as Joseph Stiglitz pointed out, they socialised losses and privatised gains. Even more galling was the news not long afterwards that Wall Street financiers were basking once again in bonus money. Executives at the insurance giant AIG, which had received $85 billion in taxpayer bailout, awarded themselves $165 million in bonuses.

The lack of accountability aggravated the sense of injustice. Prosecutions had followed the collapse of Enron, WorldCom and Arthur Andersen, but none of the chief executives who ran companies responsible for the financial crisis was punished. The 'too big to fail' philosophy at the US Treasury was matched by a 'too big to jail' mentality at the US Justice Department, which extended into the Obama administration. A mid-level banker from Credit Suisse, Kareem Serageldin, became the only Wall Street banker to be criminally prosecuted for fraudulently manipulating bond prices. Much bigger crimes went unpunished.

By the end of his presidency, Bush was so unpopular that he became the first sitting president since Lyndon Johnson not to attend his own party's convention – ironically, a hurricane led to the cancellation of the first night of the GOP convention in Minneapolis-St Paul, which meant, much to the relief of the McCain campaign, that Bush lost his speaking slot.

A video shown to the Republican faithful about 9/11 made no reference to the president.[47] Liberals had long derided Bush as a gun-slinging unilateralist, a toxic Texan, an inarticulate dunderhead,

185

a wide-eyed evangelical and a puppet of his deputy. Now, though, he was castigated from within the conservative movement for being too liberal.

Right-wingers viewed his eight years in office as a wasted opportunity. They resented his 'No Child Left Behind' education reform, because it expanded the reach of the federal government into classrooms and was passed with the help of Ted Kennedy. His Medicare prescription drugs benefit brought about the biggest expansion of this government entitlement since its foundation in the mid-'60s. His immigration proposals were too bleeding-heart. The bailouts offered undeniable proof he was a 'big government conservative'.

The younger generation of conservatives making waves on Capitol Hill was especially critical. 'Republicans controlled Washington from 2001 to 2006,' complained Eric Cantor, a rising star of the congressional party. 'They did some good things, but they also did a lot to give conservatism a bad name.'[48] Kevin McCarthy, another future leader in the House, complained about the Republicans' failure to 'rein in spending or even slow the growth of government'.[49] Just as George H. W. Bush's moderation spawned Gingrichism, so George W. Bush's pragmatism fuelled the rise of the Tea Party. As E. J. Dionne has observed: 'The Bush years are central to understanding why conservatism took such a hard right turn during the Obama years.'[50]

As the Bush administration collapsed, it became fashionable to draw parallels between the decline of George W. Bush's America and the fall of imperial Rome. A plethora of books appeared likening the president to the emperor Diocletian wrapped in a star-spangled toga. While America fiddled, China caught fire, achieving levels of economic growth without historical precedent. Unlike the Soviet Union, which had the population to challenge America but not the economic system, or Japan, which had the economy but a population of only 120 million, a resurgent Middle Kingdom, with its authoritarian capitalism, possessed both.

Globalisation had hastened its rise. Prior to joining the World Trade Organization in 2001, China had a 4.8 per cent share of manufacturing. By 2010, it was 15.1 per cent, while it had risen again by 2014 to 18.3 per cent. China was on its way to becoming the world's largest trading nation, a milestone it reached in 2012. Curiously, even the rise of China ended up having a polarising effect on US politics. Republican congressional districts with the most trade exposure to China, found the MIT economist David Autor, were more prone to elect hard-line conservatives. Those in Democratic hands were more likely to elect Democrats from the left of the party.[51]

In the summer of 2008, China celebrated its international coming out with an opening ceremony at the Beijing Olympics that made the festivities in Los Angeles look like a low budget B-movie with third-rate special effects. George W. Bush flew in to cheer on the American athletes, but his visit inevitably conferred further global approval on a regime with a horrifying human rights record. Team USA ended up with the most medals, but crucially it was China that won the most golds. Less than ten years in, the twenty-first century already looked like becoming the Chinese century. This long dormant giant was experiencing its own summertime of resurgence.

My New York commute to work takes less than 25 minutes, but skirts the broad outlines of almost 250 years of American history. After a short walk through the cobbled streets of Dumbo, I take the ferry that leaves from the wharf under Brooklyn Bridge, an engineering feat that was to the nineteenth century what the moonshot was to the twentieth. Then I cross the mouth of the East River, the swirling waters through which George Washington evacuated some 9,000 men, right under the noses of the British, when the Continental Army was reeling in the aftermath of the Battle of Brooklyn, an escape pivotal to the outcome of the Revolutionary War. On the port side of the ferry is the Statue of Liberty, a gift from the French to symbolise freedom and democracy and a beacon of hope for millions of arriving immigrants. On the starboard side, framed by the sturdy stone towers of the bridge, are the skyscrapers of Manhattan, those emblems of New World ambition.

From the ferry terminal in Lower Manhattan, I walk up Wall Street, passing Federal Hall, the site where Washington was inaugurated as America's first president. Directly across from the general's bronze statue is the New York Stock Exchange, where the market crashes of 1929 and 2008 spread such panic at home and around the world. The intersection between these two pillared buildings was the starting point for the Hard Hat Riot in 1970, when, days after the Ohio National Guard shot dead four unarmed anti-war protesters on the campus of Kent State University, construction workers beat up the hippies and school students protesting against the war in Vietnam, on the orders of their union bosses.

Across from Wall Street is the cemetery of Trinity Church, where one of the most storied founding fathers, Alexander Hamilton, is interred. Then I turn right onto Broadway, with the gothic turrets of the Woolworth Building, which was once the world's tallest tower, in front of me, and the Art Deco halo of the Chrysler Building shimmering in the far distance. A left takes me into Zuccotti Park, which in 2011 became the tent-strewn home of the Occupy Wall Street movement. Then I walk the final short stretch, to the edge of a busy but quiet plaza scattered usually with people talking in hushed tones. There, two square sunken reflecting pools mark the footprints of the Twin Towers.

Now the skyline of Lower Manhattan has been repaired. A new tower with a spire at its peak, One World Trade Center, soars to 1,776 feet, a bow to the year of the Declaration of Independence. Below ground lies a catacomb-like museum with unexpectedly sculptural exhibits – a wrecked fire truck, a burned-out jet engine, twisted girders, a concrete staircase used by survivors to flee – and the 'In Memoriam' tributes to the 2,983 lives lost on 9/11 and in the first attack on the World Trade Center eight years earlier. Inscribed with the names of the dead, the parapets of the sunken pools serve almost as altars. Bereaved relatives come from all over the world to place flowers and small flags, and to voice their quiet prayers. More than 90 countries lost citizens on 9/11.

This place has become a global gathering spot to mourn a changed world. Always there are roses and carnations. Always there is an atmosphere of binding reverence. But it is hard to pass through Ground Zero to my bureau on the far side of the memorial without thinking of the destruction of life and the loss of opportunity. All too fleeting was that rousing moment when American politics was briefly defined by a sense of togetherness. All too quickly it gave way to the destructive emotions of vengefulness and anger so dominant ever since. Even 9/11 did not slow the infernal cycle of disunion. Rather the attacks of September 11 and the financial crash of September 15 eventually made fear the great driver of US politics.

5

No You Can't

'Yes we can!' came the chants of affirmation, as revellers streamed into Lafayette Square opposite the White House, waving the Stars and Stripes as if they were finish-line chequered flags, and holding aloft 'Obama/Biden' placards like golden trophies. 'Yes we can!'

Washington can be a joyless city: one familiar with presidential comings and goings, one where passions tend to converge rather than originate. Yet when news spread through its streets that for the first time in the country's 232-year history a black man would occupy a White House built by slaves, the capital erupted. 1600 Pennsylvania Avenue became the impromptu venue for a street party. In the minds of the revellers who gathered at his gates, George W. Bush had already been evicted from the Executive Mansion. That night it was impossible to sleep for the ceaseless din of blaring horns. For those inspired by the young senator's audacious candidacy, this was the moment, to borrow from Seamus Heaney, when hope and history rhymed.

Back in 1961, the year of Barack Obama's birth, Washington remained for the most part a Jim Crow city in which racism was endemic: the rail terminus where Negro passengers arriving from the north were forced to leave their integrated carriages at Union Station to board segregated trains if they wanted to continue their journeys south; a place where the few black congressmen on Capitol Hill were barred from swimming in the 'whites only' members' pool.

Even in 2008 it remained a dishearteningly segregated city, in which white residents tended to congregate in its north-west quadrant, a safe distance from the old black ghettoes. So the joyfulness was most keenly felt amongst Washington's majority African-American population, who continued to be deprived of a lawmaker to represent them in the House of Representatives or the Senate – a constitutionally mandated act of voter suppression – but who would soon have a president to call their own.

Ahead of Election Night, I was told to prepare two reports that could run the instant a winner was declared: one for President-elect John McCain and one for President-elect Barack Obama. Since his defeat was all but inevitable, I didn't even put pen to paper for the Arizona senator, although our coverage afterwards would reflect on how his decency and refusal to play the race card contributed to his own demise. Finding words to describe Obama's victory posed a unique challenge, since they were freighted with so much history and would be broadcast all over the world, including in his father's homeland in Kenya. From a personal point of view, it also felt like I was drafting the concluding chapter of a story I had been covering for much of my adulthood – a coda, in all honesty, that I often doubted would be composed in my lifetime.

The viability of an African-American politician as a presidential candidate was a subject of such personal fascination because I had spent years conducting research into the struggle for black equality. As part of that academic journey, I got to sit down with the leaders of the civil rights movement; to visit the climactic battlegrounds, like Birmingham, Alabama, where they fought to kill off Jim Crow; and to sift through the archives of the white supremacists, all of them southern Democrats, who fought such a rearguard action to uphold the system of racial apartheid. As a student in Boston, much of my time was spent at the John F. Kennedy Presidential Library in Boston trying to make sense of why this supposed liberal icon had been a bystander to the great social revolution of his age. Fearful of opening up the schism within the Democratic Party over segregation and lacking moral seriousness, Kennedy downplayed civil rights and waited until his third year in office to push for meaningful legislation. Then it was primarily because a black rebellion threatened to overwhelm his presidency.[1]

The Kennedy brothers had even tried to cancel the March on Washington, the setting for King's 'I Have a Dream' speech, because they feared a race riot in the heart of the nation's capital. When march organisers refused, the White House ordered the biggest peacetime military build-up on American soil to guard against trouble, which meant heavily armed soldiers were on stand-by next to a fleet of helicopters as King held his audience spellbound with his paean to non-violence.

Kennedy's inaction at the start of his presidency proved to be a political miscalculation of immense scale, for it set in motion a violent chain reaction that continues to this day. White supremacists were encouraged to believe they could prolong segregation, fuelling the defiance of racist reactionaries such as Governor George Wallace, who in his 1963 inaugural address cried 'segregation now, segregation tomorrow, segregation forever'. In turn, black activists adopted more militant tactics and pressed for more radical reforms, such as affirmative action and reparations.

At the beginning of the 1960s, civil rights activists demanded equality: the right to be served at the same lunch counters, eat at the same restaurants, sit wherever they wanted on buses and trains and attend the same schools as whites. These goals had strong bipartisan and public support. Demands for affirmative action, however, were polarising. Even sympathetic white Americans found it hard to back reforms that gave the appearance of granting blacks preferential treatment.

When Kennedy entered the White House, there was an emerging consensus with growing cross-party support that segregation was morally untenable, and that black Americans should finally be granted a full menu of civil rights. Through his inaction and political faint-heartedness, he squandered this epochal chance to bring about a peaceful transition towards a more racially equitable country. Alas, that opportunity has never again arisen.

The paradox of the civil rights era for Barack Obama was that it cleared away legal obstacles impeding an African-American presidency, but also made it harder for Democrats to win. After the passage of the 1964 Civil Rights Act and the 1965 Voting Rights Act, the road to the White House became strewn with the failed candidacies of northern liberals with strong civil rights records. In 1968, Hubert Humphrey, who had made his name at the 1948 Democratic convention with a blistering speech that sparked a 'Dixiecrat' walkout led by Strom Thurmond, became the first victim of the Republicans' southern strategy. Four years later, George McGovern, who tried to make the Democratic Party more resemble multiracial America, could not even win his home state. Only southern Democrats prospered in presidential politics: Lyndon Johnson, Jimmy Carter, Bill Clinton and, many would still contend, Al Gore.

Obama was seeking to become not only the first black president, then, but also the first Democrat from above the Mason–Dixon line since Kennedy. And just as the civil rights era made it harder for him to win, so it also made it harder for him to govern because of the ultra-partisanship and polarisation that now prevailed.

To become a history-defying president, Barack Hussein Obama therefore became a history-denying presidential nominee. He decided not to locate his candidacy in the tumultuous decade into which he was born. Nor did he present his campaign as a continuation of the black struggle. Absent from his electrifying breakthrough speech at the 2004 Democratic convention, where he rejected the notion of a blue-state America and a red-state America and argued instead for a United States of America, was any mention of the civil rights era. Likewise, he eschewed the accusatory vocabulary of black resentment and recrimination, and spoke instead of his parents' 'abiding faith in the possibilities of this nation'. In common with other contemporary black high-achievers, such as Oprah Winfrey and, at that time, Bill Crosby, he never confronted or threatened white audiences. His intention was to make America feel good, not guilty.

When he declared his presidential candidacy, Obama once more de-emphasised his colour, and made clear he was not a traditional black politician with a narrow agenda. It was entirely fitting that Shepard Fairey's 'Hope' poster rendered him in red, white and blue, rather than his natural skin colour. Obama's vision of a post-partisan country, however, would prove just as illusory as the dream of a post-racial America. In becoming the first black president, Obama overcame history, but could not escape it.

———

The symbolism of Obama's victory made it a grand epic of American history. In an election that witnessed the highest turnout since 1968, the scale was also impressive. Of the 33 Democrats to seek the presidency since 1828, only three had secured a higher percentage of the vote. The freshman senator, who beat John McCain by nine million votes, was also the first Democrat in 32 years to win a majority of the popular vote.

In an election in which the share of ballots cast by white voters was the lowest in US history, people of colour made a decisive contribution – African-American support leapt from 88 per cent in 2004 to 95 per cent for Obama.[2] Yet he also attracted three million more white voters than John Kerry, and performed well in working-class communities devastated by the Great Recession. Even without the black Democratic vote banks of Detroit and Milwaukee, he would have won Wisconsin and Michigan. Also he comfortably took Macomb County, on the outskirts of Detroit, the spiritual home of Reagan Democrats. In a startling historical turnaround, this skinny guy with a funny name, as Obama called himself, also won three former slave states of the Old Confederacy: Virginia, Florida and North Carolina.

This was not just an emphatic personal victory. The Democratic Party enjoyed its best performance since LBJ's landslide in 1964. The blue wave that washed across so much of the country gave the party a net gain of 21 seats in the House and eight in the Senate. The Democrats could boast that rare thing: unified government with a filibuster-proof supermajority of 60 seats to boot.[3]

Despite such an emphatic victory, some within the conservative movement viewed Obama as an illegitimate president, a Muslim infiltrator born supposedly in some Kenyan shanty. After the Chief Justice of the Supreme Court, John Roberts, mangled Obama's swearing in, the White House even took the safeguard of repeating the oath of office to thwart any legal challenge to his lawfulness.

During his inaugural celebrations, the new president tried to evoke the post-partisan spirit of his debut speech in Boston. On the eve of his swearing in, he attended a dinner held in honour of John McCain.[4] At a concert on The Mall, Garth Brooks, the Republican country and western superstar, was asked to perform. To deliver the invocation, Obama invited the right-wing evangelist Rick Warren of the Saddleback Church in Orange County, an opponent of abortion and same-sex marriage. His inaugural speech, which was unexceptional by his standards, was a sermon of national reconciliation. 'On this day, we come to proclaim an end to the petty grievances and false promises, the recriminations and worn-out dogmas that for far too long have strangled our politics.' Yet the Obama rallying cry of 'Yes we can' instantly ran into the Republican counterblast of 'No you can't'.

On the night of his inauguration, which had drawn 1.8 million people to the National Mall, 15 Republicans gathered at the Caucus Room restaurant in Washington, including congressmen Paul Ryan, Eric Cantor, Kevin McCarthy and Newt Gingrich. Together, they plotted the downfall of the Obama presidency.

'If you act like you're in the minority, you're going to stay in the minority,' said McCarthy, who earlier in the day had asked Obama for his autograph. 'We've gotta challenge them on every single bill and challenge them on every single campaign.'

Close to midnight, as the four-hour meal drew to a close, Gingrich delivered a St Crispin's Day-style pep talk. 'You will remember this day,' he said. 'You'll remember this as the day the seeds of 2012 were sown.'[5]

Meeting Republican leaders at the White House shortly afterwards, Obama presented them with a choice: they could take marching orders from Rush Limbaugh or join him in governing. He also reminded them of his sweeping mandate. 'Elections have consequences,' he pointedly told the Republican House whip Eric Cantor, 'and at the end of the day, I won.'

Already, though, the Republicans had decided upon a strategy of total opposition.[6] Days later, House Republicans voted unanimously to block Obama's $800 billion stimulus package, a display of obstructionist solidarity in which conservatives rejoiced. At a GOP congressional retreat in Virginia afterwards, when television footage of the vote was shown on a big screen, lawmakers joined in a standing ovation.

'I know all of you are pumped about the vote,' crowed Cantor. 'We'll have more to come!' Then the Indiana congressman Mike Pence played a scene from the movie *Patton*, showing the general at his most bellicose. 'We're going to kick the hell out of them all the time. We're going to go through him like crap through a goose.'[7]

From the outset, then, the aim was to go through Obama like crap through a goose, starving him of any bipartisan successes that would help secure re-election. 'The single most important thing we want to achieve,' Mitch McConnell later admitted to the *National Journal,* in a quote exemplifying the partisan pig-headedness, 'is for President Obama to be a one-term president.'[8]

Though still a novice in the ways of Washington, Obama was never naïve enough to think the Republicans would lend him much support. Nor was he a political fantasist. Nonetheless, he was taken aback by the one-sided stimulus package vote, coming as it did in the midst of an economic crisis that still threatened to unravel the capitalist system. 'I just thought that there would be enough of a sense of urgency that at least for the first year there would be an interest in governing,' he reflected later. 'And you just didn't see that.'[9]

From the beginning of his presidency to the end, the GOP took obstructionism to unprecedented levels. Senate Republicans filibustered 30 of Obama's district court judges – 17 more than all of his predecessors combined.[10] Between 2009 and 2010, cloture, a guillotine motion aimed at halting filibusters, had to be invoked 63 times – more in two years than the total for the seven decades between 1909 and 1982. This trend had been in motion for decades.

In 1960, as the journalist Ed Luce has noted, just 8 per cent of bills were filibustered. By 2008, it was 70 per cent of legislation.[11] These blocking devices became the accepted tools of politics. Even on matters of mutual concern, such as reducing the national debt, cross-party cooperation broke down. During a temporary truce in January 2010, Republicans and Democrats created a bipartisan deficit-reduction task force, the Conrad–Gregg Budget Commission. Only a few months later, however, Mitch McConnell and other Republican co-sponsors abruptly withdrew their backing, for the simple reason that Obama indicated his support. Republican senators, rather than allow the president to burnish his post-partisan credentials, voted against a resolution they themselves had co-sponsored. Little wonder Obama's White House Chief of Staff, Rahm Emanuel, took to calling Washington 'Fucknutsville'.

The battle over the Affordable Care Act, 'Obamacare', revealed the extent to which the GOP had become the 'Party of No'. Rather than negotiate with the White House to shape and alter the legislation, Republican leaders opted for blanket opposition. Not a single GOP senator lent support. The debate also illustrated how far the GOP had lurched to the right. Republicans likened Obama's plan to European-style socialism, but it was not dissimilar to the alternative to 'Hillarycare' they had proposed in the early 1990s. Besides, the model for Obamacare was 'Romneycare' in Massachusetts, authored by a Republican governor, Mitt Romney.

The viciousness of the healthcare debate marked a new low in political discourse. When in September 2009 Obama outlined his heath proposals to a joint session of Congress, he became the first president to be heckled from the floor of the House. 'You lie!' shouted the Republican congressman Joe Wilson, a howl that prompted a death stare from Nancy Pelosi. When Obamacare was debated, Congresswoman Virginia Foxx of North Carolina railed, 'I believe we have more to fear from the potential of that bill passing than we do from any terrorist.'[12] At a mammoth rally on Capitol Hill in November, demonstrators brandished placards depicting the president as Vladimir Lenin, Che Guevara, The Joker from the

Batman movies and Adolf Hitler. Some even carried photographs of Holocaust victims from the gas chambers of Dachau.[13]

In the wake of Goldwaterism, the Reagan Revolution and the Republican Revolution of the '90s, Obama's first year witnessed the fourth wave of conservative radicalisation: the emergence of the Tea Party. The rebellion began in February 2009 in the most improbable of settings, the business news channel CNBC, when the financial commentator Rick Santelli delivered a scorching rant from the floor of the Chicago Mercantile Exchange railing against the Obama administration's plan to grant assistance to 'loser' homeowners facing foreclosure. 'We're thinking of having a Chicago Tea Party,' he shouted at the camera. When the clip went viral, aided by prominent coverage in the Drudge Report and a new social networking site called Twitter, the Tea Party came into hurried existence.

A linear descendant of the Know Nothing movement and the People's Party from the nineteenth century, it was an amorphous amalgam of deficit hawks, constitutional originalists, 'birthers', opponents of 'crony capitalism', Second Amendment advocates, web-savvy conspiracy mongers, militiamen, evangelical absolutists and right-wing eccentrics with a penchant for dressing up in the tricorn hats and powdered wigs of Revolutionary-era patriots.

Mainly white, older and male, they were united by their hatred of government, taxation, immigration and Barack Obama. The young president personified so much of what to them was alien: cool rationality, preachy secularism, Harvard elitism and metropolitan polish. Then there was his race. Not all of its members had a problem with a black president, but many did. At the first national Tea Party convention in Nashville, Tom Tancredo, a former congressman, drew cheers when he claimed that Jim Crow-era voting laws would have made it almost impossible for him to win. 'People who could not even spell the word "vote" or say it in English put a committed socialist ideologue in the White House,' he demontedly inveighed.[14]

On the eve of President Obama's first anniversary in office, the insurgency claimed its first quarry when activists in Massachusetts helped produce an upset in the special election held to replace the late Senator Ted Kennedy. The Republican Scott Brown's victory was steeped in symbolism, for it came in the birthplace of the original Tea Party, in the seat of the Senate's great liberal lion and in a Democratic stronghold that prided itself on being the only state not to vote for Richard Nixon in 1972. Almost overnight, the Democrats lost their supermajority in the Senate, which meant the filibuster became even more of a lethal weapon.

Just two days after the shock result from Massachusetts, conservatives scored an even more portentous victory. In another 5–4 decision, the Supreme Court handed down its *Citizens United* decision granting corporations, non-profits and unions unlimited political spending power in elections. With the post-Watergate legal barriers removed, political action committees known as 'super PACs' and 'dark money' non-profit groups which did not have to disclose their donors could now spend millions.

At the time, the expectation was that corporations and, to a lesser extent, unions would flood politics with money. In actual fact, a relatively small number of super-wealthy donors unleashed a tidal wave of dollars. Between two-thirds and three-quarters of all the money raised by super PACs came from 100 wealthy donors: the new plutocrats. Therefore, *Citizens United* turned the wealth gap in US society into an influence gap in US politics.

Members of the progressive super-rich, such as George Soros, the San Francisco hedge-fund manager Tom Steyer and Michael Bloomberg, backed Democratic candidates and liberal causes. The right-wing billionaires David and Charles Koch funded grassroots movements such as the Tea Party, a practice that became known as 'astroturfing'. This plutocratic populism was evident, too, in the political activities of Las Vegas casino owner Sheldon Adelson and the reclusive hedge-fund manager Robert Mercer, an early investor in Breitbart News and co-founder of the data-focused political consultancy firm Cambridge Analytica, who became Trump's biggest financial backer. The aim of all these right-wing billionaires was to make the Republican Party even more conservative, and to turn more of the country red. In the 2010 elections, the first after the *Citizens*

United ruling, a massive infusion of dark money at the local level helped the GOP capture so many state legislatures.[15]

In handing down its *Citizens United* ruling, a conservative-leaning Supreme Court once again seemed to be appropriating the constitution as much as interpreting it. So aggrieved was President Obama that during his 2010 State of the Union address he breached Washington etiquette and directly rebuked the black-robed justices ranked before him.

'With all due deference to separation of powers,' he said, 'last week the Supreme Court reversed a century of law that I believe will open the floodgates for special interests – including foreign corporations – to spend without limit in our elections.' As the justices shuffled uncomfortably in their front-row seats, he continued on with his reprimand. 'I don't think American elections should be bankrolled by America's most powerful interests or, worse, by foreign entities.'[16] In hindsight, Obama's warning seems clairvoyant.

The Tea Party movement was loosely organised and intentionally non-hierarchical, but a figurehead emerged nonetheless: Sarah Palin, the former Alaskan governor, who was seen by her legion of fans as the one bright light of John McCain's bleak 2008 campaign. Her blistering convention speech, where she asked in her folksy twang what was the difference between a Rottweiler and hockey mom (lipstick was the answer), instantly made her a right-wing pin-up.

The more the sneering left mocked her – for reportedly thinking Africa was a country, for not being able to name the newspapers she read each morning, for claiming that being able to peer across the Bering Strait at Russia from her Alaskan home vested her with foreign-policy experience – the more the right adored her. A self-styled 'mama grizzly', Palin railed against the 'lame-stream media', radical Islam, bicoastal elites, political correctness and dangerous leftists, like Obama.

At a time when celebrities were becoming politicians, Palin followed the same path trod by Jerry Springer by becoming a politician who turned into a celebrity. More than five million viewers tuned in for the debut of her 2010 reality TV show, *Sarah*

Palin's Alaska, which was produced, inevitably, by Mark Burnett. The publication of her 2009 autobiography, *Going Rogue: An American Life*, which sold a million copies in less than two weeks, again demonstrated her star power.

The press, though disparaging, could not get enough of her. 'We love Palin,' confessed Politico's Jim VandeHei and Jonathan Martin, two of Washington's most influential political weathermen. 'For the media, Palin is great at the box office.'[17]

More than just a politician, Palin became a phenomenon. With reporters displaying their customary better-story bias, the Republican presidential nomination seemed hers for the taking. Like Ross Perot and Pat Buchanan, she became another proto-Trump.

Partly because of the presence within its ranks of so many racist crackpots, it was tempting to write off the Tea Party as a 'white panic', the last hurrah of elderly white voters who felt their culture was under attack from minority groups. It seemed to be a throwback, more representative of the past than the future. In the 2010 congressional midterms, however, the Tea Party showed it had become the most potent force in US politics by powering a second Republican revolution bigger even than the first. In the largest switch in seats since the 1948 election, the GOP gained seven seats in the Senate and a staggering 63 seats in the House. President Obama, in something of an understatement, described it as a 'shellacking'.

Just as significantly, the Republicans flipped six governorships and 20 state legislatures, which gave the party a licence to gerrymander when it came to mapping out the boundaries of congressional districts after the 2010 US Census. This they did, with flagrantly unrepresentative results, in Michigan, North Carolina, Wisconsin, Florida, Ohio, Texas, New York, Georgia, Indiana, Pennsylvania and Virginia, which made it much harder for the Democrats to win back the House. Not until 2018 did Nancy Pelosi return as Speaker.[18]

The New Year started on an even uglier note, reviving memories of the political violence of the '60s and early '70s. During a constituent meeting held in a parking lot in Tucson, Arizona, a white skinhead gunned down six people, including a federal judge, and shot

Congresswoman Gabby Giffords in the head at point-blank range. As the congresswoman fought for her life, it emerged that Sarah Palin's political action committee, SarahPAC, had drawn stylised crosshairs on a map targeting Democratic lawmakers who supported Obamacare. Although no link was established between the graphic and the gunman, Giffords's congressional district in Arizona was on this provocative 'hit-list'. Palin's response to the accusation of incitement demonstrated once again how crazed public discourse had become. She called it a 'blood libel', an anti-Semitic canard.

In Washington, the attempted assassination of Giffords brought a brief halt in hostilities. At the State of the Union address two weeks later, Republican and Democratic lawmakers cast tradition aside by intermingling on the benches. Yet the comity of bipartisan 'date night', as it was called, proved fleeting. 2011 was the third consecutive year that Congress failed to pass a budget and had to rely on what were called continuing resolutions. In the 112th Congress, no Democrat in the House was more conservative than a Republican and no Republican was more liberal than a Democrat, ending the long tradition of ideological overlap.

No longer was it a case of the centre not being able to hold. There was not much left of the centre. The Blue Dog Coalition of centrist congressional Democrats, which could boast more than 50 members in 2008, dwindled to the low teens. Its moderate conservative counterpart, the Main Street Partnership, was also in meltdown.

Ahead of the 2012 midterm elections, one of the last surviving Rockefeller Republicans, Olympia Snowe of Maine, unexpectedly announced her retirement. After 33 years on Capitol Hill she could no longer stomach what she described as 'an atmosphere of polarisation and "my way or the highway" ideologies'.

Other moderates faced Tea Party primary challenges, the favoured method for terminating the careers of compromise-seeking heretics. The Indiana Senator Richard Lugar, a lawmaker since 1976, who was acclaimed for his genial bipartisanship, was defeated by the little-known insurgent Richard Mourdock. Lugar had voted in favour of Obama's first two Supreme Court nominees, backed immigration reform and supported certain restrictions on gun ownership. Yet this long history of reaching out across the aisle with Democrats became his Achilles heel. On the right especially, acts of bipartisanship had become politically ruinous.

The retirement, voluntary or enforced, of moderates who could cut deals had been a recurring problem ever since the greatest generation started to leave the stage. Now it was central to the country's crisis of governance. Pragmatists were pushed aside by radicals, Tea Partiers who joined together in what was dubbed the 'Suicide Caucus', an 80-strong rump that dragged the Republican Party even further to the right.

Moderate Democrats also tired of the putridness on Capitol Hill. In 2010, the telegenic Indianan Evan Bayh, who was often spoken of as a potential presidential contender, announced he would not be seeking a third term with a retirement speech that doubled as an indictment of Congress. 'There are better ways to serve my fellow citizens,' he said wearily.[19] On Capitol Hill, there was 'too much narrow ideology and not enough practical problem-solving'. This was now a common refrain. In 2014, the father of the House, Congressman John Dingell, retired, after a 59-year run that began during the Eisenhower administration. 'I find serving in the House to be obnoxious,' he said. 'I know how to build legislation from the centre,' he added, lamenting a skill that was now largely redundant.[20] The destructive forces in US politics were becoming more powerful than the restraining influences. Increasingly, the Senate aped the ugliness and scrappiness of the House. The moderate middle was a thing of the past.

———

Just as Gingrichism failed to throw up a credible candidate in the 1990s, so too the Tea Party struggled on the presidential stage. On Memorial Day weekend in June 2011, Sarah Palin launched what looked to all intents and purposes like a campaign for the White House when she appeared in a black helmet and leathers on the back of a Harley-Davidson at the traditional Rolling Thunder biker rally in

Washington, the full-throttled start of a One Nation tour around the country. Then it was on to Manhattan, where she sat down for pizza with her fellow media-monger Donald Trump – a photo-op ridiculed by the Big Apple tabloids because she used a knife and fork to cut her slice. By October, however, she had decided against running.

Deprived of its Alaskan Evita, star-struck movement conservatives were forced to consider less appealing alternatives. The Tea Party favourite Michele Bachmann, a Minnesota congresswoman who could almost have been Palin's twin sister, won that summer's Iowa straw poll, an early popularity contest, but faded almost immediately afterwards. This set the pattern for the Republican race, where frontrunners faltered the instant they hit the front.

In a televised debate, the Texas Governor Rick Perry shot himself in both eel-skin boots when he failed to remember which three government departments he planned to shutter. 'Oops,' he muttered in a brain freeze mercilessly replayed for days afterwards. Later he became Energy Secretary in the Trump administration, heading up a department he had wanted to abolish.

Next came the fringe candidate Herman Cain, a little-known former pizza executive who, in addition to being flummoxed by rudimentary foreign-policy questions, was hit by allegations of sexual harassment. Newt Gingrich, making his first presidential run, briefly topped the polls until he was blasted by a blitz of negative advertisements from his Republican opponents – karmic payback, perhaps, for trading in so much negativity throughout his career. Then came an improbable surge from Rick Santorum, a washed-up former Pennsylvania senator best known for equating homosexuality with incest. Like a speed-skater watching from the rear as faster rivals crashed out, Santorum had not yet lost his balance by the time of the Iowa Caucus and pulled off an unexpected victory – thus proving what has now become an iron-clad rule of the GOP nominating process, that winning Iowa is a predicator of ultimate failure.

Almost by default, Mitt Romney, an establishment favourite who four years earlier had been the runner-up to John McCain, ended up as the nominee. The Tea Party grassroots regarded the former governor of Massachusetts as a dangerous moderate, a slick well-financed RINO, a Republican in name only. To overcome their antipathy, Romney ditched the common-sense moderation of his gubernatorial career, including his landmark achievement, 'Romneycare', and portrayed himself as a hardliner on immigration. As well as calling for the construction of a fence along the southern border, he appointed the controversial sheriff Joe Arpaio as the chair of his Arizona campaign. A pragmatic governor became a *faux*-right candidate, but so weak was his opposition that he eventually wrapped up the nomination at the Texas primary in May.

That night, Romney appeared alongside Donald Trump at a fundraiser at the Trump International Hotel in Las Vegas, an event that attracted controversy because, in the days before, the billionaire had renewed his specious birther attacks on Barack Obama, claiming he had not been born in Hawaii. Ahead of their meeting, the Obama campaign ran an attack ad asking why Romney had not condemned the birther conspiracy theories and taken a stand against 'the voices of extremism'. Trump's birtherism, however, had become more mainstream within the conservative movement. A poll conducted in 2009 suggested 58 per cent of Republicans did not believe Obama was born in the United States or were not sure.[21] As Romney's visit proved, Trump was no longer an outlier. The owner of the Miss Universe pageant had become an important judge in this quadrennial Republican beauty contest.

After winning the Republican nomination, Romney followed the now familiar route of tacking towards the centre, presenting himself as a CEO with the business acumen to kick-start the economy. Briefly he surged ahead in the polls, after the first television debate in September when a bored-sounding Obama gave the impression of wanting to be almost anywhere else on the planet – a display of presidential petulance worse even than George H. W. Bush's glance at his wristwatch (not that there was a single image to capture it, which would have been replayed for days afterwards). Romney's momentum came to a shrieking halt, however, when a leaked video from a high-dollar fundraiser showed him bemoaning 'the 47 per cent who are with him [Obama], who are dependent on government, who believe that they are victims'. Thereafter, it was easy to paint him as a heartless vulture capitalist.

In the election, Obama for a second time polled more than 50 per cent, becoming the first president since Reagan to win both his presidential bids with a majority of the popular vote. Romney, by unhappy coincidence, received a 47 per cent share. The Republicans, who only 20 years earlier were thought to have a lock on the White House, had now lost the popular vote in five of the last six presidential elections.

Within conservative circles, two wholly different explanations for Romney's defeat took hold. The Republican National Committee's official autopsy called for greater outreach amongst Hispanic, black, Asian and gay Americans if the party was to avoid plunging over a demographic cliff. Nativists within the conservative movement, however, reached the contradictory conclusion. Instead, they advanced the 'missing white voter' hypothesis. Romney had lost, they posited, not because of black and Hispanic support for Obama but because too many white voters had stayed at home – a shortfall of five million voters from 2008. Rather than being too conservative, Romney had not been conservative enough. Mono-culturalism not multiculturalism offered the way forward.

Back in 2012, however, this remained a minority view. It seemed Marco Rubio, the son of Cuban immigrants, was the coming man, or maybe his mentor Jeb Bush, whose wife was Hispanic and whose speech announcing his candidacy three years later was delivered partly in fluent Spanish. In the upper reaches of the party, the notion that the GOP would turn to a candidate who launched his campaign by describing Mexicans as rapists was unthinkable. However, the mood amongst the grassroots was fractious. No longer were conservative activists prepared to countenance an establishment favourite as their presidential nominee. After the two Bushes, Bob Dole, John McCain and Mitt Romney, they were looking for someone dramatically different. A Palin, or something close. One of *them*.

Returning to live in America in the summer of 2013 after a long hiatus, it was obvious something was amiss. The country appeared to have lost its energy. Barack Obama seemed strangely listless, punch-drunk, perhaps, after being pummelled for so many years by the GOP and Fox News. The urgency and idealism of his 2008 campaign had given way to a languid and directionless presidency. Obama appeared before us now in amputated form, or as a faded poster, to borrow the Republican vice-presidential nominee Paul Ryan's pithy line from the GOP's 2012 convention. Obama's lethargy also fuelled the narrative of US decline. After all, so much of the world had expected this captivating young president to bring about a national rebirth.

Washington was even more sulphurous. The partisan line-drawing I had covered during the Clinton and Bush years had become partisan trench-digging. The sense of renewal I witnessed on the night of Obama's victory was replaced by the stench of democratic decay. Hopes in the White House that back-to-back victories would 'break the fever' never materialised. The temperature further rose. The Republicans maintained their grip on the House, even though the Democrats increased their majority in the Senate, which meant the 113th Congress ended up being even more dysfunctional than the 112th. 2013 was the least productive year in Congress since World War II. Understandably, public confidence in Congress sunk to a new low, with just a 7 per cent approval rating, the lowest Gallup had ever recorded and another indicator of institutional deterioration.[22]

That year Republican attempts to destroy Obamacare, which had been validated by the electorate at the 2012 presidential election and upheld by a conservative-leaning Supreme Court, led to the first government shutdown in almost 20 years. For 16 days, the federal budget was held hostage, as Republicans made delaying or defunding

Obamacare the condition for keeping open the government. Senator Ted Cruz conducted a solo filibuster lasting more than 21 hours, which made a global laughing stock of 'the world's greatest deliberative body' by quoting Dr Seuss's *Green Eggs and Ham*.[23]

With Congress gridlocked, the first anniversary of the Sandy Hook school shooting came and went without any legislative action on further regulating the sale of firearms. Even the death of 20 first-graders and five teaching staff could not bring about an epiphany on gun control. A compromise bill to expand background checks and impose certain restrictions on semi-automatic weapons was defeated in the Senate by Republicans and four Democrats from pro-gun states (Alaska, Arkansas, Montana and North Dakota). Astonishingly, it attracted 12 fewer votes in the Senate than the attempt in 2004 to renew the assault weapons ban.

America had decided the worst school shooting in its history should not impinge on the right of would-be killers to purchase military-style semi-automatic weapons to murder as many victims in as short a timeframe as was possible. After the vote, Obama, who described Sandy Hook as 'the hardest day of my presidency', appeared in the Rose Garden with the tearful mothers of the six- and seven-year-old victims. Gabby Giffords, who had not yet regained her full power of speech, was also at his side. This, he said solemnly, was 'a pretty shameful day for Washington'.[24]

The battle for gun control revealed Obama's strengths and weaknesses. Multiple shootings were the occasion for some of his finest orations, in Aurora, Sandy Hook and Charleston. But his failure to advance even small, incremental reforms showed also how he failed to master the cold grammar of congressional relations. Often, he had to rely on his vice-president, Joe Biden, an old Capitol Hill hand, to negotiate with GOP lawmakers. His obvious disdain for the political game did not go down well in a capital obsessed by the political game.

On gun control, the NRA remained dominant, and benefited from its decades-long campaign to turn the Second Amendment, which was drafted by the framers to protect the rights of militia, into the constitutional basis for individual gun ownership. Up until the late 1960s, it had been looked upon as the forgotten amendment, because it was so obviously obsolete. Yet the NRA brought it back from the dead. Its crowning moment came in 2008, with the landmark *Heller* ruling, when for the first time the Supreme Court concluded that the Second Amendment protected an individual's right to keep and bear arms. Once again, in a 5–4 vote, the right-leaning Supreme Court had shown itself to be the conservative movement's most valuable ally.

The country as a whole was experiencing one of its periodic funks. That July, black fury once again broke loose following the acquittal of George Zimmerman, the neighbourhood-watch volunteer who killed an unarmed African-American teenager, Trayvon Martin, by shooting him in the heart. 'No justice, no peace' was the chant, as demonstrators poured onto the streets of New York, Los Angeles, Miami, Chicago, San Francisco, Oakland and Atlanta. 'It's marching time, ladies and gentlemen,' declared Martin Luther King III, as he urged protesters to converge on the National Mall for the 50th anniversary of his father's March on Washington.[25] It was a hashtag, however, that galvanised young activists: #BlackLivesMatter.

Much of the country had little sympathy for the parents of Trayvon Martin. Even less so when Obama said his son would have looked like the teenager. This slain young man thus became a pawn of polarisation. As African-American lawmakers took to the floor of the House of Representatives dressed in the kind of hoodie he wore that fatal Florida night, a paper mock-up of that garment was marketed online as a gun-range target. Zimmerman even auctioned off the firearm he used to kill the teenager, marketing the pistol as 'an American firearm icon' and 'piece of American history'. Reportedly, it sold for $250,000.[26]

New York, where we made our home, was in a slump. All over the city were signs of decline. The decrepit subways. The rail tunnel under the Hudson River, damaged by Superstorm Sandy in 2012, in which high-speed trains were reduced to a slow-motion crawl. The antique terminals at La Guardia, described by Vice-President Joe

Biden as 'Third World', which had fallen decades behind high-tech airports in China and even India. Flying into the United States from the eastern hemisphere felt like time-travelling. The global power shift from America to Asia was perceptible, too, in Times Square, where China's Xinhua News Agency rented a giant electronic screen that towered over the Coca-Cola ad below.

Mayor Michael Bloomberg's 12-year reign, which was about to come to an end, was credited with making the city safer, cleaner and more environmentally friendly – there were bike lanes, smoke-free restaurants and a glorious High Line, an exquisitely designed park along a disused elevated railroad that became a much-copied model for urban renewal.

However, the billionaire mayor had turned the Big Apple into a rich man's fiefdom, where the green-aproned storm troopers of gentrification – the checkout staff at Whole Foods – helped transform down-at-heel neighbourhoods into high-rent havens. Skinny skyscrapers constructed for the super-rich grew skyward like stubborn and sinewy weeds, disfiguring Manhattan's cityscape and serving as emblems of the vertiginous disparities of wealth. Safety deposit boxes in the sky, they were dubbed, because so many were purchased as investment properties by absentee owners. Architecturally, some even looked like safety deposit boxes in the sky. In this modern-day tale of two cities, more than a fifth of New Yorkers now lived below the poverty line, while 50,000 residents were homeless.[27]

That sticky summer, the politics of New York seemed trashy, unserious, even unhinged. In the battle to succeed Bloomberg, Anthony Weiner, a disgraced former congressman forced to resign his seat after mistakenly sharing with his followers on Twitter 'dick pics' meant for his mistress, was the frontrunner. Now he was hit by scandal again, after it emerged he had conducted a torrid affair with a woman he had never even met – a digital dalliance which underscored how much of modern-day life played out on smartphones rather than in person.

The details, chronicled by tabloid reporters seemingly paid by the *double entendre*, were enthralling. Weiner used the *nom de plume*

Carlos Danger. His paramour was a 'Bible Belt bad girl' christened with what sounded already like a porn name, Sydney Leathers. Then there was Weiner's wronged wife, Huma Abedin, Hillary Clinton's closest aide at the State Department, who was often referred to as the former First Lady's 'second daughter'. One of my first assignments after arriving in New York was to cover her 'stand-by-my-man' news conference, where, quivering like a traumatised sparrow, she told a gaggle of baying Big Apple hacks, 'I love him, I have forgiven him, I believe in him.'

While the Clinton connection added a certain frisson, none of us in the room that afternoon had the slightest inkling of how Weiner's online antics, and his wife's laptop computer, would eventually become a dramatic storyline in the 2016 presidential election. Nor yet did we comprehend how victory in the New York mayoral election of Bill de Blasio, a Park Slope progressive who became the main beneficiary of Weiner's self-sabotage, presaged the Democratic Party's shift to the left and the rise of another Brooklynite, Bernie Sanders.

It was not just Washington and New York. Signs of waning were everywhere. Detroit, the once-great Motor City, was forced that summer to file for bankruptcy, the largest municipal insolvency in US history. In nearby Flint, residents were being poisoned by the drinking water, the kind of story I would have expected to cover in the poorer parts of Uttar Pradesh or Bihar in India. The Crystal Cathedral in Orange County, the spiritual home of the gospel of prosperity that had fascinated me as a teenager, had filed for bankruptcy.

The spirit of America had changed. Arriving in California all those years ago, I was struck by the assuredness of the American compact, the belief that hard work would be rewarded with upward mobility and a higher standard of living. That truth had always been self-evident. Now, though, surprisingly few parents believed their children would lead more abundant lives, a gut sense borne out by a welter of statistics. A man in his thirties was now earning 10 per cent less than his father at the same age in the mid-1980s.[28]

The language, once so bold and hopeful, had become more defensive. People spoke of economic security – keeping down a decent job that came with healthcare and maybe a few other fringe benefits – rather than economic advancement. I was struck by the absence even of modest aspirations – the aim of upgrading a car, buying a slightly larger house, or even taking the family out each week to eat at a cheap and casual restaurant such as Applebee's. So many Americans seemed to be living hand to mouth, pay cheque to pay cheque.

No longer was the focus on the nice-to-haves of middle-class life – a boat on the lake, a second car in the garage, the chance to visit London or cruise the Caribbean. Dreams had been downsized, or abandoned altogether. The Cadillac was now an object of envy rather than emulation. Figures released at the end of the summer showed that income inequality had actually reached its highest level since 1928. By 2014, the richest 1 per cent of Americans had accrued more wealth than the bottom 90 per cent. As Warren Buffett commented, 'There's been class warfare going on for the last 20 years and my class won.'[29]

The '1 per cent'. Now there was a nomenclature to describe the super-rich, after the Nobel Prize-winning economist Joseph Stiglitz published an essay 'Of the 1 per cent, by the 1 per cent, for the 1 per cent' in Vanity Fair, the parish pump of the international jet-set. Perhaps the most searing critique yet of globalisation, it set out how international trade deals benefited multinational corporations by fostering 'competition between countries for business'. This drove down taxes on multinational corporations, weakened health and environmental protections and undermined workplace rights, including collective bargaining. Politicians of all shades, argued Stiglitz, were complicit. After all, most Washington lawmakers were 'members of the top 1 per cent when they arrive, are kept in office by money from the top 1 per cent, and know that if they serve the top 1 per cent well they will be rewarded by the top 1 per cent when they leave office.'[30]

'We are the 99 per cent' had become the rallying cry of the Occupy Wall Street movement, which first emerged in 2011 and drew so many activists to its tented encampment in Lower Manhattan's financial district. The criticism of protesters that the Obama administration was packed with 'Corporate Democrats' who were too cosy with Wall Street had a radicalising effect on the left, just as the big government conservatism of the Bush administration had fuelled the Tea Party on the right.

The young were especially agitated, and understandably so. Going to college was now firmly associated with indebtedness, which was especially off-putting for teenagers from lower socio-economic groups during a period of wage stagnation. Between the end of the Reagan and Obama presidencies, the cost of attending higher education rose eight times more than wages.[31] Student loans now made up the largest proportion of non-housing debt, edging out credit cards and car financing. This was especially problematic because degrees were now a prerequisite of attaining so many well-paid jobs.

Nor were America's great universities any more the blast furnace of social mobility. A study of 38 colleges, including Yale, Princeton and Dartmouth, showed students from the top 1 per cent income bracket occupied more places than the offspring of the bottom 60 per cent. At Harvard almost a third of incoming students were the sons and daughters of alumni. American academia had lost the swagger I recalled from my days as a visiting scholar at MIT. Instead, it tiptoed on eggshells. The fear of offending people seemed now to override freedom of speech. Stultifying self-censorship had become a bar to academic pluralism. There was a near phobic fear of cultural appropriation. On closed-minded campuses, tales abounded of political correctness that truly had gone mad, such as the students at Mount Holyoke College who cancelled plans for a production of *The Vagina Monologues* because it discriminated against women without vaginas.[32] The identity politics of the 'woke left' became easy to mock and caricature, handing a gift to the Fox News right.

Though his country was exhausted by wars that never seemed to end, President Obama continued to pay lip service to the language of American greatness underpinned by military might.

'America remains the one indispensable nation in world affairs,' he claimed during his 2012 State of the Union address. 'Anyone who tells you that America is in decline or that our influence has waned doesn't know what they're talking about.' Hillary Clinton in 2010 had even proclaimed 'a new American moment'. However, as the locus of global economic activity shifted from the Euro-Atlantic to the Asia-Pacific, the United States showed unmistakable signs of a loss of influence. Strategically, it was overextended, and struggling financially to maintain its military dominance. The 2012 Defense Strategic Guidance admitted as much when it conceded the US military could no longer wage two wars simultaneously in different parts of the world.[33] That same year, the US National Intelligence Council projected that, by 2030, no country would be a hegemonic power. 'Pax Americana – the era of American ascendancy in international politics that began in 1945 – is fast winding down.'[34]

The summer of 2013 provided a gruesome illustration of America's retreat from the world. It came in Syria, when the Assad regime launched a nerve-agent attack in the suburbs of Damascus that killed hundreds of civilians. This murderous infringement of Obama's 'red line' warning against the use of chemical weapons made a US military response almost inevitable. Yet even after pictures emerged of the corpses of asphyxiated children lying shoulder to shoulder on hospital floors, the president failed to carry through on his threat.

Obama claimed afterwards he was 'very proud' of his decision not to bomb Syria, because it rejected the orthodoxy that America always had to respond militarily to underline its power.[35] However, it was the biggest foreign-policy climb-down of his presidency, and also one of the most consequential of the past 50 years. It showed how his post-Iraq foreign policy mantra of 'Don't do stupid shit' all too often meant 'Don't do anything at all'. After all, American hegemony had rested over the decades on the deterrent effect of the presumption that the United States was always ready to use force.

Whenever reproached, Obama had a habit of dishonestly framing foreign-policy questions and presenting false choices. Critics of his inaction in Syria were accused of being warmongers intent on wading into another Middle Eastern quagmire. This was an unfair mischaracterisation of those – including senior members of his own administration – advocating graduated responses, such as the enforcement of no-fly zones or the creation of humanitarian corridors to deliver aid and evacuate civilians.

In Syria, the void left by America was filled by Russia. Vladimir Putin became a key Middle East power player. Moreover, he was emboldened to annex Crimea, which redrew the map of Europe – and maybe to keep interfering in the 2016 presidential election. America's precipitate withdrawal from neighbouring Iraq also contributed to the rise of ISIS, a terrorist group Obama mistakenly likened to a junior varsity team, whose caliphate came to encompass land in both countries.

Had Assad not been allowed to massacre so many of his countrymen and -women with such impunity, the refugee crisis would not have been so severe. By the end of the Obama presidency, the Syrian civil war had created five million refugees, and produced an influx of asylum seekers into Europe that fuelled the rise of the populist right. Television coverage of columns of refugees making their way through Europe in 2015 contributed to the 'leave' result in the Brexit referendum, in which Britons voted to take back control of their borders. In turn, Brexit provided a fillip for Donald Trump, who claimed, falsely, that he predicted the outcome the day before during a trip to Scotland, even though he didn't touch down in Britain until the following morning, when the result was known. Obama's mishandling of Syria contributed not only to the rise of Islamic State but also to the resurgence of nativist populism.

Despite America's mounting problems, and the inability of Washington to fix them, elections continued to produce the same gridlock. In the 2014 midterm elections, the Republicans were rewarded once again for their obstructionism, achieving their best nationwide result since the pre-New Deal days of the 1920s. In the House, the GOP won its largest majority since 1928. It regained control of the Senate for the first time since 2006. It also controlled more state legislatures than at any time since the late 1920s.

I was in Kentucky that night, partly because Mitch McConnell, the obstructionist-in-chief, was thought to be vulnerable. Yet he comfortably won re-election, and vowed again to keep thwarting the White House. His *coup de grâce* came when a vacancy opened up on the Supreme Court, after the death of the celebrated conservative jurist Antonin Scalia. McConnell held up Obama's proposed replacement, Merrick Garland, a centrist in his early sixties who was among the more benign candidates that the president could have picked, for almost a year, and blocked him from ever sitting on the court.

The big-name Republicans to lose their seats that election season were victims of fellow Republicans, demonstrating once again how lawmakers were often most vulnerable to challenges from members of their own party. Most startling was the primary defeat of Eric Cantor, the House majority leader and presumed heir to the Speakership, who was beaten by a little-known Tea Party insurgent. Over the years we had grown used to moderates being ousted by hardliners in primaries, but Cantor was a staunch conservative and the prime architect of the GOP's total opposition strategy against the Obama White House. Even one-time flame-throwers were now vilified for being part of the political establishment. Hardliners were being ousted by candidates who were even more extreme.

The Democrats were decimated, and now occupied fewer state positions than at any time during most of the previous 100 years.[36] Whereas in 2009 they had controlled 59 per cent of the state legislatures, by 2017 that figure was less than a third. Over the course of the Obama presidency, the Democrats suffered a net loss of 11 senators, 62 House seats, 12 governorships and 958 seats in state legislatures.[37] No president in modern history had lost so many state legislative seats. Obama had neglected to build up his party, focusing instead on his personal political operation. As a result, the Obama coalition, with its young, multicultural base, had not become the new Democratic coalition. The character of the party also continued to change. Continuing the trend from the Clinton years, it was geared more towards the professional elite rather than the working class.

Seemingly we had entered a new political era where the Democrats, because of their demographic advantages, would dominate presidential politics, and the Republicans, because of gerrymandering and the disproportionate power of rural states in the Senate, would command congressional politics – a complete inversion of Washington's balance of power from the late '60s to the early '90s.

Whereas once we had talked about the Republican lock on the Electoral College, now we spoke of an impregnable 'Blue Wall', the 18 states, including the big-three stronghold of New York, California and Illinois, and also the Rust Belt trio of Pennsylvania, Wisconsin and Michigan, that had voted Democratic in the last five presidential elections. Behind the Blue Wall were 242 of the 270 electoral votes needed to win, seemingly protected like the gold bullion at Fort Knox. Even the party's worst result since the pre-Roosevelt era did not appear to shake the Democrats' complacency and belief in demography as destiny.

His second shellacking in a congressional midterm election did, however, galvanise Obama. Determined to demonstrate he was not yet a lame duck, he embarked on one of the more productive phases of his presidency. In the international realm, where his actions were harder for Congress to circumscribe, he normalised relations with Cuba, took the lead in negotiating the 2015 Paris climate-change accord and pulled off his signature foreign-policy achievement, the Iranian nuclear deal.

His farewell year also delivered some of the most compelling imagery of his presidency. His trip to Cuba, where the enchanting streets of Old Havana served as backdrop, was the most filmic of his time in office. On the 50th anniversary of Black Sunday in Selma, he joined arms with Congressman John Lewis, the bravest of the brave civil rights activists, to walk across the Edmund Pettus Bridge. Then there was that summer of progressive triumphs, capped by his impromptu rendition of 'Amazing Grace'.

However, his farewell year also provided some of the most haunting imagery of his years in office: the picture of Alan Kurdi, the three-year-old Syrian boy, drowned in the Mediterranean Sea, whose lifeless body was washed up on a Turkish beach; the photograph of a Black Lives Matter protester, Ieshia Evans, goddess-like as she confronted a line of policemen decked out in RoboCop-style riot gear in Baton Rouge.

Smartphones made newsgatherers out of anyone who bore witness to a newsworthy event, and in that final summer there was a spate of police shootings caught on camera that in previous times would have passed without notice. In Falcon Heights, Minnesota, the girlfriend of Philando Castile, a school worker shot seven times by a police officer, even live-streamed the aftermath on Facebook, the couple's four-year-old daughter watching from the back seat of the car.

Eight years on from the financial crash, the economic mood of the nation was still sour. In November 2016, when the country went to the polls to decide upon Obama's successor, 55 per cent of voters still thought the country was mired in recession. It had ended in June 2009, less than six months into the Obama presidency, but the micro contradicted the macro: millions of Americans were still contending with personal downturns.[38] For those who had not seen their standard of living rise over the past eight years, despite taking on multiple jobs to make ends meet, America did not feel great.

So many hopes were vested in the Obama presidency, from reviving the US economy to fixing Washington's broken politics, from ending the unending wars in Iraq and Afghanistan to shuttering Guantánamo Bay, that a sense of anti-climax was perhaps unavoidable. Just as he had seemed fated to win the White House, so he also seemed doomed to disappoint once he occupied the Oval Office. From the moment in Chicago's Grant Park when he uttered the words 'Yes we can' for the first time as president-elect, he was hobbled by unrealistically high expectations and an unreasonably obstructionist opposition party. Being the first black man to occupy the White House was always going to provide the opening line of his obituary. His presidency, it was often noted, was less historic than the fact he became president.

What the 'doomed to disappointment' argument fails to account for is that Obama entered office as the head of a unity government with a majority in the House and a supermajority in the Senate. The gridlock that beset six of his eight years as president was not preordained. Nor were those two shellackings in the midterm elections. He was the author of many of his problems, partly – and unexpectedly – because there were times when he was a poor communicator, especially when speaking without a script. His answers at press conferences could be meandering and ridiculously long-winded, and tended to appeal to the head rather than the heart. Often aloof, he lacked Clinton's empathy. Often overly cerebral, he lacked Reagan's gift for neat encapsulation.

For all the shortcomings and disappointments, his two terms in office are amongst the more consequential of the post-war years, not least because he helped rescue the US economy and saved the country from freefalling into a second Great Depression. Cars are still manufactured in Detroit, partly because of Obama's bailout of the auto industry. The Dodd–Frank Wall Street Reform and Consumer Protection Act re-regulated the financial sector. Still, his administration was noticeably more pro-Wall Street than Main Street. Rather than targeting the big banks, he shielded them. 'My administration is the only thing between you and the pitchforks,' he told a meeting at the White House involving 13 big bank CEOs. 'I'm not out there to go after you. I'm protecting you.'[39] An ethos of too big to assail.

Unemployment dropped over the course of his presidency from 10 per cent to 5 per cent, while the Dow Jones more than doubled. In the final year of his presidency, American household incomes actually enjoyed the largest gains on record. Yet that was not the widespread perception, especially in the old industrial heartland of the Rust Belt.

Obama became the first post-war president not to achieve an annual GDP growth rate of 3 per cent. Economic gains came to be unevenly spread. Income segregation became more pronounced. Between 2009 and 2013, 95 per cent of the income gains in America went to the top 1 per cent, an astonishing figure during a Democratic presidency.[40] An especial concern, as Obama himself acknowledged, was the decline in prime-age participation among male workers. In 1953, just 3 per cent of men between 25 and 54 were out of work. By 2016, it was 12 per cent.

Productivity had also slowed, which Obama blamed on a lack of public and private investment caused by the lingering effects of the financial crisis and the anti-tax ideology that had taken hold in Washington. Tellingly, however, he did not blame Ronald Reagan, or make a prolonged effort to change the anti-government zeitgeist.[41]

In enacting Obamacare, the president succeeded where Truman, Kennedy, Johnson and Clinton failed. More than 30 million uninsured Americans finally received coverage. But almost the same number remained uninsured, and the botched roll-out of the Obamacare website showed a disregard for the mechanics of government. Thereafter, his legislative accomplishments were fairly meagre. He failed to enact a comprehensive immigration reform or a cap-and-trade bill to combat climate change. Unable to breach the wall of Republican opposition, he was forced to rely on executive action to push his Clean Power Plan, the Paris climate-change accord and the Deferred Action for Childhood Arrivals, or DACA, which protected the children of illegal immigrants from deportation.

His reliance on reform through the stroke of a presidential pen meant much of his legacy was reversible, and could be wiped out by his successor's signature. Nor did he build a Democratic Party that could advance his agenda or protect his legacy. His working assumption seemed to be that the Clinton machine would soon take over the Democratic National Committee, and a second President Clinton would safeguard Obamacare and his other reforms. Too often he relied on his political celebrity rather than emphasising the drudgery of party-building, a strange oversight for a one-time community organiser. The Obama Justice Department did little to challenge Republican gerrymandered districts – although, oddly, Eric Holder, his former attorney general, tried to do so after he left office.

On Capitol Hill, all of the Congresses of his presidency, from the 111th through to the 114th, were successively more divided and dysfunctional. Obama, who eschewed personal flattery and didn't give much thought to the kind of small gestures that often could make such a big difference, was criticised for not doing enough to charm and cajole lawmakers.

Not a whisky-after-work sort of president – understandably, he preferred to have supper with his wife and daughters – even fellow Democrats complained about his standoffishness. Partly because of his cool temperament, his preternatural 'No Drama Obama' mode, often he was quiescent in the face of GOP obstructionism. Rather than rail, Truman-like, against a do-nothing Congress, he played it cool, mistakenly believing that rationality would be rewarded. Nor did he take on the Tea Party, and even avoided using the term. When Mitch McConnell blocked his doomed Merrick Garland for almost a year, Obama was far too supine.

'I understand the posture they're taking right now,' he said. 'I get the politics of it. I'm sure they're under enormous pressure from their base ... and I've told them I'm sympathetic.'[42] His response to the victory of Donald Trump, while magnanimous, was also typically phlegmatic. 'The path that this country has taken has never been a straight line,' he said dispassionately in the Rose Garden the day after the election, departing from the beloved liberal narrative of continual progress. 'We zig and zag and sometimes we move in ways that some people think is forward and others think is moving back. And that's okay.'[43]

Placing himself on the right side of history all too often became a substitute for battling to alter its course. Sometimes, on issues such as climate change, it was as if he was virtue-signalling to future generations. Winning arguments and claiming moral victories often seemed just as important to him as winning elections and enacting legislation.

Some critics, like the Yale professor David Bromwich, suggest his lack of fight stemmed from everything coming so easily to him – from the presidency of the *Harvard Law Review*, even though he hadn't ever authored a signed paper for this academic journal, to the presidency of the United States, even though he had only been a senator for three years. The black writer Ta-Nehisi Coates, noting how Obama's formative years had been spent in Hawaii, America's most racially integrated state, claimed he had not been exposed to the same level of discrimination as, say, a black kid growing up in Alabama, Mississippi or even Illinois. As a result, he underestimated the forces seeking to destroy his presidency.

Obama was never credulous enough to think he could usher in a post-racial America, a term he deliberately avoided. 'I never bought into the notion that by electing me, somehow we were entering into a post-racial period,' he told *Rolling Stone.*

The racial stalemate he spoke of in his Philadelphia race speech in 2008, which saved his imperilled candidacy when the sermons of his controversial fire-and-brimstone pastor, Jeremiah Wright, sounded like they may condemn him, was evident still when he exited the White House. Yet a recurring problem of his eight years in office was that he shied away from delivering a presidential version of the extraordinary speech that helped make him president. Obama was the poet laureate of his own presidency, but his rhetorical gifts were seldom brought to bear on race.

As for the birtherism of Donald Trump, Obama publicly laughed it off, and gave the impression of not taking it seriously. 'This all dates back to when we were growing up together in Kenya,' he joked on *The Tonight Show with Jay Leno.* 'When we finally moved to America, I thought it'd be over.' Dealing with racism through humour, however, trivialised extreme views. For Obama, irony was a means both of deflection and avoidance.

Even if he was never going to be truly transformational on the vexed question of race, the hope was he might be transitional: the leader who oversaw the peaceable demographic shift from a still strongly Caucasian America where 62.6 per cent of US citizens were white to a more ethnically diffuse nation. Four years into his presidency, for the first time in American history, a majority of newborn babies were from racial or ethnic minorities. Likewise, a record number of Americans – 12 per cent – married partners from a different race.[44] Instead, he handed over power to a white nationalist birther who played the race card from the bottom of the pack. Rather than bringing about the deracialisation of America, Obama's presidency actually contributed to its re-racialisation.

Obama's attempts to close the partisan rift also failed. Over the course of his presidency, the partisan divide became starker on every major issue. About three-quarters of Democrats approved of Obamacare, while 85 per cent of Republicans disapproved. In 2008, there was a 27 percentage-point gap between Obama and McCain supporters on whether it was more important to protect gun rights than limit gun ownership. By 2016, the gap between Clinton and Trump supporters on guns had surged to 70 per cent.

Climate change was another topic where the Democrats and Republicans grew further apart. Immigration too. Twice as many Democrats thought immigrants strengthened the country as Republicans, whereas at the turn of the century attitudes had been much the same.[45] Here again, the president's race was an important factor. If Obama was strongly associated with an issue, research by Michael Tesler of Brown University revealed, it became significantly more 'racialised' in the eyes of voters. This was especially true of the Affordable Care Act, the reform that bore his name. Voters even reacted differently to pictures of the Obamas' pet dog, Bo, after they learned the identity of its master.[46] The president's skin colour went a long way to explaining why he was such a polarising figure, with an 81 per cent average approval rating from Democrats, but just a 14 per cent average approval rating from Republicans.[47] Never before had there been such a partisan gap.

In foreign affairs, he closed the CIA's enhanced interrogation programme on his first full day in office, hunted down Osama bin Laden, revived US support for international cooperation and multilateralism and, after the Bush years, rehabilitated the rules-based international order. His landmark Cairo speech was a long overdue attempt to reassure the Muslim world that America was not engaged in a crusade against Islam.[48] His 'Asia Pivot', officially announced in a speech before the Australian parliament in November 2011, was an attempt to disentangle America from wars in the Middle East.

Those around the world who disparaged George W. Bush embraced the new president. The post-Iraq mood of anti-Americanism dissipated. In the United Kingdom, America's closest ally, confidence in the US president leapt from 16 per cent under Bush in 2008 to 86 per cent for Obama in 2009.[49]

However, he was by no means as saintly as the ridiculously early award of a Nobel Peace Prize implied. Of the estimated 3,797 people killed during his drone campaign, the cornerstone of his counter-terrorism strategy, more than 300 were civilians. 'Turns out I'm really good at killing people,' he reportedly told aides, sounding uncharacteristically trigger-happy and gung-ho. 'Didn't know that was gonna be a strong suit of mine.'[50] Obama ordered more than 500 drone strikes, compared with Bush's 52. These extrajudicial killings obviated the need for waterboarding or enhanced interrogation.

Obama went a long way towards fulfilling his promise of withdrawing US forces from Iraq and Afghanistan – the number of troops dropped from 180,000 at the start of his presidency to around 15,000 at the end. But it was a drawdown rather than a complete disentanglement, which opened him up to criticism from both hawks and doves. His failure to leave behind a residual force in Iraq directly contributed to the rise of ISIS and its capture of Mosul, then the country's third-largest city. But he failed to extricate US forces from the conflict in Afghanistan, America's longest war. This meant Donald Trump could simultaneously claim Obama was both feeble and feckless for leaving Iraq vulnerable to the threat from ISIS but not delivering complete disengagement.

Though Obama made much of the world admire America again, he had less success in making other countries bend to his will. Under his leadership, the United States lost much of its fear factor, partly because he was so reasonable, and partly because he was so reluctant to pursue a militarised foreign policy. In Syria and Ukraine, Putin ran rings around him. Bashar al-Assad, after not being punished for crossing Obama's red line, again poisoned his own people with nerve gas. The Israeli Prime Minister, Benjamin Netanyahu, a constant and bolshie irritant, regularly flouted Obama's demands to stop settlement construction in occupied territory.

Even close allies were unafraid to defy him, as Britain, Australia, South Korea and Germany did when they joined the Asian Infrastructure Investment Bank (AIIB), a Chinese initiative intended to rival the World Bank and International Monetary Fund, two of the post-war Bretton Woods institutions upon which Pax Americana had been built. Obama's first Treasury Secretary, Lawrence Summers, was alarmed by the stampede to join the new Chinese institution. 'This past month,' he wrote in April 2015, 'may be remembered as the moment the United States lost its role as the underwriter of the global economic system.'[51]

Towards the end of his presidency, Obama told a group of historians, 'I didn't make any big mistakes.'[52] His 'Don't do stupid shit' approach had, in his mind at least, been a success. Yet the Syria conflict, where by the end of his presidency 400,000 people had been killed, was a terrible blight on his record. In Libya, 'leading from behind', as an administration official described America's role in the coalition, was an unusually weak posture for the world's most powerful nation. Then, after the fall of Muammar Gaddafi, the United States remained a bystander to the chaos that followed, which created another safe haven for ISIS and led tens of thousands of refugees to take to the treacherous waters of the Mediterranean in the hope of reaching Europe. Both instances showed how Obama had overlearned the mistakes of Iraq, which led him to commit unforced errors of his own. Too much of his foreign policy was informed by an exaggerated sense of the limits of American power. To the extent there was an 'Obama doctrine', it was essentially a series of correctives for the Bush years, rather than a positive vision of global leadership. Much like Bill Clinton, Obama did not solve America's post-Cold War strategic dilemma, of how and where to project its power.

A searing rebuke of his approach came from his first Secretary of State, Hillary Clinton. 'Great nations need organising principles,' she said, when asked about the Obama doctrine. '"Don't do stupid stuff" is not an organising principle.'[53] Even more damning was Vali Nasr, an academic who had served during the first term of the Obama administration and watched US influence wane in the Middle East,

Asia, Latin America and even Africa. 'We have gone from leading everywhere, to leading nowhere.'[54]

His main corrective, of ending America's long and costly wars, was entirely understandable given the disaster of Iraq, but after eight years of disengagement Americans became wary of any kind of interventionism. This made it easier for Donald Trump to prosecute his case for America First neo-isolationism.

Obama's trade policy, centred upon the negotiation of the Trans-Pacific Partnership, a move intended to hem in China, also inadvertently played into Trump's hands. Working-class Americans rejected the argument that trade deals fuelled the US economy by opening up new markets. Instead, roughly half of voters associated globalisation with lower wages and fewer jobs. The slogan 'Make America Great Again', which Trump tried to trademark just weeks after Obama's re-election in 2012, had more resonance when about half of the country thought its global power had declined over the past decade.[55]

How did Obama change the office itself? After an eight-year pause during the Bush years, Obama revived the performative presidency. By the time he entered the White House he was not merely a global celebrity but an international cultural icon immortalised in that 'HOPE' portrait. From early on, he understood the power of his fame, and how it accrued political capital. His celebrity, and the fear it could be fleeting, played a significant part in his decision to run for the presidency in 2008, despite having served for just three years as a senator. In the Democratic primaries, his stardom also helped him dispatch Hillary Clinton, a politician with the name recognition but not the charisma of her husband.

Obama also understood media spectacle. Oprah Winfrey became his most prominent surrogate. When he delivered his acceptance speech before 80,000 people at the Mile High Stadium in Denver, the backdrop was a columned mock-up of the White House colonnade. The McCain campaign, trying to turn his global megastardom against him, put out an attack ad simply called 'Celeb', which intercut footage of Obama being fêted by a million-strong crowd in Berlin with images of Britney Spears and Paris Hilton. 'He's the biggest celebrity in the world,' the ad noted. 'But is he ready to lead?' Even in post-9/11 America, however, the question of whether voters wanted a commander-in-chief rather than a celebrity-in-chief was by no means clear-cut. The McCain ad inadvertently showcased one of Obama's strengths.

Whereas many of his predecessors looked like daggy dads dancing at a disco when they ventured into the world of entertainment, Obama made the transition effortlessly, whether mimicking Al Green, boogieing with Ellen DeGeneres, appearing on *The View* or driving around the White House grounds cracking jokes with Jerry Seinfeld on *Comedians in Cars Getting Coffee*.

To some long-time Washington watchers, it resembled a high-end version of *Keeping up with the Kardashians*. 'The Obama White House was the biggest, splashiest reality show ever,' wrote Obama biographer Jonathan Alter, 'lacking in tacky or embarrassing drama, perhaps, but still entertaining.'[56] Obama became another president who understood that politics had become pop culture, but who underperformed in the back-office aspects of the job.

By putting himself at the head of the social-media revolution, Obama took the celebrity presidency into the digital age, which was transformative. Whereas Bill Clinton had sent just two emails during his time in office, the Obama White House was downright promiscuous, joining Twitter, Facebook, Flickr, Vimeo, iTunes, Snapchat, YouTube, Periscope, Instagram, Pinterest, Friendster and Myspace. It gave the presidency online omnipresence. Racking up millions of followers, friends and likes, he became the country's most influential influencer. He used social media to persuade more young people to sign up to Obamacare and to think more seriously about climate change. It made sense to use the tools at his disposal. Yet in the absence of legislative action, it could often look like presidential clicktivism.

This online presence vested the presidency with new powers. His reliance on digital engagement allowed him to bypass the traditional media, and established the White House as a media outlet in its own right. This further weakened traditional news organisations at a time when they were already reeling. It also meant more of the national conservation played out online, although in ways that often accentuated political separatism. The use of micro-targeting – the tailoring of special messages for specific audiences – aggravated polarisation, not least because its primary intention was to mobilise existing voters rather than reach out to new ones.

There was a hipness about the Obama years that challenged the old adage 'Washington is Hollywood for ugly people', a descendant of the line 'Politics is showbusiness for ugly people'. The most photogenic First Family since the Kennedys, the Obama White House became a Black Camelot. Even the nation's sleepy capital felt fashionable, with 'permanent Washington', the commentators and journalists who make up its chattering class, starting to eye itself as more of a cultural player. The annual dinner of the White House Correspondents' Association, which became more glamorous and self-congratulatory, was a case in point. 'Nerd Prom', as it was dubbed, transformed itself into a night of a thousand stars, with a red-carpet celebrity parade beforehand, covered live on CNN, and swanky parties afterwards, one of which was hosted, Oscars-style, by *Vanity Fair*. When Stephen Colbert's roast of George W. Bush became a viral hit, it turned the dinner into a pop-culture calendar event, complete with hashtag hieroglyphics (#nerdprom). Comedians invited to speak no longer minded bombing in the ballroom, so long as they lit up Twitter.

By 2011 the dinner had become sufficiently glitzy to attract Donald Trump, who came as a guest of *The Washington Post*, a paper he came to hate. His primary role that night, however, was to be a comic prop for the president. Just days after releasing his birth certificate to the press, Obama mercilessly roasted the untitled head of the Birther Movement, and even flashed on the big screen a picture of how a Trump White House might look, with its ridiculous golden Greek columns, three extra floors and Vegas-style hoarding inscribed with the billionaire's name.

Obama's speech could also be interpreted as an attempt to re-erect a barrier between celebrity and politics, to remind people of the gulf in responsibility between a real-life president and a reality TV tycoon. He teased Trump about his 'credentials and breadth of experience', citing an irksome decision on an edition of *Celebrity Apprentice* – whether or not to fire the B-list actor Gary Busey. Twenty-four hours later, Obama's mocking words were brought into even sharper relief when he stepped solemnly before the cameras in the Grand Foyer of the White House to announce the death of Osama bin Laden.

His attempt at character assassination, however, blew up in his face. Even though Trump has since denied the Correspondents' Dinner was the moment he decided to run for the presidency, it surely aroused a desire for revenge. Moreover, it elevated his status as America's foremost anti-Obama, a useful position to occupy in a Republican Party increasingly defined by its hatred of the president.

The president's mockery of Trump continued all the way up until Election Day in 2016. Appearing on *Jimmy Kimmel Live!*, he took part in a regular segment where celebrities read out insults posted on Twitter. 'President Obama will go down as perhaps the worst president in the history of the United States,' he read, before adding the name of its author, '@realDonaldTrump'. Then Obama delivered his response, ending, rapper-like, by dropping his phone to the floor. 'Well, @realDonaldTrump, at least I will go down as president.'[57]

In the final months of the Obama presidency, as the battle to succeed him reached its unseemly climax, two weaknesses from his time in office intersected over Russia's covert operation to help Donald Trump reach the White House. The first was the president's lack of menace on the international stage, especially when it came to confronting Vladimir Putin. The second was the president's failure to extract concessions from his Republican tormentors on Capitol Hill.

In early September, when he came face-to-face with Putin at the G20 summit in China, Obama glared at the Russian president as he warned him to 'cut it out' and warned of 'serious consequences' if he didn't. Yet Putin, who had already outmanoeuvred the US president in Syria and Crimea, was undeterred. The Kremlin's meddling continued unabated. Then, when the White House sought bipartisan support to send a letter to state governors warning them to protect election infrastructure from Russian dirty tricks, the Republican congressional leadership refused, claiming it was a naked partisan play.

Not wanting to intervene so dramatically at the late stage of an election he thought his friend was going to win, Obama left it to his intelligence chiefs to sound the warning. Rather than hold a news conference, however, they did so with a written statement from the Department of Homeland Security and Director of National Intelligence, James Clapper. It landed in our inboxes at around 3.30 on a Friday afternoon, often the time in Washington when unwelcome news get buried.

In any case, 30 minutes later came a far more extraordinary October surprise: the release by *The Washington Post* of the *Access Hollywood* tape. On that same, news-packed Friday afternoon, WikiLeaks started tweeting links to emails hacked by Russian operatives from the Clinton campaign chairman, John Podesta. But even though they contained revelations embarrassing to Hillary Clinton, the tape of Trump gleefully using the words 'Grab 'em by the pussy' would surely kill off his candidacy. In what Barack Obama described that month as the 'relay race' of the presidency, it now looked certain he would hand over the baton to America's first female president. The election, most of us thought, was as good as over.

To Chicago we headed for the valedictory speech of his presidency, which he delivered in a cavernous convention centre close to the South Side streets where Obama had worked as a community organiser. For those who worked on his presidential campaign, this Windy City homecoming was also a reunion. Onto the windows of the neighbouring hotel, many of his former staffers taped posters with the words 'Fired Up, Ready to Go', the chant the then Illinois senator first heard on the campaign trail in Greenwood, South Carolina, from Edith S. Childs, an elderly African-American woman with a gold tooth and a giant Sunday-best purple hat, who had come to hear him speak on a day when his morale had been sagging.

Reflecting on his eight years in office, he ticked off his legacy items and spoke for one last time about striving for a more perfect union. Then he delivered perhaps his most honest assessment of the polarised state of the nation: of the 'great sorting' which had led people to seek refuge in their own 'bubbles'; of 'the splintering of our media into a channel for every taste'; of the rise of 'naked partisanship'; of the problems posed by 'economic and regional stratification'. There was a plea for politicians to recognise 'a common baseline of facts', and a warning against climate-change denialism.

His chief concern, though, was for the health of American democracy. Invoking George Washington, who had warned in his farewell address about the threat from political factionalism, he spoke of voting rates among the lowest in advanced economies, the corrupting impact of money, the dysfunction of Congress and the need for democratic renewal. Then, for one final time, he reprised his greatest rhetorical hit, with a retrospective change of tense:

'Yes we can. Yes we did. Yes we can.'

It was the sort of contemplative speech that demanded lengthy debate and consideration. In that cerebral way of his, carefully weighing competing arguments, Obama tried to make sense of the rise of Donald Trump, albeit without ever mentioning his name. It was hard, though, to concentrate that night, still less absorb the full import of his earnest message.

For just as Obama was about to speak, BuzzFeed released the secret dossier that many news organisations, including the BBC, had gained access to before the election but had never managed to corroborate. Compiled by a former British intelligence operative, Christopher Steele, it sketched out a possible conspiracy between the Trump campaign and the Kremlin to seize the US presidency. Some of its X-rated details made the Starr Report sound pedestrian, not least the allegation, vehemently and plausibly denied by Donald Trump, that prostitutes had urinated in front of him at the Ritz-Carlton Hotel in Moscow to defile a bed used by the Obamas during a presidential visit. Nothing spoke of the jolting transition we were about to witness more than Obama talking about his perfect union while journalists on the press riser at the back were trading lavatorial jokes about golden showers. A presidency that for Barack Obama had started out atop a mighty mountain ended in the trash-strewn valley.

6

The Donald Trump Show

Trump Tower, that totem of the '80s, now became an emblem of America's broken politics. The home of the billionaire's campaign headquarters. A venue for his victory parties, as he accumulated the delegates needed to win the Republican presidential nomination. The place he slept most nights during primary season, wherever he ended up on the trail, to spare him the encumbrance of having to stay in the states he was trying to court.

The 2016 election was supposed to be a dynastic duel between the Clintons and the Bushes, families resident in the White House for 20 of the previous 28 years. But rather than watching a restoration, we bore witness to a revolution, an insurrection that had been decades in the making – not that we understood that in the moment.

Covering this bacchanal was not unlike making a first-time visit to the Indian subcontinent, with its sensory overload, roiling chaos and bundle of contradictions: the Manhattan tycoon who became a working-class hero; the candidate maligned as a New York conman whose appeal was based on his authenticity; the feminist trailblazer rejected by a majority of white female voters. So ugly was the race that even seasoned correspondents could be forgiven for suffering from a reverse form of the Stendhal syndrome, a psychosomatic response to being exposed to great beauty that can bring on confusion and even hallucinations.

Much of it felt like tripping on political acid, whether it was that victory party at the Trump National Golf Club during primary season when the candidate-cum-impresario appeared alongside a table piled high with Trump wine, Trump steaks and Trump natural spring water; or the moment he accused Ted Cruz's Cuban-born father of being involved in the assassination of John F. Kennedy; or his rally in Birmingham, Alabama, when he claimed, speciously, to have seen footage on 9/11 of 'thousands and thousands' of Muslims in New Jersey cheering the destruction of the Twin Towers; or the televised debate where he reassured voters about the size of his appendage. If Hunter S. Thompson, the gonzo journalist who covered Nixon's campaigns through a drug-fuelled haze, had still been alive, he surely would have wondered what he had imbibed.

As well as saturating the media, Trump near-monopolised our minds and memories. Almost all my most vivid recollections from 2016 involve his candidacy, whether it was the site of the snaking queues outside his campaign events, which were made up not just of pot-bellied rednecks wearing 'Lock Her Up' T-shirts but also suburban Starbucks moms, some dressed in Lululemon yoga pants, with their lipstick-stained caffè mochas in one hand and young daughters in the other. Or the raucousness of his stadium rallies, where chants of 'USA, USA' and 'Build the Wall' were interspersed with 'Nessun Dorma' sung by Pavarotti and the candidate repeatedly purring the word 'boootiful' – which, when overlaid, sounded unnervingly orgasmic. Or the look on Melania Trump's face on the night before his victory in New Hampshire, when she followed him into the lobby of the Best Western Hotel in Manchester, where the guest rooms came with their own microwave and the breakfast area had two self-service waffle machines, an orange-juice dispenser and small sachets of Rice Krispies. Usually when a candidate is in the same budget hotel as reporters from the BBC – I was staying on the same floor, three doors away – it is a sign of their imminent demise. So here was another iron-clad rule that was about to be shattered.

From his golden escalator descent in June 2015 until Election Day in November 2016, I confess to committing most of the same analytical mistakes as my press-pack colleagues. Of thinking that launching his campaign with an attack on Mexican immigrants was suicidal when the Republican Party faced a demographic death spiral. Of viewing his attack on John McCain's heroism – which also doubled as an assault on what had long been universally accepted views about American goodness and virtue – as an act of terminal self-harm. Of predicting female voters would never back a misogynist beauty-pageant owner who scored women out of ten and who seemed to regret not being able to date his eldest daughter. Of believing right-wing evangelicals would find it morally complicated, if not sacrilegious, to back a thrice-married former casino owner who had appeared on the front cover of *Playboy* – 81 per cent of evangelicals ended up voting for him. Of assuming his puerile nicknames – Little Marco, Lyin' Ted, Crooked Hillary – would be self-belittling. Of predicting suburban soccer moms worried about school shootings would reject a candidate who suggested 'Second Amendment people' could take matters into their own hands if Hillary Clinton won the election. Of thinking polite, Rotary Club Republicans, who watch their kids play football on Friday night and attend Episcopalian church on Sunday morning, would turn up their noses at a rogue candidate who instructed rally-goers, 'If you see someone getting ready to throw a tomato, knock the crap out of them. I'll pay the legal bills.' To many of his supporters this aggression, which borrowed from the WrestleMania bouts he used to stage in Atlantic City, was appealing. It spoke of the destructive energy he promised to bring to Washington.

What to the Beltway commentariat seemed disbarring were unique selling points to his growing army of red-capped supporters. His xenophobia and racist slurs were seductive to the 72 per cent of supporters who believed the American way of life had changed for the worse since the civil rights era. His birtherism appealed to the 58 per cent of Republicans who believed Barack Obama was born outside of the United States or weren't entirely sure.[1] Attacking John McCain endeared him to movement conservatives unwilling to stomach yet another establishment pick as their presidential nominee.

Evangelical Christians saw in Trump a fellow victim of elite sneering, and thus showed forgiveness when he referred to 'Two Corinthians' rather than 'Second Corinthians', and confessed the

Bible was only his second favourite book after *The Art of the Deal*. To those who railed against political correctness, his sophomoric nicknames doubled as a poke in the eye for pious liberals. Trump bestowed respectability on their darkest innermost thoughts, which now they could express openly and unapologetically. The unsayable had become sayable.

As for his misogyny, it was not just acceptable for many of his male supporters but enviable. If only they could lurk behind the scenes at beauty pageants in the hope of catching an eyeful of nubile young flesh, or have bedded enough silicone-implanted supermodels to grade them out of ten or be in a position to tell a onetime *Playboy* playmate, as he did on *Celebrity Apprentice*, 'Must be a pretty picture, you dropping to your knees.'

Many veterans also seemed unperturbed about voting for a draft-dodger who described surviving AIDS-hit New York as his personal Vietnam, because he spoke of 'bombing the shit' out of ISIS and disentangling US forces from unending wars. The conventional wisdom deemed Trump to be too unconventional. But that, of course, was precisely what his supporters craved. Perversely, there was an underlying brilliance to all that he did.

Conservatives troubled by Trump's excesses managed to rationalise their support for him. America needed a businessman in charge. Broken Washington required an outsider to fix it. Trump might be bad, but he was better than Hillary Clinton. He wasn't truly a racist, but made racist remarks to gin up his base. As his statements became more outlandish and his behaviour more erratic, Trump became the beneficiary of his own vicious circle. The more he was criticised by the liberal media, the more it confirmed his renegade status. The more renegade he became, the more coverage and social-media comment he generated. And the more coverage he received, the higher he soared in the polls.

His grotesque boast that 'I could stand in the middle of Fifth Avenue and shoot somebody and I wouldn't lose any voters' was one of his most insightful statements during the campaign, and also his most honest. As the right-wing firebrand Ann Coulter rightly observed,

'There's nothing Trump can do that won't be forgiven, except change his immigration policies.'[2]

Even after the surrealism of his early candidacy turned into a string of primary victories, our diagnostic errors continued. When he called for a ban on every Muslim trying to enter the country, most of us continued to prophesy there simply were not enough angry white male voters to reward this kind of racial demagoguery with victory. 'It's the demography, stupid,' I wrote at the time, believing a nationalised version of the southern strategy was no longer viable. Progress begets progress, a Whiggish interpretation of the liberal flow of history premised on the first black president being followed into office by the first female president, was another flawed assumption.

The cliché of Trump's primary-season success, that the billionaire had mounted a hostile takeover of the Republican Party, was also incorrect. While there was no shortage of Never Trumpers, it was more like a merger and acquisition, with shareholder support and buy-in from a large portion of the customer base. The Republican Party's main media partner, Fox News, was on board.

We also kept on referring to the 'Republican establishment' as if it had citadel-like resilience. By 2016, however, the establishment was a ruined castle, with heirs to the throne exiles in their ancestral land. Jeb Bush could not even persuade his mother, Barbara, that yet another member of their dynasty deserved to be president. Other conventional Republicans, such as Scott Walker, the Governor of Wisconsin, Chris Christie, the Governor of New Jersey, John Kasich, the Governor of Ohio, and the Florida Senator Marco Rubio were quickly slain – spear-carriers up against a Gatling gun. Back in 1992 and 1996, the party leadership had been strong enough to rebuff Pat Buchanan. By 2016, it was easy for Donald Trump to breach its feeble defences. Tellingly, Ted Cruz put up the most resistance, an anti-establishment candidate who in the later primaries became the great white hope of the Never Trumpers. Nothing better illustrated the pitiful state of the GOP establishment than Cruz emerging as its potential saviour. Yet in a party that often felt more like a protest movement against Barack Obama, there was logic in nominating the untitled head of the Birther Movement. An anti-Obama party opted for the most anti-Obama candidate.

———

Whatever the year, whoever were the candidates, reporting on the US primary season always felt like entering the gates of a journalistic theme park and roaming its varying sectors with a notebook in one hand and popcorn in the other. Caucus-land in Iowa, with its snow-covered plains and Midwestern manners; Live-Free-or-Die-land in New Hampshire, with its white-steepled churches and ever so cranky voters; and Confederacy-land in South Carolina, with its barbeque, black churches and Stars and Bars flags.

To make sense of 2016, though, one had to visit the Old Industrial Heartland. Some Beltway commentators made do with reading the bestselling field guide, *Hillbilly Elegy: A Memoir of a Family and Culture in Crisis,* J. D. Vance's memoir, with its first-hand account of white working-class despondency and self-pity.

'We talk about the value of hard work,' Vance wrote of his fellow Appalachians, 'but tell ourselves that the reason we are not working is some perceived unfairness: Obama shut down the coal mines, or all of the jobs went to the Chinese.' To see the book come to life, all one had to do was fly to Pittsburgh and then drive out to the neighbouring valleys, with their onion-domed Russian orthodox churches, Veterans of Foreign Wars halls and windowless bars – the landscape of *The Deer Hunter.* The most relevant local landmarks were the skeletal remains of the old steelworks, with their carcass-like furnaces, and the empty shells of derelict factories that now served as echo chambers for the rallying cry 'Make America Great Again'. From 2001 to 2013, some 65,000 factories had closed across the country with the loss of five million manufacturing jobs.[3] These post-industrial landscapes provided the seedbed of Trump-land. He was a beneficiary of a malfunctioning economy where all but 200,000 of the 11.6 million 'good' jobs created since the Great Recession had gone to those with a bachelor's degree or some college education.[4]

What the billionaire told these communities aligned with their internal dialogue: politicians had sold them down the river by signing destructive trade deals; greedy corporations had betrayed them by shipping jobs abroad; cosmopolitan elites, with their sissy creed of political correctness, threatened their working-class culture; immigrants posed a threat to their national security, neighbourhood security and economic security.

Nobody in Washington cared about the opioid crisis, or understood how it had ravaged their communities. Soon we came to realise the number of discarded syringes scattered in the gutters was as accurate a political barometer of a community's allegiance as campaign posters in the windows or placards in the yards.

Trump possessed the great skill of populists and demagogues down the ages: to articulate the fears and prejudices of voters better than they could themselves, and also to offer simplistic solutions. Bomb the shit out of ISIS. End endless wars. Build new barricades, whether it was a fortified wall along the entirety of the Mexican border or protectionist trade barriers to guard against China. His manifesto could be summed up in two slogans comprised of seven words: 'Make America Great Again' and 'Build the Wall'. Nobody better gave voice to the feelings of white resentment than this adroit sloganeer.

In Braddock, Pennsylvania, where a derelict steelworks was now an industrial heritage site, the curator laughingly offered to show us the magic switch Donald Trump planned to flick the moment he became president, which miraculously would bring back tens of thousands of lost jobs. Blue-collar voters, though, were not naïve enough to look upon him as a miracle worker who could magically turn back time. But Trump made them feel seen and heard. The former Republican staffer Salena Zito put it best when she wrote in *The Atlantic*, 'The press takes him literally, but not seriously; his supporters take him seriously, but not literally.'[5]

To fight their class and cultural war, these hollowed-out communities co-opted a New York billionaire, a 'bridge and tunnel' guy from the outer boroughs who had always been mocked by Manhattan's elites. Trump intermixed the politics of grievance with the politics of vengeance, which is why the 'Lock Her Up' chant directed against Hillary Clinton became so popular. Trump wasn't so much aspirational as avenging: a vigilante candidate. He promised to settle a few scores with the political elites, China and immigrants.

Tellingly, he had nothing to say about the real job-killer: automation. From 2006 to 2013, it was estimated that trade accounted for the extinction of 13 per cent of manufacturing jobs. Robots and other factors at home killed off 88 per cent of these jobs.[6] It was easier to scapegoat NAFTA, China and Mexican immigrants, and to stoke the nostalgic nationalism that was central to his appeal. Trump was the main beneficiary of a Rust Belt revolt against robots.

Back in 2008, Barack Obama had been pilloried for describing the resentment felt in these communities. By 2016, his words sounded prophetic. 'You go into some of these small towns in Pennsylvania, and, like a lot of small towns in the Midwest, the jobs have gone now for 25 years and nothing's replaced them. Each successive administration has said that somehow these communities are gonna regenerate and they have not. So it's not surprising that they got bitter, they cling to guns or religion or antipathy to people who aren't like them, or anti-immigrant sentiment or anti-trade sentiment to explain their frustrations.' Now they were clinging to Donald Trump.

As well as visiting the Rust Belt, it was necessary to cast an eye overseas, something a self-absorbed US media failed repeatedly to do. For while Trump was an American original, his rise could hardly be described as a uniquely American phenomenon. Trumpism was part of a larger worldwide malaise, as the global economic downturn was followed by a global democratic downturn. As early as 2013, a United Nations report found that growing income inequality was responsible for growing political instability. The following year, when Pew Research conducted a survey in 44 countries about the greatest dangers facing the world, Americans ranked inequality at the top.[7]

The sense of economic vulnerability was exacerbated by fears that predominant cultures were under assault, that multiculturalism was eroding national identity, that sovereignty was imperilled. Concerns about unchecked immigration that peaked during the refugee crisis in 2015 combined the two. Technological change, and the workplace disruption it wrought, fanned the populist and nationalistic flames. At a time when the developed world was being stratified horizontally into the haves and have-nots of globalisation, and in a wired world where tech-savvy hipsters in Brooklyn had more in common with their fellow millennials in Shoreditch or Peckham than their compatriots in Cleveland or Peoria, those who had missed out sought to erect vertical barriers – walls, barbed-wire fences, tariffs. The Rust Belt was a proxy for so many post-industrial sink regions the world over.

In this rebellion of the disenfranchised and powerless, voters not only rejected politics as usual; they sought to completely upend it. Therefore, they turned to parties, movements and individuals on the extreme right and extreme left, such as Marine Le Pen in France, Syriza in Greece, Podemos in Spain, Viktor Orbán in Hungary, Rodrigo Duterte in the Philippines, the extremist Geert Wilders in the Netherlands or Rob Ford, the foul-mouthed, middle-fingered mayor of Toronto, who was a municipal forerunner of Trump. All benefited from the weakness of existing party systems.

Even before the economic downturn, mainstream political parties were already in long-term decline. In France, for the first time since the creation of the Fifth Republic in the late 1950s, neither the Socialist Party led by the then president François Hollande or the conservative party Les Républicains made it to the run-off stage of the 2017 presidential election. Up against the far-right Front National, Emmanuel Macron swept to power as the leader of En Marche, a party that had only been in existence for a year.

In Britain, fears within the Conservative Party about being outflanked by the nationalist United Kingdom Independence Party (UKIP) had prompted David Cameron to call the Brexit referendum. In 2010, the once dominant Conservatives had only been able to form a coalition government with the help of the Liberal Democrats. The Labour Party came to be led by Jeremy Corbyn, a one-time fringe player from what used to be called the 'loony left', who appeared to many voters more like a protest leader than a putative prime minister.

In many European countries, the left was in retreat. The Socialists in France. The Social Democrats in Germany. The Labour Party in Britain. Post-industrialism severed the longstanding link between the working class and its traditional tribunes. Tony Blair's centrism, which had won him an unprecedented three victories in a row, had been discredited by his support for the Iraq War. Bill Clinton's Third Way had become increasingly untenable because his policies, personality and politics had been so polarising.

A gulf was opening up between the 'wine left' and the 'beer left': highly educated, well-paid metropolitan progressives who were beneficiaries of the New Economy, and lower-paid voters in the old industrial towns who felt excluded. Modern-day issues of the left, such as transgender bathrooms and non-binary gender terminology, widened the cultural schism.

On this side of the Atlantic, the weakness of America's political duopoly, already exposed by the potency of Ross Perot's Reform Party in the '90s, now became manifest in the rise of the Tea Party, the alt-right, the Occupy Wall Street movement and Black Lives Matter campaign.

Since the turn of the century, the Green Party had also become an irritant for the Democrats. In 2000, Ralph Nader received more than 97,000 votes in Florida, taking the state away from Al Gore, the most environmentally friendly candidate ever to head a major-party ticket. In 2016, Hillary Clinton would have become president if Jill Stein's Green Party had not siphoned off so many votes in Michigan, Wisconsin and Pennsylvania.

The professionalisation of politics had created a cliquey political class who tended to speak in the jargon of their advisors and PR consultants. The ads may have been slicker, the sound-bites more fluent. Yet the language of professional politics increasingly sounded like the muzak piped into hotel lobbies. Plain-speaking figures, using a tongue that shocked the delicate sensibilities of the cosmopolitan elites, cut through and grabbed the headlines. The Johnsons. The Farages. The Hansons. The Trumps.

Those who presented problems in black-and-white terms and offered quick fixes tended to prosper. If they could be expressed in pithy, tweetable slogans, all the better. 'Take Back Control' became the mantra of Brexiteers. In the 2013 Australian election, 'Stop the Boats' and 'Axe the Tax' were the six words that helped lift Tony Abbott to victory. Decrying multiculturalism, mocking the woke left and promising to restore national greatness were common themes.

To those who blamed the global political malaise primarily on the economic downturn, Australia's churn of second-rate prime ministers suggested there were other causes. In the midst of an extraordinary 'wonder from down under' 25-year recession-free run, Canberra became the coup capital of the democratic world. As a reform era was overtaken by a revenge era, voters were spurning a political class fixated on party-room intrigue, personal vendettas, petty fights and partisan point-scoring.[8] After a long period of strong prime ministers – Bob Hawke, Paul Keating and John Howard – the talent pool started to resemble a drought-ridden billabong.

Evident in Australia, a country I observed up close for seven years as the BBC's correspondent in Sydney, was how most talented young Australians no longer gravitated towards politics. Some complained of the selection procedures for candidates being a stitch-up. Women, and many men, bemoaned the misogyny of the brutish political culture. Student politics, the stepping stone for so many, was also off-putting. For those who wanted to change the country or the world, there were easier and more attractive ways to do it, from joining an NGO to working for the United Nations or launching a start-up.

Another way in which globalisation shaped politics was by nurturing the belief among the best and brightest that they could make an impact, and more money, at a worldwide level, which often meant joining or starting transnational organisations, rather than entering politics in their home countries. What became striking about those self-congratulatory 30-under-30 and 40-under-40 high-achiever lists was how few political rising stars appeared on them.

Instead, they were populated with T-shirt-clad tech wizards, new media gurus, scientists or activists who had started charities in conflict zones, or who were running single-issue campaigns targeting global warming or sex trafficking or animal welfare, issues which transcended borders. No longer is it necessary to think globally and act locally. You can think globally and act globally. Maybe it even left the field clear for more nationalists to emerge.

With a dearth of global political talent, elections the world over were becoming 'none of the above' or 'lesser of two evils' affairs. Contests were increasingly being determined by negative partisanship, driven by animosity towards the losing party rather than any great affection for the winners. Hate had become a more powerful emotion in politics than love.

This was especially true in tribal America, and especially so in 2016. Unquestionably, Trump had an army of red-capped supporters who would happily have supported him even if he had gunned down an unsuspecting tourist outside the Tiffany store on Fifth Avenue. Yet many Republicans voted for him because they despised Hillary Clinton. In 2016, both Trump and Clinton's unfavourable ratings were much higher than their favourable ratings. According to Gallup, they headed into Election Day with the worst public images of any major-party candidates in history.[9] The campaign felt like a circus from which people were running away.

Even after the Brexit earthquake, we failed to grasp how the liquefaction would surface on this side of the Atlantic. The nostalgic nationalism, the evocation of lost greatness, was analagous. So, too, was the fear of immigration. Boris Johnson, a political showman whose rise had been assisted by his journalistic entertainment value, pulled off the same trick of becoming a blue-collar figurehead, an Old Etonian populist to Trump's billionaire populist. The Brexit parallels were not lost on Trump, who repeatedly claimed in the final days of the campaign that he was about to pull off a UK referendum-style shock.

Rupert Murdoch was another transatlantic common denominator. His media outlets, such as *The Sun* and Fox News, revelled in political disruption and chaos, and had done so much over the decades to reduce public faith in Westminster and Washington. For a time Murdoch went cool on Trump. 'When is Donald Trump going to stop embarrassing his friends, let alone the whole country?' he asked on Twitter in July 2015. Yet just as *The Sun* threw its full support behind Brexit, so Fox News celebrities such as Sean Hannity became Trump's biggest cheerleaders. A dramatic irony of the fall of Roger Ailes, who was fired from Fox News after being exposed as a workplace sexual predator, was that it came on the day Trump accepted the Republican nomination at the GOP convention in Cleveland. Few Americans had done more than Ailes to prepare the path for Trump's rise.

The billionaire was not the only home-grown manifestation of this worldwide trend. Bernie Sanders, a socialist from Vermont who had operated for years on the periphery of national politics, surfed the same populist wave. To say that now, of course, is to utter a banality. Back in 2015, however, it took us too long to link these rogue candidacies. The socialist former mayor, with his wild curly hair, black-framed glasses and mad-professor energy, could hardly have been more different from the billionaire tycoon. But these two New Yorkers, one from Brooklyn, one from Queens, were flipsides of the same coin. In the Democratic race, Sanders ended up winning 23 states, 46 per cent of the pledged delegates and 13 million votes, a stunning and entirely unexpected showing. After the election, it even became possible to construct an argument that Sanders would have been better equipped to defeat Trump, if only because he might have clung onto the safe Democrat states Hillary Clinton won and added the three key states that she lost – Pennsylvania, Michigan and Wisconsin. We now inhabited such a topsy-turvy political world, it was impossible to say with any certainty that a lifelong socialist could not become the President of the United States.

It was not just the Rust Belt. Donald Trump came to be seen as the saviour of another wreckage-strewn wasteland: the modern-day media, with its half-empty newsrooms and dried-up revenue streams. Into these parched riverbeds, Trump threw a lifeline. At a time when online news sites and apps were desperate for traffic and Google was raking in four times in advertising revenue than the entire American newspaper industry, he became the ultimate clickbait candidate. When cable channels were struggling to attract eyeballs, along came a ratings juggernaut. More than 24 million viewers watched the first Republican debate on Fox News in August 2015, the highest audience for any primary debate in television history. Attention had become the most valuable commodity of the digital age – we even spoke now of an 'attention economy'. Trump generated it in spades. Yet another irony of 2015 was that an industry devastated by the New Economy, where employment in newsrooms would plummet by 45 per cent between 2008 and 2017, failed to fully comprehend how similar disruptive forces would upend politics.

News executives echoed the words reportedly uttered by Hillary Clinton's campaign manager, Robby Mook, at her Brooklyn head-quarters whenever the billionaire appeared on screen. 'Shh, I've got to get me some Trump.'[10] A trade known for its adrenaline junkies came to be populated by Trump junkies. The result was a form of relationship addiction, almost a textbook case of co-dependency: an excessive reliance on a partner who requires support for an addiction or illness that ends up being one-sided, abusive and destructive.

On cable, he became the man not just of every hour but of every minute. Even when he wasn't on screen, CNN routinely broadcast an empty podium awaiting his arrival next to a countdown clock indicating when he would speak. On network television, the breakfast shows *Today*, *Good Morning America* and *CBS This Morning* tore up their production values to allow Trump to appear on his mobile, rather than in the studio or via satellite, the kind of 'phoners' ordinarily permitted only in the event of important breaking news.

Rock bottom was reached on the day Trump announced he would renounce his birtherism during a press conference at the Trump International Hotel on Pennsylvania Avenue in Washington, just a few blocks from the White House. The impresario turned the event into an infomercial for his new property. Then, without taking a single question, he announced perfunctorily that Obama was born in America and left. Played like a fiddle, cable news channels carried this farcical event in its entirety.

Blanket coverage meant Trump did not have to rely on the usual campaign finance model, where donations funded the ability to communicate with voters via paid advertising on television. All this he got gratis. By the spring of 2016 he had received an estimated $1.9 billion of free airtime, which meant he could bypass the establishment donor class.[11] Admittedly, much of the coverage was negative, focusing on his myriad scandals. The 15 women who accused him of sexual harassment. The fraudulence of Trump University. The refusal to hand over his tax returns. His appalling treatment of contestants in the Miss Universe pageant. Yet Trump had always lived by the maxim that any publicity was good publicity, which stemmed from a narcissistic yearning to be the centre of attention.

Trump inevitably prospered from better-story bias. Who wanted to follow 'low-energy' Jeb Bush, who sounded like he had been tranquillised and was forced, during a town hall event in New Hampshire, to plead with his audience to 'Please clap', when Trump was holding a stadium rally in the next town. Why cover a moderate candidate such as John Kasich, when the algorithms favoured Trump's extremism? No other candidate offered anywhere near the same journalistic entertainment value or dopamine hit. So many modern-day media trends worked to his advantage: from cable channels which favoured outrage and confrontation to the fact that so many journalists now virtually lived their professional lives on Twitter, a medium Trump quickly mastered and conquered – he crowned himself 'the Ernest Hemingway of 140 characters'.

As for our failure to predict his victory, it stemmed in part from what might be called 'better-America bias': the widespread belief that a candidate who stood in defiance of so many cherished American ideals, from tolerance to truthfulness, could never win; or, put another way, that Uncle Sam was better than he was. Team Trump would claim this was the usual liberal partiality from the mainstream mastheads, but in 2016 'better-America bias' was written all over the conservative press. *National Review*, the one-time mouthpiece of the right, became the intellectual home of Never Trumpism, and devoted an entire issue to explaining why he should not be allowed near the White House.

The Barnum and Bailey-like atmosphere surrounding the race, with Trump in the role of ringmaster, brought a stern admonition from President Obama. 'I just want to emphasise the degree to which we are in serious times, and this is a really serious job,' he said in May 2016 from the podium of the White House briefing room. 'This is not entertainment. This is not a reality show. This is a contest for the presidency of the United States.'[12]

But the president was swimming against a rip-tide. The mood of the media industry was best summed up by Les Moonves, the now disgraced former CBS president who was fired for sexually abusing female employees. 'It may not be good for America, but it's damned good for CBS.'

Did the media create Trump in 2016? Was the 'Frankenstein's monster' critique of the press valid? The question, of course, is legitimate, but not perhaps the best way of framing it. For this was not just a 2016 phenomenon. The media had been willing partners going back decades. Trump had been grooming reporters and proprietors all the way back to the mid-'70s, when his then attorney, Roy Cohn, set up his first meeting with the new owner of the *New York Post*, Rupert Murdoch.

Generating publicity was perhaps his greatest gift. From becoming the poster boy of Reaganism in the 1980s, to becoming a darling of the tabloids in the '90s, to remaking himself as a reality TV star in the noughties, he turned himself into a one-man content provider long before the term was even invented. From the mid-1980s, the media had almost willed him to run, and regularised the idea of him becoming president by asking him so frequently if he wanted the job. If spending a day with Donald Trump was like driving a Ferrari without the windshield, imagine spending all year with him as he careered along the road to the White House. 'One thing I've learned about the press,' he wrote in *The Art of the Deal*, 'is that they're always hungry for a good story, and the more sensational the better.'

The 2016 election showed, too, how little the traditional media understood the new media. Mistakenly we still thought traditional outlets, such as *The New York Times*, *Washington Post* and the US networks, and more recent arrivals such as MSNBC and Fox News, primarily shaped public reality. Wrongly we continued to think of news in the traditional sense: of rigorously researched stories that upheld longstanding journalistic principles of accuracy and basic truth.

What we failed to appreciate fully was how an alternative reality was being created online in the dissemination of fake news and misinformation on Facebook, Twitter and alt-right sites such as Breitbart News, 8chan and 4chan. After the election, BuzzFeed found that the 20 top-performing fake news stories, most of which were pro-Trump, generated a bigger response on Facebook than the top stories from 19 reputable news sites combined. These included the Pope endorsing Donald Trump, and Hillary Clinton selling weapons to ISIS.[13] The ratio of 'junk news' to 'professional news' on Twitter during the 2016 election was one-to-one, a team at Oxford University found. Researchers at Ohio State University found afterwards that fake news alone might have depressed her vote by 4 points, more than enough to lose her the election.

Nor did we comprehend the malign influence of Cambridge Analytica in spreading pro-Trump propaganda and the Kremlin's bot factories. A Red Cyber-army of 36,000 Russian bots tweeted during the 2016 election. More than 125 million Americans saw content on Facebook generated by the Kremlin. The Russians set up fake profiles pretending to be average Americans, with borrowed photos and concocted life stories, and fake protest groups to aggravate the familiar fault lines of guns, immigration and race. Groups such as Heart of Texas, Blacktivist, Secured Borders, United Muslims of America and Army of Jesus, which purported to be grassroots organisations, were run from St Petersburg in Russia. As part of this elaborate ballet, the Russians organised rallies, including a 'Support Hillary, Save

American Muslim' event, advertised with a poster on which was printed a counterfeit quote: 'I think Sharia Law will be a powerful new direction of freedom.' They choreographed counter-protests to coincide with protesters. They even paid a real-life American to build a cage big enough to hold an actress playing Hillary Clinton dressed in a prison uniform. The presidential election was being manipulated and hacked, but we failed to realise it until afterwards.

Unquestionably, the media gave Trump a huge assist. But it is also worth remembering that, by the time he ran for the presidency, the reality TV star was a one-man media conglomerate. In 2016, he could boast more than 8.5 million followers on Twitter, more than traditional media behemoths such as *The Washington Post*, *ABC News*, *NBC News* and new start-ups such as the Huffington Post and BuzzFeed. The traditional gatekeepers of the news were not so significant because there were no longer any gates. Few understood this better than Donald Trump. He was the new media. He grasped that the future in politics belonged to those who generated their own content.

———

No one who had sought the presidency could boast the same panoply of qualifications as Hillary Clinton – a former First Lady, New York senator, secretary of state, education expert, human-rights champion, healthcare tsar and mother. Her overriding problem in 2016 was that no one more personified the political establishment. The stellar résumé compiled during a 30-year career in public life now condemned her. She was a career politician, a platinum-card member of the Davos set, a high priestess of the East Coast elite. Not just a limousine liberal but also a Learjet liberal. Her decision to run for president, as she freely admitted in her post-election memoir, followed a holiday in the Caribbean home of the fashion designer Oscar de la Renta. In another titbit from her book which demonstrated her inability to read the room, she spoke of hiring a make-up artist on the personal recommendation of Anna Wintour.

During her tenure as secretary of state, Hillary Clinton was at her most impressive when she was at her most authentic: when she wore Coke-bottle glasses in hearings on Capitol Hill; when she ripped into Republican lawmakers in the Benghazi hearings; when she let her hair down both figuratively and literally on trips overseas; when she donned dark sunglasses on a military transport plane, Blues Brothers-style, and punched out messages on her smartphone, the viral snapshot of which suggested she was a bona-fide bad ass.

In advance of her presidential run, however, she changed her appearance to look more like a conventional candidate, and lost that sense of mischief, fun and spontaneity. She became a creature of the consultants, and, like Al Gore in 2000, got lost in her own campaign. For a public figure spoken of as presidential material since the late 1960s, when she came to national attention after delivering a blistering commencement address to her fellow female graduates of Wellesley College, she struggled to present a compelling rationale for occupying the White House. After rejecting 84 alternatives, her campaign eventually settled on the insipid 'Stronger Together' as its slogan.[14] For someone who had eyed the presidency for so much of her adult life, it was astonishing how she now struggled to articulate why she wanted the job. It reinforced the perception she was running out of a sense of entitlement, rather than purpose 'America is still great,' her rejoinder to Trump's galvanising slogan, also projected an air of arrogance, and did not ring true for those who had taken on multiple jobs just to make ends meet.

Given her troubled history with the press, her guardedness was understandable. But I mistakenly thought the friendships forged with reporters during her tenure as secretary of state would produce the kind of reset she was fond of in diplomacy. Sometimes on international trips she would share a late-night drink with the State Department press corps, a cabal of serious minded foreign-policy wonks. As soon as she launched her campaign, however, old defences were re-erected.

The tone was set when we all traipsed out to Iowa for her first campaign event, a low-key roundtable discussion at a community college. Her convoy, rather than pulling up outside the front door, where the press was waiting to film the mandatory arrivals shot, unexpectedly drove around to the back of the building, prompting a needless press stampede. Perhaps her advance team thought it had pulled off a masterstroke by outwitting the waiting press. But to what end? Running for the presidency is not a covert operation, and all it did was leave veterans of the Hillary beat sighing, 'There you go again.'

From the outset, her staffers were ridiculously overprotective. None more so than Huma Abedin, the friend whom Hillary looked upon as a comfort blanket, but who acted so often like a smothering fire blanket. Often on the campaign trail you would see Hillary talking empathetically to a supporter at the end of a speech, one of the few campaign duties she genuinely seemed to enjoy, only for the conversation to be cut short by her unsmiling aide. The connection with voters was severed. The emotions that successful campaigns feed off were suppressed.

Hillary herself could also sound snobbish and supercilious. Calling half of Trump's supporters 'a basket of deplorables' was the single biggest act of self-sabotage by a presidential candidate since Mike Dukakis climbed aboard a tank in 1988 with an oversized helmet that made him look like one of *Hogan's Heroes*. The setting for her speech that night, an LGBT fundraiser held at the glitzy Cipriani on Wall Street at which Barbra Streisand provided the entertainment, helped inflict maximum self-harm – a Tammy Wynette moment to the power of ten. That 'basket of deplorables' was another way of describing 'white trash' voters, the sole demographic Democrats thought it was still acceptable to malign. This deviation from the creed of political correctness did not go unnoticed in the Rust Belt. It should have come as little surprise that voters had such contempt for politicians when politicians publicly showed such contempt for them.

Then there was the Bill problem. Watching the former president on the stump in New Hampshire, where he spoke slowly, quietly and haltingly, showed how he had become an ambient presence rather than the mega-wattage celebrity of old. Clearly he did not want to outshine his wife, but it seemed more about conserving dwindling reserves of energy. More so than his lack of vim, it was the baggage Bill Clinton brought with him that encumbered his wife. Amidst the backlash against globalisation, he was remembered as the author of NAFTA. Amidst the Black Lives Matter campaign against mass incarceration, he was the heartless jailor and the author of a policy that had ended up being such a voter suppressant – in 2016, some six million people were prevented from casting ballots because of their convictions.[15] Amidst the revolt against Democratic centrism, he was the New Democrat sell-out. The triangulation that had saved his presidency now looked cynical, unprincipled and opportunistic. Amidst the disgust against Trump's misogyny, he was an alleged sexual predator who had taken advantage of a 22-year-old intern and allegedly molested other women.

Paradoxically, Bill Clinton still seemed more popular among female voters than his wife. Here, Hillary hatred was palpable. In Iowa and New Hampshire, Sanders outpolled her amongst women, who seemed, even when she effectively wrapped up the nomination, unexcited at this historic female first. On the morning after Super Tuesday, her crowning moment, we set out to get some vox pops from women voters in Miami. The first five we spoke to all despised her, and one by one ticked off the long list of dislikes. She was condescending and arrogant. She did not adhere to rules that applied to others. She was untrustworthy. One woman even told us Hillary Clinton did not have *any* qualifications to be president.

To understand white working-class male voters, *Hillbilly Elegy* became the touchstone book of the 2016 campaign. To understand female voters, *Lean In* by Sheryl Sandberg, the chief operating officer of Facebook, was required reading. Women were seen favourably when they advocated for others, wrote Sandberg, but unfavourably when they advocated for themselves. Hillary Clinton agreed. 'The more successful a man is, the more people like him,' she wrote after the campaign. 'With women, it's the exact opposite.'[16]

The email scandal was a further hindrance. Confessedly, when *The New York Times* first broke the story, I did not think much of it. On the Richter scale of scandal, it seemed to merit a small quiver, but nothing more. In keeping, though, with the post-Watergate mistrustfulness that turned campaign reporters into crime hacks, it was elevated into an A-grade outrage. 'It was a dumb mistake,' Hillary Clinton claimed afterwards. 'But an even dumber scandal.' For Trump, it was a gift. For disaffected Democrats, it reinforced the clawing sense the Clintons did not feel bound by normal rules.

For the media, it became a means of demonstrating impartiality, a story we could return to over and over to balance the dozens of Trump scandals. Here, the billionaire benefited from the strobe effect of his many controversies. By contrast, the email scandal was constantly in the blinding spotlight, which meant it seemed worse than truly it was. A post-election study of the mainstream media's coverage by researchers at Harvard and MIT revealed that Clinton's email-related scandals, including the hacks of the Democratic National Committee and her campaign chief John Podesta, received 65,000 sentences in newspapers such as *The New York Times*, *Washington Post* and *Wall Street Journal*. All of Trump's scandals, by contrast, were allotted just 40,000 sentences. Her coverage was also more negative than Trump's. In the final six days of the campaign, *The New York Times* ran more front-page stories on the email scandal than on policy issues during the previous two months.[17] When Gallup conducted a survey of what words voters associated with each candidate, 'email' ranked number one for Clinton.[18]

The FBI also took Hillary Clinton's emails seriously. So much so that the only two times during 2016 that I seriously thought she might lose the election were when the FBI director, James Comey, thrust them into the midst of the campaign. (Comey said Bill Clinton forced his hand to go public after the former president held a mysterious meeting with Attorney General Loretta Lynch on a plane in Arizona, prompting him to assert the FBI's independence from the Justice Department.) His first dramatic intervention came in July, on the morning when we had headed down to Charlotte, North Carolina, for Hillary Clinton's first joint appearance with Barack Obama. For 13 minutes of his scolding 15-minute statement, it sounded as if he was about to indict the former secretary of state. Then, at the end of his highly irregular statement, he said there were insufficient grounds for a prosecution – which was hardly an exoneration.

The second Comey intervention came just 11 days before the election, with what Fox News aptly called the 'October surprise on steroids'. Comey announced the FBI was reopening the investigation into the emails, because some had been found on a laptop used by Huma Abedin and her disgraced husband, Anthony Weiner. By then, however, it seemed the *Access Hollywood* tape would loom larger in voters' minds on Election Day. Here was Donald Trump's moment of accountability. Surely those well-heeled Starbucks moms who took their daughters to his rallies would desert him.

In those final days, as she criss-crossed the country, I travelled with Hillary Clinton on her plane and in her motorcade, and got to see the view from her window: as she arrived for a rally in the Florida countryside, where she was confronted by the snarling faces of pro-Trump protesters, some dressed in black-and-white prison fatigues, some waving the Confederate flag; as she addressed a floodlit night-time rally in Fort Lauderdale, where she was heckled by a Trump protester carrying a sign reading, 'Bill Clinton is a rapist'; as she arrived in Las Vegas, where her motorcade passed a golden skyscraper emblazoned with giant letters spelling 'Trump', a name she must never have expected to see on a presidential ballot paper alongside her own. With her road to the White House lined with anger, hatred and mistrust, how galling it must have been after a lifetime in public service to peer through the tinted glass of her armoured SUV to see demonstrators who wanted her locked up in a federal penitentiary. From bullets those vehicles offered a protective shell, but not from brickbats.

After *Access Hollywood*, those concluding miles should have been a cakewalk. Even after Comey's eleventh-hour reopening of the emails investigation her campaign team deliberately projected an air of invincibility. Her plane set off for Arizona, a red state that had only once gone Democrat since 1948 – a rub-his-nose-in-it campaign stop. Even neighbouring Texas was said to be in play. One day, when we flew from Florida to Las Vegas, we didn't even hear from the candidate until late afternoon, which was well after the evening news shows on the East Coast. Her reticence spoke of the 'too big to fail' complacency that had seemingly set in.

All that week I was in touch with the Clinton campaign head-quarters, where volunteers manning the phone banks found that lists of supposedly rusted-on Democratic supporters included voters who planned to back Trump. One volunteer even asked whether she had been given the correct list, thinking she was ringing the numbers of swing or Republican-leaning voters.

As Hillary's plane criss-crossed the country, it was possible to detect the same nervousness on the ground. On the fringes of a night-time rally in Florida, grassroots activists bemoaned the lack of money and attention from campaign headquarters in Brooklyn. Who knew what local Democrats were saying in Wisconsin and Michigan, states she did not even bother to visit in those final, all-important weeks? From those who occupied the front rows on her plane, however, there seemed to be no sense of panic.

Her main concession to the narrowing polls was finally to banish Huma Abedin from her personal entourage, and to change her message as she closed out the campaign. Rather than ending on high-minded appeals for national unity, the plan when she enjoyed what looked like an unassailable double-digit lead, she was forced to re-litigate the case against Trump. Rather than outlining her vision for the country, she sounded like a prosecutor making a closing argument in a scrappy trial the jury couldn't wait to end.

Palpable in those final speeches was a tone of exasperation. As she recited again her curriculum vitae – those years fighting for children as a lawyer, her tenure as First Lady, her service in the Senate co-sponsoring bipartisan legislation, those 112 countries she visited as secretary of state – she clearly could not countenance the notion that the world's most important job interview could possibly end with someone so manifestly unqualified being appointed. Nor could she seem to process fully the idea that a polyglot nation, in which millions more women voted than men, could tolerate electing a candidate whose name had become synonymous with xenophobia and misogyny.

Surely, she could never have imagined that at a campaign stop in Florida she would be introduced by a former Miss Universe, Alicia Machado, who was there to remind women voters that Donald Trump had called her 'Miss Piggy'. Nor would she have predicted that at a rally in North Carolina she would have to call on a one-time socialist, Bernie Sanders, who had managed to enthuse young female voters in ways that eluded her. It must also have been wounding to have to rely on the star power of Michelle Obama, who completely eclipsed her at a stadium rally in Winston-Salem – the sort of venue the former First Lady would have struggled to fill, had not the present First Lady been at her side. Though her crowds looked more like modern America, multi-hued rather than predominantly white, always they were smaller than Trump's.

As campaigns reach their climax, it is customary for those seeking the highest office in the land to reflect on the humbling experience of asking voters to invest them with such inordinate power. There must have been times, though, when Hillary Clinton also found it deeply humiliating. Trump contradicted her sense of America. What she looked upon as his greatest weaknesses, his supporters viewed as his greatest strengths, something she found hard to morally compute. The unspoken line of all her remarks was: 'How did it ever come to this?'

To peer out of the window in those final days, the country flashing by, was to be reminded of much that was awe-inspiring about America. Flying into Las Vegas, we looked down on the Hoover Dam, that breath-taking monument to American ingenuity and symbol of resurgence in the years after the Great Depression. From the palm-lined beaches of southern Florida to the copper-tinted mountains on the fringes of Phoenix, we witnessed its beauty. We travelled to some of the great university campuses, the academic powerhouses so central to America's technological dominance. But the end-stretch of the campaign was unlovely and unedifying. In those final days, it felt like we were travelling the low road to the White House.

Election Day began on the Upper West Side watching New Yorkers line up to vote outside a polling station housed in a 'Trump' apartment building, a pointer, some took it as, that he was about to revert to being a property developer. From the candidate himself came a final all-caps missive on Twitter, 'TODAY WE MAKE AMERICA GREAT AGAIN!' But most reporters thought they would soon be able to disable his tweet notifications on their smartphones. Some planned to 'unfollow' his account immediately.[19]

Late the night before, at an open-air concert outside Philadelphia's Independence Hall, Hillary Clinton appeared alongside the Obamas and Bruce Springsteen, and was told by America's first black president she was on the verge of a victory to historically rival his own in 2008. 'You've got this,' he whispered, as he hugged her. 'I'm so proud of you.' Campaign aides predicted the same outcome. 'You're going to bring this home,' her chief pollster assured her. After her final rally in North Carolina, this time featuring Lady Gaga, she flew back to a private airfield near her Chappaqua residence, alongside aides who uncorked champagne in anticipation of victory.[20]

At our New York bureau on Election Day, we undertook some cursory contingency planning for a Trump victory with bosses who had flown in from London, but in these private huddles I was more forthright than I dared be on air. Hillary Clinton was sure to win, I told them, because a lopsided victory in the popular vote would translate into Electoral College success. The Blue Wall would hold. I had experienced the rage of the Rust Belt. I was no stranger to Hillary hatred. I was mindful of Brexit. Not once, however, did I fly out of Pittsburgh, after touring the filmic valleys surrounding it, thinking Donald Trump would win. Even Fox News shared this view. 'Stop the bullshit,' Roger Ailes told Steve Bannon, Trump's white nationalist campaign boss, who claimed the billionaire was going to triumph. 'It's going to be a blowout. It'll be over by eight o'clock.'[21]

We filed our story on America going to the polls for our main evening bulletin and then, in glorious late-afternoon winter sunshine, walked over to the Jacob K. Javits Convention Center to report on what everyone expected to be Hillary Clinton's victory party. A stage shaped like a giant map of the United States had been constructed. It was positioned under a vast glass ceiling that she was figuratively supposed to smash. This was the night, I remember thinking, when the fever would finally break, when Newtonian rules of political gravity would reapply, when we would no longer cover US politics in a Ferrari without the windshield but instead become passengers again in a fuel-efficient sedan.

Then, after the polls shut, the votes came rolling in. From Florida, which went Trump. From Virginia, which was closer than expected. From North Carolina, which the Clinton campaign called the 'checkmate state', because victory there would make it all but impossible for Trump to win the Electoral College. Like Florida, it went for Trump. Now the Blue Wall looked vulnerable. Three of its sturdiest bricks – Michigan, Wisconsin and Pennsylvania – looked like they were about to be dislodged. A digital 'swingometer' on *The New York Times* website leant ever more decisively towards the supposed no-hoper. The beaming Clinton staffers who could hardly contain their excitement at the beginning of the evening were nowhere to be seen.

Never before in my career had a moment of realisation felt so unreal. The story could scarcely have been more riveting, but the atmosphere in the giant pressroom, if not quite funereal, was strangely numb. Journalists peered unblinking at their laptops, like traders squinting at computer screens when markets are in free-fall. Reporters who earned their living by talking were rendered speechless.

In the days beforehand, many of us had composed stories that now had a 'Dewey beats Truman' ring to them. So there was a collective sensation, at once stomach-churning and surreal, that all of us had got the election terribly wrong. The proof was in our presence. Had we read the runes more accurately, we would have been across town at the Hilton on the Avenue of the Americas, where our colleagues had gone expecting to intrude on a wake.

Hillary Clinton was holed up at her suite in The Peninsula, a hotel on Fifth Avenue almost close enough to throw shade on Trump Tower. There, aides made panicked phone calls, Bill Clinton gnawed incessantly on an unlit cigar, and, amidst all the tension, the candidate herself somehow managed to grab some sleep. By the time she woke up, states supposed to be solid blue were coloured red. When the Associated Press called Pennsylvania for Trump, it was clear he was on his way to the White House. Blue America was in a state of anaphylactic shock. She had won the popular vote by three million votes, an electorally meaningless statistic because the Blue Wall had fallen.

Then Hillary's supporters started racing through the seven stages of grief, with shock and denial displaced by anger. Never will I forget the words of an African-American Clinton supporter, as he walked out of the Javits Center into the Hell's Kitchen night. Still in my mind I can hear the pulsing fury. Still in my mind I can see his fearful face. 'America has voted for hate,' he said with dignified rage.

For her victory speech, Hillary Clinton planned to wear a white trouser suit, the colour of the suffragettes. She also intended to recount the story of her late mother, who at the age of eight was abandoned by her parents and put on a train in Chicago with her younger sister for the cross-country journey to California. President-elect Clinton would imagine travelling back in time, so she could comfort young Dorothy in that carriage. 'Look at me. Listen to me,' she would say to that vulnerable young girl. 'You will survive. You will have a good family of your own, and three children. And as hard as it might be to imagine, your daughter will grow up and become the president of the United States.' As it was, that night she never left her hotel suite.

Standing outside Trump Tower on Fifth Avenue on the morning its owner became president-elect, I watched rush-hour commuters exchange knowing glances, as if to silently affirm that some dreadful calamity had unfolded overnight that was hard as yet to articulate. This vibrant city, which had voted overwhelmingly for Hillary Clinton, seemed drained of its life force. The very place where Donald Trump once said he could shoot someone and not lose any supporters, seemed full of the walking dead. Later that day, Hillary finally delivered a concession speech, her political career ending in a rented ballroom in a faded Midtown hotel, rather than the grandeur of the White House.

Almost a year after the election, I got to spend an hour with Hillary Clinton at a hotel close to her country home in Chappaqua. Her post-election recuperation, which by her own confession had been agonising, had benefited from the novels of Elena Ferrante, the poetry of Maya Angelou, some binge-watching on the sofa (*The Good Wife*, *Madam Secretary* and, her husband's pick, *NCIS: Los Angeles*), a form of yogic breath work which involved inhaling through one nostril and exhaling through the other, and 'my share of Chardonnay', as she put it. Given the circumstances, she was in unexpectedly good spirits and smiled her bright-eyed smile as she told me she had 'come back into the light'.

Her strongest criticisms were directed at four men: Donald Trump, Vladimir Putin, Julian Assange and James Comey. Missing was the name of her husband. But she admitted the election should never have been close enough for the Russian president, WikiLeaks founder or FBI director to affect the outcome. Plainly the torment of defeat continued to inflict pain, and she admitted to making terrible mistakes, the most egregious of which was her 'deplorables' blunder.

When I brought up the speech about her mother that she never got to deliver, her face and voice were wracked with anguish. 'Yeeeeeaaaaaah, yeeeeeeah,' she said, agonisingly, as if slowing pulling off a plaster from a still septic wound. 'Putting myself in there,' she said, nodding slowly and imagining that scene in the railway carriage. 'Yeeeaaaaah.'

Painful, too, was her failure to mobilise a sizeable enough sisterhood to become America's first female president. Trump won a majority of white women, by some estimates a 52 per cent share.

261

Her performance amongst women voters overall was only one point better than Barack Obama's. Even amongst white college educated women, she managed only to get 51 per cent of the vote, a statistic I often cite to show the impossibility of predicting the outcome of the election.

Even now, I find myself sifting through a mental catalogue of missed clues. The Mexican-born Uber driver who confessed to adoring Trump, a secret he kept from his immigrant parents. The female soccer team we met practising on a pitch next to the venue of a Clinton campaign event at a university campus in Florida, whose teammates were split 50/50 for Trump/Clinton – pretty much the exact divide between white female graduates as a whole. The summer day I attended the commencement ceremony at Wellesley College, Hillary Clinton's alma mater, where Oprah Winfrey refused to say on camera whether she would support the former First Lady. The difficulty we had in finding a polling station on the campus of Duke University in North Carolina, which did not appear on Google Maps, an attempt, it seemed, to suppress voter turnout amongst the young. The long line of blue-collar workers we saw on the weekend before the election in the shadow of a cement factory in western Pennsylvania, queuing outside a community centre for food hand-outs in the biting cold. The simple historical fact the Democrats had not won three presidential elections in a row since the Roosevelt/Truman era.

Often history only reveals itself in hindsight, but it should not have come as such a shock that an era of disruptive technology would produce such a disruptive president; that an anti-Obama party selected as its nominee the most virulently anti-Obama candidate; that an anti-Washington conservative movement would back an obstreperously anti-Washington outsider; that an older and whiter GOP would pick the oldest white man in the field; that a country where racial divisions had actually widened under its first black president would pick such a racially divisive demagogue; that a nation which had witnessed such a massive redistribution of the wealth upwards would end up being run by a billionaire; that a screen- and social-media-addicted populace afflicted by so much online narcissism would plump for a narcissist; that a polity fed up with politics would select such an avowed anti-politician; that a superpower whose influence had waned over the course of the twenty-first century would pick a strongman promising to make America great again.

So rundown had America's institutions become – Congress, the Supreme Court, the criminal justice system, Wall Street, the military, the media, the main political parties and, for much of the past 20 years, the presidency itself – that disaffected voters pinned their hopes on an individual, a self-serving businessman loyal only to his eponymous brand.

As institutions became more decayed, so, too, did the safeguards against the emergence of a demagogic figure such as Trump, and the American id he embodied. The country could no longer rely for protection on good governance in Washington, corporate responsibility in US boardrooms, a regulatory framework enforced by robust federal agencies to protect against the excesses of Big Data, effective campaign-finance laws to guard against pernicious influence of Big Money, traditional conservative constraint within the GOP, a multi-faith theology promoting communitarianism and social justice or a self-confident national and local media.

All this had been brewing for years. Our failure was not just to get 2016 wrong, but also to misunderstand and downplay the transformative changes that had been overtaking America – politically, economically, culturally and technologically – for the past 50 years.

7

American Carnage

Another American pageant was unfolding – a celebration for many, a carnival of grief for others. At an outdoor concert on the eve of the inauguration, the country star Lee Greenwood reprised his old hit 'God Bless the USA' against a backdrop of the Lincoln Memorial and a wall of Jumbotron screens filled with the stars and stripes of Old Glory fluttering in slow motion. His voice sounded frailer now, and he struggled in the high register. The tone was different too. Back in the 1980s, the song exemplified the patriotism of the Reagan years and the optimistic spirit of that summertime of resurgence. Thirty years on, it sounded more nationalistic and hoarse – and not only because of the singer's frayed vocal cords. Camera cutaways showed President-elect Donald Trump heartily singing along. When the song came to an end, he punched the twilight air, as if this Reaganite anthem now belonged to him.

In advance, the Trump team let it be known that the Gipper's 1981 inaugural address had been the inspiration for the billionaire's first speech as president. As he was sworn in as vice-president, it was on Ronald Reagan's Bible that Mike Pence placed his hand. A steady chant of 'USA, USA' rose from the crowd below the inaugural stand, where the scarlet baseball caps were imprinted with that Reaganite slogan 'Make America Great Again'. There was also an '80s vibe about the Trumps. Melania and Ivanka looked like modern-day Krystle Carringtons. The lesser-known members of the incoming first family could have stepped out of the set of *Falcon Crest*.

For all the Reagan-era grace notes, Trump's inaugural was emphatically Trumpian. Determined to stamp his brand on the proceedings in the most literal sense of all, his first stop after arriving in Washington was at his new hotel in the Old Post Office building on Pennsylvania Avenue, which instantly became an administration hangout. To perform the national anthem, he chose a 16-year-old singer who came runner-up in *America's Got Talent*. Not for him a poet, cellist or opera singer, although Steve Bannon, his famously dishevelled campaign chief, did turn up wearing a suit.

Political poison polluted the Washington air, more pungent even than during the Obama years. When Hillary Clinton took the stage, the mosh pit of MAGA diehards chanted, 'Lock her up!' When the Senate Minority Leader Chuck Schumer made a plea for inclusiveness – 'Whatever our race, religion, sexual orientation, gender identity; whether we are immigrants or native-born, whether we live with disabilities or not ...' – there was a wall of boos.

Back in 1981, when Reagan stepped to the podium, the clouds parted and sun drenched the inaugural stand in perfect natural lighting, as if adhering to stage directions from some Hollywood biblical epic. When the time came for Donald Trump to speak, it started to rain. And lest you think this is fake meteorology, I was standing on the press riser off to the side, and felt those raindrops myself.

What followed was an inaugural address that could just as easily have been delivered in an aircraft hangar in Mobile, Alabama, a stadium rally in Youngstown, Ohio, or the lobby of Trump Tower after one of his primary victories. Like a revolutionary leader ransacking the capital, he opted for fiery words – the language and hellfire tone that had provided the script for his campaign. '[W]e are not merely transferring power from one administration to another or from one party to another,' he bellowed, 'but we are transferring power from Washington, DC, and giving it back to you, the people.'

While Trump was at the podium, those of us in the press stand who had provided hours of commentary in the lead-up to the ceremony were prohibited from speaking, for the entirely understandable reason that it would be distracting. For most of us, though, this directive was superfluous. This dystopian inaugural – which talked of crime-ridden inner cities and 'rusted-out factories scattered like tombstones across the landscape of our nation' – left us struggling to articulate words. 'This American carnage stops right here and stops right now,' the new president thundered. It was akin to seeing in the pulpit of some medieval cathedral a TV evangelist speaking in tongues.

Afterwards, Barack Obama was generous enough to applaud, and even pay his successor the courtesy of a compliment. 'Good job,' he said, as Trump retook his seat. A more stinging review came from George W. Bush, who further endeared himself to his one-time liberal detractors by muttering, 'That was some weird shit.'

Immediately after his election, I had wondered whether Trump would revert to being the man I met in his conference room all those years ago, before the red light of the camera activated his showman self. During an Oval Office meeting with Obama two days afterwards, he seemed respectful both of the institution of the presidency and of the man he was about to succeed. Unusually sheepish, abnormally quiescent, there were hints that day that he might be suffering from impostor syndrome. Yet his first 24 hours as president showed that Trump would be Trump. The anti-politician had morphed into the anti-president. He would change the presidency more than the presidency would change him.

Musical confirmation came at the first inaugural ball, which he and Melania visited that night, when they danced to Frank Sinatra's 'My Way'. At the second ball on his itinerary, the Freedom Ball at the Washington Convention Center, Trump asked the crowd about his presence on social media, 'Should I keep the Twitter going or not?' His question was met with a wall of affirmative cheers. It meant the Trump White House would come with its own microclimate of Twitter storms, with thunderclaps before dawn and lightning bolts before bed. The early hot take on his tweets was that they were chaff: a distractive counter-measure intended to jam our journalistic radar. Yet as his Twitter handle attested, this was the @realDonaldTrump. His tweets weren't distractions but distillations of his mind and mood. First with 140 characters and then with 280, he channelled his authentic self.

The first full day of the Trump presidency was madder still. Incensed by photographs showing his inauguration crowd to be smaller than his predecessor's in 2009, Trump ordered the National Park Service to edit aerial photographs in a way that cropped out the empty spaces on the National Mall – an extraordinary 'size matters' fit of pique. Then he dispatched his press secretary, Sean Spicer, to deliver an angry statement to gobsmacked reporters, falsely claiming Trump had attracted the biggest-ever inauguration audience – a rant that at that time stood as perhaps the most bizarre spectacle ever witnessed in the White House Briefing Room, but which ended up serving as a curtain-raiser for stranger performances to come.

Later on, during a visit to the CIA headquarters in Langley, Virginia, Trump launched a vicious attack on reporters from a presidential podium placed in front of the Memorial Wall, where 133 stars are carved into the marble to mark the intelligence officers killed in the line of service. It is hard to think of a more hallowed space in any US government building. During the presidency of Donald Trump, however, nothing would be sacred. Political no-go zones were a thing of the past.

In a bastardised version of Ronald Reagan's role of a lifetime, Trump embarked on a performative presidency in which playing the part seemed just as important as executing his practical duties. 'Twitter Trump' inevitably generated the early headlines, but it was the televisual possibilities of the presidency that seemed to animate him most. He conceived of his presidency as a television event, and of himself as a content provider as well as head of government. Not long after taking the oath of office, he instructed aides to treat every day as if it were an episode of a television show in which, as *The New York Times* reported, 'he vanquishes rivals'.[1]

The medium fixated him. Trump described his victory in 2016 as 'the biggest night in television history'. 'Welcome to the studio,' he said from his high-back leather chair at the beginning of a Cabinet meeting of 2018. In the first television interview of the presidency, he took David Muir of *ABC News* on a tour of the White House, treating it like a giant new set. 'I can be the most presidential person ever, other than the great Abe Lincoln,' he said. The essence of presidential leadership, he seemed to think, was to adopt a presidential persona, just as Ronald Reagan had done; this was as much a role-playing exercise as a practical, philosophical or moral undertaking.

Even as he assumed the most onerous job in the world, the metrics of television consumed him. That first decree-like statement from Sean Spicer, in which he sounded more like a propagandist than a press secretary, was about television ratings, false though they were. Attending his first national prayer breakfast little over a week later, Trump mocked Arnold Schwarzenegger for his poor ratings as the new host of *The Apprentice* (even as president, Trump remained an executive producer on the show). When he taunted hostile news channels, such as CNN, he frequently made fun of their 'terrible ratings!', one of the few areas in which he displayed a granular knowledge.

Major announcements, such as his choices as Supreme Court nominees, were teased on Twitter with tune-in-for-the-next-instalment expectancy. First with Judge Neil Gorsuch, then again with Brett Kavanaugh, the suspense came to an end in primetime specials broadcast from the East Room and compèred by the president. 'So, was that a surprise?' asked Trump, as Gorsuch and his wife approached the podium, treating them like contestants on a game show who had just won a Caribbean cruise.

Barack Obama, George W. Bush and Bill Clinton had announced their picks in less showy daytime roll-outs. Reagan had nominated Justice Anthony Kennedy in the evening. After Kennedy's replacement, Brett Kavanaugh, scraped through a nomination battle overshadowed by historic allegations of sexual assault and heavy drinking, Trump threw a primetime pep rally. Even the conservative Supreme Court justices in attendance looked distinctly uncomfortable about the politicisation of this White House tableau.

Trump's first State of the Union address replicated the Reagan made-for-television model. The centrepiece was his Gipper-like salute to human heroes in the balcony, among them the widow of a Navy SEAL killed in Yemen. In his 2020 State of the Union address, Trump gave the genre a personal twist, with a surprise reunion of a military wife with her warrior husband and the Oprah-style awarding of a scholarship to a beaming African-American schoolgirl. At any moment, one half-expected him to point towards one of his Cabinet secretaries and to utter his famous catchphrase 'You're fired!', or to announce that every lawmaker would return home with the keys to a new Pontiac.

Trump's campaign-style rallies were an attempt to bypass the media by producing his own programming. Fox News regularly carried these speeches in their entirety. CNN and all the other networks broadcast the highlights.

While reporters justifiably complained about the cancellation of daily White House press briefings, Trump appeared before the cameras to take questions far more than his predecessors. Oval Office sprays, when Trump fielded reporters' questions, commonly with an international leader left wordless at his side, were often so long they cut into the time allotted for face-to-face diplomacy. His question-and-answer sessions on the South Lawn of the White House before boarding Marine One were so rambling you wondered whether the helicopter might run out of fuel.

Television cameras often became flies on the wall, a documentary-like style he actively encouraged. A favourite moment of his presidency came after the Parkland school shooting in Florida, where 17 teenagers were massacred, when cameras were allowed into the Roosevelt Room to film his 64-minute meeting with Republican and Democratic leaders on gun control that was broadcast in its entirety on cable news. Despite the seriousness of the subject matter, it had the feel of the boardroom scene from *The Apprentice*.

When a cameraman was allowed to linger at an early Cabinet meeting, it provided a stream of footage that resembled state television, the Pyongyang on the Potomac moment when Cabinet officials took turns to lavish praise on their boss. Mike Pence, who early on perfected the devoted gaze of the prototypical political wife, was the most sycophantic. The then Defense Secretary, James Mattis, was the only person at the table not to bend the knee.

Always the visuals of his presidency obsessed him. Sean Spicer was instructed to wear better suits. Trump hated his National Security Advisor John Bolton's bushy moustache. An early star performer was his first UN ambassador, Nikki Haley, whom Trump commended for bringing 'glamour' to the Security Council's horseshoe table. Richard Grenell, his ambassador to Germany, became a Trump favourite not only because he publicly berated Washington's European allies but also for his angular, telegenic good looks. 'If you're not on TV, you don't really exist as far as Trump is concerned,' an associate of his second press secretary, Sarah Sanders, told *The New Yorker*.[2]

Foreign policy regularly took the form of made-for-television show diplomacy. In Saudi Arabia he happily participated in a bizarre ceremony where he placed his hands on a glowing orb that looked like a cross between a mystical, occult ritual and the draw to decide on the group tables ahead of the FIFA World Cup. When he visited NATO headquarters a few days later, he barged his way to the front of the family photo, strong-arming the Prime Minister of Montenegro out of the way, not only to assert US dominance but also to make sure he was centre-frame.

Some of the more cinematic moments of his presidency, such as when he met the plane carrying three Korean-American prisoners released by Pyongyang, were packaged into what looked like movie trailers, this one with footage in slow motion married with the stirring soundtrack of the Harrison Ford film *Air Force One*. After a trip to Iraq, his first to a combat zone, he told rally-goers, 'And I said, "Bring the cameras. I'm going to make a movie. This is the most incredible thing."' Following a visit to the Pentagon, he observed the generals were 'like from a movie, better-looking than Tom Cruise'.[3]

The artificiality of television helped create the pretence of continual achievement. This was true of his first summit with the North Korean dictator Kim Jong-un in Singapore, which was intricately choreographed so that the two leaders shook hands in front of a tableau of alternating US and North Korean flags. The imagery was arresting. The pictures appeared on front pages around the world. Tensions were reduced, but not much substantively was achieved in terms of denuclearisation.

'Little Rocket Man', whom Trump had threatened with 'fire and fury', now co-starred in a buddy movie. Kim, in one of his flowery letters to the president, likened their first meeting to a 'fantasy film'. Or was it a rom-com? After their summit, Trump told supporters in West Virginia he 'fell in love' with the diminutive North Korean. Thereafter, he treated him like an on-air spouse. No matter that the dictator has been accused, among other brutalities, of carrying out executions with anti-aircraft guns and of detaining up to 130,000 of his compatriots in gulags.

Even when events went completely off the rails, he did not seem to mind, so long as they produced good television. Trump made no attempt to shut down Kanye West's wacky, profanity-laden soliloquy when the two men met in the autumn of 2018, surely the first time in broadcast history that the word 'motherfucker' was caught on camera in the Oval Office. Trump liked what he was hearing. Kanye, who turned up wearing a Make America Great Again cap, said his headgear made him 'feel like Superman'.

As for the revolving-door turnover of his administration, it constantly introduced new characters into the mix. The only problem was when new cast members eclipsed the lead. It helped explain why Anthony 'The Mooch' Scaramucci lasted such a short time as the White House communications director, those ten glorious profanity-filled days in July 2017. Even The Mooch's protestations in an infamous *New Yorker* interview that he did not have a ticket on himself – 'I'm not Steve Bannon, I'm not trying to suck my own cock' – failed to save him.[4]

Mark Burnett, the producer of *The Apprentice*, was not much of a fan of the term 'reality show' to describe his genre of programming. Instead, he preferred the word 'dramality'. This neologism applied also to the Trump presidency.

The style of his presidency found a parallel in those trashy daytime talk shows where the aim was to stoke controversy, engineer confrontations, conjure up dramatic surprises and appeal to the basest elements of a screaming audience baying for sensation and sometimes even blood. Fist fights always got the best ratings. Trump cast himself not as the on-screen referee, the arbiter of these disputes, but rather as the central combatant: the thrower of the punches, the deliverer of the most insults and the perpetual victim.

Watching television was almost as central to his presidency as appearing on it. TV was so often the motor for his rage, his Twitter tirades, his abrupt changes in policy, his foreign policy. Trump, who described the digital video recorder TiVo as 'one of the greatest inventions of all time', was thought to consume at least five hours of television each day, starting each morning at about 5.30 with his favourite show, *Fox and Friends*, and other cable shows less to his liking, such as MSNBC's breakfast offering *Morning Joe* – 'Morning Joke', he called it.

As a candidate, he admitted TV was a primary source of information. 'Well, I watch the shows', he told Chuck Todd of *Meet the Press*, who asked from whom he got military advice. As president, it became clear his tweets came in real-time response to segments on Fox News and other cable channels. In a six-month period between the summer of 2018 and the following spring, Media Matters chronicled more than 200 instances where Trump passed on information gleaned from Fox News to his followers on Twitter. 'There is no strategy to Trump's Twitter feed', wrote the journalist Matthew Gertz, who chronicled his tweets. 'He is not trying to distract the media. He is being distracted.'[5]

Foreign diplomats quickly grasped that booking themselves on his favourite shows was the most effective way of putting a word in his ear. The then British Foreign Secretary Boris Johnson adopted this 'audience of one' strategy in a last-ditch attempt to persuade Trump against pulling out of the Iran nuclear deal, appearing on *Fox and Friends* and also, as a back-up, *Morning Joe*. In one interview, Johnson suggested Trump should be a contender for the Nobel Peace Prize for his nuclear diplomacy on the Korean peninsula, an attempt to massage his ego if he couldn't physically shake his hand.

Trump's response to some of the landmark moments of his presidency, such as the Brett Kavanaugh confirmation hearings, was often as a viewer. After mocking Kavanaugh's accuser, Christine Blasey Ford, at one of his rallies in Mississippi, he told reporters he found her televised testimony 'very compelling and she looks like a very fine woman'. Her performance on television had seemingly impressed him. When US Special Forces hunted down Abu Bakr al-Baghdadi, the leader of Islamic State, Trump described the video feed he watched near the Situation Room as 'something really amazing to see', and likened it to 'watching a movie'.

To highlight the primacy of television is not to diminish the importance to the Trump presidency of Twitter. It was through the combination of television and Twitter that Donald Trump achieved his omnipresence. It enabled him to replicate the kind of total media saturation he achieved during the campaign. Twitter gave him a platform to bypass and attack the media, needle Democrats, shame corporations, taunt foreign enemies and allies, disparage dissident Republicans and even sack members of his own administration. Rather than saying 'You're fired!' in person, Trump did it digitally. Rex Tillerson found out he had been dismissed while he was on the toilet.

Ceaselessly we were witnesses to this presidential psychodrama, and the round-the-clock availability of Twitter meant that it played out almost every waking hour of almost every day. 'It's morning again in America' took on a new connotation: rolling over in bed, picking up a smartphone and seeing who Trump had decided to vilify or smear in his latest pre-dawn attack.

It was commonplace to say that Twitter was to Trump what television was to JFK and radio to Franklin Delano Roosevelt. But it was his means of expression more than just his use of a new medium that was so norm-shattering. Back in the early '60s, televised press conferences showcased Kennedy's wit, élan and self-deprecation. Roosevelt's fireside chats soothed a nation traumatised by the Great Depression. Trump's Twitter tirades, by contrast, created a sense of perpetual crisis and anxiety, and showed how the White House was hostage to the whims and temper of its occupant. To many of his supporters, however, it offered ALL CAPS proof that he was carrying out the job they hired him to do.

So this America First president himself became an American first. Never had we witnessed a US leader who so flagrantly flouted the customs of presidential behaviour. From the juvenile nicknames ('Nervous Nancy', 'Shifty Schiff', 'Cryin' Chuck') to the ugly slurs ('Horseface' for Stormy Daniels, a former porn star with whom he was once apparently intimate). From the weird boasts (who describes himself as a 'very stable genius'?) to the wacko tweets (the photoshopped image of his face superimposed on the body of Sylvester Stallone in *Rocky* boxing garb). From the trashing of one-time colleagues (his first Secretary of State, Rex Tillerson, was as 'dumb as a brick' and the Republican House Speaker, Paul Ryan, was a 'baby', while Anthony 'The Mooch' Scaramucci was a 'nut job') to his strange fixations (he was flushed with pride after he 'aced' a simple cognitive test designed to detect signs of dementia, where he had to remember the words 'person, woman, man, camera, TV').

Never before had we witnessed a president with such a strained relationship with the truth. A running tally kept by *The Washington Post* recorded more than 22,000 falsehoods, and showed that the more time he spent in office the more prolific became his dissembling. Nor had we seen a US leader mount such a prolonged assault on members of the press, part of a deliberate campaign to delegitimise the correctors of his mistruths. Along with his daily Twitter attacks on media organisations such as *The New York Times, The Washington Post* and CNN, he praised the Montana Congressman Greg Gianforte, the 'tough cookie' who pleaded guilty to a misdemeanour assault after body-slamming a reporter from *The Guardian*. Every day brought new fights and clashes – unending confrontation.

The occupant of the White House is ideally supposed to articulate the nation's principles, personify its values and serve as a role model for the nation's children, but these were not part of the job description that he felt any need to fulfil. The Boy Scouts of America even had to apologise to parents after Trump appeared at its jamborees in the summer of 2017 and delivered a highly politicised speech railing against Barack Obama, Hillary Clinton and the fake news media.

Six weeks into his presidency, Trump transgressed yet another norm by accusing his predecessor of criminality. 'Terrible Just found out that Obama had my "wires tapped" in Trump Tower just before the victory,' he tweeted, without citing any evidence. 'Nothing found. This is McCarthyism ... This is Nixon/Watergate. Bad (or sick) guy!' Having observed a ceasefire during the transition, the anti-Obama candidate became the anti-Obama president, reverting to the vitriol of his birther crusade.

Personal vendettas became a running theme. After the death of John McCain, whose dramatic thumbs-down vote in the Senate helped save Obamacare, he refused initially to fly the flag at half-mast at the White House. Ahead of Trump's visit to Japan, the Navy and Air Force even received a request to hide the USS *John S. McCain*, which was named in honour of him, his father and grandfather, so that its presence in a Tokyo naval base would not upset the president.

This was a presidency of the here and now. Trump was preoccupied by the moment. Frenetic and impulsive, there was something fast and furious about almost everything his administration did. Like Reagan, his focus on the presentational aspects of the presidency meant he often floundered at the back-office aspects of the role. As he lacked the curiosity or patience to digest briefing papers, aides often provided information in diagrammatic form – classroom-style visual aids. Decision-making was offhand, and he was not always a full participant in his own administration. As Bob Woodward reported in his pull-back-the-curtain bestseller *Fear: Trump in the White House*, senior officials routinely decided not to act on his orders in the hope he would forget ever having made them. Orderly long-term policy-making was cast aside. Quick policy fixes were often botched.

The Trump White House flunked its first two attempts to institute a travel ban restricting the entry of immigrants from mainly Muslim countries. The president also failed to repeal and replace Obamacare, one of his core campaign promises. On healthcare, the dysfunction of the Republican Party – which could not agree on how to kill off Obamacare despite seven years of trying – mirrored the dysfunction of the West Wing.

Even though the GOP controlled the presidency, Senate and House, it struggled to advance its agenda, and found it difficult to transition from being a party of opposition to one of government. The Party of No remained the Party of No, as House Speaker Paul Ryan despairingly conceded: 'We were a 10-year opposition party. Being against things was easy to do.'

Gridlock was ordinarily the consequence of divided government, but the healthcare debacle suggested it had become endemic. Without the unifying presence of Barack Obama in the White House, Republican discipline in the early phase of the Trump presidency sometimes fell apart.

Despite promising to bring his business skills to Washington, Trump proved to be a poor chief executive. The chaos of administration staff turnover – four White House chiefs of staff, four National Security Advisors, three secretaries of defense, two secretaries of state, two attorneys general and a revolving door of senior West Wing aides – was without precedent. We were introduced to the phrase 'kakistocracy', meaning the rule of the incompetent, and reminded of the warning from Jeb Bush: 'He's a chaos candidate and he'd make a chaos president.' Adults in the room were either shown the door or headed for it themselves. Afterwards, they made little attempt to conceal their true feelings towards their former boss. Tillerson called him 'a fucking moron'. Gary Cohn, his economy tsar, labelled him 'a professional liar'. John Kelly, his one-time chief of staff, described him as an 'idiot' and 'unhinged'. James Mattis noted: 'Donald Trump is the first president in my lifetime who does not try to unite the American people.'

Early on it became clear that this would be by far the most obviously improper presidency of the modern era. Conflicts of interest abounded. This was so much the case that it became hard to differentiate where the presidency ended and the family business began. China's decision to grant trademark rights to Ivanka Trump during Xi Jinping's visit to Mar-a-Lago was a case in point. Foreign diplomats wanting to curry favour with the Trump White House booked into his Pennsylvania Avenue hotel. The president even announced that the G20 summit of international leaders would be held at a Trump resort in Miami, before the outcry forced a rare climb-down.

The self-styled billionaire repeatedly refused to release his personal tax returns, presumably to save himself from financial embarrassment. *The New York Times* revealed that he had paid just $750 in income tax in 2016 and 2017, and also that his business had haemorrhaged hundreds of millions of dollars over the previous 20 years. Continually, he was the litigant president, fighting, among other things, claims that he had violated the emoluments clause of the constitution, barring personal enrichment. The swamp that Donald Trump promised to drain became even more saturated and putrid.

Not since the Reagan years and Iran-Contra had a presidency been hit by so many criminal indictments, including his first National Security Advisor, Michael Flynn, his one-time campaign chief, Paul Manafort, and his long-time political advisor Roger Stone, who celebrated his arraignment by flashing a Nixon-style victory salute. When his former lawyer Michael Cohen was arrested and agreed to cooperate with federal prosecutors, the president spoke like the boss of a crime family. Deploying the lingua franca of the Mafioso, he described his one-time fixer as 'a rat'.

The overall effect was to turn the White House into a hub of unceasing agitation and anxiety, rather than a place, as it should be, of competence and calm.

Under Trump, the economy continued its post-Great Recession rebound. Unemployment declined further. The stock market continued to grow. Journeying into the Rust Belt, there was a sense of economic revival. The Ohio River, which was almost empty of traffic when we visited in 2016, was buzzing again with coal barges. Workers in heartland towns told us their prospects had improved. What was striking about the Trump presidency, however, was its failure to tackle many of the deep-rooted problems, such as income inequality, that got him elected. His boasts of a 'blue-collar boom' were contradicted by statistics suggesting the growth in middle-class income had fallen to 2.7 per cent, down from 5.8 per cent during Obama's final two years in office. Wage growth dropped in 48 out of 50 states.[6]

Largely because of the Trump trade war, the steel industry continued to shed jobs – almost 2,000 since he took office. It was estimated that tit-for-tat tariff fights cost 175,000 manufacturing jobs. The trade war also meant pain for farmers, who had to be given massive cash hand-outs from Washington to compensate for the drop in exports – precisely the kind of big government conservatism that brought the Tea Party into existence.

The tax cuts from this populist president benefited the rich far more than the middle class. According to the non-partisan Congressional Research Service, the wealthiest 20 per cent saw their post-tax income rise by 2.9 per cent, compared with just 1.6 per cent for middle-income earners.[7]

Trump failed to make much headway with his vaunted wall along the southern border, eventually resorting to siphoning funds from the Pentagon, sparking a constitutional showdown in the process when Congress blocked funding to build a 110-mile section of fencing.

Even draconian measures that drew widespread international condemnation, such as separating immigrant children from their families at the southern border, failed initially to end the refugee crisis. The wire cages of the detention centres became the Guantánamo watchtowers of the Trump presidency.

The controversy and bedlam did not concern his base. They had not sent him to Washington to play by normal rules. Negative headlines were dismissed as fake news, the jaundiced coverage of a liberal press out to destroy his presidency. Having voted for the billionaire partly to punch sneering bi-coastal liberals in the nose, there was also gratification in seeing elite blood shed with such profusion. Awards ceremonies such as the Oscars, when stars queued up to skewer Trump, were catnip to his red-capped supporters.

Donald Trump could also point to a significant record of right-wing accomplishment. Tax cuts. Two right-wing Supreme Court nominees elevated early on to the bench (and a third by the time he left office). The travel ban – eventually. The bonfire of federal regulations.

He claimed to have achieved more than almost any other administration in history. However, a poll of nearly 200 political science scholars, which routinely placed Republicans higher than Democrats, ranked him 44th out of the 44 men who have occupied the post. Conservative scholars who identified themselves as Republicans placed him 40th, a humiliating ranking for a president who likened himself, unabashedly, to Abraham Lincoln.

Among historians the Trump presidency was starting to be viewed as an aggregation of the lesser traits of his predecessors. The bullying of Lyndon Baines Johnson, who demeaned White House aides and even humiliated his vice-president, Hubert Humphrey – forcing his deputy once to recite a speech on Vietnam while he listened, legs akimbo, trousers round his ankles, on the toilet. The intellectual incuriosity of Ronald Reagan. The shameless lying of Bill Clinton. The paranoia of Richard Nixon. The incompetence of George W. Bush. The historical amnesia of Gerald Ford, who asserted during the sole 1976 presidential debate that Eastern Europe was not dominated by Moscow. The strategic impatience of Barack Obama, whose instinct always was to withdraw US forces from troublesome battlefields, such as Iraq and Afghanistan, even if it meant leaving behind a mess. The distractedness of Jack Kennedy, who whiled away afternoons in the White House swimming pool with a bevy of young women to sate his libido, an X-rated version perhaps of Trump sitting for hours in front of his flat-screen TV watching friendly right-wing anchors bowing down before him.

Those same historians struggled to detect the kind of virtues that offset his predecessors' vices: the optimism of Reagan; the inspirational rhetoric of JFK; the legislative cunning of LBJ; the governing pragmatism of Nixon; the decency of Ford; the foreign-policy insight of Bush senior; the empathy of Clinton; the racial inclusivity of Bush junior; or the personal rectitude of Obama. Rather than being viewed as the reincarnation of Ronald Reagan, Trump was cast as a modern-day James Buchanan or Franklin Pierce, the worst of presidential worsts.

Because Donald Trump was unwilling to accept that he was anything other than an A+ president, the grade he frequently bestowed on himself, he was not prepared to adopt the kind of course corrections that saved troubled administrations. This was not a learning presidency. Trump lacked the self-awareness to admit he was wrong, still less alter course. Incumbents can benefit from self-doubt, a trait Donald Trump seemed to regard as a character flaw.

A master of blame transference, he always lashed out at others, whether members of his administration, such as Jeff Sessions, or the chairman of the Federal Reserve, Jerome Powell, his own hand-picked appointee. Whereas Harry S. Truman used to say, 'The buck stops here', Trump's version of it, which he revealed on the South Lawn in January 2019, was 'The buck stops with everybody.' Presidents also usually grow in office. But while there were physical signs the septuagenarian had aged, there was little evidence he had matured.

For many of his supporters, however, the fact that he became president was as consequential as his presidency itself – the racial reverse of how African-Americans construed the victory of Barack Obama. In perhaps the ultimate expression of negative partisanship, their man occupied the White House and the Democrats did not. Like Reagan's and Obama's, this was a hugely symbolic presidency, but whereas the Gipper signified resurgence and Obama embodied renewal, Trump represented revenge.

———

On the morning after Trump took the oath of office, two very different Americas passed each other by at Washington's Union Station, as bleary-eyed revellers who had danced long into the night at the inaugural balls made their way back to New Jersey and New York with hang-up bags slung over their arms and incoming trains disgorged female demonstrators by the carriage-load. The first mass protest of the Trump era took place less than 24 hours after his swearing in, and many of the empty spaces on the National Mall from the day before were now packed shoulder-to-shoulder with women in a pink blossoming of the 'Trump Resistance'.

The organisers of the march had not much liked the idea of women knitting pink pussy hats, but they came to be instantly iconic. So too did some of the banners, especially those carried by women who had marched over the decades in favour of *Roe v. Wade* and the Equal Rights Amendment. 'My arms are tired from holding up this sign since the 1960s,' read one. 'I can't believe I still have to protest this shit,' sighed another.

The country was irrevocably split. Like the ink blots of a Rorschach test, how you reacted to the Trump presidency determined which America you inhabited. The most deliberately divisive president of the modern era, Trump governed in a manner designed to reward those who voted for him and to neglect, or even punish, those who backed Hillary Clinton.

In an attempt to guarantee his re-election, he pursued a more extreme version of George W. Bush's 51 per cent model: a 30-state strategy to safeguard the 304 votes he won in the Electoral College. The aim was to consolidate his base, rather than significantly expand it – to build a Trumpian wall, in effect, around the states that voted Trump.

His travel schedule early in his presidency suggested he would be a sectional rather than national leader. Shortly after winning the presidency, he embarked on a 'victory tour' that took in Ohio, North Carolina and Iowa, three states he carried on Election Day. Of the ten states Trump visited first as president, seven helped send him to Washington. His trips to the three Democratic states were unavoidable. Virginia was the home of the CIA and Pentagon. Delaware was the site of the Dover Air Base, where Americans killed in combat are repatriated. His first trip to Maryland was to attend a conference of the Conservative Political Action Conference (CPAC). The blue state he visited most was New Jersey, to play golf at one of his country clubs.

Not until May did he return to New York, a blink-and-you-miss-it foray for a commemorative dinner to mark the Battle of the Coral Sea with the then Australian Prime Minister, Malcolm Turnbull. Avoiding the city of his birth for fear of massive demonstrations, he did not step through the doors of Trump Tower until August. His preference was for political comfort zones, and the worshipping crowds they brought.

The make-up of his administration was emphatically partisan. Trump dispensed with the tradition of appointing a high-profile figure from the opposing party to run a government department. Gary Cohn, a former head of Goldman Sachs, became the most high-ranking Democrat in the White House, with a seat at the Cabinet table, but was derided by the president as a 'globalist' and resigned in early 2018.

Nominating Jeff Sessions as his attorney general was particularly provocative, for the Alabama senator had faced accusations of racism in the 1980s that cost him a federal judgeship. Sessions would have joined the Ku Klux Klan, he allegedly said, had its ranks not included pot smokers. Yet accusations of racism and Islamophobia were no bar to entry into the administration. Steve Bannon had been the executive editor of the Trump fanzine Breitbart News, 'the home of the alt-right'. The president's first National Security Advisor, Michael Flynn, who had to step down because of his ties with Russia, had once tweeted that the 'fear of Muslims is rational'. Stephen Miller, the main architect of the Trump administration's hard-line immigration policies, promoted white nationalist literature from alt-right websites and bemoaned the loss of Confederate symbols in the aftermath of Dylann Roof's racist gun rampage in Charleston.

Trump's policies rewarded red states and penalised the blue. His attempt to repeal Obamacare would have resulted in a massive redistribution of funding from blue states that had expanded Medicare eligibility under the Affordable Care Act to red states that had not. His 2017 tax reforms hit Democratic states especially hard, because of the state and local tax reduction known as SALT. The ten states with the highest SALT deduction all voted for Hillary Clinton. Trump targeted the so-called sanctuary cities obstructing his deportation policy by withholding federal law enforcement funds. His municipal enemies list included the Democratic strongholds of Boston, Chicago, Los Angeles, New York and Washington DC.

California and New York, those bi-coastal bastions of the Trump resistance, were singled out. Trump revoked a waiver allowing the Golden State to set its own emission standards that had been renewed repeatedly since the Nixon years. He pressured Republicans in Congress to block federal funding for a new rail tunnel under the Hudson River between New Jersey and New York, which had been ranked by the Obama administration as the number one infrastructure project in the country, because the existing tunnel was in danger of failing. The Trump administration even blocked New Yorkers from enrolling or re-enrolling in trusted traveller programmes that speeded up international travel at John F. Kennedy International Airport.

The 'with me or against me' principle applied to the federal government. Trump expected top-ranking officials to put personal allegiance to him over their oaths to serve the American people and uphold the US constitution, a loyalty culture that added to the sense of chaos. The FBI Director, James Comey, was fired when he refused to drop the Russian collusion investigation into Michael Flynn. Almost daily for a time, the president humiliated Jeff Sessions with abusive tweets for recusing himself from the Russian investigation, which paved the way for his deputy, Rod Rosenstein, to appoint a special counsel. 'I'm fucked,' said Trump, when he heard the news. Sessions, the first senator to back Trump's candidacy, had been sent to the Justice Department precisely because of his presumed loyalty.

Even as he became the head of government, Trump escalated his attacks on the institutions of state. He assailed his intelligence services, the FBI and the 'deep state' for raising legitimate questions about his links with the Kremlin and Moscow's support for his candidacy. He berated his generals. 'You're all losers,' he told them during a meeting at the Pentagon. 'You don't know how to win any more.' He gave *carte blanche* to Rex Tillerson, the former Texan oil man, to hollow out the State Department, which he thought was populated with 'globalists', liberal interventionists and Hillary Clinton sympathisers. After the exodus of career diplomats and the difficulty in attracting new Foreign Service Officers, its headquarters in Foggy Bottom looked more and more like a derelict shell. This is precisely what Steve Bannon meant when he spoke of 'the destruction of the administrative state'.

Governmental institutions that ordinarily transcended politics, and which dealt with hard facts, were treated like extensions of his personal organisation. After Trump mistakenly claimed Hurricane Dorian would hit Alabama, the White House pressed the National Oceanic and Atmospheric Administration to 'correct' the forecasters who contradicted the president. The National Archives, the repository of the country's history, altered a photograph of the women's march that was critical of Trump. The federal judiciary was a frequent target. His criticism of the 'Obama judges' who blocked his travel ban earned a rare rebuke from the Chief Justice, John Roberts. 'We do not have Obama judges or Trump judges, Bush judges or Clinton judges,' he pointedly asserted.

Taking on blue America often meant maligning black and brown America. In doing so, Trump relied on the political business model that helped him reach the White House, which meant inflaming America's angriest fault line: race. His first travel ban targeted immigrants from seven Muslim-majority countries. Continually, he assailed black athletes in the 'Take a knee' protests, which unfolded during the playing of the national anthem before American football games. He retweeted anti-Muslim videos from a fringe far-right group, Britain First, and repeatedly attacked Sadiq Khan, London's Muslim mayor. Immigrants from Haiti and African nations, he told senators in an Oval Office meeting, came from 'shit-hole countries'.

African-American lawmakers, such as the late Elijah Cummings, the much-loved chairman of the House Oversight Committee, also became his target. Cummings's district in Baltimore, tweeted the president, was 'a disgusting, rodent and rat-infested mess'. His attack fitted a long-established pattern in which he depicted black neighbourhoods as pathologically unhygienic and unsafe, playing on racist stereotypes that for generations had portrayed African-Americans as dirty and inferior. After the Cummings controversy, Trump claimed to be 'the least racist person there is anywhere in the world', but his words and actions going back decades belied that outlandish boast.[8]

In the summer of his first year in office, it took him 48 hours to specifically condemn the white-supremacist violence in Charlottesville, Virginia, where torch-carrying neo-Nazis shouted 'Jews will not replace us!', and where a counter-protester was killed when a racist deliberately rammed his car into the crowd. In an extraordinary press availability held a few days afterwards in the lobby of Trump Tower, he claimed there were 'very fine people' on both sides, suggesting a moral equivalence between neo-Nazi protesters and their opponents. Standing next to me in the press huddle that surreal afternoon was an African-American cameraman who abandoned his tripod to join reporters in hurling questions, something I had never before seen in 25 years as a journalist (cameramen never leave their rolling cameras in press conferences and leave the questions to reporters). 'What should I tell my children?' he shouted. 'What should I tell my children?'

When Trump hosted events at the White House intended to be more inclusive, often they had the opposite effect. A ceremony in the Oval Office to honour Navajo veterans took place in front of a portrait of Andrew Jackson, the president who had signed the Indian Removal Act leading to the forced eviction of Native Americans from their land, a calamity known as 'The Trail of Tears'. Trump compounded this error by telling the bewildered veterans, 'We have a representative in Congress who has been here a long time – longer than you – they call her Pocahontas,' yet another dig at Senator Elizabeth Warren, who claimed Native American ancestry.[9]

After the Democrats won back the House of Representatives in the 2018 congressional midterms, Trump was presented with new targets for his racist attacks: four women of colour – Alexandria Ocasio-Cortez, Ayanna Pressley, Rashida Tlaib and her fellow Muslim congresswoman Ilhan Omar, a group that called themselves 'The Squad'.

'Why don't they go back and help fix the totally broken and crime infested places from which they came,' tweeted Trump in the summer of 2019, even though three of the four were born in the United States. Rekindling notions of selective citizenship from nativist panics of the past, Trump was not just assailing these women for being un-American, but suggesting they were non-American.

Days later, he crossed another behavioural threshold when he followed up his racist tweets with ugly racial demagoguery at a stadium rally in North Carolina. After singling out the members of The Squad in turn, and ending on Congresswoman Omar, who, he had earlier suggested, falsely and outrageously, had married her brother, Trump did nothing to quell the crowd as it chanted, 'Send her home, send her home.' Never before had a modern-day US president publicly used such nativist language. Not since George Wallace's campaign for the presidency in 1968 had we seen this kind of rabble-rousing – the former segregationist governor, who ran as an independent, got nowhere near the White House.

The politics behind the attack was not hard to unpick. Trump wanted to make these four women the face of the modern-day Democrats: to create four new hate figures, or four new Hillary Clintons. 'Send her home' sounded like it was about to become the 'Lock her up' mantra of the 2020 race, until GOP leaders made it clear, via Mike Pence, that the party of Lincoln could not be defined by those words.

The night of the infamous North Carolina rally I was on the National Mall and watched Marine One swoop in over the Tidal Basin and fly past the Washington Monument, before dropping the president on the South Lawn of the White House. The obelisk was illuminated with a gigantic projection of Apollo 11, a spacecraft that still inspired awe. At the very moment the country was celebrating the 50th anniversary of the moon landing, a unifying national mission detached from earthly politics, an American first of such noble ambition, the president was actively sowing the seeds of disunion. How far off that Sea of Tranquillity seemed now.

It came as little surprise that America witnessed an alarming increase in hate crimes from the moment Trump won the presidency. Between 9 November 2016 and 31 March 2017, the Southern Poverty Law Center recorded 1,863 incidents, the biggest spike since the aftermath of 9/11. This was brought home to my own family when the playground my children regularly went to after school was daubed with Nazi swastikas and the pro-Trump graffiti 'GO TRUMP'. By the end of 2020, hate crimes had reached their highest level in more than a decade, and hate killings were the worst on record.

Sometimes it appeared that a line could be drawn between the president's words of incitement and racial violence. In August 2019 a white nationalist whose online manifesto vowed to end the 'Hispanic invasion' shot dead 23 people at a Walmart store in El Paso, Texas. Trump had used that very word 'invasion' at a Florida rally in May, and had then asked his supporters, 'How do you stop these people?' When someone shouted, 'Shoot them,' he laughed.

After the 2018 synagogue mass shooting in Pittsburgh, when 11 people were killed by a gunman armed with an AR-15 assault rifle shouting anti-Semitic slurs, a coalition of local Jewish leaders issued a letter telling Trump he would not be welcome in the city until he denounced white nationalism. I was in Pittsburgh that awful weekend – the Tree of Life synagogue was located in the neighbourhood where the children's TV star Fred Rogers used to live – and heard for myself from community members who regarded the president as a purveyor of hate. Trump's own rhetoric made it impossible for him to assume the traditional mantle of 'mourner-in-chief'.

A vigilante president encouraged vigilantes. 'A Trump super fan' is how prosecutors described Cesar Sayoc, who posted 16 bombs to people he deemed to be enemies of the president, including prominent Democrats and CNN. Arrested in Florida, his white van was festooned with pro-Trump stickers and pictures of Hillary Clinton and Barack Obama overlaid with the crosshairs of a rifle. Not long afterwards, a picture emerged of him at a Trump rally holding aloft a home-made banner reading 'CNN sucks'. President Trump's first hate tweet had targeted 'Fake News @CNN', while he had also retweeted a crazed video of himself tackling and punching a man at a WrestleMania event, with a CNN logo superimposed on his opponent's face.[10]

Political violence made an unwelcome reappearance. In December 2016, a 28-year-old from North Carolina launched a gun attack on a pizzeria in Washington DC, which a spate of fake 'Pizzagate' news stories on alt-right sites claimed was imprisoning sex slaves who were victims of a child-abuse ring operated by Hillary Clinton. Nor was the violence solely confined to the right. In the summer of 2017 a left-wing activist who was a supporter of Bernie Sanders carried out a gun attack on a Republican congressional baseball team practising in

Alexandria, Virginia. The House Majority Whip Steve Scalise became the first sitting member of Congress to have been shot since Gabby Giffords.

As the country continued to rip itself apart, the president sought to appropriate America's birthday, 4 July, and turn it into a personal celebration. Trump's 2019 Salute to America, which looked to all intents and purposes like a MAGA rally on the National Mall, provided yet another reminder of the over-politicisation of American life. The pictures from this pageant were quickly packaged up into campaign advertisements. And what pictures they were. The Lincoln Memorial was decorated not just with red-white-and-blue bunting but also with martial trappings – two 60-ton M1 Abrams tanks and a pair of armoured Bradley Fighting Vehicles. A B-2 Stealth Bomber, F-22 Raptors, the plane used as Air Force One and the Navy's Blue Angels Flight Demonstration Squadron soared overhead. This was Make America Great Again as a military tattoo.

It was no wonder that sales of dystopian literature soared, as worried citizens compiled a crisis reading list that included George Orwell's 1984, Margaret Atwood's The Handmaid's Tale and Philip Roth's The Plot Against America. Roth's novel imagines a President Charles Lindbergh, the aviator who became the spokesman of the America First Committee in the early years of World War II. In answer to the question posed by all three novels – 'Could it happen here?' – concerned readers responded with an emphatic 'Yes'.

Invocations of a modern-day Third Reich were hysterical and overblown. They showed how anger had warped political discourse. Donald Trump's America was not Gilead, although when I interviewed Margaret Atwood in Toronto she thought it was easy to imagine Mike Pence as one of the theocratic commanders. Just as the billionaire unwisely compared himself to the heroes of history, so his more strident critics overreached when they likened him to history's worst villains.

Nonetheless, there were parallels with the tales from the autarchic canon. Trump's response to the aerial photographs from his inauguration, in which he asserted a 'truth' that defied the evidence of our eyes, was eerily Orwellian. Orwell himself could have coined the phrase 'alternative facts', mouthed by the president's aide Kellyanne Conway in defence of his truth-twisting.

Addressing a convention of Veterans of Foreign Wars, Trump even argued that reports of his trade war with China hurting the US economy, an almost uniformly held view in corporate America, were false. 'What you're seeing and what you're reading is not what's happening', said Trump, prompting a wave of memes quoting one of the better-known passages from *1984*. 'The party told you to reject the evidence of your eyes and ears. It was their final, most essential command.'

Trump also displayed authoritarian impulses. Repeatedly he claimed an 'absolute right' to exert control over the Justice Department, and was convinced of his immunity not just from federal and state prosecution but from any form of oversight. Frequently he gave the impression his presidency was not constrained by the law. 'I have an Article II, where I have the right to do whatever I want', he declared in the summer of 2019, which was reminiscent of Richard Nixon's infamous assertion during his interviews with David Frost: 'when the president does it, that means that it is not illegal.'

With the courts and Congress constraining the Trump White House early on, and with the constitutional checks and balances seemingly working as the framers intended, the fandom surrounding the founding fathers reached new heights. They were cast as positively prophetic for anticipating a president like Trump. Going to watch the musical *Hamilton*, which celebrates the brave early years of the fledgling republic, and cheering at the line from the French General Lafayette 'Immigrants, we get the job done', became an act of resistance. However, the veneration of the founding fathers once again blinded Americans to how their flawed constitution had contributed to the country's downward slide.

All the living ex-presidents, regardless of party, received a Trump Bump. None more so than George W. Bush, who, having made it clear he did not vote for the billionaire, benefited from a dizzying revisionism. Now the 'Toxic Texan' looked like an elder statesman. Iraq and Katrina no longer seemed so heinous. His impish friendship with Michelle Obama, sealed again with the discreet handover of a sweet at his father's funeral, stood in such marked contrast to the humourlessness of his Republican successor. As with the fawning over the framers, it created the misleading sense that ex-presidents were blameless in the rise of Donald Trump.

Clinton, Bush, Obama. America had seen a succession of schismatising leaders. But Trump instantly became the most polarising president of them all. There was a staggering 79 per cent gap in his approval ratings between Democrats and those of Republicans. For blue America he was a national embarrassment. Much of red America, though, still saw him as a national saviour.

So extreme was the temperature on the afternoon Donald Trump announced America's withdrawal from the Paris climate change accord that the journalists seated in the White House Rose Garden, awaiting his emergence from the Oval Office, noticed the red thermometer warning symbol appear on our smartphones – 'iPhone needs to cool down before you can use it' – and our laptops start to overheat.

In keeping with his reality TV advisory to West Wing staffers, he tried to create the greatest possible suspense before giving his statement. 'I will be announcing my decision on Paris Accord, Thursday at 3.00 pm,' he teased in a tweet beforehand. The White House even laid on a military jazz quartet, sweltering in their scarlet tunics, to serenade the waiting administration officials and press corps. This inevitably invited comparisons with the string orchestra that kept playing as the *Titanic* nosed beneath the waves, though it was melting icebergs which this time were potentially calamitous.

The remarks prepared that day sounded like a teleprompter version of a rally speech. Elucidation as rant. 'The Paris Agreement handicaps the United States economy in order to win praise from the very foreign capitals and global activists that have long sought to gain wealth at our country's expense,' he bellowed, revisiting his decades-old themes of national victimhood and humiliation. 'They

291

don't put America first. I do, and always will,' he stressed. 'I was elected to represent the citizens of Pittsburgh, not Paris.' (We drove to Pittsburgh the following morning, a forward-thinking city with a Democratic mayor and cutting-edge environmental policies.)

Early on in his presidency, it became clear the Trump doctrine was primarily an anti-Obama doctrine, aimed at demolishing his predecessor's foreign-policy legacy. More a deal-breaker than a deal-maker, one of his first acts as president was to withdraw the United States unilaterally from the Trans-Pacific Partnership, Obama's geopolitical gang-up intended to contain China. Likewise, the Paris climate change accord, Iranian nuclear deal and rapprochement with Cuba were Obama legacy items. The new president bombed targets in Syria partly to show his preparedness to enforce the very red lines prohibiting the use of chemical weapons that had proved so elastic for Obama.

Trump's view of international leaders was shaped to a large extent by how they got on with his predecessor. The German Chancellor, Angela Merkel, was given short shrift, because she was the international leader whom Obama most respected – the departing president made his last foreign visit to Berlin, where they dined together for three hours. Nor did it help that *Time* magazine named her 'Person of the Year' in 2015, and acclaimed her as 'the leader of the free world'. The Canadian Prime Minister, Justin Trudeau, another Obama favourite, was a regular target of Trump's tweet tirades. Obama's foes, most notably Benjamin Netanyahu, became bosom buddies.

'America First meant America alone' was our standard line as reporters. I parroted it myself from the White House after he jettisoned the Paris accord. That, however, was only part of the story. While relations soured with longstanding allies as Trump abdicated America's traditional role as the leader of rules-based international order, he lent support to an informal axis of authoritarians.

In Saudi Arabia he spoke with almost fatherly pride of the country's de facto leader, Crown Prince Mohammed bin Salman, even though he had been implicated by US intelligence in the murder of the dissident journalist Jamal Khashoggi, who was decapitated with an electric saw. He praised Egypt's autocratic president, Abdel

292

Fattah el-Sisi, as 'a fantastic guy'. He complimented Rodrigo Duterte, the president of the Philippines, for an 'unbelievable job on the drug problem', even though the crackdown resulted in the extrajudicial killing of an estimated 12,000 suspected drug dealers and users. Recep Tayyip Erdoğan of Turkey received 'very high marks', despite his increasingly authoritarian rule. The far-right president of Brazil, Jair Bolsonaro, the so-called Trump of the Tropics, received a brotherly welcome at the White House. After a 21-year break, the Prime Minister of Hungary, Viktor Orbán, the face of European ultra-nationalism, was invited back to the White House. International strongmen seemed to make Trump go weak at the knees.

Vladimir Putin occupied a special place in Trump's affections, and from the very beginning the president exhibited an almost phobic aversion to any form of criticism of the Russian leader. This inevitably raised suspicions over Russia's interference in the 2016 election. After Russian agents launched a nerve-agent attack targeting a KGB defector in the UK, in the cathedral town of Salisbury, the president fumed at aides for pushing him to expel 60 Russian diplomats and suspected spies in retaliation and favoured a far more limited response. At a summit in Helsinki with Putin, Trump sided with the former KGB spymaster over his own intelligence agencies on the question of Russian collusion – jaw-dropping remarks he had to walk back on after his return to Washington following a rare outcry from normally obsequious Republicans.

Trump actively sought to expand this network of nationalist fellow travellers. Ahead of the French presidential election in the spring of 2017, Trump backed the far-right candidate Marine Le Pen, tweeting 'she's the strongest on borders and she's the strongest on what's been going on in France'. Before becoming president, he announced in a late-night tweet that Nigel Farage would make an excellent UK ambassador in Washington, which sent a lightning bolt through Whitehall.

When it came to relations with Washington, the world's authoritarians and nationalists had rarely had it so good. Certainly, a US president had never before showered them with such praise or given them such licence. In the red, white and blue of America First, autocrats saw a green light to act with impunity.

Though it may be premature to speak of the creation of a new world order bringing together nationalists and authoritarians, the old post-war order was crumbling under the weight of Trump's wrecking ball. The transatlantic alliance, the bedrock of the international system, faced its most severe stress test since the Suez Crisis in 1956. As Downing Street desperately eyed a post-Brexit trade deal, the special relationship came to look more like a servile relationship.

Traditional alliances now meant little. In his first telephone call with Malcolm Turnbull, Trump tried to tear up the agreement reached with the Obama administration over the resettlement into the United States of refugees from Australia's offshore detention centres. On his first trip to Europe, he berated NATO allies over burden-sharing, with a scorched-earth speech at the alliance's new headquarters in Brussels that turned into the most humiliating public dressing-down of allies ever witnessed from a US president. Standing in front of a lump of twisted metal retrieved from Ground Zero, Trump markedly failed to endorse Article Five of the NATO charter, the provision invoked by America's allies after September 11 to rally to the defence of any member under attack.

Trump attended historical commemorations, such as the 75th anniversary of the D-Day landings, but there was something ahistorical about his approach – as if the alliances forged in blood on the battlefields of the two world wars were now expendable. Perhaps his true feelings surfaced when he failed to visit the Aisne-Marne American Cemetery near Paris in 2018, which officials at the time said was because of bad weather. 'Why should I go to that cemetery?', *The Atlantic* magazine reported him as asking aides. 'It's filled with losers.' In another conversation during that trip, he reportedly referred to the 1,800 US Marines who had lost their lives at the Battle of Belleau Wood as 'suckers'.

The gathering he seemed to least enjoy was the G7, largely because it brought together Washington's longest-standing friends. He stormed out of the summit in Quebec City, refusing to sign its communiqué. In

Biarritz, he complained the gathering was focusing on 'niche issues' such as climate change, and bemoaned the ongoing exclusion of Vladimir Putin in punishment for his annexation of Crimea. The message conveyed in all these settings, when America's closest allies were at his side, was that there was no longer a joint Western project. Trump did not seem to believe in the concept of the United States standing at the head of a free world, the cornerstone of US policy since the war.

America's post-war dominance was based on the strength and durability of its alliance system, which was a product of careful diplomatic design. Yet whether it was Australia, Britain, Canada, Japan, South Korea, Germany, France, Mexico, Ukraine or NATO, Trump was trashing these vital relationships and guilty of a betrayal of trust, the sine qua non of diplomacy. In Syria, Trump threw the Kurds who had fought alongside US Special Forces in the campaign against Islamic State to the wolves by green-lighting the Turkish invasion of north-eastern Iraq. This betrayal showed that America was no longer a trustworthy friend, and also indicated how Trump sometimes failed to understand the might of US military power: in this instance, how a tiny deployment of just 50 American Special Forces troops could maintain stability in northern Syria and prevent Turkey and the Kurds from engaging in all-out war.

The conduct of foreign affairs became unusually personalised. Whereas in recent decades America's influence has been defined in terms of soft power and hard power, the new president pinned his faith in 'Trump power'. An 'I alone can fix it' approach: 'America First' as 'Me First'. Often it was predicated on his egotistical view that international leaders would put the alchemy of good personal chemistry with him ahead of their country's vital national interests.

There were obvious drawbacks. This belief in 'Trump power' created the misleading sense that a friendly relationship would inexorably lead to positive policy outcomes, which was manifestly not the case in the trade dispute with China or the nuclear diplomacy with North Korea. This highly personalised approach also undercut traditional forms of diplomacy. 'I told Rex Tillerson, our wonderful Secretary of State, that he is wasting his time negotiating with Little Rocket

Man,' he wrote on Twitter, while Tillerson was working through back channels with Pyongyang and before Trump's infatuation with the North Korean despot had begun.

Foreign governments no longer knew who spoke for the United States. The word of secretaries of state, national security advisors and ambassadors all over the world could be undercut with a single tweet. Besides, Trump often instructed his son-in-law, Jared Kushner, and personal lawyer, Rudy Giuliani, to be his emissary.

For all that, Trump restored a fear factor to US diplomacy absent during the Obama years; a bringing together of a twentieth-century view of American power, based on the preparedness to use military might, and a nineteenth-century sense of American manhood, based on the disposition towards physical violence – a kind of John Wayne doctrine.

The Assad regime hesitated before ordering another chemical strike – although it continued its use of barrel bombs, which killed far more civilians. NATO allies started to stump up more cash. At the United Nations, the constant threat that the organisation's biggest donor could withdraw funding provided fresh impetus for US-led reform, especially of the bloated peacekeeping operations.

When I interviewed the new Secretary-General, António Guterres, in his wood-panelled suite of offices on the 38th floor of the United Nations in New York, which looks onto a Trump apartment building, he was so afraid of insulting the former property tycoon that he told me afterwards he never referred to him publicly by name. Instead, he spoke generically of 'the US government'. Trump, after all, could bankrupt the United Nations with a single tweet.

There were times when Trump's unpredictability was a national security asset. After he gave the order to assassinate Iran's second most powerful leader, Qasem Soleimani, critics drew parallels with the killing of Archduke Ferdinand in Sarajevo, the spark that ignited World War I. Yet Iran's initial response – to launch missile strikes on two US bases in Iraq – was relatively mild, because they feared a disproportionate response from the US commander-in-chief.

This dread of Trump had shades of Nixon's 'Madman Theory', where friends and foes alike feared his irrationality and volatility and could not entirely rule out the awful possibility of him pressing the nuclear button. Yet here again was a paradox: in an inversion of President Theodore Roosevelt's famous dictum, he spoke loudly and rarely reached for the big stick. Trump sounded like a warmonger, but he did not want to wage war.

Frequently, in a kind of Trump-versus-Trump doctrine, the president contradicted himself, as his macho compulsions vied with his isolationist impulses. Having given the go-head for an attack on the Iranians in June 2019 for downing an unarmed American drone, he made a last-minute decision not to retaliate militarily.

Though the president was feared, often he was ridiculed. During his 2018 speech to the United Nations General Assembly, his extravagant boasts about how he had made America great again were met with open laughter from the diplomats arrayed before him. At a Buckingham Palace reception during the 2019 G7 summit, he was mocked in a huddle of world leaders that included Justin Trudeau, Boris Johnson and Emmanuel Macron – a slight caught on camera that prompted yet another early exit from a G7 gathering.

His extremism meant he was also reviled. The then Speaker of the House of Commons, John Bercow, announced Trump would not be welcome to address a joint session of parliament, a courtesy extended to Xi Jinping only a few years earlier and an astonishing snub from America's closest ally. His Muslim travel ban was denounced not just by adversaries such as Iran but also by allies such as France and Canada. No longer did the world look to America for moral leadership. No longer did the United States actively pursue a human rights agenda. In an interview early on with the disgraced Fox News anchor Bill O'Reilly, when asked why he was so fond of 'a killer' like Putin, he scoffed at the idea that America had ever offered the ethical lead. 'There are a lot of killers. You think our country's so innocent?' It was true, but no US president had been prepared to admit to the amorality of US foreign policy, partly for fear of the legitimising message it would send to authoritarians.

Yet another way of understanding Trump's foreign policy was through the prism of electoral politics, for much of what he did in foreign affairs was with an eye on re-election. True to this doctrine of political self-preservation, and true to his pledges as a candidate, he avoided military entanglements. He launched a trade war against China. He relocated the US embassy in Israel from Tel Aviv to Jerusalem, a popular move among evangelicals. 'Promise made, promise kept' became something of a guiding principle in foreign policy, and lent a measure of consistency to an often haphazard approach. In his memoir, *The Room Where It Happened*, John Bolton observed how he was 'hard-pressed to identify any significant decision during my Trump tenure that wasn't driven by re-election calculations'.

The summer of 2019 offered a case study of Trumpism on the global stage. On the eve of the G20 summit in Osaka, Vladimir Putin declared in an interview with the *Financial Times* that the Western-style liberal order had 'become obsolete'. Trump seemed intent on proving him right. As he flew into Japan, there was the now almost ritualistic hazing of the host.

'If Japan is attacked, we will fight World War III, but if we're attacked, Japan doesn't have to help us at all,' he complained in an interview, before heading for Osaka. 'They can watch it on a Sony television.'

Attacking Shinzo Abe seemed especially cruel, for the Japanese Prime Minister had been the most slavish practitioner of the child-monarch approach to the US president, taking calculated flattery to the point of craven obsequiousness. In the lead-up to Osaka, Abe even produced a simplistic colour chart for Trump showing how much Japan invested in America, not that it granted Abe any diplomatic immunity from the schoolyard bully.

In Osaka, Trump showered praise on Mohammed bin Salman. When an American pool reporter allowed into the room asked about the murdered journalist Jamal Khashoggi, the press were immediately shown the door, with Trump pretending not to hear the question. In his first meeting with the Russian president after the publication of the Mueller Report, Trump was even chummier with Vladimir Putin. 'Don't meddle in the [2020] election,' he said laughingly when invited by a reporter to admonish the Russian president, treating the Kremlin's interference as if it were an adolescent prank.

Nor was he troubled by Putin's requiem for Western-style liberalism. Bizarrely, at his end-of-summit news conference he did not even appear to understand what was meant by the term, confusing it with West Coast liberalism. '[Putin] sees what's going on, I guess, if you look at what's happening in Los Angeles. And what's happening in San Francisco and a couple of other cities which are run by an extraordinary group of liberal people.' Invited to defend democracy, he attacked the Democrats. Offered the chance to contradict Putin, he condemned Pelosi.

In his bilateral meeting with Xi Jinping, Trump also demonstrated how his transactional approach to foreign policy merged with the electoral. The president pleaded with his Chinese counterpart to purchase soybeans from hard-pressed US farmers in key battleground states.

The most surreal moment in Osaka came with the president's unexpected, early morning offer to Kim Jong-un for a quick meet-and-greet at the demilitarised zone on the Korean Peninsula: 'if Chairman Kim of North Korea sees this,' he tweeted, 'I would meet him at the Border/DMZ just to shake his hand and say Hello (?)!'

If the impromptu invitation felt like a diplomatic form of online dating, the staging of the meeting itself owed more to *The Bachelor*. At this brief encounter, a starry-eyed Kim Jong-un gambolled down the steps on the northern side of the armistice line while Donald Trump emerged, with a self-satisfied smile, from a building on the south through its mirrored glass doors, the most theatrical entrance on offer. Ordinarily, moments of history are sealed with a handshake, but here it was with a footstep. Donald Trump left his Secret Service security detail behind to stride out alone into what for decades had been enemy territory, a country that less than two years earlier he'd threatened to wipe from the map. The North Korean leader had gone from mortal foe to chirpy tour guide.

The shortest presidential foreign trip on record lasted little more than a minute. Yet by crossing a geographic threshold no other occupant of the White House had ever stepped over, he lent legitimacy to a totalitarian regime with one of the worst human rights records in the world and granted a murderous despot the imprimatur of

American acceptance. As for nuclear diplomacy, 'Little Rocket Man' retained his arsenal of weapons capable of reaching the West Coast.

This was the first instalment in what became a tale of two Kims, with the amorousness at the DMZ followed in short order by the president's frigid reaction to the leak of critical diplomatic cables from the UK ambassador in Washington, Sir Kim Darroch. Inept, incompetent and insecure was the diplomat's assessment of the president and his administration, supposedly secret words spelt out in bold tabloid font on the front page of *The Mail on Sunday*. With his gossamer skin pierced, Trump made the White House a no-go zone for the ambassador of America's closest ally. Here his famed catchphrase, 'You're fired!', was superfluous. Fearing a trial by tweet, Darroch resigned shortly afterwards, knowing his position had become untenable.

Now in the final weeks of her prime ministership, Theresa May bore the brunt of his fury. Via Twitter, Trump mocked her negotiating skills on Brexit as 'a disaster'. So a relationship that began in Washington shortly after his inauguration with a gentle tap on the hand from the president as the two walked down the colonnade that connects the West Wing to the Executive Mansion ended with repeated kicks in the teeth.

Before the summer's end there were more eccentricities. Trump intervened with the Swedish Prime Minister on behalf of the rapper A$AP Rocky, held for alleged assault, following a lobbying campaign from Kanye West and Kim Kardashian. In a meeting with the Pakistani Prime Minister, Imran Khan, another celebrity politician, Trump talked casually about wiping Afghanistan off the map and killing 10 million people, something he said he ideally did not want to do. 'Kabul seeks clarification on Trump talk of wiping out Afghanistan,' read the headline the next day from Reuters, which sounded more like it belonged on the satirical website The Onion. He even raised the possibility of buying Greenland – something, admittedly, the Americans had proposed doing three times before – and cancelled a visit to Copenhagen at the last minute after the Danish Prime Minister called his real-estate offer 'absurd'.

There were a few countries, such as Israel and India, where Trump was popular, but most of his signature policies were rejected around the world: the wall along the Mexican border, the withdrawal from the Paris climate change accord and the Iranian nuclear deal. In a shocking illustration of how US prestige had suffered under his leadership, Vladimir Putin had a higher international approval rating (33 per cent), according to Pew Research. Trump's 29 per cent was just one point better than China's Xi Jinping.[11] Three decades on from the end of the Cold War, an authoritarian Russian president who regularly flouted international law apparently commanded more global respect than the president of the United States.

The snaking lines outside high schools in the commuter belt of Philadelphia were a portent of political change. It was the morning of the midterm congressional elections, and we were witnessing a pre-dawn suburban revolt. Many of the well-heeled Republicans who in 2016 had backed Donald Trump, but held their noses as they did so, were now expressing voters' remorse. Many of those Starbucks moms now had regrets. Two years after the detonation of the blue wall, a blue wave now swept across much of the country It lifted the Democrats to a majority in the House of Representatives.

From that moment on, it seemed inevitable that the Trump presidency would include the spectacle of impeachment, even if the returning House Speaker, Nancy Pelosi, was initially reluctant to take this rarely used option, mindful of the backlash against the GOP in 1998 and how it had cost two of her predecessors as House Speaker their jobs.

Those who wanted to rid the White House of Donald Trump clung to the belief that Robert Mueller's investigation into Russian meddling would provide the grounds for his removal from office by uncovering evidence of a conspiracy or of obstruction of justice. The chatter in Washington was that the former FBI director was masterminding a slow and deliberate game of three-dimensional chess, while Donald Trump was playing hungry hippo. A string of

301

high-profile indictments and convictions – Flynn, Manafort, Stone, Cohen, the former Trump campaign advisors Rick Gates and George Papadopoulos and 12 Russian intelligence officers – suggested the king might soon be under threat.

Far from moving in for the kill, however, Mueller made choices that greatly diminished the president's legal jeopardy. After Trump reneged on an agreement to be interviewed at Camp David, the special counsel decided not to subpoena him. Nor did he obtain Trump's tax returns or examine his financial ties with Russia. Crucially, he adhered to the Justice Department guideline that a sitting president could not be indicted, which meant he soft-pedalled the findings in his report. Russian meddling had been sweeping and systematic, he concluded. Links were uncovered between Trump campaign officials and individuals with ties to the Kremlin. Yet the investigation did not find sufficient evidence to conclude beyond reasonable doubt that the campaign had coordinated and conspired with the Russian government. On the issue of the obstruction of justice, Mueller found 'multiple acts by the President that were capable of exerting undue influence over law enforcement investigations'. These included 'efforts to remove the Special Counsel'. In damning terms he had accused the president while stopping short of a formal indictment.

Unveiling the 448-page report, the Attorney General, William Barr, wilfully distorted its findings, providing important political cover and lending official credence to the Trump boast that there had been 'no collusion and no obstruction'. Amid this miasma of misrepresentation, Mueller felt the need to correct the record in a press conference, the first time he had broken his silence. 'If we had had confidence that the president did not commit a crime,' he stressed, 'we would have said so.' Yet Trump continued to enjoy the undying support of Republican leaders and had the protection of an attorney general who exhibited the loyalty of a personal lawyer. For now, impeachment was off the table, and the president emerged emboldened.

Perhaps it was a sense of impunity that encouraged Donald Trump to propose his quid pro quo to the new Ukrainian president, Volodymyr Zelensky: the release of nearly $400 million in congressionally authorised military aid to Kiev in return for political dirt on Joe Biden and his son Hunter.

This time Nancy Pelosi was more willing to pursue impeachment. After all, using an instrument of US foreign policy for personal political gain was precisely the kind of abuse of presidential power that the framers had anticipated in laying out the grounds for removal from office.

Trump, of course, claimed his famed call in July 2019 with Zelensky, a fellow celebrity politician, was 'perfect', but the partial transcript suggested a classic shakedown. 'I would like you to do us a favour,' he said, immediately after discussing the question of military aid. 'There's a lot of talk about Biden's son [Hunter], that Biden stopped the prosecution, and a lot of people want to find out about that, so whatever you could do with the attorney general would be great.' When the transcript was released in September 2019, the momentum driving impeachment became unstoppable.

So much of what was wrong about American politics was resident in the trial of Donald John Trump. The hyper-partisanship of Republicans and Democrats was evident in the party-line votes to impeach and acquit that made its outcome so very predictable. Not one House Republican broke ranks on the articles of impeachment. Just two Democrats voted against the abuse of power article, while three were against the obstruction of Congress charge – in 1999, during Bill Clinton's impeachment, 81 Republicans helped kill off an abuse of power charge, although admittedly, the charge in this instance was easier to justify.

So coarse and ugly was the political discourse that Chief Justice John Roberts, who presided over the trial, told both sides to dial back the rhetoric. There was also no shortage of hype and sensation, although it never lived up to the melodrama of Clinton's impeachment, partly because Zelensky was no Lewinsky.

A low point was the negative statecraft of Senate Majority Leader Mitch McConnell, who used parliamentary procedures to bar witnesses from even appearing in the trial – a case of jurors actively obstructing justice. Embracing his role as a wartime *consigliere*, McConnell's loyalty to the White House was never in question. For a Senate leader who managed to block Merrick Garland's Supreme

Court appointment for almost a year, preventing the Democratic House managers who prosecuted the case in the trial from calling witnesses hardly required breaking sweat.

Constantly it has been remarked upon how Trump has trashed presidential norms, but the impeachment process underscored how the previous three years had destroyed the shared sense of what those norms should be. Washington could not even agree, as it had done during Watergate, on what constituted right and wrong. Between red and blue America, there was no longer agreement on the difference between black and white.

In many aspects, the impeachment of Donald Trump felt like another rerun of the O. J. Simpson trial. Just as O. J. appealed to the racial allegiance of African-American jury members, so Trump relied on the tribalism of Republicans. Just as O. J.'s legal team railed against the Los Angeles Police Department and its rogue officer, Mark Fuhrman, so Trump complained about the Democratic 'dirty cops' led by the former California prosecutor Adam 'Shifty' Schiff. As with 'The Juice', so with 'The Donald': the facts of the case were ultimately secondary to the feelings aroused by it. It turned on the question of whose side you were on.

Even the cast list included a familiar name. The celebrity law professor Alan Dershowitz, who had been part of the O. J. defence team, now appeared on the floor of the Senate to defend Donald Trump. Astonishingly, he tried to advance the argument that, because Trump believed his re-election was in the public interest, he was justified in his quid pro quo with Ukraine. Not only did that contradict a central tenet of the president's defence – that there was no favour for a favour – but Dershowitz was essentially claiming that a sitting president could do anything to get re-elected, a banana-republic defence.

To give the trial even more of a throwback feel, Bill Clinton's accuser, Kenneth Starr, was given a cameo by the president. Remarkably, he used his speech to the Senate trial to bemoan 'the age of impeachment' which he himself had helped usher in.

The president's 'Read the transcript' mantra even had echoes of the O. J. defence team's 'If it doesn't fit, you must acquit' description of that bloodied black glove: a successful attempt to turn the most damning evidence into the most exculpatory. Democrats complained that the Republicans had turned the Senate into Fifth Avenue, the place where Trump boasted he could shoot someone without losing any support. Only one Republican senator refused to play the partisan game by voting for removal. Mitt Romney's tearful speech sounded almost like a requiem for moderate Republicanism.

The Senate jury reflected America's polarised divide. Of its 100 members, 85 came from states that had voted for their party's presidential nominee in the 2016 election, the highest proportion in history. At the same time, however, the body could hardly be described as representative. Senators sent to Washington from states with 152 million Americans voted to acquit. Senators representing 170 million Americans found Donald Trump guilty.

After his acquittal, some moderate Republican Senators suggested Donald Trump would be chastened by impeachment, that it would be a teachable moment. However, the president's first post-trial tweet suggested he regarded it as proof of his omnipotence. To his 70 million plus followers, he posted an animation of election placards reading 'Trump 2020, Trump 2024, Trump 2028' and beyond an age of Trump stretching endlessly into the future. Not once did he display any contrition.

His victory rally in the East Room of the White House the morning after his acquittal, where Republican jurors stood to applaud the president, was another definitive moment: when the party of Reagan truly became the party of Trump. They had fallen into line, becoming his loyal soldiers. It was noticeable that the term GOP, an abbreviation for the Grand Old Party, was no longer so commonly heard. It was almost as if commentators no longer thought the party was deserving of that historic title.

Striking, too, during that ceremony was how the Attorney General, William Barr, got up from his seat to clap and salute Trump's legal team. The gesture suggested that the firewall between prosecutors at the Justice Department and political operatives at the White House had been incinerated, and that Barr was the arsonist.

The president's post-impeachment purge was quick in coming. Instantly, he ousted administration officials who had testified against him. Trump fired his Ambassador to the European Union, Gordon Sondland, who claimed during his explosive testimony that 'everyone knew' about the quid pro quo with Ukraine. He even subjected Lieutenant Colonel Alexander Vindman, a decorated veteran who listened in on the Zelensky call and testified against his commander-in-chief, to the dishonour of being marched out of the White House by security guards.

Above all, the impeachment saga illustrated how partisanship had nullified one of the most important constitutional checks and balances. Removing a president required 67 votes, an impossibly high threshold when Senators vote by party. The process therefore no longer held presidents to a higher ethical standard. If anything, it ran the risk of promoting presidential bad behaviour. Incumbents now know they enjoy a certain degree of impunity if they command the loyalty of just 34 of the 100 senators.

The 2020 State of the Union address, delivered on the eve of his acquittal, showed how acidic the air in Washington had become. It began with the president refusing to shake Nancy Pelosi's hand, and ended with her angrily ripping up his speech – both infantile gestures. Yet the moment that truly encapsulated America's chronic state of disunion came half-way through, when Trump awarded the Presidential Medal of Freedom to the conservative radio host Rush Limbaugh. An honour bestowed on Nelson Mandela, Mother Teresa and the astronauts who first flew to the moon now hung around the neck of the high priest of American polarisation. Truly this was the age of Trump.

8

2020

There were no longer any fresh flowers at the 9/11 Memorial. An American altar usually decorated with roses, carnations and postcard-sized Stars and Stripes was sequestered behind a makeshift plastic railing. Broadway, the 'Great White Way', went dark. The subway system was a ghost train. The Jacob K. Javits Convention Center, where Hillary Clinton had intended to shatter that glass ceiling, was now an emergency field hospital. Staten Island ferries kept cutting through the choppy waters of New York Harbour, passing Lady Liberty on the way in and out of Lower Manhattan, but scarcely any passengers were on board. Times Square was devoid of people. In the midst of a planetary pandemic, nobody wanted to meet any more at the 'Crossroads of the World'.

New York, a place known for its infectious energy and life abundant, was now in a coma-like state. The ceaseless din of sirens turned the city that never sleeps into the city that couldn't sleep. With more cases than any other American conurbation, this city once more became Ground Zero, a haunting term no New Yorker ever wanted applied here again. Our world was turned upside down, just as it had been on September 11.

In those first fretful weeks it felt like the headlines were crowding in on us. The coronavirus had reached America. It had come to the outer suburbs of New York. There were cases in the Bronx, Brooklyn, Queens and Manhattan. By now, the news was coming word of mouth. Someone had tested positive in our downtown office complex. A tenant in a neighbouring apartment building had been laid low. Our children's school was shutting. All the schools were shutting. The whole of New

York was soon in lockdown. Back then I remember thinking how different this was from stories I had reported on in the past. With wars and disasters there was always a refuge at the end of a harrowing ordeal. With Covid-19, however, the entire world was a trouble spot.

This was also the first time my family was living the same calamitous story that I had to cover. They were subject to the same risks and dangers. They felt the same tensions and concerns. And for us there was an extra layer of anxiety. My wife, Fleur, was in her final trimester. So some of those headlines now came like thunderbolts. A top New York hospital was barring partners from being present at the birth. Other maternity wards followed suit. Delivery rooms were being placed in Covid isolation: women sequestered from their partners, partners sequestered from their newborns. The magical realism of birth was becoming something altogether more dystopian.

In pre-pandemic times – how quickly we adopted the language of the before and after – many New Yorkers suffered from a paranoia known as FOMO: the fear of missing out. But the virus was something that everyone wanted to avoid: the talk of the town that nobody wanted to speak of from first-hand experience.

My symptoms presented on a Friday night, a weariness that I put down to weeks of covering the outbreak, and the new parental juggle of home-schooling our kids. Then came the muscle pain, the cough, the numbing of my taste buds. More worryingly, Fleur was developing a fever. Then she had the cough, what felt like a weather system on her lungs, the chronic fatigue and the tell-tale shortness of breath. New York attracts optimists. We both believed we'd be among those who only experienced mild symptoms. But Fleur's condition was deteriorating. We feared those sirens outside our windows might soon be outside our door.

With the coronavirus, darkness brought more menace. Symptoms worsened as the day went on. And late one night, when Fleur was finding it hard to breathe properly, we feared we would have to call 911. Few things are more frightening than watching a loved one struggle to finish a sentence for lack of breath, especially when that sentence is a matter of life and death.

Sleep usually brought some comfort, and did so again. Thankfully Fleur rallied. Her breathing improved. Her blood oxygen level crept back up. She avoided hospitalisation. Slowly, over the next few days, the clouds began to part, and eventually came the brilliant sunshine of recovery. We could be counted among the fortunate, and became even more mindful of the dead, and the loved ones they left behind.

Donald Trump's response to Covid-19 was entirely predictable. He did not change. He did not grow. He did not admit errors. He did not show humility or even sufficient humanity. For the America already horrified by his presidency, all its hallmarks were on agitated display. The implausible boasts – he awarded himself 10 out of 10 for his handling of the crisis. The politicisation of what should be the apolitical – early on, he toured the Centers for Disease Control wearing a campaign cap emblazoned with the slogan 'Keep America Great'. The truth-twisting – the specious claims that America was faring better than any other country, even though it had 4 per cent of the world's population but 24 per cent of the world's Covid-19 deaths. The attacks on the 'fake news' media, including a personal assault on a White House reporter who asked what his message to frightened Americans was: 'I tell them you are a terrible reporter.'

His attacks continued on government institutions at the forefront of battling the crisis. 'The Deep State Department' is how he described the State Department from his presidential podium the morning after it issued its most extreme travel advisory, urging Americans to refrain from all international travel. He hyped remedies, declaring the combination of hydroxychloroquine and azithromycin to be 'one of the biggest game-changers in the history of medicine', even as government health officials warned against offering false hope or untested drugs. He continued to disdain science. Astonishingly, he even suggested Americans might inject themselves with disinfectant, a snake-oil suggestion that earned him the nickname 'Domestos Don'.

His authoritarian impulses surfaced once again. Threatening to ride roughshod over the state governors, he claimed at one point to have 'total authority' over the decision to reopen the country, a blatantly unconstitutional assertion. More ominously, he threatened to adjourn both houses of Congress, something no previous president had ever done.

What was also striking was his lack of empathy. *The Washington Post* studied 13 hours of press briefings from the president and found he had spent just four-and-a-half minutes expressing sympathy for the victims. Rather than soothing words for relatives of those who had died, or words of encouragement and appreciation for those in the medical trenches, Trump's daily White House briefings commonly started with a shower of self-congratulation. After he had spoken, his loyal vice-president usually delivered a paean of praise to the president in that Pyongyang-Pence style he had perfected over the previous three years. Trump's narcissistic hunger for adoration seemed impossible to sate. Instead of a wartime president, he sounded at times like a sun king.

The coronavirus crisis gave this TV president his own nightly show with healthy viewing figures, which he joyfully pointed out rivalled the season finale of *The Bachelor*. 'President Trump is a ratings hit,' he tweeted on the day when his top health officials predicted as many as 200,000 Americans could die – an overly optimistic estimate, as it turned out.

Then there was the xenophobia that had always been the sine qua non of his political business model – repeatedly he described the disease as the 'Chinese virus' and even the 'Kung flu'. Initially treating the coronavirus more as an immigration problem rather than a health emergency, he closed America's border to foreign nationals who had travelled to China. As events turned out, restricting travel was an entirely rational move, but studies suggested that strains of the novel coronavirus first came to America from Europe. The China travel ban was announced on 31 January. Transatlantic travel from Europe was not restricted until 11 March.

His attempt at economic stewardship was more convincing than his mastery of public health. A lesson from financial shocks of the past, most notably the meltdown in 2008, was to 'go big' early on. That he tried to do. But here, as well, there were shades of his showman self. He seemed to have rounded on the initial figure of a trillion dollars for the stimulus package, because it sounded like such a gargantuan number – a fiscal eighth wonder of the world. In the end, of course, much more money was required.

The coronavirus outbreak posed a diabolical challenge to governments the world over, and required the kind of multi-pronged approach and long-term thinking that seemed beyond the US president. Instead, he repeatedly downplayed the threat, despite admitting to Bob Woodward that he understood the fatal potentialities. 'I wanted to always play it down,' he told Woodward. He claimed he did not want to spread panic, but his overriding fear seemed to be of spooking the markets.

The Trump presidency was so often about the pretence of progress. But the marketing skills of the sloganeer did not work here. This was a national emergency that could not be tweeted or nicknamed away. Nor could he blame it on 'fake news'. The facts were inescapable: the soaring numbers of the dead.

What did its response to this pandemic tell us about the United States? First of all, we saw the enduring goodness of this country. As with 9/11, we marvelled at the selflessness and bravery of its first responders – the nurses, doctors, medical support staff and ambulance drivers who turned up to work with the same sense of public-spiritedness shown by the firefighters who rushed towards the flaming Twin Towers. One of the most touching sights in New York was to see firefighters standing alongside their trucks outside hospitals to applaud the doctors and nurses, the heroes of 9/11 saluting the superheroes of Covid-19.

We witnessed the ingenuity and creativity of schools that transitioned to remote, online teaching without missing a beat. We saw a can-do spirit that kept stores open, shelves stocked and food being delivered. In other words, most Americans showed precisely the same virtues we saw in every country brought to a halt by the virus.

As for the American exceptionalism on display, much of it was negative. The queues outside gun stores. The spike in online sales of firearms – Ammo.com saw a 70 per cent increase in business. The panic-buying of AR-15s. The gun lobby even managed to persuade the Trump administration to categorise firearms stores and shooting ranges as essential businesses. At least there were no school shootings in March 2020, the first time month without one since 2002.

Once again, those who lived in developed nations were left to ponder why the world's richest country did not have a system of universal healthcare. When people lost their jobs – and more than 20 million were made jobless within weeks – they also lost their health insurance. One of the most heart-wrenching utterances of the coronavirus outbreak came from a man in a New York hospital gasping for breath before he died, whose last moments were consumed with worrying about the cost of his treatment: 'Who's going to pay for it?' he asked.

Coronavirus exposed America's racial divide and economic inequalities. Trends witnessed first in New York City were replicated nationally. Black people were six times more likely than white people to be hospitalised as a result of Covid-19. They died at twice the rate.

Poverty was a propagator of the pandemic. Hardship was a super-spreader. In Queens, the borough of New York that became the epicentre of the epicentre, I saw low-income workers line up around the block for hours, in scenes that looked like they belonged in the Great Depression. Even in the lace-curtain suburbs we saw queues of high-end cars, including Mercedes and luxury SUVs, waiting for over five hours so their owners could receive hand-outs from a local church.

At the other end of the income spectrum, the emperors of the New Economy increased their wealth. In the first three months of shutdown, the Amazon founder Jeff Bezos saw his net worth rise by an estimated $48 billion. By the end of the Covid summer, Apple had become the first US company with a market capitalisation of $2 trillion. Even as the US economy experienced its steepest decline since the Great Depression, the S&P 500 stock market index reached a record high, demonstrating once again the disconnect between share values and economic realities on the ground.

Rather than uniting the country in the face of a common enemy, the pandemic became an accelerant of polarisation. In the early weeks of the outbreak, Republicans were twice as likely as Democrats to view coronavirus coverage as exaggerated. Democrats were more likely to wash their hands thoroughly. Many conservatives rejected the epidemiology of the disease. To prove there was no virus, a pastor in Arkansas boasted that his parishioners were prepared to lick the floor of his church. Sean Hannity accused the Democrats and the media of inflating the severity of the coronavirus 'to bludgeon Trump with this new hoax'. The Medal of Freedom recipient Rush Limbaugh likened coronavirus to the common cold. So, as well as a pandemic, America was contending with an infodemic, much of it disseminated by the misinformation super-spreaders on Fox News and talkback radio.

Shutdowns became politicised. 'In your more politically conservative regions, closing is not interpreted as caring for you,' the Reverend Josh King told *The Washington Post*, 'it's interpreted as liberalism.' Tea Party-style rallies protesting against stay-at-home orders were held across the country, egged on by the president. 'LIBERATE VIRGINIA! LIBERATE MICHIGAN! LIBERATE MINNESOTA!' he tweeted. An armed militia group took up his call to arms, and stormed Michigan's state capital when the Democratic governor, Gretchen Whitmer, extended her emergency powers to combat the virus. Later in the year, the FBI arrested members of a Michigan militia over a plot to kidnap Governor Whitmer and put her on trial for treason.

Wearing a mask became a badge of political identification. Trump mocked as 'politically correct' a reporter who was wearing a simple face mask, and refused, save for a few occasions, to wear one himself.

Even the political geography of America affected how people were physically exposed to the virus. Four out of five of the worst-infected states initially – New York, New Jersey, California and Michigan – were Democrat. Florida, whose Republican governor, Ron DeSantis, refused to shut the state's beaches during spring break, was the only red state in the top five. By the end of the summer, however, as Covid-19 spread to the more rural parts of the country, seven out of ten of those who contracted the virus lived in red states.

For American liberals, Dr Anthony Fauci, the director of the National Institute of Allergy and Infectious Diseases, became the subversive hero of the hour. Offering an antidote to this post-truth presidency, Fauci stuck to scientific facts. After repeatedly contradicting Donald Trump over the seriousness of the outbreak, he came to be viewed with a measure of the same affection and reverence as the liberal Supreme Court jurist Ruth Bader Ginsburg.

The coronavirus outbreak led momentarily to an end to the gridlock on Capitol Hill, since legislators had no other choice but to legislate, given the severity of the economic crisis. But the passage of a stimulus package felt more like freak-out bipartisanship than patriotic cooperation, the legislative equivalent of panic-buying. Besides, when it came to the negotiation of a second stimulus package, the usual partisan acrimony, point-scoring and brinkmanship quickly returned.

The paradox here was that the coronavirus crisis initially erased philosophical lines, just as the financial meltdown had done in 2008. Ideological conservatives once again became operational liberals. Those who ordinarily detested government came to depend on it. Corporate America, generally so phobic towards federal intervention, was in desperate need of government bailouts. Trickle-down supply-siders became Keynesian big spenders. Even universal basic income, a fringe idea popularised by the Democratic presidential candidate Andrew Yang, went mainstream. The US government gave $1,200 one-off payments to every American who earned under $75,000 a year. Trump insisted on putting his signature on each of the cheques, a self-indulgence that not one of his predecessors had ever demanded and one that delayed the delivery of the urgently needed money.

Covid-19 underscored how the federal government had been run down over the past 40 years. The Centers for Disease Control and Prevention had been repeatedly targeted for funding cuts by the Trump administration, including a 16 per cent reduction in the 2021 budget proposal, although Congress came to its rescue.

The team responsible for dealing with pandemics on the National Security Council at the White House had been disbanded in the spring of 2018 and not replaced. A USAID programme known as PREDICT, which was aimed at spotting zoonotic viruses that passed from animals to humans, was shut down.

As with the attacks of September 11, warnings were repeatedly ignored. In recent years there had been numerous exercises to test the country's preparedness for a pandemic that identified exactly the areas of vulnerability that were now exposed: one, codenamed Crimson Contagion, involved a respiratory virus originating from China. Between 2003 and 2015, at least ten government reports highlighted the chronic shortage of ventilators and other life-saving equipment.[1]

As with Hurricane Katrina, the Federal Emergency Management Agency struggled to deliver essential supplies. As ever, there were tensions between federal agencies and the states. The institutional decline of government that led so many Americans to pin their faith on an individual, Donald Trump, was again plain to see, whether in the shortage of masks and protective gowns or the dearth of early testing. 'How did the US end up with nurses wearing garbage bags?' asked *The New Yorker* in a jolting headline. The answer lay in the hollowing out of government going back decades, and the problem of the federal government being in the hands of those who so deeply mistrusted government.

America's claim to global pre-eminence looked less convincing by the day. While, in previous crises, the world's most powerful nation might have mobilised a global response, nobody expected that of Trump's United States. The neo-isolationism of three years of America-Firstism had created a geopolitical form of social distancing, and this crisis reminded us of the oceanic divide that had opened up, even with Washington's closest allies.

Take the European travel ban, blocking visitors flying in from the Continent, which Trump announced during an Oval Office address to the nation without any prior warning to the countries affected. As American infection rates worsened, the EU retaliated by imposing a travel ban on US citizens travelling across the Atlantic.

In another act of extreme unilateralism, Trump suspended US funding for the World Health Organization, the lead UN agency battling the pandemic. Noting the absence of US leadership or even much active involvement, the former Swedish Prime Minister Carl Bildt lamented, 'This is the first great crisis of the post-American world.'

Images of the nuclear-powered aircraft carrier, the USS *Theodore Roosevelt*, limping into port in Guam, its captain stripped of his command by the Pentagon for decrying the inadequate response from Washington to a serious coronavirus outbreak aboard his ship, showed how much the superpower had been hobbled. The United States offered a case study of dysfunction. Much of the world looked on in shock and pity.

So many of America's long-term ailments intersected and metastasised in this fatal moment: its democratic sickliness, its inoperative government, its ugly polarisation, its income disparities, its racial inequality and its rejection of rationality. Alas, when Covid-19 hit, America was among the most vulnerable.

In the midst of the pandemic, a video went viral. It showed a black man, George Floyd, being suffocated by the knee of a white police officer; a killing that lasted more than eight minutes. It was an allegedly murderous act that came to epitomise how African-Americans have long been held down and smothered by systemic racism. Once again we were witnessing the scourge of police brutality, a disease America has never been able to cure.

Across the country, fury broke loose. In Minneapolis, the city where George Floyd was killed, protesters torched the local police station. There was violence in Atlanta, Georgia, the birthplace of Martin Luther King. In New York shops, including Macy's department store in the heart of Midtown, were looted. Deserted streets filled with protesters. Social distancing was temporarily elbowed aside by social unrest. The ambulance sirens we had heard for months were now drowned out by chants of protest. Cities already made combustible by Covid erupted.

The United States was confronted by three simultaneous convulsions: a public health crisis that disproportionately affected people of colour; an economic shock that disproportionately affected people of colour; and civil unrest sparked by police brutality that had always disproportionately affected people of colour. A shattered mirror was being held up to a fractured country.

At the same time there was American beauty in this moment, as the country was engulfed by its largest multi-racial and multi-generational mobilisation since the 1960s. Protesters converged on the Lincoln Memorial in Washington, the pulpit from which Dr King had delivered his most celebrated sermon, a paean to non-violence that spoke of a dream that had long been deferred. Marchers streamed across the Brooklyn Bridge in New York and the Golden Gate Bridge in San Francisco, part of a movement that quickly established a footprint in all 50 states. Even in small, rural towns never before touched by racial turbulence, protesters took a knee.

The relics of the Confederacy, the totems of that lost cause, came under renewed assault. Memorials celebrating the fight to prolong slavery were replaced with new landmarks. The Mayor of Washington decreed that a block of 16th Street should become Black Lives Matter Plaza. So those words were painted in giant yellow letters on the very doorstep of the White House. The same motif was daubed on Fifth Avenue outside the entrance to Trump Tower, more eye-catching than the skyscraper's golden signage.

For a time we wondered whether this was another Parkland moment, a cloudburst of activism that failed to change the political weather on gun reform. Yet the anti-racism protests felt more meaningful and profound. Black Lives Matter, a movement rejected by most Americans when it started in 2013, now enjoyed majority support. Its leaders told me they were witnessing an historic attitudinal shift: white Americans – indeed, white people the world over – were finally understanding and acknowledging their privilege.

Even Donald Trump, the one-time leader of the Birther Movement, felt compelled to act. In another of his Rose Garden ceremonies, he added his signature to an executive order paving the way for a national database to bar police officers accused of brutality moving from one force to another. His priority response, however, was to crack down on the protests. This meant adopting the 'law and order' language and posture of Richard Nixon's winning presidential campaign in 1968, the year of the assassination of Martin Luther King and the last time the country had witnessed racial protests on this scale. 'You have to dominate the streets, he said in a call with the nation's governors. 'They're gonna run over you. You're gonna look like a bunch of jerks.'

To demonstrate his dominance, Trump staged a melodramatic photo-opportunity in Washington DC, choreographed with the assistance of federal law enforcement officials, who fired stun grenades and mounted baton charges to disperse a crowd of peaceful protesters from outside the White House. Violently a path was cleared so the president could stride the short distance to a church that had been daubed with Black Lives Matter graffiti, outside which he held aloft his testamental prop, a leather-bound edition of the Bible. With the chairman of the Joint Chiefs of Staff, General Mark Milley, at his side, dressed in camouflage fatigues and combat boots, he could claim a pyrrhic victory in the Battle of Lafayette Square.

Later that night came more intimidating security theatre, when two military helicopters hovered low over the protesters in the heart of the capital, the downward thrust from their blades whipping up shards of glass and creating winds with the force of a tropical storm. Then, the following evening, members of the District of Columbia's National Guard, acting on orders from the Pentagon, formed a phalanx on the steps of the Lincoln Memorial. Images of them standing sentinel in body armour, combat helmets and sinister-looking face coverings instantly went viral. The country seemed to be unravelling.

As around us this epic history swirled, the due date loomed for the birth of our baby daughter, our first American child. Demonstrations were taking place below our windows. New York imposed a curfew. Having opted for a home delivery to avoid the restrictions imposed by Covid-riddled hospitals, we now feared our routes to the nearest emergency room might be cut off and also that our midwife might not be able to reach us. A city immobilised by the pandemic was now paralysed by protest.

After months of living in the worst-affected city in the worst-affected country our anxiety had become habitualised. But this was altogether more frightening. Looping in my mind was the fear of something going calamitously wrong. Alas, the curse of being a foreign correspondent is to have witnessed too many worst-case scenarios.

As my wife went into labour, NYPD helicopters circled above our Brooklyn apartment building. Our midwife's assistant was questioned by policemen outside our door. Looking out from our windows onto Brooklyn Bridge down below, I saw a convoy of police squad cars darting into Lower Manhattan. It felt like something out of the novel *The Year of Living Dangerously*, but that is what 2020 had become.

Inside our makeshift birthing suite, our cocoon away from the chaos, my wife maintained her extraordinary fortitude and calm. After a four-hour labour, we got the first glance of our baby daughter. Usually parents cry tears of joy when first they see their newborn. For us, they came with a flood of relief. Our baby's safe arrival marked the lifting of months of mental siege: respite after sleepless nights of pre-traumatic stress. Then Honor Wood Bryant gulped her first lungfuls, as protesters across the country chanted 'I can't breathe'.

––––––––

To think that we began 2020 supposing the US presidential election would be the foremost news event of the year: the story that would monopolise our journalistic attention; the travelling carnival that would see us clocking up tens of thousands of miles; the democratic spectacle that would distance us from our families. With that expectant air, we headed out from airports crowded still with mask-less travellers to the battlegrounds of Iowa and New Hampshire, where we sized up the Democratic field.

Joe Biden was a front-runner who felt like he had done his dash. Speeches, often delivered in a near-whisper, became rambling soliloquies – a reminiscence from his Senate career here, the name-drop of a friendly international leader there. Anecdotes did not make any political point, something that could not be explained by the stammer he struggled to overcome since childhood. Surrogates, many of them retired politicians themselves, upstaged him. Still he could flash his illuminative smile, but when he opened his mouth nobody could be entirely sure what would come out. On the stump, he was worse even than Jeb Bush in 2016. The former Florida governor could at least complete a cogent sentence, even if nobody applauded when it came to an end.

Bernie Sanders, with his manic energy, still drew the largest crowds. Even though he was 78 years old and had recently suffered a heart attack, he was loved by the young. At the other end of the age spectrum, Pete Buttigieg seemed prematurely old. Still, he offered the promise of generational change, which has always been so seductive for Democrats who prefer to fall in love rather than in line. Even though 'Mayor Pete' was no Jack Kennedy, the 38-year-old spoke in perfectly formed sentences, which it sounded like he had been rehearsing in the womb. The former mayor of South Bend, Indiana, also had a stellar CV, which included a Rhodes Scholarship and service in the US military. With immaculate articulateness, the first openly gay presidential candidate managed to persuade Iowa Caucus-goers that he was the best candidate on offer.

Had it not been for the chaos of caucus night, when glitches on a smartphone app designed to tabulate the votes delayed for a week the declaration of his victory, Buttigieg might have stormed into New Hampshire with 'big mo' behind him. As it was, the Iowa caucus quickly became old news, and Bernie Sanders narrowly won the first-in-the-nation primary, profiting from a field that continued to divide moderate Democratic voters.

The casualty of those early contests was Joe Biden. Fourth in Iowa and fifth in New Hampshire, perhaps the time had come for him to don his trademark Aviator shades and ride off westward into the sunset. Instead, of course, he headed to South Carolina, where the endorsement of the influential black Democratic congressman Jim Clyburn helped bring about a Lazarus-like return.

After his victory in the South Carolina primary, centrist rivals, such as Buttigieg and Senator Amy Klobuchar of Minnesota, exited the race. Faced with the alarming prospect of Sanders, a one-time socialist, seizing the party's nomination, Democrats smashed the emergency glass in the hope that amiable Joe could put out the firebrand.

Days later, following his cascade of victories on Super Tuesday, pundits marvelled at how Biden had triumphed in states where he had not even campaigned. Yet the opposite was more probably true. His absence helped explain his success. The lesson from Iowa and New Hampshire, after all, was that the more voters saw of him, the less likely they were to vote for him. His stealth candidacy ahead of Super Tuesday helped him wrap up the nomination.

After the Covid lockdown, and for much of election year, he became a virtual recluse, but the 'Biden in the bunker' strategy worked well. The pandemic took the heat out of the ideological battle within the Democratic Party. He could claim to be taking the safe road to the White House. Social distancing even helped neutralise an issue that, in the #MeToo era, posed a threat to his candidacy: that he was creepily touchy-feely with women. Most importantly, Biden's invisibility meant the focus was always on Donald Trump. After the near-death experience of the early contests, it was as if the coronavirus had given Biden political antibodies offering protection from his own underlying conditions.

His personal narrative also found a mournful echo in these sorrowful times. Just after winning election to the Senate in 1972, he suffered the trauma of losing his first wife, Neilia, and 13-month-old daughter, Naomi, in a car accident. Then in 2015 he watched his son, Beau, a survivor of that car crash, die from a rare form of brain cancer. Naturally empathetic, Biden found himself on the same emotional plane as the tens of thousands of families who had suffered bereavement.

His geniality also made him impossible to demonise, and hard to portray as a Hillary Clinton-like hate figure. His easy-listening moderation made him difficult to depict as a tribune of the radical left.

Elections are often framed as a choice between continuity and change. Yet a selling point for Biden was that he offered voters a version of both. After Trump's chaotic handling of the coronavirus, he could plausibly present himself as a candidate of change. At the same time, by pledging to serve as a conventional president, he represented a continuum. As the campaign went on, he appeared to performing the job he was essentially hired to do: to win back white working-class voters in the Rust Belt and female voters in the suburbs.

While Biden remained sequestered at his Delaware home, Trump was impatient to resume campaigning as quickly as possible. For his first public campaign event since shutdown, his team booked a basketball arena in Tulsa, Oklahoma, for 19 June – an insensitive choice of venue in the midst of so much racial turbulence because the city had been the scene in 1921 of a race massacre, and an insensitive choice of date since it coincided with Juneteenth, a day of celebration marking the emancipation of slaves. After switching the date to the following night, the Trump campaign claimed that more than a million supporters had requested tickets. But they had been duped by an online army of TikTokers. The stadium was half-empty. Solitary Trump supporters sat amid banks of empty seats, like fans of a non-league football team on a wet Wednesday night – easy pickings for photographers depicting the desultory mood.

The television images from later that June evening also lodged in the mind. They showed the president stepping off Marine One looking unusually dishevelled, his crimson silk tie draped casually around his neck, his red cap held limply in his hand – it looked almost like a political walk of shame.

Later in the summer, the Covid convention season mirrored the surrealism of the times. For their virtual convention, the Democrats staged what felt like a public television pledge drive, with the kind of compromised production values – blurry Zoom links and speakers not quite sure whether their microphone was on or off – that we had all become accustomed to during lockdown. Yet the messaging was clarion clear, whether it came from Michelle Obama delivering a fireside chat from the sofa of her living room or her husband sermonising from a constitutional museum in Philadelphia that looked like a temple of democracy: the election was a struggle between good and evil. Declaring himself to be 'an ally of the light', Joe Biden's acceptance speech followed that same Manichaean path: 'May history be able to say that the end of this chapter of American darkness began here tonight, as love and hope and light joined in the battle for the soul of our nation.'

The Republican convention, with its superabundance of US flags, perfect teeth and presidential offspring, could hardly have been more different. Given the presence of so many family members, it felt like a night of a thousand Trumps. Camelot meets the Kardashians. There were even shades of Evita, when Ivanka Trump introduced her father on a stage built in front of the floodlit White House, which doubled that night – controversially and arguably illegally – as a political prop. Inevitably, the theatrics were compared to reality television, but it all seemed so divorced from reality, not least because the coronavirus was so often spoken of in the past tense.

Trump's keynote speech was unexpectedly low-energy. It was as if he was still struggling to come up with a persuasive re-election message. From this master sloganeer, there was no equivalent in 2020 of 'Build the Wall' or 'Lock Her Up'. 'Keep America Great Again' sounded misplaced. 'Make America Great Again Again' fell flat. Moreover, it reminded voters of the here and now. The Republican convention did not even come up with a policy platform, an attestation not just of how Trump completely dominated the party but also of his failure to formulate a programme for his second term.

Four years earlier, he had brilliantly articulated the grievances of his supporters. Now, though, he gave voice to his own frustrations: venting about having to contend with 'the China virus'; lashing out against public health officials, assailing Democratic governors whose state shutdowns had paralysed the Trump economy, an onslaught he continued even after Governor Whitmer was targeted in the kidnap plot; complaining about the press for spending too much time on 'Covid, Covid, Covid'.

Trump succeeded in 2016 because he presented himself as an anti-Obama and an anti-Hillary candidate. Part of the reason Joe Biden led in the polls was because he so easily fitted the role of the anti-Trump. For so much of the campaign, however, it was more a case of Trump versus Trump. The president was his own political enemy: not taking the coronavirus seriously enough at the start; inviting ridicule for speculating whether bleach might offer a cure; re-tweeting video of a Trump supporter in The Villages retirement community in

Florida shouting 'white power' from his golf cart; and, in what felt like a throwback to the 1950s, telling suburban women, such a vital demographic, that he was getting their husbands back to work.

For those already dismayed by his behaviour, his undermining of the democratic process represented a dangerous new low. In addition to making baseless claims that postal voting would lead to massive voter fraud, he encouraged supporters in the swing states of North Carolina and Pennsylvania to vote twice. As well as threatening to delay the election, which he did not even have the constitutional authority to do, Trump repeatedly refused to affirm that he would accept the outcome of the vote or even agree to a peaceful transfer of power. We were used to a leader who revelled in rejecting presidential standards, but challenging democratic norms represented a troubling new departure. Seemingly we had reached the point where an American president posed a threat to American democracy.

After Labor Day came a series of shocks that could hardly be described as surprises. On a Friday evening in mid-September we learned of the death of Supreme Court Justice Ruth Bader Ginsburg, which raised the spectre of a constitutional paroxysm to add to the list of 2020 convulsions. Her dying words instantly became a liberal mantra: 'My fervent wish is that I not be replaced until a new president is installed.' The unsentimental calculus of Washington power suggested otherwise, of course, and within hours of the 87-year-old's death, Mitch McConnell nullified every syllable of her deathbed wish. President Trump's nominee would receive a vote on the floor of the United States Senate, declared the Senate Majority leader. Speed was essential, Republicans openly admitted on Fox News that night, because of the need to replace a liberal with a conservative in case the presidential election came to be settled in the Supreme Court. No attempt was made to camouflage their thinking.

Two weeks later, Donald Trump announced his replacement for Ruth Bader Ginsburg at a Rose Garden ceremony that will be remembered not for the unveiling of the conservative judge, Amy Coney Barrett, an acolyte of Antonin Scalia, but for becoming a super-spreader event. Indeed, future generations might find it hard to comprehend the scene of jubilant Republicans hugging, shaking hands, sitting shoulder-to-shoulder and mainly not wearing masks in the midst of a pandemic that by that stage had killed more than 200,000 Americans. It was triumphalist, hubristic and, unsurprisingly, led to the infection of numerous members of the president's inner circle. Afterwards, the White House started to resemble one of those rural meatpacking plants that became hotspots of transmission.

Days later came the first televised debate, a verbal slaughterhouse. Over the course of 90 minutes, Trump interrupted Joe Biden or the moderator, Chris Wallace, 128 times. The former vice-president called the president 'a clown'. Broadcast globally, it was a ghastly advertisement for US democracy, a real-time rendering of American decline.

The most stunning moment of the campaign was yet to come. Two nights later, we learned that the president had Covid – breaking news, imparted via Twitter at one o'clock in the morning, that had the jolting effect of drinking Red Bull from a fire hose. I was in Michigan at the time, and spoke the next morning to Democrats who believed the president was faking it and to Republicans who still thought the coronavirus was a hoax – yet another reminder of how America had become a country where there was no longer an agreed-upon set of facts.

For a few days, the campaign felt more like a vigil. We waited on news of the president's condition, and weren't entirely sure whether we could trust the medical updates from his White House doctor. We even wondered whether his brush with mortality might bring about some kind of Trumpian epiphany, especially after he tweeted out the word 'LOVE!!!' in all caps.

Yet Trump remained Trump. As ever, he was alert to the televisual possibilities of the moment, and summoned his presidential motorcade to parade him in front of supporters gathered at the gates of the Walter Reed National Military Medical Center. Yet this drive-past was a mere curtain-raiser.

Days later, in a departure devised to coincide with the evening news shows, he left through the golden Art Deco doors of the hospital, boarded Marine One and then flew the short distance to the South Lawn of the White House. Then he strode purposefully across the lawn, climbed the steps to the balcony, dramatically removed his mask and stood ramrod straight as he saluted in the direction of the departing helicopter. Within minutes, this triumphant homecoming was packaged up into a short film, with slow-motion videography and the usual rousing Hollywood music (although the president decided against ripping off his shirt to reveal a Superman T-shirt, an idea that *The New York Times* reported he had discussed with aides).

To Trump devotees, it must have looked like the happy ending of an action movie. To his detractors, it was more like a scene from a comic opera. This became a defining moment of the Trump presidency not just because it borrowed from the visual grammar of reality TV but also because it was so instantly polarising. Were you watching an all-American hero returning after vanquishing a deadly enemy or the self-satirising theatre of some American Mussolini? How you answered that question most probably determined how you would vote.

And what a vote it turned out to be. In Texas we filmed cars and pick-up trucks lined up at drive-in polling stations that looked like Covid test sites, a new innovation that made voting, with the necessary proof of identification, as easy as ordering a burger and fries. In Georgia there were snaking lines, their length a measure of the determination, especially among African-Americans, to make their voices heard. Outside a polling station near Madison Square Garden, the queue was so long it looked as if tickets had just gone on sale for Bruce Springsteen's last ever concert. Because of the extension of early voting, the reliance on postal ballots and the resolve to participate in the most consequential presidential contest of our lifetimes, turnout in the coronavirus election was the highest in more than 100 years.

Just as election day turned into election month, so election night turned into election week. Since Donald Trump had encouraged his supporters to turn up in person, Republican votes tended to be counted first. Because Joe Biden had urged Democrats to use postal ballots to avoid exposure to Covid-19, his votes tended to be counted later. It therefore came as no surprise that Trump took an early lead. Nor should it have been much of a shock to hear him claim victory on the night, a move he had telegraphed for months beforehand. Still, it was astounding to listen to the words he delivered from the presidential podium at his East Room pseudo-victory party (a gathering that, inexorably, became another super-spreader event). 'Frankly, we did win,' he claimed, even though he was nowhere near accumulating the 270 Electoral College votes needed. More alarmingly, he equated continuing to count the vote with stealing the election. 'This is a fraud on the American public,' he falsely declared.

As the counting continued, the momentum shifted firmly in Biden's favour. By Thursday morning he had taken the lead in Georgia, where the votes of African-Americans from the late Congressman John Lewis's district enabled him to surge ahead. The Democrats also had what looked like an unassailable advantage in Pennsylvania, a state Donald Trump simply could not afford to lose. By early evening the Associated Press projected wins for Biden in Wisconsin and Michigan, the other two Rust Belt states that ordinarily went Democrat but which had voted for Trump in 2016.

Now facing almost inevitable defeat, Donald Trump called a press conference in the White House briefing room where he unleashed such a blizzard of falsehoods that the three major broadcast networks – ABC, NBC and CBS – cut away half-way through. No longer were they willing to broadcast the president's lies.

On Saturday morning, after a new batch of votes had been counted in Philadelphia, the cradle of American democracy, the networks finally called Pennsylvania, and with it the election. Joe Biden was now president-elect. The American electorate had fired Donald Trump. History will record that his last tweet before being declared the loser read: 'I WON THIS ELECTION, BY A LOT.'

All week, the warriors of the right assumed their usual battle formations. Newt Gingrich urged Donald Trump to pursue a scorched-earth legal strategy. 'The president should be prepared to file suit in every single state,' he told Fox News. Sean Hannity, by peddling various outlandish conspiracy theories, launched another misinformation campaign. Rudy Giuliani convened a press conference at what Donald Trump described on Twitter as the 'Four Seasons'. But rather than the luxury hotel, baffled reporters found themselves outside Four Seasons Total Landscaping, a Philadelphia gardening business sandwiched between a crematorium and a sex shop.

As Trump's power drained away, his baseless claims became more desperate and nonsensical. The dozens of defeats he suffered in lawsuits aimed at overturning the election made him a serial loser. Even after the Electoral College officially crowned Biden the victor, Trump pressed on with his campaign to subvert democracy. 'I just want to find 11,780 votes', he told Georgia's Republican Secretary of State, during an intimidating phone call that sounded even more impeachable than his Ukrainian hustle. When that failed, he pressured Mike Pence to break the law by thwarting Congress when it met to tally the Electoral College votes, an act of disenfranchisement that his deputy obviously did not have the constitutional authority to carry out.

The storming of the Capitol that January day was unprecedented in modern times. This sanctum had not been breached since the British ransacked Washington in 1814. Incited by Donald Trump at an open-air rally, a mob of his supporters mounted an insurrection – a deadly Trumpian insurgency. Lawmakers, initially placed in lockdown, had to be evacuated to an undisclosed location, a phrase from the 9/11 days. Police drew guns on the floor of the House of Representatives, its damaged doors now barricaded. Protesters smashed windows, scaled walls with climbing ropes, brandished Confederate flags and vandalized offices. Pipe bombs were recovered nearby. Five people lost their lives, including a police officer. These anarchic scenes made the institutions of US government look pathetically fragile. The country witnessed one of its sorriest ever days.

In this culminating moment, American democracy was in crisis. Covid-19 was rampant. The city upon a hill looked like a disease-ridden ruin. Were this a different country on a different continent, we would be speaking in terms of a failed state.

Conclusion: Present at the Destruction

I still keep in touch with the family that hosted me in California all those years ago, although the last time we broke bread together was early on in the Obama presidency. Over lunch at one of those Sizzler-style restaurants that they liked to eat at on Sundays after church, they told me of their fears about what they regarded as a flood of illegal immigrants coming over the border less than a 90-minute drive away, and claimed that Obamacare acted as a magnet.

The president, they suspected, had not been born on American soil and was most probably a Muslim. If not, why had he bowed before that Saudi king? In the 2016 presidential election, Orange County, a fortress of Reaganism and the home of Richard Nixon's presidential library, went Democrat for the first time since the Great Depression, partly because of an influx of non-white voters. My friends voted Trump.

Looking back over the period since I first sat on their poolside terrace drinking Mountain Dew, the temptation is to divide it into a boom-bust cycle of two divergent phases. The final 16 years of the twentieth century could be seen as a time of American dominion. The first 16 years of the twenty-first century could be looked upon as a period of rapid American decline. In 2016 Trump could be construed as a product of the dissonance between the two, a protest candidate for the millions of voters who mourned a future that never happened and a past that looked sunnier by the day.

Yet the history of the United States over these past four decades, and past six presidencies, has been linear more than cyclical, with downward trend-lines in almost every aspect of national life. The problems facing the Biden administration are the same as those the Trump administration faced, failed to deal with and, in many cases, made worse.

Since the 1980s, the US economy has become chronically imbalanced, with an ever-widening divide not just between the rich and poor but also between the super-rich and the rest. By 2016 America had the second-highest poverty rate among OECD countries. Even before Covid, food insecurity was at crisis levels. More than 37 million Americans – or 11 per cent of the population – do not earn enough income to regularly buy sufficient food.

American health has deteriorated badly, despite healthcare spending accounting for 18 per cent of GDP, twice the average of industrialised nations. Even after the enactment of Obamacare, more than 25 million Americans remain uninsured. Junk food has contributed to an obesity epidemic, with more than two-thirds of adults either overweight or obese.[1] Dentists talk of 'Mountain Dew mouth', a form of tooth decay caused by drinking excessive quantities of sugary soft drinks.

Life-expectancy dropped for three consecutive years between 2014 and 2017. American fertility rates have been in steep decline since the 2008 financial crash and reached a record low in 2018. This raises questions about the country's ability to replenish its workforce and look after its elderly, a problem Japan has been crippled by for the past 30 years.[2]

The pandemic temporarily slowed down the gun epidemic, but 15,292 people were fatally shot in 2019. There were more mass shootings than days in the year. America also has by far the highest incarceration rate of any nation, with more than a fifth of the world's prisoners. Even though African-Americans account for just 13 per cent of the population, 40 per cent of those held behind bars are black. By their 23rd birthday, more than half of African-American men will have been arrested. Spending on prisons and jails grew by 141 per cent between 1986 and 2013. Over the same period, spending on higher education rose by just 6 per cent.[3] These are not the metrics of national greatness.

Whereas in 1990 America ranked sixth in the world for education, now it is 27th. Its maths scores place it 38th. Because of localised funding and gaping disparities between the tax bases of rich and poor communities, all too often the quality of a child's education is determined by the five digits of their parents' zip code.

America's infrastructure has become an international disgrace: a D+, according to the American Society of Civil Engineers. Its dams, levees, airports, air traffic control systems, hazardous waste facilities, energy grid and drinking water all received D grades. The heart sinks at the thought of boarding an American airliner for a long-haul flight from a US airport, a complete reversal from the pioneering days of aviation.

A philistinism and an anti-intellectualism pervade national life, which has devalued knowledge, learning and rationality. All too often, expertise is pilloried as an elitist conceit. Self-evident truths are contested, whether they relate to Barack Obama's birth certificate, the science of climate change, the coronavirus or the result of the 2020 election. American culture, while still capable of artistic transcendence, has become trashier, more celebrity-obsessed and narcissistic. For every *Sopranos* and *Breaking Bad*, there is a *Tiger King* and *Real Housewives of Orange County*.

In the post-Cold War world, America has either tended to overextend itself, as in Iraq and Afghanistan, or failed to project its might, as in Rwanda and Syria. Favouring correctives over creeds, successive presidents have taken office with a sense of what US global leadership should not look like – the essence of Obama's 'Don't do stupid shit' doctrine in the wake of George W. Bush and Trump's attempts to unravel all that his predecessor did – but no coherent sense of an alternative. Polarisation at home has undercut US leadership abroad by producing so many discontinuities in policy: what has been labelled 'reset-button' or 'control-alt-delete' diplomacy.

To bastardise Dean Acheson's biting quote about Britain losing an empire and failing to find a role, the United States lost an enemy and failed to find a post-Cold War mission. Nor is America so dominant militarily. China already has the military strength, and in particular the long-range missile capability, to overwhelm the United States in the Indo-Pacific region.[4] It is hard to think of a single region of the world where America is pre-eminent. All of its strategic rivals and enemies – China, Russia, Iran and North Korea – have seen their influence grow.

Some of the determining moments of America's past half-century are so glaring that they will leap from the pages of history for centuries to come. The war in Iraq. The deregulation of Wall Street. The fraudulent marketing and over-prescription of OxyContin and other painkillers, leading to an opioid epidemic. The United States' mismanagement of coronavirus, which may rank as the most catastrophic domestic policy failure of the post-war years. Others, such as the repeal of the Fairness Doctrine or the failure to regulate the new economy adequately, became ever more apparent over time.

Nor are inflection points hard to spot. The 1984 Reagan landslide, which panicked Democrats into granting so many ideological concessions to Reaganism, changed the way Americans thought about government, heightened the deregulatory impulse and shifted the country to the right. The end of the Cold War, which coincided with the shift in national leadership from the Greatest Generation to the Baby Boomers, brought to an end the era of patriotic bipartisanship. The attacks of September 11 eroded the belief in immigration as a force for economic good and religious pluralism as the basis for successful multiculturalism. For millions at the bottom of society, and many in the once prosperous middle, the 2008 financial crash killed off the American Dream.

Shifts over time, more than singular events, are the key to understanding the country's downward spiral: the widening wealth gap; the widening influence gap, compounded by the *Citizens United* Supreme Court ruling, which enabled the super-rich to flood politics with so much unregulated money; the weakening of once trusted institutions, such as Congress and the overly politicised courts; the ideological clustering of the Big Sort, and the political distancing it has wrought; the decline of reason; the discord between a knowledge-based economy and a knowledge-free polity;

the failure to concur on an agreed body of facts, a prerequisite for a healthy democracy; the all-powerfulness of the internet, which has helped turn politics, and society, into such a rage-filled ruckus. The fact that so much of national life plays out online speaks of the breakdown of traditional institutions. Perhaps a reason why 'cancel culture' has become so virulent is that young people especially no longer believe they can seek redress through politics or the criminal justice system.

For decades, the lack of corporate responsibility in American boardrooms has been destructive and has exacerbated an array of interlocking problems: the vast disparities in pay, corporate tax avoidance, heartless outsourcing, the supremacy of shareholder value and the mistaken belief that the stock market is an accurate barometer of economic health. Likewise, lax regulation has been a recurring problem, whether it involves guns, prescription drugs, derivatives, broadcasting, clean water, the internet or the New Economy more broadly. Too often over the last 30 years, regulators have primarily seen their role as not to regulate.

The decades-long assault on government has produced a crisis of governance, thus intensifying the assault on government, a destructively circular problem. Small wonder that, between 1958 and 2015, those who professed to 'basically trust the government' fell from 73 per cent to 19 per cent.[5] Donald Trump's repeated attacks on the 'deep state' were a natural next step after 50 years of shrill anti-government invective. Again, too often those in government have had no ideological investment in making government work.

America's broken politics and its malfunctioning economy are inextricably linked. As income polarisation has increased over the past 50 years, so too has political polarisation. They have moved in tandem. Moreover, there is a growing body of academic evidence to suggest that, far from being coincidental, this is causal. Growing inequality has contributed to both parties vacating the centre ground of politics, and led voters to adopt more hard-line positions. Political polarisation, and the gridlock it engenders, causes further income inequality by making it harder to find common ground on policies that address these disparities in wealth, such as increases in the minimum wage or more equitable taxation.

Washington has become even more dysfunctional. Traditional checks and balances have become weaponised to such an extent that even the nuclear option of impeachment is in danger of becoming routine. Having witnessed only one president being put on trial in the previous 223 years, we have seen two in the past 21.

Legislatively speaking, congressional leaders are no longer willing to grant their opponents any political victories, which increasingly is how bipartisanship is perceived. With partisanship overriding everything, and with paralysis now the default setting, America has gone 25 years without a properly functioning federal government.

The last 15 years have also been 14 of the most polarised in US political history, judged by comparing Gallup presidential approval ratings with party identification. For the past ten years, the president's average approval rating from supporters of the opposing party has not topped 13 per cent, which reveals how much Republicans hated Obama and how much Democrats despised Trump.[6] This kind of negative partisanship is a symptom of a sick polity.

Occupants of the Oval Office almost always leave their mark on the presidency. After the torpidity of the Eisenhower years, Kennedy made the office more youthful and glamorous. Johnson, that shrewd 'Master of the Senate', brought the executive and legislative branches into closer alignment. Nixon consolidated more power in the White House, creating 'the imperial presidency'. Ford sought to reverse that process in a way that downsized the office. Clinton made the presidency more touchy-feely, narrowing the emotional distance between the presidency and the people. Obama set a new standard for ethical behaviour – a reign of virtue motivated in part by the African-American mantra of working twice as hard to get half as far – and made the presidency more hip.

Donald Trump, by abrogating so many behavioural customs, made the presidency more uncouth, aggressive and lawless. While it is hard to imagine his successors unleashing the same barrage of insults, there are already signs of a 'Trump effect' on political discourse. In America and around the world he has encouraged politicians to step up their attacks on the media in ways that have made the objective politically subjective – a reminder that you don't need to dress in an oversized suit or wear an over-long tie to be a Trump impersonator.

Trump may well have the effect on values and behaviour that Reagan had on attitudes towards government and wealth. What is known as the Overton Window, the broadly agreed parameters of acceptable public discourse, has not only shifted to the right: it has had a brick hurled through it. I vividly remember the moment during the 2016 campaign when an email from Team Trump dropped into our inboxes, announcing that he would ban all Muslims from entering the United States. So far was it outside the mainstream of American political orthodoxy that initially we thought it was a hoax. Now, though, the Muslim ban has been normalised.

Equally long-lasting could be the debasement of facts as the basis for debate and policy formulation. After all, an unsettling lesson of the Trump presidency is that post-truth politics can be highly effective, especially in shoring up a political base. True believers happily embraced a distorted view of reality.

Most alarming was Donald Trump's refusal to accept defeat in a clear-cut election, a flagrant attack on the very idea of democracy. After decades of voter suppression, a Republican president and most of the Republican Party opted for reality suppression. In this lurch towards authoritarianism, the anti-politician who became the anti-president became the anti-democrat. Now this dangerous precedent has been set, will others attempt similar acts of daylight electoral robbery? Will other mobs try to storm the Capitol?

In America's downward slide, journalists are far from blameless. Our conflict-driven panel discussions. Our obsession with trivialities. Our fixation with the modern-day metrics of news – ratings, hits, clicks. Our cynicism and mocking tone. Our better-story bias, especially evident in enabling the Trump phenomenon. Our Beltway myopia and neglect of the heartland, which blinded us to the reasons for his rise. Our horse-race coverage of elections, which stops us focusing on the problems, such as income inequality, that make the political weather. Our sensationalist reporting of set-piece news events such as hearings on Capitol Hill, whether the chairs are occupied by Oliver North, Brett Kavanaugh or Robert Mueller. Our glorification of celebrities. Our frenzied tone and 'BREAKING NEWS' banners, which can risk giving the impression of a perpetual state of crisis. The danger of spending too much of our professional lives on Twitter, rather than speaking to people face-to-face. Our self-absorption, fuelled by Twitter, Facebook and Instagram (and, yes, evident in passages of this book that at times leaned towards memoir more than commentary).

The internet threatened to kill journalism, so we embraced its cannibalistic fury. Undeniably, there has been a welter of brave, brilliant and forensic reporting, but so much of the modern-day news industry has become more about entertainment than elucidation. That extends to politics: we yearn for presidents and presidential candidates with maximum journalistic entertainment value. We hate the idea of a presidency on in the background. Yet the theatrics of America's modern presidency have played a significant role in its decline. The Oval Office needs administrators not actors, seriousness not sensation.

Because this is such a polycentric country, with vital centres of power spread throughout the land, there has always been an extent to which the USA has been Washington-proof and president-proof. This may be the chief benefit of its decentralised, federal system. Yet over the past five years so many of these power hubs have themselves been in a state of almost continual crisis.

Hollywood has been impacted by the meteor effect of the #MeToo movement and the grotesque behaviour of some of the movie industry's leading men, such as Harvey Weinstein. The major TV networks have been devastated by online streaming services such as Netflix and Hulu, and thus lost their old convening power to bring the country together. So many local and regional newspapers, which did so much to nurture a sense of community, have been wiped from the media map.

Silicon Valley has created almost as many problems as it has solved. Facebook, as well as connecting families and reuniting old friends, has turned out to be a destructive propagator of disinformation and divisiveness. Uber has transformed urban travel and offered flexible new working options, but it has also shown the limitations of the gig economy, where low-paid drivers serve as independent contractors rather than members of staff, and are deprived of the benefits and protections of traditional employment. Most of us have come to rely on Amazon, for some a guilty online retail pleasure, but it has been slammed for its anti-competitive practices, tax avoidance and treatment of low-paid workers.

Giants of the old economy have also been hobbled. Blue-ribbon retailers such as Sears and J. C. Penney have been decimated by the slow death of the American shopping mall. Boeing, the US aerospace behemoth, has been shamed for the engineering flaws and mismanagement that led to the crashes of two of its 737 Max aircraft, killing 346 people in Indonesia and Ethiopia. Wells Fargo, America's fourth-largest bank, has been hit by a scandal involving fraudulent sales practices and fake accounts.

The Catholic Church, one of the great pillars of American life, has been disgraced by the paedophile priest scandal. The Boy Scouts of America had to file for chapter 11 bankruptcy protection because of a wave of sexual assault lawsuits. Many of the sporting codes have also been mired in controversy or scandal: American football (the epidemic of permanent brain damage), baseball (with banned steroids) and US gymnastics (the sexual abuse scandal which affected more than 368 female athletes). The music industry has been rocked by the abhorrent behaviour of its most bankable star, Michael Jackson, who since his death has been labelled a serial paedophile. National events that once showcased the best of America have become accident-prone: the power outage at the 2010 Super Bowl in New Orleans that stopped play for 34 minutes, and the envelope screw-up at the Oscars.

Since the grounding of its shuttle programme in 2011, NASA has struggled to stir the national imagination. Instead, New Economy titans such as Jeff Bezos and Elon Musk have been in the vanguard of space travel. Donald Trump's announcement of a mission to Mars sounded like bluster, while his creation of a Space Force descended into farce when fans of *Star Trek* noticed its new logo bore striking similarities to that of Captain Kirk and the crew of the starship USS *Enterprise*.

America's great universities remain centres of excellence and hubs of innovation, but they could hardly be described as engines of inter-generational mobility. An income gap has created an education gap. The Varsity Blues admissions scandal involving stars such as the *Desperate Housewives* actress Felicity Huffman revealed how higher education has been corrupted by the same pay-to-play mentality that bedevils politics. Besides, so many of those who make it to university end up being crippled by debt.

Virtually every sector is in a reputational ditch.

Many of America's great cities are also beset by problems. To report on gang violence in certain neighbourhoods of Chicago requires some of the same safety precautions as venturing into Kabul or Baghdad – and the city is not even the murder capital of America, a position currently held by St Louis. In New York, one only has to descend into the city's subway stations to witness its decrepit infrastructure or peer skyward to see how the relaxation of zoning regulations has disfigured the cityscape with pop-up residential skyscrapers for the super-rich.

Miami faces an existential threat because of rising sea levels, as does New Orleans. Much of Houston has been constructed on flood plains, making it vulnerable to the kind of once-in-a-century weather events, such as Hurricane Harvey in 2017, that now come along every few years. Some once great US metropolises, including Detroit, Memphis, Milwaukee, Baltimore and Atlanta, top the list of distressed cities, judged in terms of unemployment rates, educational attainment and poverty levels.[7]

There remain some beacons of good municipal governance. High-performing cities, such as San Diego, Phoenix and Philadelphia, have fuelled hopes of a bottom-up revival in politics, starting in the municipalities and percolating through to Washington. Yet a central reason why government functions effectively in these cities is that the Big Sort has made them more ideologically cohesive. Alas, the municipal template does not offer a remedy for the partisan battlefield of Washington.

The veneration of the constitution, and the lionisation of the framers, has had an immobilising effect on America. Dangerous though it is to speculate on what the founding fathers might nowadays think – although that is the philosophical basis of originalist jurisprudence – they might well be surprised that so much of their founding charter remains unaltered. After all, the framers themselves warned that a rigid party system and political factionalism would render government unworkable. Nor did they intend the separation of powers to produce stalemate.

The composition of the Senate – a constitutionally mandated act of malapportionment – feeds this dysfunction because it has enshrined minoritarian rule. It has given the smaller states, and the Republicans who predominantly represent them, such a disproportionate amount of power. The two years between 1997 and 1998 are the only time Republican Senators have represented a majority of the American people, if you assign half of each state's population to each senator.

The constitutional equilibrium between the three branches of government, moreover, is completely out of kilter. Because of the gridlock on Capitol Hill, successive presidents have been forced to rely more heavily on executive actions, which are usually subject to constitutional challenge in the Supreme Court. This has vested a disproportionate amount of power in the hands of five of the nine justices, all of whom have lifetime tenure and can now be elevated to the court on a party-line vote. The effect has been to turn the court into something more akin to a third legislative body, with an exclusive group of unelected members.

The heightened power of the Supreme Court is especially problematic now that it has a 6–3 conservative majority, a right-titled balance of power unrepresentative of the country as a whole. *Roe v. Wade* may now be imperilled, even though polls routinely suggest that two-thirds of the American people do not support its complete overturning. The court has lurched to the right at a time when the country has a more tolerant majority, as evidenced by the rising support for same-sex marriage. The fact that the Democrats have won the popular vote in seven out of the last eight presidential elections but the Republicans have nominated 15 of the last 19 justices underscores the need for a thoroughgoing national debate about the modern-day validity of an old-fashioned constitution.

That is why talk of a reboot or reset of the current obsolete operating system is so misplaced. Yet a drastic constitutional overhaul will never transpire, because the founding fathers made the constitution so hard to change.

As any student of this country knows, the notion of American decline is as old as America itself. Paradoxically, this has been especially true of the post-war years, when the United States was truly in the ascendant. Sputnik, Vietnam, the domestic upheaval of the 1960s, the malaise of the 1970s, the rise of Japan in the '80s and early '90s, the rise of the rest. America has routinely been cast as a has-been nation, often at the very moment it was making a comeback.

There is a vital difference, however, between then and now. The national turnarounds of the '50s, '60s, '70s and '80s relied on a level of political collaboration in Washington largely absent today. Faced with the post-Sputnik panic in the 1950s, patriotic bipartisanship flourished. Faced with a black revolt in the '60s that threatened to tear the country apart, right-minded Democrats and Republicans came together to pass the landmark civil rights acts. Faced with a criminal presidency during Watergate, there was eventually a cross-party push to force Nixon from office.

Alas, a solutions-based politics has given way to a conflict-based politics. Problem-solving has given way to partisan point-scoring. Just about the only thing politicians in Washington have in common is that they breathe the same toxic air. Now, even catastrophic events such as 9/11, Hurricane Katrina and the coronavirus have become accelerants of polarisation.

We are no longer talking merely about decline, a strain of thought I resisted until returning to live here in 2013, when the body of evidence became too overwhelming to ignore. This has become about disintegration, the breakdown of national cohesion. America now feels like a continent rather than a country, a geographic expression rather than a properly functioning state. Shared land occupied by antagonistic tribes. The electoral map, with the west coast and north-east coloured blue and the states in the middle of the country shaded red, looks partitionist. The very term United States is oxymoronic. There are two Americas with two very different realities.

Since the turn of the century it has become fashionable to talk of a post-American world. My fear now is of a post-America America. Its state of ceaseless conflict brings to mind the old adage that the only thing capable of defeating America is America itself. But that, I fear, is where we are, in the midst of a cold civil war.

Travelling through this country, I struggle to identify where politically, philosophically or spiritually it will find common ground. Not in the guns debate. Not in the abortion debate. Not in the healthcare debate. Not at weddings, where more than a third of Republicans and almost half of Democrats say they would be unhappy if their children married a partner from the other party, compared with 5 per cent in 1960.[8] Not in the singing of the national anthem at American football games. Not when the United States wins the women's soccer World Cup, which erupted into a war of words between Trump and the team's lesbian captain, Megan Rapinoe. Not on 4 July, now that tanks have rumbled onto the National Mall and Donald Trump has turned the Lincoln Memorial into a makeshift campaign stage. Not in the midst of a pandemic. Few national events are politically benign, ideologically neutral or detached from the culture wars. No longer are there demilitarised zones in US politics.

Unifying ideas that have been elemental to the success of America have been rejected or challenged, not least the benefits of immigration. 'America is full,' stated Donald Trump, a short-sighted statement in a century when his country's best hope of pre-eminence may be attracting the world's most innovative minds. The American Dream is no longer a uniting precept.

How can politics be deradicalised? Making the presidency boring again would be a start. A return to the days when legislators headed to Washington with a sense of national purpose would help. Not insignificantly, the 2018 congressional midterm elections saw a surge in the number of veterans elected to Congress who had served in Iraq and Afghanistan, and who tended to be more centrist and bipartisan – the 9/11 generation of lawmakers. However, young Democrats seem more energised by the radicalism of Congresswoman Alexandria Ocasio-Cortez than by the pragmatism of Pete Buttigieg. A moderate conservative would find it impossible to win the presidential nomination of the Trumpian Republican Party.

The economic, technological and demographic trend-lines all point to politics becoming more polarised and extreme. Demographic changes will turn America into a majority-minority country by mid-century and make many white people feel even more embattled and susceptible to racial demagoguery.

Automation and artificial intelligence will continue to be serial jobs killers. Over the next 15 years, some 40 per cent of US jobs could be lost to computers and machines. Visiting Pittsburgh these days, it is noticeable how many men who used to work in the steelworks now sit behind the wheels of Uber cars. Worryingly for them, America's one-time 'Steel City' has become a centre of excellence for robotics, and is where Uber is road-testing its driverless cars. For the second time in their working lives, automation is coming for their jobs.

Moreover, the decimation of those Rust Belt factories is a forerunner of the decimation of offices in every American community. Over the next five years artificial intelligence is expected to transform some 500 million jobs worldwide. The blue-collar revolt we witnessed in 2016 could be followed by a white-collar rebellion.

The destructive forces that led to the presidency of Donald Trump will outlive his years in office. The earthquake that erupted in 2016 will continue to shake the land beneath our feet. That is why using a 'perfect storm' metaphor to describe his surprise victory in 2016 was always flawed. Storms pass. The clouds quickly part. This was a seismic event, as his strong showing in 2020 proved.

When I started writing this book, I began to think about what a 16-year-old beginning that slow descent over the mountains into Los Angeles would make of America today. What thoughts would run through her mind as she passed through the arrivals hall and saw the official portrait of America's reality-TV president: a leader who denied the science of global warming, the most pressing issue for the youth of today; a man who had become for so many around the world the face of the ugly American? Would she be drawn here, as I was in the 1980s, by the conviction that no other country so stirs the imagination or offers such possibility?

Perhaps if she wanted to see the most thrusting nation in the world, China might be the place to visit – though one would hope she would recognise the cruel authoritarianism of the Chinese system. If she wanted to experience the highest living standards, she might find them in Australia, the lifestyle superpower of the world. As for visiting Tomorrowland, Asia's mega-cities offer a glimpse of the future rather than their US counterparts. Would she even want to come to America at all, after the mass shootings at Sandy Hook and Parkland?

As I was reaching the end of this book, that 16-year-old was replaced in my mind by our own daughter, Honor. So this question has become more personal and less abstract. Every word was freighted with more meaning, and asked of me the question: what should I tell our daughter about the land of her birth, the country that beguiled her father so?

First, I will assure her there is so much still to love. So much still to savour. There is American splendour in the poetry of Maya Angelou, the librettos of Lin-Manuel Miranda, the desert art of Georgia O'Keeffe, the paeans to friendship penned by Patti Smith, the fugues of Leonard Bernstein, the ballads of Ella Fitzgerald, the anthems of Elvis Presley and the siren call of George Gershwin's hypnotic clarinet. There is American beauty in the granite thunderdomes of Yosemite, the russet hues of the Shenandoah Valley in the fall and the red rock towers of Monument Valley. There is American joy in the street theatre of Manhattan, the cheap seats on Broadway and the pews of African-American churches.

I will tell her there is an American symphony to hear and see in New York, the city of her birth, a melting pot she will become immersed in every time we take the subway, a city that never sleeps – although we hope she will not take that too literally.

There are places we can visit to reflect on the goodness of this land. We can take the boat to Liberty Island, to be reminded of the words of Emma Lazarus that are imprinted at the base of the Statue of Liberty – 'Give me your tired, your poor, Your huddled masses yearning to be free' – noble intentions overridden intermittently throughout history by nativist panics. We can sit at twilight on the steps of the Lincoln Memorial to dwell on the 272 words delivered at Gettysburg by the Great Emancipator and the mesmerising dream of Martin Luther King. When she is older, we can go to see *Hamilton*, to be reminded of the revolutionary fervour that brought this country into existence, and to marvel at a multiracial cast which showcases how American identity changes constantly over time in ways that renew and replenish.

When the time feels right, I will remind her of her good fortune: that she was born into a family with good health insurance, that her brother and sister do not have to pass through a metal detector to attend class, that her light skin grants her the presumption of innocence from most police forces in the land. But there are subjects I will avoid. Honor does not need to know she has been born into the school mass-shooting generation, one where American schoolchildren hide in cupboards to practise 'shelter in place'.

When should I tell my daughter America was great? I myself have not addressed the question that Trump never answered satisfactorily in 2016. The 1950s had an economy that benefited almost everyone – the exception rather than the rule in US economic history – but most African-Americans were treated as second-class citizens. The 1964 Civil Rights Act was a crowning achievement, but came in the midst of the Vietnam War, a national nadir. There was so much to admire about the first response to the attacks of September 11, but the noble instincts they aroused proved to be so fleeting. The truth is the notion of American greatness has always struggled under the weight of America's contradictions. Slavery in the land of the free. Enduring poverty in what has been since the late nineteenth century the richest nation in the world. So, rather than in eras or epochs, I will encourage her to look for greatness in America's collective endeavours and shared historic achievements: the civil rights movement with its brave and glorious anthems about overcoming oppression; the moon shot, with its sense of astral ambition; the female fight for equal rights, another great social revolution of the '60s; even the Los Angeles Olympics in 1984, which felt binding and patriotic rather than bullying and nationalistic. That sense of shared enterprise, driven by the pursuit of communal goals and mutual advancement, has been missing in the modern era, this age of confrontation.

Greatness will never be this country's defining characteristic while so many of its compatriots are at loggerheads; when mistrust, dislike and hatred are the drivers of politics; when the spirit of joint endeavour is displaced by the venom and even nihilism that now pervades so many aspects of national life.

So my hope for my daughter's America, unambitious though it may seem, is for a pause: a respite from the hostility that might induce a period of reflection, restoration and renewal. Los Angeles is hosting the Olympics again in 2028. Not enough time for a turnaround. But is it too much to yearn at least for an American pageant that nurtures once more a sense of commonality and inspires global awe? Not a summertime of American resurgence. Rather, a season of American unification. Alas, I fear more American carnage.

Acknowledgements

Perhaps the greatest gift of my journalistic life has been to have a seat in the stalls for many of the most extraordinary moments in modern American history: the Reagan Revolution, the Bush interregnum, the Clinton years, 9/11 and the lead-up to war in Iraq, the victory of Barack Obama and the defeat of Hillary Clinton. As I was writing this book, however, and the coronavirus crowded in on us in New York, I confess to wanting to escape. The Covid-19 crisis became a coda to the book I wish we all could have avoided. It made me yearn even more for the America I fell in love with as a teenager during that carefree Californian summer.

The idea for *When America Stopped Being Great* came from an essay I wrote for the BBC, which began with that first westward journey. Early one Friday evening, I started putting pen to paper on the Acela Express as it pulled out of Union Station in Washington, and was still writing when the sun rose in New York on Saturday morning. Much to my surprise, this bundle of thoughts and reminiscences became something of a viral sensation, so my thanks to the more than three million people who read that essay and unwittingly helped bring this book into existence.

Our digital team in Washington, led by Tom Geoghegan, Ben Bevington and Jude Sheerin, has always promoted my writing, and always found a home for the longest of long reads. Thanks as well to Finlo Roher in London, who came up with the headline for that piece, which I purloined for the title of this book.

My BBC boss in Washington, Paul Danahar, a dear friend since our days covering the 9/11 beat in South Asia, has always been a wise and brave editor. He casts a thoughtful eye over almost every word I write, and defends us to the hilt. The BBC's former foreign editor Jon Williams posted me to New York in the first place, and then, happily, became our neighbour in Brooklyn. Thanks as well to my friend Andrew Roy, the BBC's present foreign editor and former Washington bureau chief from the Clinton years, and the BBC's head of newsgathering Jonathan Munro for letting me see how the Trump years played out.

My New York producers, Nada Tawfik, Chris Gibson, Tony Brown, Lynsea Garrison and Ashley Semler have been a joy. My shooter Andrew 'Sarge' Herbert is an Aussie legend. My friend Andrew Blum filmed that first interview with Donald Trump. My thanks, as well, to our producers and camera crews in Washington and beyond. The lovely Tara Neil, Kate Farrell, Sarah Svoboda, John Landy, Ian Druce, Ron Skeans, Pete Murtaugh, Chuck Tayman, James Cooke, Maxine Collins, Maria Byrne, Mat Morrison, Aiden Johnson, Gringo Wotshela, Ed Habershon, Kat Stefanie, Samantha Granville, Harry Low, Brajesh Upadhyay, Lindle Markwell, Aiden Johnson, Sam Beattie, Morgan Gisholt Minard, Bill McKenna, Allen McGreevy, Joni Mazer Field, Jonathan Csapo and Rozalia Hristova. Much of the book was discussed over various dinners in the home of my good friends Katty Kay and Tom Carver. Our office manager John McPherson has long been a BBC treasure.

My correspondent colleagues Jon Sopel, Barbara Plett Usher, James Cook, Anthony Zurcher, Aleem Maqbool, Gary O'Donoghue, Laura Bicker, Chris Buckler, David Willis, Laura Trevelyan and Jane O'Brien have been wonderful fellow travellers. Thanks, as well, to our happy band in the BBC New York bureau: Michelle Fleury, Samira Hussain, John Mervin, Natalie Sherman, Bahman Kalbasi, Zoe Thomas, James Cooke and Tom Brook.

I have also benefited from the work of a squadron of historians and political reporters who have covered or written about the last six presidencies with such distinction, foremost amongst them Lou Cannon, H. W. Brands, Gil Troy, Jon Meacham, John Harris, Joe Klein, Hendrik Hertzberg, Jean Edward Smith, E. J. Dionne, Jonathan Alter and Steve Kornacki.

The biggest treat of writing this book was to reconnect with the professor who examined my doctoral thesis all those years ago, my fellow Bristolian Tony Badger, the former Paul Mellon Professor of American History at Cambridge University and one of the nicest men in British academia. Our transatlantic email exchanges took on the feel of a fun evening in one of those cosy Cambridge pubs where the conversation could have extended way beyond closing time. Tony was generous with his insights, anecdotes and encyclopaedic knowledge. Richard Partington, the senior tutor at Churchill College, who has done so much to encourage kids from similar backgrounds to me to feel that Cambridge is their academic home, was also supportive.

For his thoughts on the manuscript, I am indebted to Allan Little, the BBC's poet laureate of news. Allan, who has always been supportive of my long-form writing, is the kind of correspondent we all want to emulate. The BBC's Ben Wright, another of our finest wordsmiths and a friend since the George W. Bush days, popped up in New York at just the right time with his discerning eye and generous encouragement. I owe an enormous debt to Malcolm Balen, the BBC tsar who checks every word we prepare for outside consumption. It is to his great credit that Malcolm wields his blue pencil so lightly and so deftly. I am thankful for his wise counsel and encouraging words.

It was also my good fortune to work with Jamie Birkett at Bloomsbury, who was not just a great advocate for the book but such a talented and helpful editor. In these socially distanced times, we quickly developed a close working relationship, even though we have yet to come face-to-face. The Bloomsbury team was exemplary: Jude Drake in publicity, Lizzy Ewer and Rosie Parnham in marketing, Sutchinda Thompson, who designed such a striking cover, Rayshma Arjune, who looked after publicity on this side of the Atlantic, and Matthew Taylor who was such a diligent copyeditor.

For the Australian edition, I am grateful to the indefatigable Nikki Christer at Penguin Random House, who once again brought a book into existence based on what was essentially a one-line pitch. It was a pleasure to work with the editor Patrick Mangan, a fellow Pom, and my tireless publicist Jessica Malpass.

Gordon Wise, my agent in London, deserves a special word of thanks, for believing in this book from the outset and for pushing so strongly for a pre-history of the Trump presidency that took a step back from the frenzied here and now. Pippa Masson, his colleague from Curtis Brown in Sydney, is always a joy to work with.

My dear mum and dad, Janet and Colin Bryant, have always encouraged my American travels, even though it has meant me living most of my adult life beyond British shores.

Words of thanks to my children, Billy and Wren, double as an apology: for the time I spent reading history books on holiday when I should have been splashing around in the pool; for allowing Netflix to do some of my early morning weekend parenting so I could sit at my laptop. Though they are usually in the same room when I write, many are the times when I have been absent. Still, I have watched them blossom into charismatic little New Yorkers, with all the spirit, imagination, open-mindedness and internationalism that entails. Beautiful Honor, the calmest of babies, has been the most joyous of distractions.

The final and most heartfelt words of appreciation go to my wife Fleur, who agreed to leave behind her beloved Australian homeland in 2013 so I could pursue my latest American dream. Not for the first time, completing a book meant burning too much midnight oil. Not for the first time, some of my early deadlines coincided with a due date. No one, though, has encouraged my writing more than Fleur, and done more in a loving and practical way to help make it happen. For years to come we will talk about the months spent in lockdown during New York's coronavirus outbreak, and reflect on how the experience brought us even closer together as a couple and as a family. Forever we will remember the spring and summer of 2020, mindful of those who lost their lives and thankful for the magic of new life.

NOTES

INTRODUCTION: FACE TO FACE WITH 'THE DONALD'

1 Remarks by the president, 26 June 2015. White House Press Secretary.
2 *Politico*, 31 July 2016.
3 With neither candidate reaching the necessary 270 Electoral College votes to win – they would have been tied on 269 – the election would have been thrown into the House of Representatives, where the Republicans hold the majority of state delegations. Trump, therefore, would have won.

CHAPTER 1: IT'S MORNING AGAIN IN AMERICA

1 Gil Troy, *Morning in America: How Ronald Reagan Invented the 1980s* (Princeton University Press, 2005), p. 161.
2 *The New York Times*, 9 January 1983.
3 Steve Kornacki, *The Red and the Blue: The 1990s and the Birth of Political Tribalism* (HarperCollins, 2018), p. 20.
4 Ibid., p. 58.
5 *Newsweek* Election Extra, November/December 1984.
6 John Micklethwait and Adrian Wooldridge, *Right Nation: Conservative Power in America* (Penguin, 2004), p. 43.
7 *Los Angeles Times*, 6 June 2004.
8 H. W. Brands, *Reagan: The Life* (Anchor, 2016), p. 146.
9 Lou Cannon, *The Role of a Lifetime* (Public Affairs, 2000), p. 26.
10 Alistair Cooke, *Letter from America, 1946–2004* (Knopf, 2009), p. 276.
11 Brands, p. 168.
12 Joe Klein, *Politics Lost* (Crown, 2007), p. 19.
13 Brands, p. 194.
14 Klein, *Politics Lost*, p. 62.
15 Joe Klein, *The Natural: The Misunderstood Presidency of Bill Clinton* (Crown, 2003); Klein, *Politics Lost*, p. 96.

16   E. J. Dionne, *Why the Right Went Wrong: Conservatism from Goldwater to Trump and Beyond* (Simon & Schuster, 2016), p. 234.

17   Cannon, p. 5.

18   Ibid., p. 32.

19   Donald Ritchie, 'Who Moved the Inauguration? Dispelling an Urban Legend', Oxford University Press blog, 22 January 2009.

20   Cannon, p. 120.

21   Ronald Reagan, *The Reagan Diaries* (HarperCollins, 2007), p. 258.

22   *The New York Times*, 29 July 1984.

23   Kurt Andersen, *Fantasyland: How America Went Haywire: A 500-Year History* (Random House, 2017), pp. 255–6.

24   UPI, 5 July 1985.

25   Cannon, p. 40.

26   Hendrik Hertzberg, *Politics: Observations & Arguments, 1966–2004* (Penguin, 2004), p. 71.

27   Cannon, p. 98.

28   *Hollywood Reporter*, 6 January 2017.

29   Norman Mailer, *Mind of an Outlaw: Selected Essays* (Random House, 2014), p. 450.

30   Douglas Brinkley, *Gerald R. Ford* (Henry Holt, 2017), p. 122.

31   Cannon, pp. 81–2.

32   Ibid., p. 37.

33   Brands, p. 219.

34   *The New York Times*, 21 January 1981.

35   Cannon, pp. 76–7.

36   Ibid., p. 40.

37   Andersen, *Fantasyland*, p. 255.

38   *Salon*, 7 February 2015.

39   Arthur M. Schlesinger, *The Cycles of American History* (Mariner, 2009), p. 294.

40   Cannon, pp. 8–9.

41   Troy, p. 123.

42   Cannon, p. 8.

43   *Yahoo*, 22 September 2017.

44   *Politico*, 'What I Learned Watching *Back to the Future* with Ronald Reagan', 27 February 2018.

45   Jill Lepore, *These Truths: A History of the United States* (W. W. Norton, 2018), p. 704.

46 Ed Luce, *Time to Start Thinking: America and the Spectre of Decline* (Abacus, 2012), p. 49.

47 *The New York Times*, 4 April 1984.

48 *New York* magazine, 29 January 2016.

49 *Fortune*, 1 December 1986.

50 *Time*, 16 January 1989.

51 The Daily Beast, 21 October 2015.

52 *The New York Times*, 21 November 1986.

53 *The New York Times*, 7 August 1983.

54 *The New York Times*, 25 September 1988.

55 *The New York Times*, 4 April 1984.

56 Donald Trump, *The Art of the Deal* (Random House, 1987), p. 176.

57 *The New York Times*, 4 April 1984.

58 Cooke, p. 339

59 *The Washington Post*, 2 September 1987.

60 *The New York Times*, 7 September 1987.

61 *The New York Times*, 5 October 1987.

62 *Politico*, 25 October 2015.

63 *The New York Times*, 8 September 2015.

64 Jon Meacham, *Destiny and Power: The American Odyssey of George Herbert Walker Bush* (Random House, 2016), p. 326.

65 Trump, p. 58.

66 Troy, p. 16.

67 *The Atlantic*, February 2010.

68 *Forbes*, 15 September 2015.

69 *The Atlantic*, February 2010.

70 Dionne, p. 32.

71 Ibid.

72 *Los Angeles Times*, 6 June 2004.

73 Brands, p. 539.

74 Troy, p. 321.

75 *The Washington Post*, 4 February 2011.

76 Schlesinger, p. 294.

77 *The New York Times*, 10 June 2004.

78 Ibid.

79 *Politico*, 16 January 2008.

80 *Time*, 27 January 2011.

81 Cannon, p. 9.

82 *The New York Times*, 5 March 1992.

83 *The Atlantic*, 30 June 2019.

CHAPTER 2: GOODBYE TO THE GREATEST GENERATION

1   Meacham, p. 495.

2   Ibid., p. 462.

3   *The New York Times*, 2 March 1991.

4   Meacham, pp. 471–2.

5   Ibid., p. 466; *The New York Times*, 2 March 1991.

6   *The New York Times*, 2 March 1991.

7   Meacham, p. 468.

8   Ibid., p. 469.

9   Tom Friedman and Michael Mandelbaum, *That Used to Be Us* (Farrar, Straus & Giroux, 2011), p. 13.

10 Troy, p. 301.

11 Micklethwait and Wooldridge, p. 33.

12 Ibid.

13 Meacham, p. 117.

14 Ibid., p. 124.

15 Ibid., p. 325.

16 *Newsweek*, 19 October 1987.

17 Klein, *Politics Lost*, p. 101.

18 Ibid.

19 Ibid., p. 103.

20 Ibid., p. 98.

21 Kornacki, p. 81.

22 Meacham, p. 357.

23 Micklethwait and Wooldridge, p. 8.

24 Meacham, p. xxxiii.

25 John Lawrence, 'How the "Watergate Babies" Broke American Politics', *Politico*, 26 May 2018.

26 David Osborne, 'The Swinging Days of Newt Gingrich', *Mother Jones*, 1 November 1984.

27 *The Washington Post*, 23 March 1989.

28 *Los Angeles Times*, 1 June 1989.

29 *The Washington Post*, 2 December 2018.

30 Kornacki, p. 111.

31 John F. Harris, *The Survivor: Bill Clinton in the White House* (Random House, 2006), p. xxii.

32 Kornacki, p. 85.

33 Meacham, p. 472.

34 Kornacki, p. 91.

35 *The New York Times*, 5 February 1992.

36 Kornacki, p. 153.

37 Ibid., p. 154.

38 *Los Angeles Times*, 13 May 1992.

39 *The Washington Post*, 29 February 1992.

40 Kornacki, p. 157.

41 *The American Conservative*, 30 May 2018.

42 Dionne, p. 107.

43 Kornacki, p. 167.

44 Ibid., p. 162.

45 Ibid., p. 191.

46 Ibid., p. 173.

47 Dionne, p. 108.

48 Kornacki, p. 209.

49 *The Washington Post*, 2 December 2018.

50 Associated Press, 5 December 2018.

51 *Politico*, 5 December 2018.

52 Meacham, p. 498.

53 Ibid., p. 511.

54 Ibid., p. 522.

CHAPTER 3: BILL AND NEWT

1 Harris, p. 9.

2 Kornacki, p. 216.

3 *The New York Times*, 2 February 1993.

4 Harris, p. 5.

5 Ibid., p. 329.

6 Klein, *The Natural*, p. 52.

7 Kornacki, p. 272.

8 Ibid., p. 266.

9 *The Atlantic*, November 2018.

10 Harris, p. 143.

11 Ibid., p. 82.

12   Kornacki, p. 261.

13   Ibid., p. 262.

14   *Baltimore Sun*, 27 July 1995.

15   'Did Bill Clinton Hold up LAX Air Traffic for a Haircut?', Snopes, 27 July 2016.

16   Ken Jennings, *Planet Funny: How Comedy Took Over Our Culture* (Simon & Schuster, 2018).

17   Pew Research Center, 4 February 2016.

18   UPI, 2 April 1993.

19   Cooke, p. 354.

20   Harris, p. 147.

21   George Packer, *Our Man: Richard Holbrooke and the End of the American Century* (Knopf, 2019), p. 312.

22   *The Washington Post*, 25 August 2016.

23   Harris, p. 115.

24   *The New York Times*, 3 October 1993.

25   *The Washington Post*, 25 August 2016.

26   Micklethwait and Wooldridge, p. 68.

27   *Time*, 7 June 1993.

28   Dionne, p. 118.

29   Kornacki, p. 248.

30   Klein, *The Natural*, p. 103.

31   *The Atlantic*, November 2018.

32   Kornacki, p. 291.

33   Ibid., p. 287.

34   *The New York Times*, 11 May 1995.

35   *The New York Times*, 7 November 1996.

36   Klein, *The Natural*, p. 8.

37   Packer, p. 311.

38   James Macgregor Burns and Georgia J. Sorensen, *Dead Center: Clinton-Gore Leadership and the Perils of Moderation* (Scribner, 1999), p. 219.

39   Dionne, p. 134.

40   Kornacki, p. 340.

41   Author interview with Toni Morrison.

42   *The Atlantic*, November 2018.

43   Klein, *The Natural*, p. 16.

44   Ibid.

45   Harris, p. 342.

46 Ibid., p. 347.

47 Lepore, p. 711.

48 *The New Yorker*, 11 March 2019.

49 Lepore, p. 707.

50 Klein, *Politics Lost*, p. 16.

51 Lepore, p. 714.

52 Fareed Zakaria, *The Post-American World* (W. W. Norton, 2008), pp. 36, 222.

53 Kurt Andersen, 'The Best Decade Ever? The 1990s, Obviously', *The New York Times*, 6 February 2015.

54 Joseph Stiglitz, 'The Roaring Nineties', *The Atlantic*, October 2002.

55 Klein, *The Natural*, p. 13.

56 *USA Today*, 30 June 2014.

57 *The New York Times*, 28 April 1994.

58 Michael Burleigh, *The Best of Times, the Worst of Times: A History of Now* (Pan Macmillan, 2018), p. 257.

59 *Salon*, 11 September 2016.

60 ThoughtCo, 28 February 2019.

61 *The New York Times*, 20 October 2002.

62 Berkshire Hathaway Annual Letter, 2002.

63 Justice Department News, 29 January 1998.

64 'One Nation, Interconnected', *Wired*, May 2000.

65 *The New York Times*, 4 September 2018.

66 Andersen, pp. 357–60.

67 *Foreign Affairs*, 1 October 2018.

68 *USA Today*, 21 August 2016.

69 *The Atlantic*, 22 August 2016.

70 Luce, p. 266.

71 Harris, p. 283.

72 *Foreign Affairs*, November/December 1998.

73 *The Guardian*, 19 June 2019.

74 Harris, p. 206.

75 *Esquire*, 17 June 2015.

76 *Fortune*, 22 July 1996.

77 Reuters, 17 July 2016.

78 *Fortune*, 22 July 1996.

79 Kornacki, p. 411.

80 Ibid., p. 412.

81 Ibid., p. 413.

82 Ibid., p. 412.

83 *Politico*, 25 October 2015.

84 *The New York Times*, 14 February 2000.

85 Ibid.

86 Dionne, p. 158.

CHAPTER 4: THE THREE CONVULSIONS

1 Jean Edward Smith, *Bush* (Simon & Schuster, 2017), p. xx.

2 Meacham, p. 553.

3 Dionne, p. 171.

4 *The Atlantic*, 27 August 2018.

5 Thomas Mann, *Brookings Institution*, 1 January 2001.

6 *Vanity Fair*, 19 March 2014.

7 *Nation*, 28 July 2015.

8 Smith, p. xxi.

9 Kornacki, p. 419.

10 Ibid., p. 422.

11 Ron Brownstein, *The Second Civil War: How Extreme Partisanship Has Paralyzed Washington and Polarized America* (Penguin, 2008), p. 265.

12 *The Washington Post*, 11 September 2017.

13 *The New York Times*, 10 April 2005.

14 Lepore, p. 745.

15 *The New York Times*, 15 November 2001.

16 *The Atlantic*, 4 September 2013.

17 Klein, *Politics Lost*, p. 226.

18 *The Washington Post*, 11 September 2017.

19 *The New York Times*, 26 September 2006.

20 Joseph Stiglitz, *The Great Divide* (W. W. Norton, 2016), p. 5.

21 Smith, p. xv.

22 NPR, 5 April 2019; *Forbes*, 27 June 2014.

23 Burleigh, p. 11.

24 *The New York Times*, 1 July 2019.

25 Smith, p. 384.

26 *Weekly Standard*, 7 November 2001.

27 Friedman and Mandelbaum, p. 156.

28 *The New York Times*, 4 March 2001.

29 Lepore, p. 740.

30 *Vanity Fair*, 22 January 2016.

31 Ibid., March 2005.

32 Smith, p. 392.

33 Ibid., p. 415.

34 *Washington Examiner*, 3 September 2005.

35 Bill Bishop, *The Big Sort: Why the Clustering of Like-Minded America is Tearing us Apart* (Mariner, 2009), p. 6.

36 Ibid., p. 12.

37 Amy Chua, *Political Tribes: Group Instinct and the Fate of Nations* (Penguin 2018), p. 166.

38 Bishop, p. 38.

39 *The New Yorker*, 27 December 2018; *Fortune*, 8 September 2016.

40 Smith, p. 441.

41 Ibid., p. 432.

42 *The New York Times*, 28 October 2016.

43 Luce, p. 272.

44 Friedman and Mandelbaum, p. 72.

45 *The New York Times*, 26 October 2011.

46 Governing.com, 29 January 2020.

47 Smith, pp. 636–7.

48 Dionne, p. 233.

49 Pew Research Center, 23 July 2009.

50 Dionne, p. 223.

51 David Autor and others, 'Importing Political Polarisation: The Electoral Consequences of Rising Trade Exposure', December 2017.

CHAPTER 5: No You Can't

1 Nick Bryant, *The Bystander: John F. Kennedy and the Struggle for Black Equality* (Basic Books, 2006).

2 Dionne, p. 287.

3 Ibid., p. 292.

4 CNN, 19 January 2008.

5 Robert Draper, *Do Not Ask What Good We Do: Inside the US House of Representatives* (Free Press, 2012), p. xviii.

6 *The New York Times*, 14 January 2017.

7 *Politico*, 4 December 2016.

8   *National Journal*, 23 October 2010.

9   Jonathan Alter, *The Promise: President Obama, Year One* (Simon & Schuster, 2010), p. 129.

10   *Politico*, 4 December 2016.

11   Luce, p. 180.

12   *CBS News*, 2 November 2009.

13   Alter, p. 408.

14   *New York Daily News*, 5 February 2010.

15   *Salon*, 29 December 2019.

16   CNN, 28 January 2010.

17   Laura Flanders, *At the Tea Party: The Wing Nuts, Whack Jobs and Whitey-Whiteness of the New Republican Right – and Why We Should Take It Seriously* (OR Books, 2010), p. 239.

18   *New York Review of Books*, 19 December 2019.

19   *ABC News*, 15 February 2010.

20   *The New York Times*, 25 February 2014.

21   *The Guardian*, 29 May 2012; *Politico*, 31 July 2009.

22   Gallup, 19 June 2014.

23   *Politico*, 24 September 2013.

24   *The Washington Post*, 17 April 2013.

25   Reuters, 30 July 2013.

26   BBC News, 22 May 2016.

27   *New York Review of Books*, 23 May 2019.

28   Stiglitz, p. 30.

29   *Vanity Fair*, 31 May 2012.

30   Ibid., May 2011.

31   *Forbes*, 24 July 2018.

32   *New York Magazine*, 27 January 2015.

33   Burleigh, p. 261.

34   National Intelligence Council Global Trends 2030: Alternative Worlds, December 2012.

35   Interview between Barack Obama and Jeffrey Goldberg, *The Atlantic*, 30 August 2013.

36   *Politico*, 9 February 2017.

37   *Vox*, 10 January 2017.

38   Burleigh, p. 285.

39   *The New York Times*, 17 October 2004.

40   *Wall Street Journal*, 10 September 2013.

41 Barack Obama, 'The Way Ahead', *The Economist*, 8 October 2016.

42 *New York Review of Books*, 19 December 2019.

43 Statement by Barack Obama, 9 November 2016.

44 Michael Dimock, 'How America Changed During Barack Obama's Presidency', Pew Research Center, 10 January 2017.

45 Ibid.

46 *Slate*, 11 June 2012.

47 Molly Reynolds, 'President Obama's Legislative Legacy and What It Means for the Next Generation', *Brookings Institution*, 30 December 2016.

48 Alter, p. 224.

49 Dimock.

50 'Obama's Final Drone Strike Data', Council on Foreign Relations, 20 January 2017.

51 Gideon Rachman, *Easternization: Asia's Rise and America's Decline from Obama to Trump and Beyond* (Other Press, 2017), p. 82.

52 *The New York Times*, 17 January 2017.

53 *The Atlantic*, 10 August 2014.

54 Rachman, p. 164.

55 Dimock.

56 Alter, p. 279.

57 *The New Yorker*, 18 November 2016.

CHAPTER 6: THE DONALD TRUMP SHOW

1 *Politico*, 30 July 2009.

2 Lepore, p. 777.

3 Burleigh, p. 285.

4 CNN, 30 June 2016.

5 Salena Zito, 'Taking Trump Seriously, Not Literally', *The Atlantic*, 23 September 2016.

6 *Fortune*, 8 November 2016.

7 Pew Research, 'Greatest Dangers in the World', 16 October 2014.

8 Nick Bryant, *The Rise and Fall of Australia: How a Great Nation Lost Its Way* (Random House, 2014).

9 Gallup, 8 November 2016.

10 *The New York Times*, 29 February 2016.

11 Ibid., 15 March 2016.

12 CNN, 6 May 2016.

13 BuzzFeed, 16 November 2016.

14 *The New York Times*, 19 October 2016.

15 Hillary Rodham Clinton, *What Happened* (Simon & Schuster, 2017), p. 125.

16 Vox, 15 November 2019.

17 *Columbia Journalism Review*, 5 December 2017.

18 CNN, 8 November 2016.

19 *The Atlantic*, 15 September 2020.

20 CNN, 8 November 2016.

21 *The New Yorker*, 11 March 2019.

Chapter 7: American Carnage

1 *The New York Times*, 9 December 2017.

2 *The New Yorker*, 17 September 2108.

3 CNN, 23 December 2019.

4 *The New Yorker*, 27 July 2017.

5 *Politico*, 5 January 2018.

6 *Salon*, 29 February 2020.

7 *Newsweek*, 9 October 2019.

8 Bloomberg, 31 July 2019.

9 CNN, 27 November 2017.

10 The Daily Beast, 7 July 2017.

11 Pew Research Center, 8 January 2020.

Chapter 8: 2020

1 *Business Insider*, 3 August 2020.

Conclusion: Present at the Destruction

1 *The Week*, 13 October 2019.

2 *The New York Times*, 27 November 2019.

3 *New York Review of Books*, 23 July 2020.

4 'Averting Crisis: American Strategy, Military Spending and Collective Defence in the Indo-Pacific', US Studies Centre, 19 August 2019.

5 Lepore, p. 726.

6 *The Washington Post*, 16 January 2019.

7 *Business Insider*, 9 July 2015.

8 Public Religion Research Institute, 21 February 2019.

Index

Abbott, Tony 243
ABC 121, 327
Abe, Shinzo 298
Abedin, Huma 212, 252, 255, 256
abortion 28, 56, 146, 153
Abu Ghraib 170
Adams, John Quincy 158
Adelson, Sheldon 200
Affordable Care Act, *see* Obamacare
    (Affordable Care Act)
Afghanistan 164, 167–8, 225, 300
Agnew, Spiro 27
AIDS epidemic 60
Ailes, Roger 26, 71–2, 95, 124, 245,
    258–9
Al Qaeda 131, 139–40
Albright, Madeleine 126
Alter, Jonathan 228
America Online 123, 138
American Civil Liberties Union
    (ACLU) 162
Americans with Disabilities Act 94
Andersen, Kurt 137
anti-Semitism 146, 285–6
Apple 312
Apple, Johnny 112
Apprentice, The 4, 8, 142, 269
    Celebrity Apprentice 25, 229–30,
    236
Arafat, Yasser 130
Arbatov, Georgy 68
Arkansas Project 103
Armey, Dick 109
Arpaio, Joe 206
Ashcroft, John 163
Asian Infrastructure Investment Bank
    (AIIB) 226

al-Assad, Bashar 215–16, 225
Assange, Julian 261
astrology 35
astroturfing 200
Atwater, Lee 53, 71
Atwood, Margaret: *The Handmaid's
    Tale* 289
auto industries 137–8
Autor, David 182, 187

Bachmann, Michele 205
al-Baghdadi, Abu Bakr 274
Baird, Zoë 99–100
Baker, Howard 75
Baker, James 38, 92–3, 102, 126, 166
Baker, Peter 123
Bakker, Jim and Tammy Faye 28, 70
Bannon, Steve 181, 258–9, 266, 283,
    284
Barak, Ehud 130
Barr, William 302, 305
Barrett, Amy Coney 324–5
Barrett, Rona 50
Bayh, Birch 30
Bayh, Evan 204
Beck, Glenn 124, 139, 181
Bell, Daniel: *The End of Ideology* 22
Bentsen, Lloyd 81
Bercow, John 297
Bezos, Jeff 312, 337
Biden, Hunter 302–3
Biden, Joe 209, 210–11, 302–3
    2020 presidential election 9, 10,
    11–12, 319, 320–1, 323, 326–7
Bildt, Carl 315
bin Laden, Osama 164, 165, 174,
    230

Note on the Author

Nick Bryant is one of the BBC's most senior foreign correspondents and has covered the past four US administrations. He has been posted in Washington DC, South Asia, Australia and, most recently, New York. He is the author of *The Bystander: John F. Kennedy and the Struggle for Black Equality*, *Confessions from Correspondentland* and *The Rise and Fall of Australia*. Nick studied history at Cambridge and has a doctorate in American history from Oxford. *The Washington Post* has noted: 'Bryant is a genuine rarity. A Brit who understands America.' He lives in New York with his wife and children.

Note on the Type

The text of this book is set in Minion, a digital typeface designed by Robert Slimbach in 1990 for Adobe Systems. The name comes from the traditional naming system for type sizes, in which minion is between nonpareil and brevier. It is inspired by late Renaissance-era type.